Public Issues:
A Geographical Perspective

Public Issues:
A Geographical Perspective

edited by
Jean Andrey and J. Gordon Nelson

Department of Geography Publication Series

Series Editor Bruce Mitchell
Editorial Assistant Kate Evans
Cover Design Gary Brannon
Cartography Barry Levely
Printing Graphic Services
University of Waterloo

Geography and Public Issues Series

Canadian Association of Geographers Public Issues Committee
Heritage Resources Centre, University of Waterloo
Series Editor J. Gordon Nelson
Publication Number 2
Editors Jean Andrey and J. Gordon Nelson

Canadian Cataloguing in Publication Data

Main entry under title:

Public Issues : a geographical perspective

(Department of Geography publication series ; no. 41)
Papers presented at a special session on public
issues at the annual general meeting of the
Canadian Association of Geographers held in
Vancouver, May, 1992.
Includes bibliographical references.
ISBN 0-921083-49-1

1. Human geography - Canada - Congresses.
2. Human geography - Congresses. I. Andrey, Jean
Clara, 1955-   . II. Nelson, J. G. (James Gordon),
1932-   . III. University of Waterloo. Dept. of
Geography. IV. Canadian Association of Geographers.
V. Series.

GF511.P83 1993   304.2'0971   C94-930075-6

Preface

The Canadian Association of Geographers (CAG) Public Issues Committee was formed in the late 1980s to bring important public issues to the attention of the geographical community for their use in education and further studies, and to demonstrate the contribution that the discipline of geography can make to issues of importance in Canada and other countries. The committee has organized special sessions at each of the past five annual meetings of the CAG, one of which resulted in the first CAG Public Issues Committee monograph, *Water Diversion and Export: Learning from Canadian Experience* by J. C. Day and Frank Quinn (1992).

The current monograph is the second in the CAG Public Issues publication series. It is based on papers presented in nine special sessions on "Geography and Public Issues" at the 1992 annual meeting of the CAG held at The University of British Columbia. Unlike the Day and Quinn book, which focuses on a specific public issue, this volume discusses a wide range of issues at a variety of scales.

The monograph is entitled, *Pubic Issues: A Geographical Perspective*, and consists of 19 substantive chapters plus an introduction. These chapters represent the contribution of 27 geographers, working and studying in academic and governmental institutions across Canada. The chapters are organized into three parts - *Understanding Change and Its Implications for Planning; Assessing Responses to Change; and Working for Improvement*. As one reads through the various chapters, the tone becomes less descriptive and analytic and more evaluative and normative.

The book serves to illustrate the range of topics and approaches that are of interest to geographers involved in research on public issues, and hopefully will foster more research in the public issue arena.

Acknowledgements

This monograph was prepared with financial support from the Royal Canadian Geographical Society and the Social Sciences and Humanities Research Council to whom we are grateful. Financial and other support was also provided by The Heritage Resources Centre, The University of Waterloo.

We would also like to extend thanks to the two reviewers for their helpful comments, to Kate Evans for preparing such a professional manuscript, and to Barry Levely and Gary Brannon who prepared the maps and book cover.

Table of Contents

viii

List of Figures

List of Tables

Introduction

Understanding, Assessing and Adapting to Change

J. Gordon Nelson and Jean Andrey

Motivation

Humankind faces many changes in Canada and other parts of the world today. These changes are wide-ranging, complex and frequently marked by uncertainties. The changes include such things as economic restructuring, population growth, environmental degradation, climate variability, shifts in political boundaries and priorities, and increasing disparity between the developed and developing worlds. It is doubtful if humans have ever faced so many complex changes at any time in their history on earth. Indeed many observers believe that these changes pose major threats to human and other life forms now and increasingly so in future.

All these changes can be considered as public issues in the sense that a relatively large number of individuals or groups are concerned about their effects on well-being in economic, social, environmental or other terms. In other words the changes become issues when people are aware of them and wish to understand and plan for them and their effects in better ways.

As a result of the wide scope and diverse nature of the issues at hand, they can be viewed, understood and dealt with from many different perspectives. Certain views or approaches are more generally recognized and used than others. Economics, political science and engineering are examples of approaches or fields of knowledge that are commonly thought of as especially useful and applicable to public issues.

Even a brief examination of the papers and bibliographies in this volume shows that geographers have long been interested in and have made strong contributions to understanding and responding to public issues of various kinds. Examples include work in hazards, resources and urban affairs. Yet the value of the geographic perspective and contribution is not well known among citizens and decision-makers, and is not as appreciated as it should be, even among geographers. In fact, many geographers are not strongly motivated to make contributions to public issues, to take advantage of the opportunities available to them and their scientific, scholarly and professional capabilities, and to work for improvement.

Geographers do share many research tools with other scholars and professionals, in both the social and natural science arenas. Geographers, however, have a stronger interest than many scientists in techniques for identifying, measuring and interpreting information about topics and issues in an integrated way, for example in the complex context of places, areas, or regions. In fact one of the trademarks of the geographical approach is the heavy emphasis on the relationships among features and processes, and the collection and analysis of a wide array of human and natural information in order to understand change or issues in a very broad context as well as in more specialized ways. In other words geographers tend to want to understand the whole picture and how a particular change or issue fits into that picture, especially in terms of changes in space and time. In this sense, most geographers also have an interest in trends and future directions, and rates of change and their implications for human and environmental well-being.

The Approach in this Study

Concern about opportunities for geography to make contributions to the many public issues facing humankind led to a decision by the Canadian Association of Geographers (CAG) Public Issues Committee to hold a special session on public issues at the CAG annual meeting in Vancouver, May 1992. The CAG Public Issues Committee was established in 1988 to foster interest in public issues and to demonstrate the contribution that geographers can make toward problem resolution. The Committee has organized sessions at previous annual meetings of the CAG, primarily on water diversions and other environmental issues, but the 1992 sessions were intended to cover the broad range of public issues in which geographers are involved.

Invitations were sent to about 50 geographers in Canada asking them to consider presenting a paper on an issue of special knowledge and interest to them. They were also requested to circulate the invitation to others who might be interested in the opportunity. About 30 geographers accepted the invitation and presented papers in a series of Public Issues sessions at the CAG meeting. Other geographers expressed support for the idea but said that they had agreed to present a paper at another session to be held at the conference. Subsequently some of these geographers agreed to have their papers included in the articles published in this volume.

In the original invitation, correspondents were asked basically to describe how geography had contributed to a public issue and how a geographic approach made it possible to do so. It was also suggested that the history and future prospects for contributions by geographers should be discussed. Such information was thought to be useful in demonstrating and stimulating relevant geographical work. The results would also be useful in educational activities related to geography and public issues.

The Results

The papers in this volume show the nature and value of the geographic contribution to public issues, although not always in the sense that had originally been expected. Most papers focus more on the issue that is being addressed than on the concepts, methods and techniques used in doing so. However, the papers do make a strong contribution to the better understanding of an array of public issues. With study, they also reveal how the conceptual and methodological approaches of the geographer can provide for such a contribution.

While some of the papers deal with general issues, most authors adopt a case study approach either in framing the chapter or in terms of the illustrative materials used to argue a point. The power of such case studies is in their ability to bring together or synthesize all the complexities of contemporary public issues. Case studies can show how interested persons use different types of information as well as different scientific, technical and political processes and methods in learning and making decisions. Case studies show how different ways of knowing are brought together on the ground in seeking responses to public issues. Case studies are therefore a valuable tool for people interested in learning about how to deal with issues. They do have some difficulties, however, for example making generalizations or more wide-ranging conclusions based on one or two cases.

To illustrate all of this as clearly as possible we have divided the 19 papers into three groupings which are linked to one another in thinking about and addressing public issues. The three groupings are: Understanding Change and Its Implications for Planning; Assessing Responses to Change; and Working for Improvement. The papers allocated to each of these groupings fit them rather well but inevitably have some overlap with the other headings. The groupings outline a simple way of thinking about the broad kinds of contributions that geographers can make to public issues.

The papers show that geographers stress a number of concepts and methods which are very useful in understanding and dealing with public issues. The basic concepts include an interest in:

1) a holistic or comprehensive view of the situation or context in which issues arise;

2) human-environment interrelations or interactions;

3) the array of natural, economic, social, technical, land and resource use, institutional, political and other processes at work in any situation of interest and the relations among them;

4) changes in the history and spatial distribution of these processes and their effects on or relations with any issue of concern;

5) the differing scales involved in change, for example local, regional, national and international;

6) the way in which changes and issues typify or relate to a place or area, and how they can be compared among places;

7) the nature and rate of change;

8) the implication of changes for the future, this interest sometimes extending to an active interest in planning, management and adaptation.

The papers also show that especially in the last two to three decades geographers have shown a growing interest and active involvement in a range of challenging problems. Geographers bring a wide range of conceptual frameworks and methodological approaches to the study of public issues that enhance greatly our capacity to assemble, analyze, synthesize and interpret information and to monitor, assess, plan, manage and adapt to change. Overall then the complexities and uncertainties associated with the present human and global condition offer unusual opportunities for geographers to contribute as individuals or as members of multidisciplinary teams. Geographers can build on the kinds of contributions exhibited in the papers in this volume.

Part I - Understanding Change: Implications for Planning

Understanding involves a conceptual framework or set of ideas for interpreting and adapting to the world around us in an individually and socially effective way. In other words the interpretations and responses involved in understanding should have survival value for individuals and groups attempting to cope with the changing world around us. The first six papers in the volume are good illustrations of the ways in which a geographic perspective or approach can contribute to such understanding of various aspects of change. All of the papers in this section deal with general policy issues, although two of them are couched in terms of empirical case studies.

The first paper by Sanderson is entitled, "Climate Change and Its Implications for Water in the Great Lakes Basin." This paper provides a vivid overview of the nature of climate change and its future implications. It stresses the kind and distribution of temperature and other changes which are expected, their effects on lake levels and other aspects of the environment, and their implications for various human activities. Sanderson enhances our understanding of these changes by discussing them at different scales — global, regional and local. Complexity and uncertainty are central themes throughout the paper — the complexity of the systems involved and uncertainty in terms of both future climates and related impacts. Sanderson ends the paper by highlighting the potential role of geographers in this high profile, yet controversial, public policy issue primarily because of their ability to understand the inter-relationships between natural and human systems.

The second paper, by Nash and Perout, serves as a further illustration of the wide-ranging effects of global climatic change by advancing the idea that many more environmental refugees will move among different parts of the world as a result of any such changes. This paper is based on the collection and synthesis of spatial migration data from the United Nations and other standard sources, and is valuable in drawing attention to an emerging major issue that is not yet sufficiently appreciated. Although refugees are a global phenomenon, this issue emerges from and has its greatest potential effects at the local and regional levels, for example in the various cities and places where refugees tend to congregate. The paper makes a strong argument for a more pro-active stance by the Canadian government on both pragmatic and ethical grounds.

Troughton's discussion of Canadian agriculture also highlights the spatial and historical dimensions of an emerging crisis — this time at the national scale. Troughton's paper clearly articulates the nature of change in the agricultural sector and discusses the importance of various factors — especially technology and governmental policies — in fostering these changes. Troughton's paper is a powerful critique of the piecemeal way in which agricultural policy has traditionally evolved and offers a variety of insights into Canadian land use and landscape change over the past century, and more generally into global economic restructuring and environmental change as they relate to free trade.

Andrey's paper helps us to understand another public issue, traffic and transportation planning. Andrey's paper includes a review of how geographers have responded to transportation issues. Their views and responses have ranged from a relatively narrow one in which traffic flow and other changes were approached through research and policy focusing on "technical fixes" to a broad approach involving research and policy dealing with the architecture and layout of cities, the planning of land use, and consideration of social and environmental effects. The major transport challenges facing North American society are discussed and priority areas for future study are identified.

The fifth paper in this section is an empirically rich and thoughtful overview of the role of commuting in the Canadian mining industry, written by Storey and Shrimpton. The paper begins with an overview of the factors that have altered the ways in which the mining industry in Canada operates. Then the authors draw on both primary and secondary research to describe the social and economic implications of an emerging trend toward commuter mining, in which the work place is so isolated from the workers' homes, that food and accommodation are provided at the work site and employees rotate between work site and home site on a fixed schedule. The paper has a strong spatial theme and "sense of place" is key to understanding both the motivations and implications of this type of employment arrangement. As in Andrey and in Troughton, the importance of technology and the growing concern over environmental and social impacts of human activities are highlighted.

Another paper with a strongly spatial theme is offered by Mensah and Ironside on employment opportunities of the urban poor. The paper is based primarily on survey work in Edmonton, Alberta. Results lend support to the "spatial mismatch hypothesis," which argues that recent economic and land use changes are creating inner city areas characterized by skilled jobs and low-skilled workers. One of the underlying themes of the paper is that of equity in social planning. Again, the issues of economic restructuring and urban transport are discussed, albeit in the context of the case study.

Part II: Assessing Response to Change

All seven papers in Part II focus more explicitly on the assessment of public and private response to change. By assessment we mean going beyond understanding to interpreting and making judgements about the nature and effects of responses, especially by public authorities. By public responses we mean the ways in which governments react to changes through the passing of laws; the establishment of policies and guidelines; the creation of regulations; the provision of subsidies or other economic measures; the development of agencies, staff and budgets; education and training; and other social guides intended to steer society in the direction judged to be most apt under the circumstances. Here we are basically dealing with ways of organizing for and making decisions amidst conflicting perceptions, attitudes and values. Political systems, the roles of interest groups, citizen participation and other aspects of decision-making are all involved in these situations. Underlying themes that emerge are the importance of place/locale and the need to deal with complexity and cumulative economic, social or environmental impacts of projects, programs and policies in assessing response.

Sharpe in his paper entitled "Community Futures in Ontario" assesses the ways in which the boundaries of local economic development areas for a major government program are established and the effects that this has on program results. Sharpe provides an overview of both the institutional context for local economic development in Canada and of the Community Futures Program, which is the Canadian government's major local economic development policy mechanism. The issue of locality is examined through two case studies, one focusing on the Norfolk District in southern Ontario and the other on Superior East in north central Ontario. Results indicate the sensitivity of program success to the character of places.

In the next paper, Bunting and Filion assess the effects of urban renewal programs in terms of the often insufficiently recognized conflicts among policies, programs, and priorities of different government agencies and interest groups. The inconsistencies and contradictions among these programs and public decisions are analyzed and assessed in terms of their effects on the ground, notably in contributing to the decline of Kitchener's downtown. Throughout the study, the importance of place and the need for a holistic vision of different planning activities are highlighted.

The papers by Slack, and Georgison and Day on ports contribute a very useful comparison of geographic approaches to a similar problem. Slack's approach is more comprehensive and top-down, focusing on the role and effects of senior governments in Canada and particularly on their response to economic and technological changes, which are recognized in many of the papers in this volume as major causes of change and of conflict in public issues. Slack explains the current complexity of port administration in Canada and demonstrates that recent major changes in technology, for example through container shipment, alter our general understanding of ports to include not only coastal but inland locations such as Denver.

Georgison and Day's study is a more focused one, using case studies of "port as place." The analysis and assessment is undertaken from a broad human ecological perspective. This involves some understanding of the physical geography of areas, their institutional and economic histories, and other variables which give places their character and provide a context in which pollution and other costs become issues. Georgison and Day also provide an example of a basic methodology used by geographers and that is the comparative method. In complex land use and environmental situations such as ports, it is frequently the case that there is little overriding theory which can be used to provide a basis for undertaking, predicting and assessing changes in terms of any ideal model. Meaning in such case studies is frequently derived by comparing the situation in two or more places. In this case Vancouver is compared to Seattle and Canadian policies to those in the United States. In the assessment context, this approach is often referred to as "learning from the experience of others."

The paper by Sundstrom on the Oldman Dam interprets and evaluates the role of the environmental assessment process itself in meeting the concerns of the public and various agencies about the desirability of building an irrigation dam on the Oldman, a tributary of the South Saskatchewan River, Alberta. Sundstrom's methodology is basically to examine the reports and documents produced in the assessment and planning process and to evaluate them in terms of their effects on the actions of governments, including the Cabinet and the Legislature. In his wide-ranging historic assessment Sundstrom analyzes the adequacies and inadequacies of economic and other specialized evaluations made by the governmental proponents of the dam and the determination of the province to proceed with the project in spite of any evidence to the contrary. The illusory nature of any rational, science-based planning approach involving attempts at comprehensive understanding of needs, project alternatives and their effects, is very clear here, as is the frequently highly political nature of resources and environmental decision-making.

In the next paper on "First Nations Strategies," Wolfe follows Sundstrom in analyzing a wide range of reports and other documentation of changing government responses, in this case to native issues in Canada. She assesses the responses in terms of their effects in leading to new policies, programs and projects. In interpreting the evolution of government policy and the responses of aboriginal peoples, she shows the value of linking the responses to basic differences in value systems, particularly as these relate to the way land is perceived and valued in relation to economy and society. Aboriginal peoples perceive land, economy and society as basically inseparable and necessary to provide for a capacity to sustain and endure as a people, while other Canadian interests often do not . Another important contribution that Wolfe makes is to help the reader appreciate the value of a wide-ranging human ecological perspective in which various technical, economic, social and other changes can be understood in relation to one another. Wolfe also makes good use of the concept of strategy to summarize various means of adapting to and planning for change. These include the setting of goals, as well as criteria or standards for judging success, and the development of programs and projects for implementation. The idea of strategy underlies Wolfe's analysis and assessment of the natives' response to public policy. Their approach has been to press for and increasingly to organize their own strategies for survival in the future in response to government measures which they perceive as often to the contrary. In this context also Wolfe illustrates the value of a historical analysis in assessing government policies, effects and native responses.

Greer-Wootten's paper on "The Politics of Interest Groups in Environmental Decision-Making" is a very fitting one with which to end this section on assessing responses because it describes the historical evolution of a very fundamental shift in the approach to public issues in Canada and many other countries. In this context, Greer-Wootten analyzes the historic experience of various groups in regard to different environmental issues in different situations. What emerges is a trend toward more complex responses to public issues by non-government groups and organizations. A top-down, hierarchical and linear approach involving identification of issues and development of policy and other responses by government for people was typical during the 1950s and to a lesser extent the 1960s and 1970s. It is being replaced by a situation in which many citizen interest groups and an array of different government agencies interact and adapt in identifying and responding to public issues in environmental and related fields. The situation is viewed as being much more complex and pluralist in character than formerly. These findings by Greer-Wootten indicate a need for basic rethinking of some of the models which we have used to understand, assess and implement responses to public issues. There appears to be a case for moving toward a more interactive or adaptive model rather than the rational one that many scholars and professionals continue to propound today.

Part III: Working for Improvement

The previous remarks lead rather readily to the papers concerned mainly with working for improvement in regard to public issues in Canada. By working for improvement we generally mean creating and implementing research, educational, planning, and management responses to public issues.

The paper by Chapman and Hardwick is an excellent illustration of working for improvement in that it involves research by geographers on public issues and also involvement in the planning and implementation of results. Chapman and Hardwick observed the influence of population, economic and urban growth on the educational system in the United States in the 1950s and 1960s. They also observed the research, planning and implementation procedures undertaken to respond. They undertook similar studies of change in British Columbia (B.C.) and concluded that a new educational system similar to the responses developed in the United States was needed there. This involved moving from a single university situated in Vancouver to a set of universities and colleges distributed throughout the growing province. Hardwick in particular became involved in detailed B.C. government efforts to implement such a system, along with other geographers who had worked with him and Chapman earlier. The Chapman and Hardwick paper is of additional interest in that it shows the value of having people who were involved in the study, planning and implementation of change, undertake a review of their experience for the public record. Such reviews and assessments enhance understanding of research, planning and management responses by scholars and practitioners. They also allow for further critical reviews and can lay the groundwork for assessment and improvement by others.

The paper by Nelson and Lawrence is of interest in several respects. First, the authors accept the need for a more diverse and interactive approach to the understanding, assessment and improvement of public issues. In their view, this approach should involve all major concerned groups in and outside of government, and especially the people likely to be directly affected by changes. The authors and their colleagues have developed a methodology for doing this. The method involves geographers and other scholars and professionals working closely with interested citizens in collecting information, in assessing this information, and especially in considering ways to improve the situation for as many groups and individuals as possible. A key element in this interactive and adaptive approach is the use of the ABC resource survey or assessment system to identify, collect, analyze, evaluate and interpret information on public issues. The ABC system is basically a system of mapping human ecology. Examples in the Nelson and Lawrence paper include the application and development of the method in the Great Lakes area.

The paper by McLellan and Baker moves beyond the ideas of Nelson and Lawrence to recognize and attempt to deal explicitly with the diverse demands placed by various groups on each other and upon other people and the environment. They recommend dealing with this pluralist situation by conflict resolution methods which involve negotiation and mediation. Through workshops and other techniques they seek to identify common interests as well as ways of compensating for or mitigating losses for all those concerned about the decisions. This study centres on aggregate mining issues, a field in which McLellan has been a pioneer in approaches that have wide-ranging applicability to many of the complex land use, resource and environmental issues now facing us.

Bardecki's paper on policies and procedures for cumulative impact management is a radical one in that it views a problem from a perspective that is different than the prevailing mode and so provides a useful avenue for possible improvement. Thus, Bardecki notes that many land use and other issues have been addressed in the last two decades through environmental assessments. These evaluations began in the environmental decade of the 1960s.

More recently it has frequently been recognized that assessment of one project or an interrelated group of projects, programs or policies is inadequate because such changes interact with other changes already underway in an area, so that it is difficult to separate, study, plan for and manage the changes independent of one another. A new kind of assessment, termed cumulative impact assessment, has therefore been promoted and developed This is proving to be a very demanding method which involves scoping and studying many kinds of projects, programs and changes in an area. It is very costly and difficult to do. Bardecki turns the problem on its head by saying that historically we have developed procedures for handling such diverse changes and their effects through regulatory procedures, and that regulation could be more rewarding and useful than devoting further effort to cumulative impact assessment, which is not as well linked to planning and management as it could be anyway.

Manning's paper takes a more normative tone in that it calls for a shift to a new way of making decisions on natural resources and, by inference, on related social and environmental matters as well. Manning's paper builds upon the fundamental concept of sustainable development which has recently been advanced as a powerful basis for dealing with the many complex problems facing Canadians and other people. The previous concept of unlimited economic growth which has been the basic one since the 1950s is thought to underlie many of the climatic change, pollution, coastal and other issues that face us now. Manning follows the 1987 Brundtland Commission report in supporting the idea of sustainability as the new ideology needed to guide the way we live, plan, manage and do research. In many ways then Manning's paper can be seen as that of an advocate, a geographer who on the basis of much thought, research and field experience in various federal government agencies, is not only arguing for sustainability but also presenting details on the principles to be applied in planning, management, research and related activities if the idea of sustainability is to be implemented effectively. His is a more prescriptive contribution than the others.

Finally, in the context of an interest in monitoring and assessment, Nelson and Serafin study some key concepts and networks which have been developed and used in research, planning and management over the last three decades in Canada and other countries. Nelson and Serafin argue on the basis of general experience, a wide-ranging literature review and some detailed case studies, that the popular rational planning model is not a workable and effective way of thinking about and attempting to improve approaches to research, planning and management. Essentially the rational approach is simplistic in focusing on one issue or concern — one project, program or policy — and attempting to identify and decide upon the alternative ways in which it should be planned and implemented. Difficulties arise in separating one issue or project from others, and in assembling sufficient information to understand the array of possible alternatives, and their socio-economic and environmental effects. There is the additional problem of dealing with the acceptability of any proposed change to the array of parties or interests affected by such change. Nelson and Serafin suggest an approach that is more sensitive to knowledge limits and to the pluralist and political character of most decision-making situations. They refer to this as an interactive and adaptive — or civics — approach.

Some Concluding Comments

We have been able to arrange for the publication of 19 case studies by geographers that were obtained opportunistically by convening a set of special sessions at a professional annual meeting. In doing so we have not been able to anticipate and guide the nature and organization of the contributions to the extent that was initially desired. Yet the results seem very worthwhile to geographers and others interested in understanding, assessing and improving human and environmental conditions, locally, nationally and internationally.

One very fundamental point in this regard is that the rational approach to public issues is of increasingly limited value for research and planning purposes. Some of the reasons have been outlined previously and include a narrow view of an issue or problem, inability to assemble information sufficient to understand all alternatives and effects, and difficulties in implementing alternatives in complex political circumstances as well as in monitoring the results. The idea that a preferred alternative and its effects can be monitored and adjustments made to deal with unanticipated effects and "surprises" is generally inapplicable because most projects, programs and policies are not monitored and because of staff, budget and other limitations; bureaucratic and political resistance; and other obstacles.

Another difficulty or obstacle posed by the rational approach is that the results are very difficult to analyze and assess, in large part because of the simplistic nature of the model. The model does not deal in any detail with the way a problem or issue is defined, how it is selected from among others, how it gets on the public agendas and so forth. Nor does the model provide consistent guidelines for the evaluation of the large array of alternatives applicable to any issue and who decides among these and how.

This is not the place to consider alternative ideas, concepts, paradigms or approaches in any detail. What may be needed, however, is a radical change which would allow us to consider research, education, planning and management in much more interactive, adaptive and political terms. Overall the impression gained from study of the papers in this volume is that the key concept and one that has a long history in geography and human ecology is not so much management as adaptation to change by all involved parties. In this sense, as part of this approach, considerable focus should be placed on continuous assessment and adaptation by all parties to constantly changing situations.

The civics approach which is described in the Nelson and Serafin paper does not address all of the foregoing and challenges by any means. But it does include a set of processes that are seen as necessary to decision-making. Nelson and Serafin describe these as understanding, communicating, assessing, planning, implementing, monitoring and adapting. These could be used as criteria in analyzing and assessing any public issue or in decision-making more generally.

Waterloo, 19 October, 1993.

Part I

Understanding Change:

Implications for Planning

Chapter 1

Climatic Change and Its Implications for Water in the Great Lakes Basin in Ontario

Marie Sanderson
University of Waterloo

Introduction

Many geographers in Canada and elsewhere are concerned about the possibility of climate change and are actively engaged in studying the possible impact of such change on various sectors of the economy. Water resources were the topic of a paper by Cohen (1986) and agriculture by Smit (1987). This present paper presents the results of two research projects on the impact of climate change on water in the Great Lakes basin in Ontario. The discussion of climate change is based on the following facts:

1) The concentrations of CO_2 and other "greenhouse" gases in the world's atmosphere are increasing, as shown by evidence from measurements at Mauna Loa in Hawaii beginning in 1957 (Figure 1.1).

2) The greenhouse gases in the atmosphere are known to absorb long wave radiation from the earth's surface and re-radiate it to the earth, thus potentially increasing surface temperature.

3) The analyses of ocean sediment cores, representing evidence of climates thousands of years ago, indicate that high levels of CO_2 in the atmosphere have always been associated with warmer periods in the earth's history.

It is important to state that the longest records of air temperatures measured at climate stations throughout the world, are about 100 to 150 years. Averaging all world temperature records shows a distinct warming trend (0.5°C) in the last 100 years (Figure 1.2). Scientists have constructed three-dimensional models of the world's atmospheric circulation to simulate the present world climate patterns and have then added the factor of increased greenhouse gases to simulate the future world climate that might occur

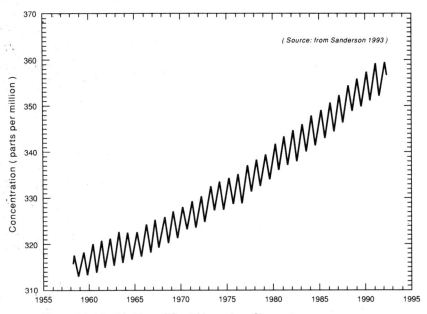

Figure 1.1: Monthly Mean CO_2 at Mauna Loa Observatory

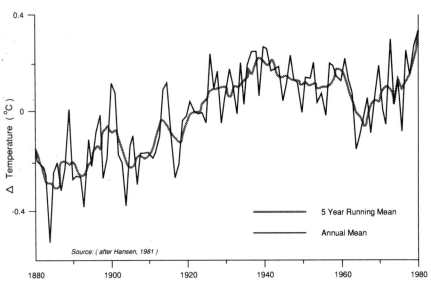

Figure 1.2: World Air Temperatures 1880 - 1980

when CO_2 concentrations are expected to be double pre-industrial revolution values (2 x CO_2 climate). These general circulation models (GCMs) are not predictions, but projections of possible world climates about the middle of the 21st century.

The focus in this paper is on changes in the climate of the Great Lakes basin as projected by several GCMs, some possible impacts and some planning implications. The first part of the paper describes research conducted by the Great Lakes Institute on climate change and Great Lakes levels and the subsequent impacts on shipping and hydro power industries (Sanderson, 1987). The second part outlines research carried out by the Water Network on the impact of climate change on water resources in the Grand River basin in southern Ontario.

The Impact on Great Lakes Levels

The Great Lakes (Figure 1.3) contain 20 per cent of the world's fresh water, an amount which could flood all North America including Mexico to a depth of one metre. The Great Lakes basin occupies a total area of 770,000 km^2, almost as large as the whole unified country of Germany. However, the water in the Great Lakes is a one-time gift of the last ice age, and these vast quantities of water are not renewable. The renewable portion of the water in the lakes must be re-supplied annually by nature. This renewable resource, called the net basin supply (NBS), represents about 75 cms on the surface of the lakes annually, and is the result of precipitation (P), the rain and snow that fall on the lakes, minus the evaporation (E) from the lake surfaces plus the runoff (R) from the land areas of the basin (NBS=P-E+R).

The average monthly amounts of these three variables as well as the average monthly water levels are shown in Figure 1.4 for Lake Erie. Precipitation (Graph B) is rather uniform throughout the year, while evaporation from the lake surface is low in winter and spring and reaches a maximum in early fall (Graph B). Runoff from the land areas peaks in early spring and is at a minimum in the autumn (Graph C). This figure shows that lake levels (Graph A) are lowest in winter when water is stored on the land surfaces in the form of snow, and highest in summer when snow melt runoff from the land surfaces has occurred and evaporation is low.

Lake levels are of vital importance to a great many people. The shipping industry prefers high levels, since ships are loaded to a maximum depending on the levels of the lakes. Hydro electric power companies also prefer high levels since their ability to generate power depends on the difference

Figure 1.3: The Great Lakes Basin, Showing the Location of 10 GISS Data Points

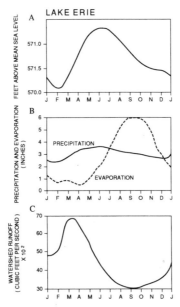

Figure 1.4: Average Monthly Lake Level, Precipitation
and Runoff for Lake Erie

of levels between lakes. On the other hand, lake shore dwellers prefer low levels to give them wide beaches and reduce erosion.

Lake levels have been measured at several locations along the shorelines of each lake for more than 100 years by the governments of Canada and the United States. Figure 1.5 shows the average annual level (the average of 365 days) that have occurred for each year for the period 1900 - 1985 for Lakes Michigan - Huron (considered one lake hydrologically), St. Clair and Erie. Long term changes are apparent: low levels in the 1930s, highs in the 1950s, extreme lows in the 1960s and all time highs in the 1980s. The range between measured extreme high and low levels has been two metres in these lakes.

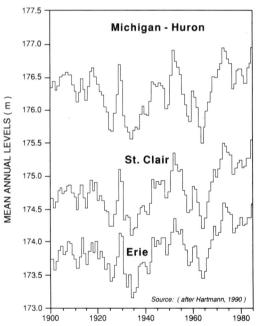

Figure 1.5: Annual Levels of Michigan - Huron, St. Clair and Erie

What will lake levels be in the future? Certainly they will vary in the future as they have in the past as a result of the variability of precipitation, evaporation and runoff. The impact of climate change on these factors and ultimately on lake levels is the topic of the research described here. Table 1.1 shows the changes in temperature and precipitation projected by the Goddard Institute of Space Studies (GISS) climate change scenario (Hansen et al., 1981) for point 1 north of Lake Superior and point 10 southeast of Lake Ontario (see Figure 1.3). The projected average temperature increase is about 4.5°C, with a larger increase in winter than in summer. Precipitation is not so well understood in the models. The GISS scenario projects a precipitation increase in the northwest of the basin, and a decrease in the southeast.

Table 1.1
Present and Projected Future Mean Monthly Temperature and
Precipitation in the Great Lakes Region (Grid Points 1 and 10)

	(1) Temperature °C			(1) Precipitation (cm)			(10) Temperature °C			(10) Precipitation (cm)		
	Norm	CH	2xCO2	Norm	Effect	2xCO2	Norm	CH	2xCO2	Norm	Effect	2xCO2
Jan	-20.2	5.6	-14.6	1.2	117.6	1.4	-4.5	5.6	1.1	2.4	104.2	2.5
Feb	-17.5	5.6	-11.9	1.1	116.7	1.2	-5.5	5.1	-0.4	2.7	104.2	2.8
Mar	-9.5	5.3	-4.2	1.2	109.7	1.3	-2.5	4.8	2.3	3.2	100.0	3.2
Apr	0.2	4.5	4.7	1.4	107.7	1.5	4.5	4.5	9.0	3.5	100.0	3.5
May	7.8	3.6	11.4	2.1	103.2	2.2	13.0	4.0	17.0	3.4	100.0	3.4
June	14.5	3.0	17.5	3.0	110.0	3.3	18.0	3.8	21.8	3.3	103.3	3.4
July	17.0	2.9	19.9	3.0	111.1	3.3	21.0	4.0	25.0	4.0	103.8	4.2
Aug	14.8	3.1	17.9	2.9	113.0	3.3	18.5	4.3	22.8	3.7	95.2	3.5
Sept	9.5	3.7	13.2	2.9	110.0	3.2	15.0	4.4	19.4	3.3	77.8	2.6
Oct	4.0	4.6	8.6	2.1	116.7	2.5	10.0	4.5	14.5	3.2	70.0	2.3
Nov	-6.0	5.2	0.8	1.8	123.5	2.3	1.5	5.0	6.5	3.3	78.3	2.5
Dec	15.5	5.5	-10.0	1.3	123.5	1.6	-4.0	5.6	1.6	2.4	88.0	2.1
Mean	4.4			113.5			4.6			93.7		

NORM = 1951-80 normals
CH = magnitude of change between 1951-80 normals and 2 x CO_2 normal
2 x CO_2 = projected normals under 2 x CO_2 conditions

These climate data can be used to project future lake levels. A hydrologic model using climate data that simulates past levels and flows in the Great Lakes has been developed by the Great Lakes Environmental Research Laboratory (GLERL) in Ann Arbor, Michigan (Hartmann, 1990). This GLERL model and the period 1900 to 1977 was used as the base case. The hydrologic model was run using the GISS scenario to arrive at new series of lake levels for the period 1900-1977, levels that would have occurred during the period 1900-1977 under GISS climate change conditions. These hypothetical levels compared with actual measured levels are shown for Lake Erie in Figure 1.6. It is observed that under the GISS scenario (Case 2 in Figure 1.6), the average level of the lake would decline by about one half metre and the frequency of low levels, as in the 1960s, would increase to 70 per cent of the time. If the International Joint Commission predictions of increased consumptive use (water withdrawn from the lakes and not returned) are added to the model, the levels would decline further (Case 3 in Figure 1.6).

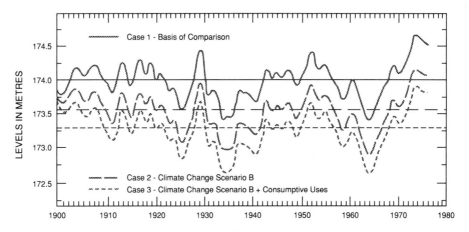

Figure 1.6: Yearly Mean Levels - Lake Erie

The impact of these levels on hydro electric power generation and the Canadian shipping industry on the Great Lakes was then evaluated with the following results (Sanderson, 1987):

- Average annual costs to Canadian Great Lakes shipping companies for the four principal cargoes, iron ore, grain, coal and limestone would increase (by approximately 30 per cent) under climate change.

- The frequency of years when shipping costs equal or exceed those of the period of low lake levels of 1963 to 1965 would increase to nine years in ten.

*   For the Canadian hydro generating stations on the Great Lakes, climate change plus the associated increased consumptive use would result in a loss of 4,165 gigawatt hours of power generation. Replacing the lost production with a mix of nuclear and fossil fuel generation would cost Ontario Hydro $111 ($ Canadian 1984) annually.

The Impact on Water in the Grand River Basin

The second part of this paper is concerned with climate change and the impact on water resources in the Grand River basin: on surface water, groundwater recharge and water deficiency.

The present climate for the city of Cambridge in the central part of the basin is illustrated in Table 1.2. This city has four months with below freezing mean temperatures, while the precipitation is fairly uniform throughout the year, totalling about 900 mm. The northern areas of the basin are a little colder and wetter and the southern and eastern sections a little warmer and drier than at Cambridge.

Table 1.2
Average Climate Data Cambridge (1951 to 1980)

	J	F	M	A	M	J	J	A	S	O	N	D	YR
Mean Daily Temperature °C	-6.0	-5.8	-1.0	6.4	13.0	17.8	20.6	19.6	15.5	9.3	3.4	-3.2	7.5
Precipitation (mm)	71	55	74	86	79	65	81	97	78	70	70	73	899

The changes in temperature and precipitation projected by three climate change scenarios — GISS, GFDL (Geophysical Fluid Dynamics Laboratory: Washington and Meehl, 1983) and CCC (Canadian Climate Centre: Boer, 1990) — are shown in Table 1.3. The changes in mean temperature range from 4.7°C (GISS) to 5.7°C (CCC) and all scenarios project increases in temperature that are greater in winter than in summer. As far as precipitation is concerned, the CCC projects a decrease (6 per cent) in precipitation in the basin while the other two scenarios project slight increases.

Table 1.3
Projected Changes in Monthly Temperature (C°) and Precipitation
(% Change) by Scenario for the Grand River Basin

Month	GISS Temp.	GISS Precip.	GFDL Temp.	GFDL Precip.	CCC Temp.	CCC Precip.
J	5.80	10.0	6.50	15.0	10.00	2.0
F	5.50	12.0	6.40	0.0	10.50	10.0
M	5.10	11.5	6.30	10.0	9.00	2.0
A	4.40	11.1	3.95	10.0	7.00	7.5
M	3.70	7.1	3.70	10.0	5.10	2.5
J	3.20	9.0	3.30	10.0	4.60	-5.0
J	3.40	8.1	5.50	-20.0	4.60	19.0
A	4.10	-3.0	5.60	-10.0	4.80	-18.0
S	4.90	-14.0	5.35	-15.0	4.30	-28.0
O	5.10	-9.0	5.40	0.0	3.60	-23.0
N	5.40	2.0	6.00	-5.0	2.10	-35.0
D	5.80	-11.5	5.50	0.0	2.50	-9.0
Mean	4.70	1.9	5.30	0.4	5.70	-6.3

The Thornthwaite water balance model (Thornthwaite and Mather, 1955) was used to estimate the monthly water loss from the surface to the atmosphere during the period of historical record for the 25 climatic stations in the basin. The locations of these stations are shown in Figure 1.7. During the period of record, in some cases more than 100 years, about two thirds of the precipitation in the basin, or about 600 mm, is evaporated, while one third runs off directly or recharges the groundwater table and eventually makes its way to the Grand River. The flows in the Grand River, measured since the 1940s, confirm that the percentage of precipitation that becomes river flow averages 33 per cent.

To estimate future changes in water in the basin, the three climate change scenarios were applied to the data for the 25 climate stations. The changes projected by the various scenarios are shown in Table 1.4. With increased temperature, the annual water loss to the atmosphere or evapotranspiration is projected to increase by 15 to 18 per cent. The river flow is estimated to decrease by 20 per cent for the GISS scenario and up to 39 per cent for the CCC climate change scenario. The amount of water that

Figure 1.7: The Grand River Basin showing the Location of Climatic Stations

recharges the groundwater table is estimated to decrease by 20 to 40 per cent. Table 1.4 also indicates that with increased temperature the amount of moisture deficiency (drought) would increase by 15 per cent (GISS) to 36 per cent (CCC). This would mean increased demand for water for irrigation (Sanderson and Smith, 1990).

Table 1.4
Climate Change Impact on Water Resources Grand River Basin:
Change in Per Cent

Scenario	Precipitation	Evapotrans-piration	Drought	Discharge in River
BASE	0	0	0	0
GISS	+2	+18	+15	-20
GFDL	+0.4	+15	+16	-22
CCC	-7	+17	+36	-39

Planning Implications and Conclusions

The government of Canada, like that of other countries, is taking the prospect of climate change very seriously. To try to reduce the increases in greenhouse gases in the atmosphere, Canada signed the United Nations Framework Convention on climate change at the United Nations conference on environment and development in Rio de Janiero in 1992. The object is to stabilize concentrations of anthropogenic greenhouse gases in the atmosphere. However, because some global warming seems inevitable, indeed has already occurred because of increased CO_2 levels, the government is funding a good deal of climate change research and has identified the Great Lakes basin as an area where the socio-economic impacts of climate change are to be evaluated (Mortsch et al., 1993).

In spite of scientific evidence to the contrary, many people believe that the levels of the lakes are manipulated by government agencies. During the period of high levels of the 1970s and 1980s, shore dwellers were concerned that governments were keeping the levels high by increasing the diversions into Lake Superior and by the regulation of that lake to benefit the hydro and shipping companies. As a result of intense lobbying by shore owners, the governments of Canada and the United States requested the

International Joint Commission to study methods of alleviating the adverse effects of fluctuating lake levels. The results of this study will be available later this year. A similar reference by governments to the International Joint Commission was made in the 1960s when extreme low levels occurred. In future, if lower lake levels occur with much greater frequency than at present, it is likely that the users of the lakes, especially the shipping and hydro power companies, as well as boaters and marina operators, will pressure the governments of the United States and Canada to "do something" to restore the lakes to their former levels.

If average lake levels decline by as much as two metres, as predicted by one U.S. study (Hartmann, 1990) the coastlines of the lakes will be very different from the present, most notably for the shallower lakes, Erie and St. Clair. With a decline in level of two metres, the actual water area of Lake St. Clair would decrease by almost 50 per cent. The management of shoreline areas would certainly see some changes if lake levels continued to be low for a period of time, since most present management efforts are concerned with erosion resulting from high lake levels, as a result of the long period of high levels during the 1970s and 1980s. What would the management policies be for the additional areas of coastal lands exposed by the lowered lakes?

Doubtless some previous large-scale water transfer projects would be reexamined. Mega schemes to divert water into the Great Lakes from other watersheds, e.g. the Grand Canal proposal, which entails diverting water from James Bay into the Great Lakes to stabilize levels (Bourassa, 1985) may be considered very seriously.

Climate change will have negative effects on water resources in the tributary Great Lakes basins, such as the Grand, as we have shown. Many municipalities depend on river flows for their water supply and, if urban population continues to increase and if the normal low summer flows are further reduced by 15-36 per cent under climate change, there could be problems of water supply. With the decreased ground water recharge, there would be problems with shallow wells. With increased irrigation demand, along with decreased river flows under the warmer climate conditions, it will be an interesting question as to who has the priority rights to the water — the farmer upstream or the municipality downstream. The option of building pipelines from one of the lakes to inland cities to augment the water supply, as was done from Lake Huron to London, Ontario, is already being considered by many municipalities. If climate-related problems include polluted local water supplies, there will be increased interest in such pipelines.

With the issue of climate change, geographers have a challenge that they are uniquely qualified to pursue, to examine physical geography problems and evaluate their impact on human activities. The research needs are enormous and the tasks exciting for geographers willing to undertake the challenge.

References

Boer, G. (1990) "Results of a 2 x CO_2 simulation with the Canadian Climate Centre GCM," in Wall, G. and Sanderson, M. (eds.), *Proceedings Conference Climate Change: Implications for Water and Ecological Resources*, Occasional Paper 11, Waterloo, Ontario: Department of Geography, University of Waterloo, 45-49.

Bourassa, R. (1985) *Power from the North*, Scarborough: Prentice-Hall.

Cohen, S. (1986) "Impacts of climate change on water resources in the Great Lakes basin, *Climate Change*, Vol. 8: 135-153.

Hansen, J.D. et al. (1981) "Climate impact of increasing atmospheric carbon dioxide," *Science,* Vol. 213: 957-966.

Hartmann, H. (1990) "Climate change impacts on Laurentian Great Lakes levels," *Climate Change*, Vol. 17: 49-67.

Mortsch, L., Koshida, G. and Tavares, D. (eds.) (1993) *Adapting to the Impacts of Climate Change and Variability,* Proceedings of a Workshop, Québec City, February 7-11.

Sanderson, M. (1987) "Implications of climatic change for navigation and power generation in the Great Lakes," *Climate Change Digest,* 87-103, Environment Canada.

Sanderson, M., Ekern, P., Giambelluca, T., Nullet, D., Price, S. and Schroeder, T. (1993) *Prevailing Trade Winds: Weather and Climate in Hawaii,* Hawaii: University of Hawaii Press.

Sanderson, M. and Smith, J. (1990) "Climate Change and Water in the Grand River Basin, Ontario," in McNeil, R.Y. and Windsor, J.E. (eds.), *Innovations in River Basin Management*, Cambridge: Canadian Water Resources Association, 243-261.

Smit, B. (1987) "Implications of climate change for agriculture in Ontario," *Climate Change Digest*, 87-102, Environment Canada.

Thornthwaite, C.W. and Mather, J. (1955) "The water balance," *Publications in Climatology*, Vol. 8(1).

Washington, W. and Meehl, G. (1983) "General Circulation Model experiments on the climatic effects due to a doubling and quadrupling of CO_2," *Journal of Geophysical Research,* Vol. 88: 6600-6610.

Chapter 2

Environmental Refugees : Some Issues for Canada

Alan Nash and Alena Perout
Concordia University and Vanier College

Introduction

There has been a growing concern about the topic of "environmental refugees" in recent years, sparked by the parallel developments of a growing
public concern for the environment, and news of repeated ecological crises
across the globe.

However, this concern has not translated itself into any meaningful debate
about the policy issues that problems of environmental refugees raise. In
this paper, we attempt to consider some of these issues: first, by distinguishing carefully between "political" and "environmental" refugees; second, by considering Canada's obligations towards environmental refugees
in particular; third, by discussing Canada's record of achievement with regard to refugees in general; and, finally, by discussing the significance of
environmental refugees for Canadian public policy.

Refugees: "Political" and "Environmental"

Under the terms of the International Convention relating to the Status of
Refugees, refugees, or "Convention refugees" as they are more formally
termed, are defined as any person who

> "...owing to well-founded fear of being persecuted for reasons of
> race, religion, nationality, membership of a particular social group
> or political opinion, is outside the country of his origin and is unable
> or, owing to such fear, is unwilling to avail himself of the protection
> of that country; or ... owing to such fear, is unwilling to return to it"
> (Article 1(A)(2) para.2; United Nations, 1983: 11).

Since the enactment of the Convention in 1951, the problem has changed
from being mainly a European phenomenon to a Third World dilemma, and
has grown enormously. Thus, in 1984 the Office of the United Nations High

Commissioner for Refugees (UNHCR) estimated there were 10.8 million Convention refugees worldwide; by 1990 the estimate was over 15 million (UNHCR, 1984; World Women's Congress, 1991). As Figure 2.1 shows, these people were mostly located in the developing world, and more specifically in the African continent and parts of Asia (see also Nash, 1989).

The factors causing this growth in refugee flows and its changing distribution are, to quote the United Nations Group of Governmental Experts on International Co-operation to Avert New Flows of Refugees, "a result of a number of complex and often interrelated political, economic and social problems related to, and influenced by the overall international situation" (UN, 1986: paragraph 63).

In one very useful categorization, Zia Rizvi (1988) has sought to divide the factors responsible for refugee movements in general into three groups, as follows: "primary factors," which include those violations of human rights enumerated in the 1951 international Convention relating to the Status of Refugees that are direct grounds upon which to claim refugee status under the Convention, as in the case of the 15 million noted above; "secondary factors," such as civil war, that are partly enumerated in the 1969 Convention adopted by the Organization of African Unity and becoming more widely accepted by the international community as additional basis on which to define a broader refugee status; and, finally, "auxiliary factors" which, Rizvi argues, are newly recognized and considered excluded from traditional international concepts of refugee status. These include economic, demographic and ecological factors.

According to Rizvi (1988), such "auxiliary factors," or "root causes" as they are more generally known, are increasingly dominating the refugee scene. They will continue to do so for two reasons: first, through an indirect and complex causal relationship in which such root causes result in persecution on the five grounds defined in the 1951 Convention; second, through the direct generation of mass movements of people fleeing economic, demographic or ecological crises in their own countries in order to seek desperately needed succor elsewhere.

As an example, if we define "ecological" or "environmental refugees" as

> "...individuals who have been forced to leave their country of origin due to the deterioration of their surrounding environment, which no longer provides basic elements needed to sustain life" (Perout and Nash, 1992)

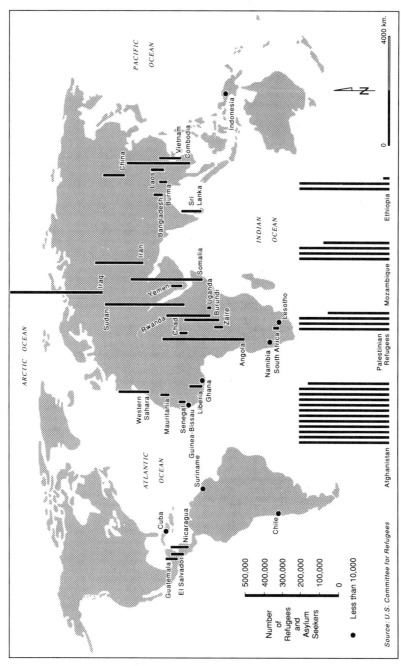

Figure 2.1: Refugees and Asylum Seekers in need of Protection and / or Assistance by Source Country, 1989

one writer has estimated that as many as 10 million migrants can be considered environmental refugees (Jacobson, 1988: 6), a figure that nearly doubles the world's total number of refugees and, of course, would signifi cantly increase the size of the problem to be faced by the global community.

But the point is that this definition has not been accepted. Rizvi's "auxiliary factors" may trigger movement because of a denial of rights that are guaranteed by the International Covenant on Economic and Social Rights, but environmental or economic causes in themselves are not recognized by the 1951 Convention as ones defining refugee status (Hathaway, 1991). Thus, environmental or economic migrants cannot earn either the official designation of "Convention refugee" or the protection from refoulement and the financial assistance that this situation affords. Nevertheless, their movement challenges the global community, not only because they are a growing phenomenon but also because they lie outside the traditional framework that the world has developed to resolve refugee issues (Rizvi, 1988). It is this challenge that we propose to address in this paper, taking the case of "environmental refugees" in particular and considering the situation from a Canadian perspective.

Canada's Obligations Towards Environmental Refugees

Having defined the phenomenon of environmental refugees and indicated the dilemma of their position, that is on the one hand, their need for assistance, but on the other their current lack of international recognition, it is necessary now to examine how Canada responded to the challenge they pose. This will be done here by analyzing two basic questions: first, why should Canada be concerned about the plight of such people and, second — if it appears that Canada should be concerned — what, in terms of practical policy, can this country do?

The first question — should Canada be concerned about the existence, and growing number, of environmental refugees — can be dealt with on two levels, using what Adelman (1988), writing about the case of refugees in general, has recently called the principles of "self-sacrifice" and "self-interest." Using the principle of self-sacrifice, it could be argued on a moral or ethical level that, whoever we are and wherever we may be, we should be concerned with the plight and suffering of other people, because they are a part of our shared humanity — a view perhaps best expressed by the metaphysical Anglican cleric John Donne when he wrote that "any man's death diminishes me because I am a part of mankind." Indeed, as Adelman himself has argued

"At its limit, self-sacrifice entails the sacrifice of the individual out of universal obligation to all mankind. Some call it charity when the self-sacrifice is limited to a limited portion of one's personal bounty. Rawls and Walzer call their principle mutual aid since the principle of helping strangers who happen to cross your path is qualified even further by minimal risk to oneself (1971, 114; 1983, 45). Nevertheless, the principle of self-sacrifice, the principle of charity, and the principle of mutual aid all proceed from a source opposite to self-interest — even if self-interest qualifies them to different degrees — the duty to sacrifice self for the benefit of others" (Adelman, 1988: 84; author's emphasis).

The alternative principle of self-interest relies, at least in its general sense, on the fundamental principle of justice, that every individual is entitled to the protection of a state in a territory where they can earn the necessities of life. As Adelman has argued

"States that share that principle must collectively extend that principle to those who are the victims of states that do not live up to the principle. If they do not accept the principle as a universal obligation, that is, if they do not apply the principle to all mankind, they would not be entitled to claim that belief as a principle of justice. It is precisely by making their particular beliefs a universal obligation of all and to all mankind that self-interest is built into a principle of justice" (Adelman, 1988: 84).

He extends this reasoning by arguing that a concern for the preservation of international order — surely the concern of most nation states — derives directly from this principle. Thus

"...it is in the self-interest of states that adopt the duty to protect their individual members to extend that protection to individuals outside the protection of any state, lest these stateless individuals create disorder in their quest for the necessities of life and for protection and thereby threaten the international order" (Adelman, 1988: 84).

Otherwise, as Adelman has noted elsewhere, "the nations will de facto encourage the stateless to take explosive measures to demonstrate the hazards of their statelessness" (Adelman, 1991a: 19).

Beyond these general arguments, self-interest is also engaged in the specific case of environmental refugees because of the obvious point that we are all part of one global interacting environmental system. In brief, the movement of environmental refugees from areas that can no longer sustain habitation may increase the pressures of population and promote accelerated decay in the surrounding territories to which they move, and so may ultimately prompt further migrations ever further afield. In addition, because of the complex interrelatedness of the world's ecosystem, a deterioration in one part of that system may ultimately have environmental ramifications across the whole global system. In this way, Canada is affected by practices far outside its borders, for both the initial circumstances which caused the environmental refugees to move, and the stresses that their subsequent movements place upon other areas will affect the global ecosystem of which this country is a part. Thus, for example, Third World deforestation not only partly influences local populations to migrate to neighbouring locales where they, in turn, put additional stresses upon the local environment, but may also contribute to global warming and sea level increase, which could have profound effects upon the ability of Canada's environment to support its own population.

This elaborate chain of events may appear surprising but a brief consideration of the processes involved clearly demonstrates the connections. Thus, it is well-known that the so-called "greenhouse gases" — methane, nitrous oxide, ground-level ozone, chlorofluorocarbons and, principally, carbon dioxide — trap the warmth of the sun before it is radiated out into space by the earth. Without this "greenhouse effect," the earth's average temperature would drop to about -18°C. Just as importantly, increasing amounts of greenhouse gases in the atmosphere are expected to result in an increase in global mean temperatures of between 2.6 and 5.8°C over the next century and in increases in sea level — due to the melting of the ice caps and, principally, to the expansion of water held in the oceans — of between 0.3 and 1.0 metres over the same period (MacNeill et al., 1991). This would pose what the Brundtland Commission identifies as a "threat to life-support systems" (World Commission on Environment and Development, 1987: 33) and what Linda Starke (1990) refers to as "disaster" in her recent book *Signs of Hope.* She observes that

> "[p]rime agricultural areas could suddenly find that crops will no longer thrive there. After decades of investment, irrigation systems could be useless, or in the wrong place. Tropical systems are expected to increase in number and severity. Low-lying delta regions and islands are particularly threatened by the expected global sea-level rise. In fact, the President of the Maldives ... recently invited

the Commonwealth Heads of Government to hold their meeting in the Maldives in 2030, but warned that it might have to be under water" (Starke, 1990: 20).

Of course, the case of the Maldives serves as a remarkable and perhaps extreme example of what might happen, but the possible impact of these phenomena on countries such as Canada, while perhaps less severe, should not be overlooked. This is recognized in the Canadian government's recent *Green Plan* where the possible effects of global warming are shown on a map of Canada[1] and listed as follows:

> (1) northern British Columbia: "warmer temperatures could cause changes in fish populations"; (2) central Alberta: "changes in rainfall patterns could increase drought in the Prairies"; (3) southern Saskatchewan: "water supplies in Southern Canada could decline significantly"; (4) central Saskatchewan: "soil degradation and erosion of prairie land may increase due to moisture loss"; (5) Ontario: "Great Lakes winter ice system may disappear"; (6) northern Quebec: "forest region could shift northward, with deciduous trees growing as far north as James Bay"; (7) Gulf of St. Lawrence: "many coastal areas could be flooded"; (8) Nova Scotia: "inshore fisheries season could be extended"; (9) Southern Ontario: "snow seasons could disappear" (Environment Canada, 1990: 99).

MacNeill et al. add that "[g]lobal warming will also increase the probability of severe droughts in the agricultural heartlands of ... North America" and highlight southern British Columbia on their map entitled "Coastal areas vulnerable to sea-level rise" (MacNeill, Winsemius and Yakushiji, 1991: 15-16). On a smaller scale, future problems appear similarly compelling. As but one example, the *Green Plan* notes that a one metre rise in sea level would affect more than 250 houses in Charlottetown, Prince Edward Island, and would contaminate local ground water sources with sea water (Environment Canada, 1990: 99).

From this discussion it appears that considerations of both self-interest and self-sacrifice should compel Canada to be concerned with the plight of en-

---

1   The numbering and location of the quoted phenomena are exactly as given on the *Green Plan's* map; however, it is clear from the wording used by Environment Canada that a number of the possible changes described would affect wider areas of Canada.

vironmental refugees. It is because both motives are involved in this case that the argument can be put this strongly. Otherwise, Canada's record, as measured by its current overseas aid budget or Convention refugee programs is not one that would lead us to suggest that motives of self-sacrifice on their own would be sufficient to prompt this country into extensive action on behalf of environmental refugees. However, the additional threat of large numbers of people arriving on our borders due to the collapse of their environment, and the effects of that collapse on the ability of the global environment to sustain Canada's ecosystems must surely prompt a government response — if only out of a sense of responsibility to the Canadian people. The principle of self-interest demands it.

Having suggested that Canada should be concerned with the plight of environmental refugees, in order to deepen an understanding of the strategies that this country might use to alleviate their problems, it is necessary now to briefly consider Canada's traditional response to refugees before turning to a discussion of future policy options.

Canada's Traditional Response to Refugees

Only after the end of the Second World War does it become possible to examine in detail the flow of refugees to Canada. Indeed, this coincides with increased activity in this field, the establishment of Canadian refugee and humanitarian programs, the increasing number of refugees worldwide seeking asylum and the development of international responses following the 1951 Convention. The data indicate that nearly one third of a million refugees and beneficiaries of humanitarian programs landed in Canada between 1947 and 1980 (see Table 2.1). The predominant components of this movement were the post-war flow from Europe between 1947 and 1957 (some 186,000 individuals) and the Indochinese Refugee Program of 1979-1980 (60,049). These two movements accounted for 74 per cent of the total flow between 1947 and 1980.

In terms of origins, between 1947 and 1980, using the regional definitions of Employment and Immigration Canada (EIC), 235,942 refugees arrived from Europe (71 per cent of the total flow), 69,337 from Southeast Asia (21 per cent), 9,169 from Africa (2.7 percent), 7,025 from Latin America (2.1 per cent) and 11,419 from the Middle East/West Asia region (3.4 per cent). This period was thus one that was heavily influenced by a European bias — originating in the post-war exodus, but continued by events such as the Hungarian and Czech uprisings. This trend was modified somewhat towards the end of the period by events in Southeast Asia, but other regions of the world were largely ignored.

Table 2.1
Special Refugee and Humanitarian Movements
1947 - 1980

Year	Movement	No. of Refugees
1947-1957	Post-war European Movement	186,150
1956 & 1957	Hungarian Movement	37,149
1968 & 1969	Czechoslovakian Movement	11,943
1970	Tibetan Movement	228
1972 & 1973	Ugandan Asian Movement	7,069
1973-1979	Special South American Program	7,016
1975	Cypriot Special Program	700
1975-1978	Special Vietnamese/Cambodian Program	9,060
1976	Iraqi Kurdish Movement	98
1976 & 1977	Angola/Mozambique Returnees	2,100
1976-1979	Lebanese Special Program	11,321
1978	Argentinian Political Prisoner Program	9
1979 & 1980	Indochinese Refugee Program	*60,049
Total		332,892

Source: EIC, 1982: 32
Note: * Separate totals for 1979 and 1980 Indochinese refugee intake sum to 60,069 (EIC, 1982: 32)

Over the period 1981 to 1987, 140,869 individuals were admitted or landed in Canada under refugee and humanitarian programs (see Table 2.2). Of this total, 116,775 were admitted as refugees (Convention Refugees and members of the Designated Classes, either government or privately-sponsored) and 24,094 (or 17 per cent of the total) under the humanitarian programs. The regional origins of this flow, for the years 1982-1987 are presented in Table 2.3. From this, it can be seen that over the period, Eastern Europe and Southeast Asia each represented a third of all refugee flows into Canada and thus dominated the picture. Latin America contributed 17.6 per cent while Africa (5.8 per cent), the Middle East (4.3 per cent) and others (2.5 per cent, principally Sri Lanka and Afghanistan) were minor contributors to the total. However, this overall picture conceals some significant short-term variations. In 1979 and 1980 the bulk of Canada's refugee intake came from Indochina (EIC: 1982, 32), but by 1982 Eastern Europe contributed 57.4 per cent of the total and Southeast Asia's proportion had fallen to 32.2 per cent. Latin America (4.8 per cent), the Middle East (1.6 per cent), Africa (2.3 per cent) and others (1.2 per cent) were all minor

Table 2.2
Canada's Refugee and Humanitarian Programs
1979 - 1987, By Annual Totals

| | Year | Refugee Admissions[a] | | Special Program Landings[b] | Refugee Claims in Canada Landings[c] | Special Review Committee[d] | Total |
		Gov't Sponsored	Privately Funded				
	1979	13,730	13,781				[e]27,879
	1980	19,237	21,111				40,348
	1981	10,592	4,387				14,979
Total, 1979-1981		**43,559**	**39,279**				**83,206**
	1982	11,352	4,859	5,307	697		22,215
	1983	8,941	4,076	4,236	626	192	18,071
	1984	10,547	3,893	5,206	960	167	20,773
Total, 1982-1984		**30,840**	**12,828**	**14,749**	**2,283**	**359**	**61,059**
	1985	11,559	3,795	3,196	1,196	139	19,885
	1986	12,146	5,064	2,794	1,412	92	21,508
	1987	12,223	7,008	2,606	1,442	159	23,438
Total, 1985-1987		**35,928**	**15,867**	**8,596**	**4,050**	**390**	**64,831**
Total, 1979-1987		**110,327**	**67,974**	**23,345**	**6,333**	**749**	**209,096**

Sources: Employment and Immigration, Policy and Program Development Branch, Refugee Affairs Division 1983, 4; 1984, 37; 1985, 34; 1986, 60; 1987a; 1987b, 39-40; data for 1979 to 1981 and unpublished preliminary data for 1987 provided by David White, Employment and Immigration, Policy and Program Development Branch, Refugees Affairs Division, 1 March 1988.

Notes:

[a]Before 1982 data show landings; after 1982 they show admissions because they include persons arriving at ports of entry with immigrant visas and, where known, those processed abroad on an emergency basis (who enter on the strength of a Minister's Permit, and who are not granted permanent residence ('landing') until full compliance with the 1976 Act and the Regulations is demonstrated).

[b]Persons who were neither Convention refugees nor Designated Class immigrants, but who were assisted under the special humanitarian programs for El Salvador, Poland, Lebanon, Iran, Sri Lanka and, from 1984, Guatemala. No Special Program Landings occurred before 1982.

[c]Persons who were found to be Convention refugees under the provisions of the refugee determination process in Canada and who were subsequently granted permanent residence. Refugee claims in Canda Landings are included under government - and privately sponsored refugee admissions for 1979 to 1981.

[d]Special Review Committee Approvals: Persons from countries benefitting from Canada's humanitarian programs who were permitted to apply for permanent residence in Canada without undergoing a refugee determination.

[e]The 1976 Immigration Act did not come into force until 1978; this total includes 368 refugees who were processed according to the previous legislation and who, consequently, cannot be distinguished as government or privately-sponsored refugee admissions.

*1987 data are preliminary

Table 2.3
Canada's Refugee and Humanitarian Programs
1982-1987, By Region

Region	Year	Refugee Admissions[a]		Special Program Landings[b]	Claims in Canada Landings[c]	Special Review Committee[d]	Total
		Gov't Sponsored	Privately Funded				
Eastern	1982	6,054	3,258	3,302	68		12,682
Europe	1983	2,649	1,558	2,893	67	164	7,331
	1984	2,641	909	2,217	63	121	5,951
	1985	2,517	1,288	761	46	123	4,735
	1986	3,404	1,952	192	20	87	5,655
	1987*	3,713	2,912	—	19	121	6,765
	Total	**20,978**	**11,877**	**9,365**	**283**	**616**	**43,119**
Southeast	1982	4,091	1,202	—	86		5,379
Asia[e]	1983	3,013	1,647	—	12	8	4,680
	1984	3,749	2,090	—	10	16	5,865
	1985	4,406	1,703	—	6	3	6,118
	1986	3,931	2,059	—	11	5	6,006
	1987*	2,995	2,698	—	3	9	5,705
	Total	**22,185**	**11,399**	**—**	**128**	**41**	**33,753**
Middle	1982	61	196	506	61		824
East[f]	1983	296	388	621	100	—	1,405
	1984	584	368	1,631	79	—	2,662
	1985	440	283	1,363	328	—	2,414
	1986	305	342	1,636	418	—	2,701
	1987*	520	345	1,906	270	3	3,044
	Total	**2,206**	**1,922**	**7,663**	**1,256**	**3**	**13,050**
Latin	1982	732	47	1,499	418		2,696
America	1983	2,164	139	690	348	20	3,361
	1984	2,545	241	478	580	30	3,874
	1985	3,133	247	665	401	13	4,459
	1986	3,422	232	704	377	—	4,735
	1987*	3,688	273	408	342	26	4,737
	Total	**15,684**	**1,179**	**4,444**	**2,466**	**89**	**23,862**
Africa	1982	288	84	—	22	—	394
	1983	653	170	—	64	—	887
	1984	861	177	—	69	—	1,107
	1985	786	171	—	90	—	1,047
	1986	846	318	—	83	—	1,247
	1987*	795	473	—	109	—	1,377
	Total	**4,229**	**1,393**	**—**	**437**	**—**	**6,059**
Others[f]	1982	126	72	—	42	—	240
	1983	166	174	32	35	—	407
	1984	167	108	880	159	—	1,314
	1985	277	103	407	325	—	1.112
	1986	238	161	262	503	—	1.164
	1987*	512	307	292	699	—	1,810
	Total	**1,486**	**925**	**1,873**	**1,763**	**—**	**6,047**
Total 1982-1987		**66,768**	**28,695**	**23,345**	**6,333**	**749**	**125,890**

Source: Employment and Immigration, Policy and Program Development Branch, Refugee Affairs Division, 1983, 4; 1984, 37; 1985, 34; 1986, 60; 1987a; 1987b, 40; unpublished preliminary data for 1987 provided by David White, Employment and Immigration, Policy and Program Development Branch, Refugee Affairs Division, 1 March 1988.
Notes:
aIncludes persons arriving at ports of entry with immigrant visas and, where known, those processed abroad on an emergency basis (who enter on the strength of a Minister's Permit, and who are not granted permanent residence ('landing') until full compliance with the 1976 Act and the Regulations is demonstrated).
bPersons who were neither Convention refugees nor Designated Class immigrants, but who were assisted under the special humanitarian programs for El Salvador, Poland, Lebanon, Iran, Sri Lanka and, from 1984, Guatemala.
cPersons who were found to be Convention refugees under the provisions of the refugee determination process in Canada and who were subsequently granted permanent residence.
dSpecial Review Committee Approvals: persons from countries benefitting from Canada's humanitarian programs who were permitted to apply for permanent residence in Canada without undergoing a refugee determination.
eIn 1982, and from 1986, this category is called 'Indochina'.
fFrom 1985, data for Afghanistan were moved from the category 'Others' and placed in the category 'Middle East' which then became known as 'West Asia'. However, in order to ensure consistency in this table, Afghanistan's data have been included in the category 'Others' for the whole period 1982 to 1987. In 1987, Afghanistan's data were distributed as follows: government-sponsored admissions, 372; privately-sponsored admissions, 216; and refugee claims in Canada landings, 174.
*1987 data are preliminary.

source regions. By 1987, Eastern Europe's contribution had fallen from its 1982 level to 34.4 per cent, and Southeast Asia's contribution had also diminished to 29.6 per cent. All other world regions saw increases; the share arriving from the Middle East rose to 4.5 per cent, Africa to 6.6 per cent and others rose to 4.3 per cent. The largest increase was recorded by Latin America, whose contribution rose to 20.6 per cent by 1987, suggesting that this region is becoming the third principal source of Canada's refugee flows.

Table 2.4 presents data on the breakdown of these flows by country for 1986 and shows that the regional picture just discussed is determined largely by one major source country in each region and is founded on the contributions of a very limited range of countries. Thus, while Eastern Europe contributed 31 per cent of Canada's refugee intake in 1986, Poland alone was responsible for 21 per cent. Vietnam contributed 21 per cent, Kampuchea 9 per cent, El Salvador 13 per cent and Ethiopia 5 per cent. No other country recorded over 4 per cent. Interestingly, as Figure 2.1 suggests, these figures are at marked variance with these countries' shares of the total world refugee population; nevertheless, these five countries alone were responsible for 60 per cent of all refugee admissions into Canada from abroad in 1986.

Future Policy Options

Having shown the extent of Canada's response to those that fit the traditional definitions of "refugee," it is now possible to consider the policy options that this country has available with regard to environmental refugees. These fall under three broad headings: first, recognize the plight of environmental refugees by including them within the criteria of those eligible for refugee assistance; second, deal with the root causes of their plight; and, third, promote an international response.

In terms of the first, Canada could take rapid and imaginative steps to include environmental refugees within the definition of those it treats as refugee and humanitarian cases. The majority of such cases currently admitted to Canada are not, in any case, Convention refugees but rather enter under one of this country's humanitarian programs. These programs are targeted at "quasi-refugees", individuals whom Canada would like to help but who fall outside the strict definitions of the 1951 Convention definition (Adelman, 1991b: 210-217). To do this, the 1976 Immigration Act allowed for the establishment, by regulation, of the Special Measures programs and the Designated Classes, an authority which has been used extensively by the government since then (Nash, 1989: 39-41). Indeed, it is estimated that 75

Table 2.4
Total Refugee Admissions From Abroad
By Source Country, 1986

Country of Last Permanent Residence	Refugee Admissions From Abroad (a)		Special Program Landings (b)		Total (c)	
	No.	%	No.	%	No.	%
Eastern Europe						
Poland	3,591	20.86	192	6.87	3,783	18.91
Czechoslovakia	684	3.97	-	-	684	3.42
Hungary	543	3.15	-	-	543	2.71
Romania	438	2.54	-	-	438	2.19
U.S.S.R.	40	0.23	-	-	40	0.20
Others	60	0.35	-	-	60	0.30
Total	**5,356**	**31.12**	**192**	**6.87**	**5,548**	**27.73**
Southeast Asia						
Vietnam	3,680	21.38	-	-	3,680	18.39
Kampuchea	1,641	9.53	-	-	1,641	8.20
Laos	602	3.50	-	-	602	3.01
Others	67	0.39	-	-	67	0.33
Total	**5,990**	**34.80**	-	-	**5,990**	**29.94**
Latin America						
Chile	183	1.06	-	-	183	0.91
Argentina	3	0.02	-	-	3	0.01
Others	9	0.05	-	-	9	0.04
South America	**195**	**1.13**	-	-	**195**	**0.97**
El Salvador	2,186	12.70	230	8.23	2,416	12.08
Guatemala	537	3.12	474	16.96	1,011	5.05
Nicaragua	646	3.75	-	-	646	3.23
Others	58	0.34	-	-	58	0.29
Central America	**3,427**	**19.91**	**704**	**25.20**	**4,131**	**20.65**
Cuba	30	0.17	-	-	30	0.15
Haiti	2	0.01	-	-	2	0.01
Others	-	-	-	-	-	-
Caribbean	**32**	**0.18**	-	-	**32**	**0.16**
Total	**3,654**	**21.22**	**704**	**25.20**	**4,358**	**21.78**
Middle East						
Afghanistan	302	1.75	-	-	302	1.51
Iran	450	2.61	469	16.79	919	4.59
Iraq	125	0.73	-	-	125	0.62
Lebanon	22	0.13	1,167	41.77	1,189	5.94
Others	50	0.29	-	-	50	0.25
Total	**949**	**5.51**	**1,636**	**58.55**	**2,585**	**12.92**
Africa						
Ethiopia	876	5.09	-	-	876	4.38
Uganda	49	0.28	-	-	49	0.24
Sudan	18	0.10	-	-	18	0.09
Nigeria	1	*	-	-	1	*
South Africa	51	0.30	-	-	51	0.25
Others	169	0.98	-	-	169	0.84
Total	**1,164**	**6.76**	-	-	**1,164**	**5.82**
Others						
Sri Lanka	26	0.15	262	9.37	288	1.44
Others	74	0.43	-	-	74	0.37
Total	**100**	**0.58**	**262**	**9.37**	**362**	**1.81**
TOTAL	**17,213**	**100%**	**2,794**	**100%**	**20,007**	**100%**

Source: Employment and Immigration, Policy and Program Development Branch, Refugee Affairs Division 1987b, 42-43.

Notes:
a. "Refugee admissions from abroad" includes those arriving at ports of entry with immigrant visas and, where known, those processed abroad on an emergency basis who enter on the strength of a Minister's Permit pending landing after full compliance with the 1976 Act and Regulations is demonstrated.
b. "Special program landings": persons who were neither Convention refugees nor Designated Class immigrants, but who were assisted under the special humanitarian programs for El Salvador, Poland, Lebanon, Iran, Sri Lanka, and Guatemala.
c. "Total": total refugee admissions from abroad and Special program landings.
* Percentage too small for tabulation.
Due to rounding, sub-totals may not sum to exactly 100 per cent.

per cent of Canada's entire refugee and humanitarian landings fall into these categories. Special Measures programs have, for example, assisted many Poles to reach Canada, while the Indochinese Designated Class facilitated the entry of thousands of Vietnamese boatpeople into this country during the late 1970s and early 1980s (Hathaway, 1988). This being the case, it is clear that Canada could easily extend its assistance and protection to environmental refugees — beyond the additional and necessary policies of expanding in situ humanitarian assistance to affected areas in order to counter massive potential movements of such people — simply by creating another humanitarian landing program to accommodate them. Having said this, it is worth adding that because Canada would only be able to admit a limited number of such individuals, not only because Canada obviously cannot provide a home for all the world's environmental refugees but also because of the ever-present fear of engendering a public backlash against immigration, the country's attention would be best focused upon specific areas of the world where such action could achieve the most effect.

Research is urgently needed to identify such "strategic" areas but one example can be quoted here to illustrate the argument. If it is the case that human-induced environmental degradation in parts of the Himalayan highlands in Bhutan are responsible for the increased intensity and severity of flooding further downstream in Bangladesh (Karan, 1987: 15), one possible solution to the problem might be for Canada to provide resettlement opportunities for the small Himalayan population involved. This would not only immeasurably improve the lot of these people but also would remove the threat of future difficulties for the far larger populations of those parts of Bangladesh downstream.

To provide more than mere alleviation, Canada must, of course, begin to address the root cause of the problem — to address one of Rizvi's "auxiliary factors" that cause refugee movements — the degradation of the environment that has and will occasion the production of environmental refugees. In this regard, Canada should consider eliminating CIDA projects that are environmentally unsound and, instead, create "sustainable development aid"; the provision of "clean up" project funding for Third World and Eastern European countries that need it; the promotion and provision of environmental education in countries where it is required; the promotion and provision of equipment that encourages sustainable practices such as solar ovens in refugee camps in Africa or the provision of non-CFC refrigerant technology to China; the encouragement of research and development in environmentally-sound endeavours that can then be used to benefit the wider world community; and, "early warning" research to pinpoint regions of the world that might be affected most by future changes in the environment and where the potential for refugee flows might be greatest unless action is taken.

Lastly, in terms of domestic response, it is important not to forget that Canada's own treatment of its environment has to be considered. This is not only because the overconsumption of resources and production of pollution by Canadians threatens the world's fragile ecosystem but because the pressures of Canada's growing population itself threatens — both in a real and a perceived sense — the sustainability of the Canadian environment and therefore, perhaps ironically, its ability to provide a home for Canadians and a safe haven for those fleeing the collapse of environments elsewhere in the world.

The areas of Canada under threat in this way — through the increasing pollution of water supplies, urban expansion, the greater use of toxic chemicals in farming and manufacturing, the overexploitation of natural resources on land and sea — can be easily pinpointed by the use of three examples at different scales. At the broadest scale, of course, the whole country is affected as but a cursory glance at the *Green Plan* makes clear. At a regional level, the Great Lakes - St. Lawrence system with its 17 priority "hot spots" and 42 "areas of concern" stands as an example of the insidious effects of years of pollution (Environment Canada, 1990: 32-33). At a metropolitan level, as long ago as 1976, the report *Human Settlement in Canada* remarked that

> "[t]he majority of urban growth in Canada is taking place in three of the nation's most fertile areas: south-central Ontario, the St. Lawrence lowlands in Quebec, and the Lower Mainland in British Columbia. Together these three areas contain 24 million acres of the finest agricultural land in Canada. Much of it is unique because of mild climate, good rainfall, and excellent soil. There can be no doubt that significant tracts of this land are threatened by the expansion of settlement" (Canadian Habitat Secretariat, 1976: 52).

Yet, there is extreme reticence to examine the effects of growing numbers of people in Canada because, as Regier and Bales have recently argued,

> "...the population question is tied directly to immigration, an activity with which many environmentalists are historically sympathetic. To demonstrate the deleterious effect of expanding population numbers on the health of terrestrial and aquatic ecosystems, and to implicate immigrants, may attract an undesirable group of supporters — the so-called 'red necks' " (1991: 2).

Already such concerns have begun to surface in fora as various as the Canada Employment and Immigration Advisory Council, where we are told that "it would be worthwhile in a proactive sense to delve deeper into the issue [of environment and immigration] before the perception settles that immigrants damage the environment" (CEIAC, 1991: 31), or the anti-growth lobby group known as Zero Population Growth (1991: 2) which notes that "our social and environmental problems will worsen as long as we continue to allow a rate of high migration...more people means more severe problems." Undoubtedly, if this challenge is to be met, not only will existing environmental educational programs for Canadians have to be made effective but also similar programs must be established for new immigrants, renewed attention must be given to the issues of the country's ultimate carrying capacity under a range of technologies, and regional policies for immigration within Canada must be considered.

Canada cannot solve the plight of environmental refugees on its own, and for this reason the final set of initiatives must include those of international response and burden-sharing — responses that require a world commitment but in which, obviously, Canada might be able to play more than its part through exercising its traditional leadership in humanitarian issues or by galvanizing the many world bodies of which it is a member. Policies in this respect include the renegotiation of the 1951 Convention refugee definition so that environmental refugees might be eligible for the protection and assistance of the UNHCR and all countries party to such an agreement. Interestingly, the noted legal scholar Guy Goodwin-Gill has recently argued that the current meaning of the principle of non-refoulement "must now be understood beyond and apart from its formulation in article 33 of the [1951] Convention." He continues, "[t]he range of relevant situations could arguably encompass all in distress, whether from natural disaster, from human misadventure, or so-called man-made disaster" (Goodwin-Gill, 1991: 28).

Other international responses include the rejection by multilateral bodies, such as the World Bank and the International Monetary Fund, of non-sustainable development projects; agreement on a set of environmental initiatives that will comprise an Earth Charter at the 1992 United Nations Conference on Environment and Development; the linking of foreign policy and external trade issues with not only humanitarian issues, as Canada has recently championed, but also with environmental practice; and, lastly, a resolution of the Third World debt crisis before many of the nations involved have destroyed all their natural resources in order simply to service their huge loans.

To conclude, the above responses to the challenge of environmental refugees form part of a set of enlightened long-term solutions that are needed. What is greatly to be feared now is that the Canadian government will continue to concentrate its efforts on the largely ineffectual short-term strategies that it currently employs, such as confining its attention to the prevention of entry into Canada of such people, rather than dealing with the larger dimensions of the problem of which it apparently is fully aware. This awareness is highlighted by the fact that the Intelligence Advisory Committee, in a confidential Canadian Intelligence Estimate report to the Cabinet that was recently leaked to the Canadian Press, noted that nearly all the world's environmental problems will have major effects on Canada. It foresaw major ecological disaster or North-South conflicts over the issue and concluded that

> "Canada can expect to have increasing numbers of environmental refugees requesting immigration to Canada, while regional movements of the population at home, such as from idle fishing areas, will add further to population stresses within the country" (quoted in Mooney, 1991: A2).

Yet, despite these conclusions, the government has had nothing to say with regard to responsible, sensitive solutions and, elsewhere we learn, is not even prepared to consider broadening the international definition of refugee because, according to a spokesperson for Bernard Valcourt, the Minister of Immigration, "if the refugee definition is drawn too broadly, we risk defining the problem into complete unmanageability" (quoted in Oziewicz, 1991).

In the case of Convention refugees, it is possible that Canada — in conjunction with the other nations of the West — can continue to avoid the consequences of such strategies of avoidance and exclusion. However, in the case of environmental refugees, as we have seen in this paper, this can only be a vain hope. Their current plight is intimately connected with our future predicament; and, if only because of this, their plight has to be faced.

Acknowledgement:

The authors wish to thank Professor S. Robert Aiken for his help and advice.

References

Adelman, H. (1988) "Obligation and refugees," in Nash, A. (ed.), *Human Rights and the Protection of Refugees under International Law*, Ottawa and Montreal: Institute for Research on Public Policy & The Canadian Human Rights Foundation, 73-92.

Adelman, H. (1991a) "Refuge or asylum: A philosophical perspective," in Adelman, H. and Lanphier, C.M. (eds.), *Refuge or Asylum: A Choice for Canada*, York: York Lanes Press, 12-26.

Adelman, H. (1991b) "Canadian refugee policy in the postwar period: An analysis," in Adelman, H. (ed.), *Refugee Policy: Canada and the United States*, York: York Lanes Press, 172-223.

Canada Employment and Immigration Advisory Council (CEIAC) (1991) *Immigration in the 1990s*, Ottawa: Canada Employment and Immigration Advisory Council.

Canadian Habitat Secretariat (1976) *Human Settlement in Canada*, Ottawa: Urban Affairs Canada.

Employment and Immigration Canada (1982) *Indochinese Refugees: The Canadian Response, 1979 and 1980*, Ottawa: Supply and Services.

Employment and Immigration Canada, Policy and Program Development Branch Refugee Affairs Division (1983) *Refugee Perspectives, 1983-1984*, Ottawa: Employment and Immigration Canada.

Employment and Immigration Canada, Policy and Program Development Branch, Refugee Affairs Division (1984) *Refugee Perspectives, 1984-1985*, Ottawa: Employment and Immigration Canada.

Employment and Immigration Canada, Policy and Program Development Branch, Refugee Affairs Division (1985) *Refugee Perspectives, 1985-1986*, Ottawa: Employment and Immigration Canada.

Employment and Immigration Canada, Policy and Program Development Branch, Refugee Affairs Division (1986) *Refugee Perspectives, 1986-1987*, Ottawa: Supply and Services.

Employment and Immigration Canada, Policy and Program Development Branch, Refugee Affairs Division (1987a) *Refugee and Humanitarian Programs, December 31, 1986*, Ottawa: Supply and Services.

Employment and Immigration Canada, Policy and Program Development Branch, Refugee Affairs Division (1987b) *Refugee Perspectives, 1987-1988*, Ottawa: Supply and Services.

Environment Canada (1990) *Canada's Green Plan*, Ottawa: Supply and Services.

Goodwin-Gill, G. (1991) "International law and the search for solutions to the refugee problem," in Adelman, H. and Lanphier C.M. (eds.), *Refuge or Asylum: A Choice for Canada*, York: York Lanes Press, 27-42.

Hathaway, J. C. (1988) "Selective concern: An overview of refugee law in Canada," *McGill Law Journal*, Vol. 33: 676-715.

Hathaway, J. C. (1991) *The Law of Refugee Status*, Toronto: Butterworths.

Jacobson, J. J. (1988) *Environmental Refugees: A Yardstick of Habitability*, Washington: Worldwatch Institute.

Karan, P.P. (1987) "Environment and development in Bhutan," *Geografiska Annaler*, Vol. 69B: 15-26.

MacNeill, J., Winsemius, P. and Yakushiji, T. (1991) *Beyond Interdependence*, New York: Oxford University Press.

Mooney, P. (1991) "Third World disaster foreseen: Report warns of new refugees," Toronto: The Globe and Mail, A1, A2.

Nash, A. (1989) *International Refugee Pressures and the Canadian Public Policy Response*, Ottawa: Institute for Research on Public Policy, Discussion Paper 89.B.1.

Oziewicz, E. (1991) "Canada objects to redefining refugees," Toronto: The Globe and Mail, A5.

Perout, A. and Nash, A. (1992) "Environmental refugees and Canadian immigration policies," Montreal: Department of Political Science, Concordia University, Discussion Paper.

Rawls, J. A (1971) *Theory of Justice*, Cambridge, Mass.: Belknap Press.

Regier, H. A. and G. Bales, A.G. (1991) "Environmental impacts of immigration: A preliminary examination," Ottawa: Employment and Immigration Canada.

Rizvi, Z. (1988) "Causes of the refugee problem and the international response," in Nash, A. (ed.), *Human Rights and the Protection of Refugees under International Law*, Ottawa and Montreal: Institute for Research on Public Policy & The Canadian Human Rights Foundation, 107-120.

Starke, L. (1990) *Signs of Hope*, Oxford: Oxford University Press.

United Nations (1983) *Convention and Protocol Relating to the Status of Refugees,* Geneva: Office of the United Nations High Commissioner for Refugees, (UN Document HCR/1P/10/ENG).

United Nations (1986) *Report of the Group of Governmental Experts on International Co-operation to Avert New Flows of Refugees*, New York: United Nations (UN Document A/41/324).

United Nations High Commissioner for Refugees (1984) "UNHCR: world refugee map," *Refugees*, Vol. 12: 24-25, Geneva: Office of the High Commissioner for Refugees.

U.S. Committee for Refugees (1990) *World Refugee Survey: 1989 in Review,* Washington, D.C.: American Council for Nationalities Service.

Walzer, M. (1983) *Spheres of Justice, A Defence of Pluralism*, New York: Basic Books.

World Commission on Environment and Development (1987) *Our Common Future,* Oxford: Oxford University Press.

World Women's Congress for a Healthy Planet (1991) *Official Report,* Proceedings and interviews, Miami, Florida.

Zero Population Growth (1991) "Canadian population and immigration," Population and Environment Issue Sheet, Version 1.0, Ajax, Ontario: Zero Population Growth of Canada Inc.

Chapter 3

Canadian Agriculture in the 1990s: A System Under Siege

Michael Troughton,
University of Western Ontario

Introduction

During the last 50 years Canadian agriculture has undergone a series of restructurings that, while oriented towards increased production and economic efficiency, have also resulted in a massive contraction of its constituent units, fragmentation and polarization of production and returns, increased control by an oligopolistic agribusiness sector, and a decoupling of agriculture from the remainder of the rural system (Troughton, 1992). Paradoxically then, despite efforts to strengthen the system, Canadian agriculture enters the 90s in a weakened state and highly vulnerable to a further set of economic and political pressures, especially external, which could result in a system that is merely a marginalized remnant. While the situation in Canada is not unique among agricultural systems in many developed countries, the swiftness of the change and the acuteness of its problems, make Canadian agriculture of particular interest in the debate about the role of public policy in helping to create the situation and in devising possible alternatives. This paper reviews the characteristics of the restructuring process, including the successive stages of mechanization and industrialization, and with an emphasis on the increasingly dominant role of institutions and institutional arrangements beyond the farm gate. An underlying question is whether the process was and is inevitable, or whether critical choices still exist that could result in a more sustainable agricultural system?

The Dominant System

To appreciate the critical nature of the present agricultural system, it is useful, very briefly, to note its characteristics when it was the dominant national activity and land use. The shape of the Canadian ecumene is largely a product of the period of agriculturally-based settlement, which was at its peak in eastern Canada in the late 1800s and in the west as recently as the 1930s (Troughton,1982). The result was a system of over 70 million hectares (ha) comprised of over 730,000 individual, and overwhelmingly family farms. The farming system was at the heart of a dominantly rural, national economic and social system, in which rural settlement (farm and non-farm) and agriculturally-based employment were of particular significance in political and institutional, as well as socio-economic, terms. As late as the 1920s, Canada exhibited more the characteristics of a yeoman society based on "Jeffersonian principles" than existed even in the U.S.A. On the other hand, while the system was based on local, small-scale units of production and processing, it was fully open to technological innovation. Throughout the period until the 1930s, federal and provincial governments, which were very small by today's standards, pursued policies that, while encouraging expansion, saw their role as non-interventionist. Meanwhile, in the eastern heartland areas of southern Ontario and southern Quebec, and in the recently settled Prairies, agricultural settlement, land use and its social, economic and political linkages defined Canada (Harris & Warkentin,1974; Zimmerman & Moneo,1971).

No systems are unchanging, least of all economic and technologically driven systems such as modern agriculture, but the degree of change from "dominant" to "residual" status has been most marked. In spite of increased productivity, the agricultural system has declined substantially in numbers from its peak: losing over 65 per cent of farms, 75 per cent of farm population, virtually all rural processing and associated employment, and up to 50 per cent of the farmland base in eastern Canada. The changes have been part, of course, of the major, overall shift in Canada from a rural to an urban-industrial society and economy, but the shift has been more marked and drastic in terms of rural decline because virtually the only rationale employed for retention within and of the system has been that of economic efficiency. Canadian agriculture was always a utilitarian endeavour, in which financial success was the key to ongoing activity, but the general lack of other reasons to maintain the system have been conspicuous by their absence as far as governments and other controlling institutions have been concerned.

The Initial Restructuring: Mechanization

Mechanization first became a dominant factor in the regions last settled, i.e. the Prairies. Successful cultivation of the grassland demanded new technologies in ploughing and in the organization of production and marketing. On the other hand, prior to World War II even Prairie farms remained generally small (under 100 ha) and horses supplied the majority of energy applied to farm fields. However, stimulated by the war and its demands, and by wartime and post-war labour shortages, mechanization proceeded apace in the 1940s and 1950s, increasing both the scale of farm operations and stimulating greater specialization of production (Auer, 1970; Wilson, 1981).

Mechanization is really the surrogate term for the much broader shift to use of a whole new set of manufactured inputs to farming, not only new machines, but fertilizers, agricultural chemicals and the widespread application of science and technology to production. Its justification lay in huge increases in productivity; per hectare, based on new seeds and fertilizers; per farm, as fewer, larger units emerged; and per person employed, as the labour force shrank. In some regions this initial restructuring process produced a system that was generally more streamlined and operationally efficient, even though, by shedding labour, it left a smaller farm or farm-related rural population. In other regions, however, the result was the breakdown of agriculture and the associated agrarian system, as farms on poorer land were unable to utilize or afford the new inputs, and thereby became uncompetitive. Widespread farm abandonment — up to 80 per cent in the Maritimes and over 50 per cent in eastern Canada — was the result (Troughton, 1981). The rural, farm-based system contracted everywhere and in some regions virtually disappeared. In the late 1950s and during the 1960s, farm and farmland abandonment and associated rural poverty were the major foci of government programmes under the Agricultural Rehabilitation and Development Act (ARDA) (Buckley & Tihanyi, 1967). However, the problems were "solved" more by the completion of the abandonment process than by any rehabilitation (Fuller & Lapping, 1985).

One characteristic that emerged during this initial restructuring, and which has continued to affect even those farmers who were able to adapt to the new technological and economic parameters, was the "cost-price squeeze"; the downward pressure on output prices versus the rising costs of and dependency on non-farm inputs. One response by farmers operating under conditions of "pure competition" was to attempt to achieve a collective role in the marketplace through the establishment of cooperatives and producer marketing boards. The former resulted in the establishment of the provincial grain Pools in the mid-1920s (Fowke, 1957), the latter in some enabling legislation for most provinces by the late 1930s (Troughton, 1989). Despite these endeavours, however, increasing advantages lay with an emerging agribusiness, i.e. the input suppliers and output processors and distributors. The latter have become increasingly centralized and powerful, and after World War II began to rapidly absorb small local agricultural supply and processing firms, and to move manufacturing and processing out of the rural area (Mitchell, 1975). Again, these moves were justified in terms of economic rationalization, but were not accompanied by any attempts to offset the impacts on the rural economy or communities.

Further Restructuring: Industrialization

After the initial shake-out of farms following World War 2, there was some feeling that the restructured system would stabilize, based on a smaller set of larger, full-time, increasingly mechanized operations (Special Committee on Farm Income,1969). However, in the last three decades the pace of change has, if anything, accelerated, with further restructuring based on what has been termed the "industrialization of agriculture" (Gregor, 1982; Troughton, 1986). Industrialization may be viewed as the next stage of mechanization in terms of the farm operation, but the key lies in two other factors, namely, much greater fragmentation and polarization within the farm production sector, and the passage of control of a larger horizontally and vertically integrated agri-food system into the hands of agribusiness and government.

The increasingly integrated structure of "the total agricultural and food system" in Canada was recognized by the Federal Task Force on Agriculture in its seminal 1969 Report, *Canadian Agriculture in the Seventies*. This report, written mainly by agricultural economists and bureaucrats, described an increasingly specialized and tightly integrated system, based on the application of a model which combined the goals of economic efficiency and the application of technology to achieve production at lowest unit cost. The report identified the key system elements, namely, a reduced set of specialized production units, the agribusiness supply and processing sectors, and governments acting as the facilitator and regulator, ostensibly on behalf of the consumer.

At the farm level, the industrial model is based on a smaller set of full-time, efficient units which are typified by their increased scale of operation (area and/or numbers of livestock), their intensive use of capital, and their specialized production. Overall, these farms represent only a minority of all remaining farm units but dominate commercial production; less than 30 per cent of all Canadian farms produce over 85 per cent of marketed output. Polarization of production is reflected in the ownership of a high proportion of the capital resources and income based on farm receipts (Brinkman,1988; Statistics Canada,1992). Most remaining farms are effectively part-time or "hobby" operations and are of marginal economic significance. Specialization is the key to success; individual farms concentrate on a very narrow range of crop and especially livestock products, often employing "factory farm" methods. Farmers, consequently, operate within a production sector which is fragmented into the different types of specialized production. Each specialized type (e.g. dairy, broiler chickens, tobacco) has specific operational norms and marketing arrangements which are increasingly determined by a combination of agribusiness firms and governmental institutional arrangements (Mitchell, 1975; Troughton, 1989, 1992).

Agribusiness has followed the characteristic path of other industrial sectors, becoming increasingly based on a small number of very large firms, many of which are multinationals operating in many different markets, and diversified across agricultural and non-agricultural sectors (Wallace & Smith, 1985). These firms comprise a series of oligopolies which have come to control both the inputs to farming (e.g. oil and chemical companies, machinery manufacturers and banks), and each of the production-processing sectors (e.g. grain-milling, distilling and brewing, oilseed crushing and vegetable oil processing, red meat and poultry slaughtering and packing, and fruit and vegetable processing). In addition, many of the same firms control the majority of food distribution and retailing (Kneen, 1989; Warnock, 1978).

While it is in the general interest of agribusiness to maintain an efficient production system, there is little or no interest in the maintenance of family farming, nor of specifically Canadian sources of raw materials. The Federal Government, while professing to reflect and encourage family farming and domestic self-sufficiency has generally been in thrall to agribusiness and has shared its general ideological stance. This has become most apparent in the present circumstances surrounding free trade which has been advanced by government and generally supported by agribusiness which, in turn, becomes footloose and able to restructure itself in continental or global marketplaces.

Government and Institutional Arrangements

As noted, Canadian governments traditionally saw their role as one of encouragement in areas of agricultural settlement and commercial activity, but of minimal interference in the operation of the market. This led to rejection of most of the numerous pleas by western farmers between 1890 and 1930 for protection against the oligopolistic power of agribusiness in the wheat economy (i.e. the railways, elevator companies and the Winnipeg grain exchange) and, eventually, to farmers establishing their own provincial cooperative grain Pools (Fowke, 1957). Similarly, in eastern Canada, producers faced reluctant governments in their efforts to establish the first producer's marketing boards. However, with the economic Depression of the 1930s and the near collapse of western Canadian agriculture, the federal government was forced into an era of greater intervention which resulted in the establishment of government run marketing arrangements, culminating in the establishment of the Canadian Wheat Board (CWB) in 1935 (Morriss, 1987). This has been identified as the beginning of a policy direction that has had price and income stabilization as key objectives (Fulton, 1987). At that time, at least, agribusiness also saw government intervention as desirable and began the process of manipulating it to its advantage (Finkel, 1979).

Although governments have greatly increased their level of intervention in agriculture during the last 50 years, their operating premise has been almost exclusively that of an economic or commercial focus, structured according to the industrial efficiency model. Only twice, in the 1930s and in the 1960s, have social and environmental goals assumed greater prominence. In the 1930s the Prairie Farm Rehabilitation Administration (PFRA) was established with the objective of the amelioration of physical (drought-related) and socio-economic (depressed product prices and farm incomes) conditions affecting Prairie farms (Buckley & Tihanyi, 1967). But, in reality, it was the end of the drought and the economic stimulus of war that "rehabilitated" the region, which then embarked on its first major restructuring.

By the mid-1950s, and especially in eastern Canada, mechanization was leading both to widespread abandonment and to poverty among the remaining farm and rural non-farm residents in many physically marginal areas. Under ARDA and related legislation, an attempt was made to alleviate the conditions using programmes modelled on the PFRA (Buckley & Tihanyi, 1967). However, these problems too were largely solved by continued farm abandonment and out-migration, and there was no commitment to any form of rural maintenance policy. This was, and is, in sharp contrast to policies in the European Community and in Scandinavia which have been explicitly directed at the retention of farming and rural communities in peripheral and physically marginal regions (Clout, 1984). By the late 1970s the federal government had switched its regional development to an urban-industrial strategy (Department of Regional Industrial Expansion) and henceforth based support for agricultural activity purely on economic criteria.

Increasingly the primary area of government involvement has been in attempts to maintain income on "economically viable farms" and to develop the most efficient means of production to supply processors and consumers. Besides broad policies of stabilization, the main feature during the 1970s was support for the establishment of national farm product marketing agencies and provincial marketing boards, culminating in the application of the most stringent model, that of supply management. Although, ostensibly, marketing boards were designed to help farmers offset the weight of processors in the market and were seen by some farmer groups as being the means to preserve farm numbers, the results of their establishment and operation hardly bear that ideal out. Farm marketing legislation specifies the establishment of boards to regulate the marketing of specific products, thereby encouraging farm level specialization. Even though farmers may negotiate or, as with supply management, actually be involved in setting prices, they must still deal with the oligopolistic structure of the various processing sectors, whose members, in turn, benefit from the efficient production of a high quality product under guaranteed supply conditions. Although the creation of marketing boards may have delayed somewhat the decline of numbers of farms in specific areas, they have also contributed to the drastic 'weeding out' of many smaller producers and to the creation and maintenance of distinctions between the minority of producers within a board and operating under supply management and the majority operating outside in uncontrolled sectors. Marketing boards, although giving protection to some producers, do not, by and large, offset the continuing cost-price squeeze, which exacerbates the push for individual farmers to become ever more oriented to the industrial model, and it does not alter a situation whereby many farmers, especially the commercial minority, are actually competing against one another for a larger share of an inelastic market demand (Troughton, 1989).

Social and Environmental Impacts of Modern Agriculture

Unanticipated, and certainly unplanned, but nevertheless a significant aspect of agricultural restructuring in Canada, has been a series of social and environmental impacts which have been integral aspects of the progressive decline and weakening of the system, and which have, at last, begun to elicit some concern. Mention has been made of the widespread farm loss and abandonment, especially in marginal areas. This has led to the virtual demise of the agricultural system in much of Nova Scotia and New Brunswick (Troughton, 1988b), throughout eastern and northern Quebec and on the Shield in both southern and northern Ontario (Parson, 1985; Troughton, 1983), as well as along the northern Prairie margins. The malaise is more widespread, however. In virtually all agricultural areas there have been steep declines in farm population, and where this has been the dominant component of the rural population, as for example in the Prairies, a major weakening of the whole social and settlement system has occurred (Baker, 1958; Wilson, 1981; Paul, 1992). Even in the less extensive heartland areas like southern Ontario, there has been both outright loss and widespread decoupling of the farm from the non-farm sector. While decoupling is to some extent economic, as farmers bypass local supply and processing facilities, it has an impact on the overall rural fabric and contributes to the decline of erstwhile agrarian societies (Fuller, 1985).

Paralleling the social impacts, have been the widespread incidences of the environmental impacts of increasingly intensive and specialized agriculture which concentrates its activity on an ever smaller segment of the land base (Coote, 1983). The results of increased inputs of machinery, fertilizers, chemicals, irrigation systems, and intensive livestock raising, have been increased soil erosion, especially associated with intensive and near-monoculture of row crops and removal of field boundaries and natural vegetation, problems of soil compaction and lowered nutrient status and toxicity, salinization (Sparrow, 1984), and both local and general problems of soil, water and air pollution. While some adjustments have been made and new waste management techniques introduced, the problem is bound up with the need for farmers to produce more efficiently in the short term and the resultant lack of time and money for them to play their traditional role as stewards or to employ capital in a more conserving fashion (Hill & Ramsay, 1976).

The Situation in the 1980s

The various elements of change outlined above, i.e. two successive phases of system restructuring, culminating in the emergence of the industrial model, controlled by agribusiness and underpinned by legislation and institutional arrangements, and their links to an array of social and environmental problems, were all apparent by the early 1980s. The Canadian agricultural system had moved from being a reasonably coherent entity to a much reduced and highly fragmented set of sub-sectors, with its role in any larger rural context diminishing rapidly, and with virtually no rural planning or policy that either recognized or dealt with the situation (Troughton, 1988a).

Notwithstanding these structural weaknesses, the prevailing opinion of those in control — agribusiness and government and the agricultural economist community — was that an economically efficient and internationally competitive agricultural system had been fashioned (Brinkman, 1987). Government was congratulating itself on the application of strict systems of supply management to domestic dairy and poultry production and was contemplating its extension to other sectors (Agriculture Canada, 1981). Increased production of grains and oilseeds for export was being emphasized, in relation to a perception of rising global demand, and the value of farm real estate was increasing rapidly, keeping ahead of rising input costs. The system had consolidated into two major components, the export sector, concentrated on grains, oilseeds and red meat, and dominant in the Prairies, and the domestic sector producing dairy, poultry, pork and horticultural products under varying degrees of protection and concentrated closer to the centres of population in the southern areas of Ontario, Quebec and British Columbia.

Again, there seemed to be the essence of some stability in operational and economic terms which, it was hoped, would allow remedial action to address some of the more problematic environmental impacts. This, however, was not to be. In the mid-1980s a combination of circumstances acted to reveal the inherent weaknesses of the system, in terms of both its domestic and export orientations (Brinkman, 1987). While external factors were critical, notably a worldwide economic depression in the early 1980s, and uncertainty in global agriculture markets created by other major players, the decade also saw the Canadian government make a radical switch in policy that threatened its own agricultural institutional structure and left large parts of the system vulnerable to external pressures. This latter shift from some protection of domestic production and processing to one of continental free trade is exacerbating other pressures on the system and creating further divisions.

The global recession of the early 1980s was felt particularly in terms of a drastic fall in both farm values and farm income. Many farmers who had been encouraged to invest in more intensive operations, albeit at very high rates of interest, saw the values of their investment fall. Many went bankrupt, and many more operated heavily in debt. Some suggested that this "rationalization" was producing a "leaner and more efficient system" but many of those in financial difficulties were young farmers on whom the future system should have been built. To make matters worse, the anticipated recovery, that was experienced by other sectors of the economy in the mid '80s, was not forthcoming in agriculture. This was a result of several factors, including overproduction and reduced effective global demand and, especially significant in the Canadian context, the onset of the so-called "trade war" between the United States and the European Community, with its depressive effect on world market prices for grains (especially wheat) and oilseeds (Olesen, 1987). The impact on Canadian exports was drastic; from a situation of expanding volume at prices which contributed to both reasonable farm incomes and a positive balance of trade, to a situation where prices fell below the cost of production and both sales and farmer income have had to be underwritten by government support payments (Fulton et al., 1989). This, in turn, called into question the long term viability of the policies of agricultural stabilization and has meant that, as the economic recession of the late '80s and early '90s occurred, Prairie farm income was derived largely from government payments, which while covering the short-fall between the cost of production and the world commodity prices, leave farm incomes very depressed. The result has been a further steady erosion of the ranks of Prairie producers, and little or no possibility of reversing the associated environmental and social problems of the region.

Until 1985, the situation in eastern Canada and in British Columbia was somewhat better, thanks to the operation of supply management and other tariff arrangements that safeguarded both the domestic market and the incomes of major sets of producers, although those outside supply management suffered similar declines in farm value and income. However, in 1985 the federal government reversed a stand on trade that had been in effect for nearly a century, and began negotiations with respect to a free trade agreement with the U.S.

The free trade negotiations involved the whole Canadian economy and were conducted at governmental level. As such, the agricultural sector became part of the overall negotiating framework with little or no attention being paid to its particular characteristics and needs. Free trade in agriculture was "sold" on the basis of improving access to U.S. markets and enhanced export opportunities (External Affairs Canada, 1987; Allen & Macmillan, 1988), even though only a small proportion of Canadian agricultural exports are destined for the U.S., and U.S. imports to Canada are already larger and involve a wider array of sectors. It was implicit, though never clarified, that a free trade agreement with the U.S. would help to resolve the "trade war" in grains.

It was recognized that Canadian domestic agricultural arrangements, especially supply management, were antithetical to free trade, and they had already been identified as such and targeted by the U.S. Department of Agriculture (USDA, 1987; Miner & Hathaway, 1988), but the Canadian version of the free trade document stated that these arrangements would (somehow) be safeguarded (External Affairs Canada, 1987). This attempt to woo western farm support by the promise of increased exports, especially of red meat, and to assuage eastern farmer's fears by promising to maintain supply management, only highlighted the overall weakness of the system and the inherent problems of the dual government commitment. It should also be recognized that, perhaps commensurate with its reduced economic and political significance, agriculture's position received little public exposure or meaningful debate.

The Canada - U.S. Free Trade Agreement (FTA) was signed on January 2, 1989, and it soon became apparent that, rather than enhancing the situation of Canadian agriculture, especially at the farm level, the Agreement was acting to make it increasingly vulnerable to both U.S. and wider international pressure. One of the elements of the FTA was an undertaking to "work together with the U.S.A. to further the GATT (General Agreement on Tariffs and Trade)" (External Affairs Canada, Article 11). One of the U.S. objectives in its GATT negotiations was to eliminate all "trade-distorting" arrangements, notably those of foreign nations operating under GATT Article XI which sanctions domestic arrangements such as Canada's supply management. Thus, Canada was pursuing a policy designed to help eliminate arrangements which it had promised its farmers it would uphold ! That this problem could arise was realized by various observers prior to the FTA (Warley & Barrichello, 1987), but by 1990 it became an uncomfortable reality.

The System under Siege

To be viable, the agricultural system should combine the strengths of its parts, and operate to fulfill its various objectives — economic production, environmental stewardship and community organization — in an integrated and reasonably self-sufficient fashion. Canadian agriculture has increasing problems reaching and supporting any one of these objectives because of fragmentation and weaknesses in its internal structure and external support framework.

In economic terms, only a small fraction of farm operations are viable. The majority of farm family income is derived off the farm (Statistics Canada, 1992), and under present circumstances even farm income is heavily maintained by government support payments. Prairie farmers' real farm income is calculated at below the levels of the 1930s Depression (Fulton et al., 1989), while the income of those farmers in supply managed sectors are increasingly uncertain in the face of U.S. and GATT pressure and the federal government's projected switch to a weak form of tariff protection (Agriculture Canada, 1989). Many farmers, including the majority of those under 40, are carrying a heavy debt load, and substantial numbers are dropping out annually.

One of the attractions of farming is the "farm way of life", which is a product not only of a satisfactory income but of the rural farm community and the amenity of the countryside. All of these are currently in doubt. Rural communities, especially away from the larger urban places, and particularly in the Prairies, are in decline. Reduced numbers of farms and farm population mean insufficient numbers to support many social and commercial activities. Many rural service centres are in decline or stagnant as farm services are centralized and the farm operation is decoupled from the local community. At the extreme, many Prairie settlements are on the verge of extinction as rail and elevator closures remove their economic base, and/or as key institutions such as the school are closed (Paul, 1992). In the rural-urban fringe, despite the contrast of growth through "repopulation", farm populations are increasingly outnumbered by newcomers. Although communities may be revitalized and there are both economic and social opportunities, these tend to operate more in an exurban than in an agrarian milieu (Walker, 1987). To make matters worse, very little planning and virtually no governmental programmes are based upon the ideal of a rural-agricultural perspective, and most services and links emanate from and often within an urban-regional context (Troughton, 1988a).

As noted, the style of modern commercial agriculture tends to work against both environmental quality and the amenity of the rural landscape. Larger farms with fewer buildings and larger fields, few livestock out of doors, hedgerow and woodlot vegetation removal, and chemical spraying all combine to create less attractive landscapes, and in some cases situations that are ecologically unsustainable (Hill & Ramsay, 1976). Problems of waste management alienate other residents and create problems with soil and water systems. Chemicals are suspected of possibly harming the quality of agricultural products. Farmers are caught in the difficulty of trying to maintain short term gains in productivity while observing the decline in environmental quality, and possibly the long term viability of their countryside. An added, though as yet unspecified, problem is what will be the impact of climatic change (Smit, 1989).

Added to the above threats are the uncertainties and breakdowns affecting the institutional structures and arrangements of the system, both nationally and internationally. Operational control of Canadian agriculture lies increasingly with agribusiness, which although not as involved at the (farm) production level as in some sectors of U.S. agriculture, determines the direction of the industrial model through control of inputs and, especially of processing (Kneen,1989). Canadian agribusiness, however, has some fundamental weaknesses that impact on the health of the system; significant portions are parts of multinational companies with headquarters outside Canada, primarily in the U.S. These "branch" operations were established not only to service Canadian agriculture but also because it was necessary and profitable to operate within the protected Canadian market (Mitchell, 1975). With the advent of free trade, that market is now open to competition and able to be served from outside. Already, many companies have used the threat of moving to the U.S. as a lever to press for lower commodity prices, and several have already relocated, including fruit and vegetable processors. The demise of local processing facilities could mean an end to local production of several high value field and horticultural crops (OMAF, 1987).

It is impossible to predict what will happen, but it is certain that the system is weakly structured both in terms of the pressures on individual family farms and by virtue of the sectoral fragmentation which makes collective action difficult to achieve, and thus plays into the hands of agribusiness. Several major production areas, most notably poultry and dairying, are threatened by the probable termination of supply management (Bergeron, 1988) and by the potential inroads being made by large vertically integrated U.S. farm corporations. Likewise, a continuation of depressed prices and the inability of government to sustain the huge subsidy payments could spell the end of viable agriculture and the (rural-farm) community system in the Prairie wheat belt region.

So what has been the role of public policy? Unfortunately, its role has been to fashion, and at times exacerbate, the current situation, through an over-whelming adherence to the economic-industrial model, and more recently to an international rather than a nationally-based political frame of reference. It has been noted that during the half century from about 1935 there developed a more or less consistent national policy approach to agriculture based on various measures of price and income stabilization. Although this was never fully spelled out or rigorously maintained, it did reflect an emphasis on the distinct national system which differed quite markedly from that operating in the U.S. (Fulton, 1987). The switch to free trade represents a radical shift which, at the very least, undermines any purely national policy based on stabilization, and likely makes untenable much of the structure that has evolved to meet Canadian needs and circumstances. While bring-ing Canadian agriculture more into line with the U.S., it does not create "the level playing field" mentioned in the FTA, and seems to ignore the difficulty of competing either economically or politically with a system 10 times as large and operating on a much more productive base (Field, 1968; Trough-ton, 1991; Troughton & Chiotti, 1992).

It is significant that, although there are eleven government agricultural min-istries in Canada, they have never attempted to develop a national policy in concert, and the federal role has always been less than comprehensive because of provincial jurisdiction over many operational aspects. Perhaps more significant, in terms of the overall system, is the fact that there exist no rural ministries that might fashion agriculturally-centred or agriculturally involving rural policies to try to maintain the wider system, as is being attempted in parts of western Europe. In turn, there is very little meaningful rural planning anywhere in Canada; that which does exist is significant as an anomaly rather than the perceived basis for wider application. Governments, planners, and probably many rural folk have very little left to hold onto, in either ideological or practical terms.

Sustainability: An Alternative?

One could end by predicting the demise of the Canadian agricultural system and perhaps of much of the ecumene it has defined. However, there is probably some general, if vague, agreement that this should not happen. Agriculture, after all, is about food production and that will continue to be a necessity. Although, for the near future at least, Canada could probably be supplied from outside, perhaps more cheaply for the consumer, it is assumed that the future will include the need to utilize Canada's agricultural production capacity to feed some portion of the world's population. Given that ultimate requirement, one may begin to fashion a set of goals for the rehabilitation of the existing system. Home grown production and self-sufficiency of supply has value in terms of security, including control over quality. The rural and even the farm way of life have attractions for many, but cannot exist without some basis for economic and social stability. Underpinning all is the fact that ideally, agricultural production is based on the use of renewable or sustainable resources. For this to be maintained, attention must be paid to the physical base and to the necessary ecological relationships.

All these ideas revolve about a model of sustainability in a total systems context in which the protection of the soil (agronomic sustainability) would support the individual family farm operation (micro-economic sustainability) which would be the basis for agricultural-rural communities servicing and utilizing the farm base and its production (social or community sustainability). This vested hierarchy of agrarian structure would support and be supported by a macro-economic system which has sustainability as its prime objective and whose institutions and arrangements recognize what is necessary for its maintenance (Lowrance, 1990). To achieve this situation, however, would require radical decisions to effect the necessary restructuring of the present set-up (Hill, 1985). There are only two circumstances under which those decisions might be taken; the first is when or if the present system is in fact on the verge of collapse and it becomes obvious to Canadian society that the present direction will destroy rather than rebuild. The second reason would be if it were demonstrated that the agriculture and food system is the one in which ecological sustainability and sustainable development, as defined by the Brundtland Commission (WCED, 1987), could find a common basis. Unfortunately, public awareness and policy instruments of anything other than conventional economic development are so weak in Canada that one feels on stronger ground predicting the fall of the system, rather than a lifting of the siege.

References:

Agriculture Canada (1981) *Canada's Agrifood System: An Overview*, Ottawa: Supply & Services.

Agriculture Canada (1989) *Growing Together: A Vision for Canada's Agri-Food Industry*, Pub. 5269/E, Ottawa.

Allen, K. and Macmillan, K. (eds.) (1988) *U.S. - Canadian Agricultural Trade Challenges: Developing Common Approaches*, Resources for the Future/C.D.Howe Institute, R.F.F.Washington DC.

Auer, L, (1970) *Canadian Agricultural Productivity*, Staff Study No.24, Ottawa, Economic Council of Canada.

Baker, W. B. (1958) "Changing community patterns in Saskatchewan," *Canadian Geographical Journal*, Vol. LV1(2): 44-56.

Bergeron, J. B. (1988) "Implications of trade liberalization for the Canadian food industry," *Market Commentary*, 165-170.

Brinkman, G. L. (1987) "The competitive position of Canadian agriculture," *Canadian Journal of Agricultural Economics*, Vol. 35(2): 263-288.

Brinkman, G. L. (1988) *The Structure of Canadian Agriculture,* Paper, Agricultural and Rural Restructuring Group, Experts Meeting, Regina (mimeo).

Buckley, H. and Tihanyi, E. (1967) *Canadian Policies for Rural Adjustment: A Study of the Economic Impact of ARDA, PFRA, and MMRA*, Special Study 7, Ottawa: Economic Council of Canada.

Clout, H. (1984) *A Rural Policy for the EEC?,* London: Methuen.

Coote, D. R. (1983) "Stresses on land under intensive agricultural use," in Simpson-Lewis, W. (ed.), *Stress on Land in Canada*, Folio 6, Ottawa: Lands Directorate, Environment Canada, 227-257.

External Affairs Canada (1987) *Trade: Securing Canada's Future (The Canada-U.S.Free Trade Agreement)*, Ottawa: Government of Canada.

Federal Task Force on Agriculture (1969) *Canadian Agriculture in the Seventies*, Ottawa: Queen's Printer.

Field, N. C. (1968) "Environmental quality and land productivity: A comparison of the agricultural land base of the USSR and North America," *The Canadian Geographer*, Vol. 12(1): 1-14.

Finkel, A. (1979) *Business and Social Reform in the Thirties*, Toronto: Lorimer.

Fowke, V. C.(1957) *The National Policy and the Wheat Economy*, Toronto: University of Toronto Press.

Fuller, A. M. (ed.) (1985) *Farming and the Rural Community in Ontario*, Toronto: Foundation for Rural Living.

Fuller, A. M. and Lapping, M. B. (1985) "Rural development policy in Canada: An interpretation," *Community Development Journal*, Vol. 20(2): 1607-1608.

Fulton, M. (1987) "Canadian agricultural policy," *Canadian Journal of Agricultural Economics*, Vol. 34(1):107-125.

Fulton, M., Rosaasen, K. and Schmitz, A. (1989) *Canadian Agricultural Policy and Prairie Agriculture, A Study for the ECC*, Ottawa: Supply & Services.

Gregor, H. F. (1982) *Industrialization of U.S.Agriculture: An Interpretive Atlas*, Boulder, Colorado: Westview Press.

Harris, R. C. and Warkentin, J. (1974) *Canada before Confederation*, Toronto: Oxford University Press.

Hill, S. B. (1985) "Redesigning the food system for sustainability," *Alternatives*, Vol. 12(3/4): 32-36.

Hill, S. B. and Ramsay, J. A. (1976) *Limitations of the Energy Approach in Defining Priorities in Agriculture*, 'Energy and Agriculture Conference', Washington: University of St.Louis (mimeo).

Kneen, B. (1989) *From Hand to Mouth: Understanding the Food System,* Toronto: NC Press.

Lowrance, R. (1990) "Research approaches for ecological sustainability," *Journal of Soil and Water Conservation,* Vol. 45(1): 51-57.

Miner, W. M. and Hathaway, D. E. (eds.) (1988) *World Agricultural Trade: Building a Concensus,* I.R.P.P. & I.I.E., Halifax.

Mitchell, D. (1975) *The Politics of Food,* Toronto: Lorimer.

Morriss, W. E. (1987) *Chosen Instrument: A History of the Canadian Wheat Board,* CWB/Reidmore Books, Edmonton.

Olesen, B. T. (1987) "World grain trade: An economic perspective on the current price war", *Canadian Journal of Agricultural Economics,* Vol. 35(3): 501-514.

OMAF (Ontario Ministry of Agriculture & Food) (1987) *Canada - U.S. Trade Negotiations: Implications for Ontario's Agriculture, Food and Beverage Sector,* OMAF, Toronto (mimeo).

Parson, H. (1985) "Marginal agriculture on the Canadian Shield," in Bunce, M.F. and Troughton, M. J. (eds.), *Pressures of Change in Rural Canada,* Geographical Monograph 14, Toronto: Atkinson College, York University, 73-91.

Paul, A. H. (1992) "The popper proposals for the Great Plains: A view from the Canadian prairies," *Great Plains Research,* Vol. 2(2): 199-222.

Smit, B. (1989) "Climatic warming and Canada's comparative position in agriculture," *Climatic Change Digest,* Atmospheric Environment Service CCD 89-01, Ottawa: Environment Canada.

Sparrow, Sen. H. O. (1984) *Soil at Risk: Canada's Eroding Future,* Report of Standing Committee on Agriculture, Fisheries & Forestry, Ottawa: Senate of Canada.

Special Committee on Farm Income in Ontario (1969) *Report: The Challenge of Abundance,* Toronto: Ontario Ministry of Agriculture & Food.

Statistics Canada (1992) Cat. 93-350, Ottawa: Statistics Canada, Agriculture Division.

Troughton, M. J. (1981) "The policy and legislative response to loss of agricultural land in Canada," *Ontario Geography*, Vol. 18: 79-109.

Troughton,.M. J. (1982) *Canadian Agriculture,* Geography of World Agriculture 10, Akademiai Kiado, Budapest.

Troughton, M. J. (1983) "The failure of agricultural settlement in northern Ontario," *Nordia*, Vol. 17(1): 141-151.

Troughton, M. J. (1986) "Farming systems in the modern world," in Pacione, M. (ed), *Progress in Agricultural Geography*, London: Croom Helm, 93-123.

Troughton, M. J. (1988a) "Rural Canada: What future?," in Dykeman, F.W. (ed), *Integrated Rural Planning and Development,* Sackville, N.B.: Rural & Small Town Research & Studies Program, Mt. Allison University, 3-20.

Troughton, M. J. (1988b) "From nodes to nodes: The rise and fall of agricultural activity in the Maritime Provinces," in Day, D. (ed), *Geographical Perspectives on the Maritime Provinces,* Halifax: St. Mary's University, 25-46.

Troughton, M. J. (1989) "The role of marketing boards in the industrialization of the Canadian agricultural system," *Journal of Rural Studies*, Vol. 5(4): 367-383.

Troughton, M. J. (1991) "Canadian agriculture and the Canada - U.S. Free Trade Agreement: A critical apraisal," *Progress in Rural Policy & Planning*, Vol. 1: 176-196.

Troughton, M. J. (1992) "The restructuring of agriculture: The Canadian example," in Bowler, I.R., Bryant, C. and Nellis, D. (eds.), *Contemporary Rural Systems in Transition: Vol.1 Agriculture and Environment,* CAB International, Wallingford, U.K., 29-42.

Troughton, M. J. and Chiotti, Q. (1992) *An Uncertain Future: Canadian Agriculture within the Canada - U.S. Free Trade Agreement,* Carleton Geography Discussion Papers, 9, Ottawa: Carleton University, 25 pp.

USDA (United States Department of Agriculture) (1987) *Government Intervention in Agriculture*, E.R.S. Staff Report 229, Washington, DC.

Walker, G. E. (1987) *An Invaded Countryside: Structures of Life on the Toronto Fringe,* Geographical Monograph 17, Toronto: Atkinson College, York University.

Wallace, A. I. and Smith, W. (1985) "Agribusiness in North America," in Ilberry, B. and Healy, M. (eds.), *The Industrialization of the Countryside,* Norwich: Geo-Books, 57-74.

Warley, T. K. and Barrichello, R. R. (1987) "Agricultural issues in a comprehensive Canada - U.S. Free Trade Agreement: A Canadian perspective," *Canadian Journal of Agricultural Economics*, Vol. 34: 213-227.

Warnock. J. (1978) *Profit Hungry: The Food Industry in Canada,* Vancouver: New Star Books,.

Wilson, B. (1981) *Beyond the Harvest: Canadian Grain at the Crossroads,* Saskatoon: Western Producer Prairie Books.

WCED (World Commission on Environment & Development/Brundtland Commission) (1987) *Our Common Future,* Oxford: Oxford University Press.

Zimmerman, C. C. and Moneo, G. W. (1971) *The Prairie Community System*, Ottawa: Agricultural Economics Research Council of Canada.

Chapter 4

Geography and Transportation Planning

Jean Andrey
University of Waterloo

Introduction

Transportation systems exist to facilitate the flow of goods and people within and between regions. Their economic and social importance is enormous. This paper is an exploration of the field of transportation and especially of the contributions that geographers have made and can make to transportation research, planning and policy. While some of the comments pertain to transportation in the broadest sense, much of the discussion focuses on road transport, and especially road passenger transport, in North America. The paper begins with an historical overview of transport planning in North America and then discusses some of the main transportation challenges that we face as we enter the twenty-first century. Next the development of the subdiscipline of transport geography is reviewed, drawing parallels with the broader multi-disciplinary field of transport planning where appropriate. Finally, a general framework is suggested to provide direction for future geographical studies of transportation problems.

The Evolution of Transport Planning in North America

The history of transportation in North America may be viewed as a staged evolution governed by changes in technology, settlement, and policy. In the early years following colonization, technology was limited, settlement was sparse, and transport policy was "... interwoven with national and regional economic and social policies developed to satisfy non-transport objectives and concerns" (Gillen, 1990: 2). Central governments played a major role by providing land grants and construction subsidies to both individuals and private firms, usually on a project-by-project basis, to develop the national transport infrastructure of the nineteenth century, which included canals, railways, and roads. In urban areas, the development of transport infrastructure was less deliberate. Urban settlements tended to be compact agglomerations of mixed commercial and residential activities, and urban transport was based primarily on walking and privately operated transit services.

The advent of the private automobile in the late nineteenth century changed mobility in a remarkable way, creating in essence a "transportation revolution" (Bardou et al., 1982). Although the first automobiles were purchased primarily for rural and recreational travel, the popularity of the private car grew rapidly. In 1920 there were approximately eight million registered passenger cars in the United States and 400,000 in Canada. By the end of the second world war there were four times as many and by the early 1960s the number had doubled again. Transportation investment and planning concentrated their efforts on this relatively new mode of travel. In fact, the 1950s and 1960s has been labelled "the highway era", as both federal and lower levels of government spent massive sums of money on the expansion of infrastructure, including the construction of the U.S. Interstate System, the TransCanada Highway, Ontario's Highway 401, and numerous metropolitan beltways. Initially, highway planning was largely preoccupied with technical questions of how to improve the design and operation of individual transport facilities, but, as pointed out in Weiner (1987, 11), a number of breakthroughs in analytic techniques in the 1950s laid the groundwork for a more comprehensive approach to urban transport planning in the years that followed.

Comprehensive transport planning began in the Detroit and Chicago area studies in the 1950s. This new approach to urban transport planning involved massive data collection exercises, and used trip generation and traffic assignment computer models to forecast future trips and thus plan for infrastructure needs. Studies were long-term (usually 20 years) and region-wide in scope, as dictated by the U.S. Federal Aid Highway Act of 1962. These forecasts quickly became both the backbone of urban master plans and the justification for new or expanded expressways throughout North America.

Late in the 1960s, however, this quantitative, demand-based approach to transportation planning was challenged by a group of citizenry, who among other things resented the intrusion of these expressways into their neighbourhoods. A period of social activism followed, where concerns were voiced over a number of transport issues including safety, air and noise pollution, inadequate transportation for disadvantaged groups, the energy crisis, and the need to revitalize urban core areas. In response, procedures and standards were modified, and although transport planning in more recent years has continued to rely heavily on computer modelling (Lewis et al., 1990), there has been increased emphasis on public participation and on using a wider range of criteria for evaluating transportation options.

But more than just the planning process has changed over the past two decades. Both modal split and travel patterns have been changing in response to land use and demographic trends, economic restructuring, and regulatory reform within the transport industry. The main effect has been a greater demand for road transport at a time when there is less money available for road maintenance and construction, and more concern over the environmental consequences of transportation activities.

Challenges Going Into The 21st Century

As we enter the twenty-first century, there are a number of transportation challenges that we face. The transportation sector is enormous, however, and the issues vary for inter-city versus urban transport, for users versus operators versus communities, for freight versus passenger services, and across the various modes. Although it is impossible to do justice to all the various transportation issues in a single paper, considerable insight is provided by considering two of the major challenges that cut across all the various perspectives mentioned above. These are the challenges of providing acceptable levels of mobility and at the same time reducing the negative environmental and social impacts associated with our transportation systems.

Ensuring mobility is the "raison d'etre" for both transportation facilities and transport planning activities. Its importance is encapsulated in the titles of the new national transportation policies in North America — "Moving America" in the United States and "Freedom to Move" in Canada. But the North American public has come to expect and demand incredible levels of personal mobility, and the inability of our current infrastructure to keep pace with demand has, in many people's estimate, given rise to a major mobility crisis. In fact, traffic congestion and the threat of incipient gridlock has been a cover story in most major newspapers in North America, and surveys taken in a variety of places in the United States indicate that traffic congestion is the top concern for a majority of citizens (Larson, 1988). Of course, road congestion is not a new concern. In fact, it has been a nearly continuous concern for urban core areas since the 1930s, but our mobility patterns have changed, and so have the nature and magnitude of the congestion problem. First, people are more mobile now; vehicle ownership rates continue to rise and the distances travelled per vehicle show the same upward trend. Truck transport has also grown considerably over the past two decades both in absolute and relative terms. Second, residential and commercial growth has increasingly taken the form of low density developments in suburbia. Together, these have resulted in increased traffic volume and especially cross-commutes at a time when road infrastructure expansion has slowed or stalled and in a way that conventional mass transit finds it impossible to compete with the private auto.

In some metropolitan areas of the United States, especially in California, the congestion problem has spawned an anti-growth backlash (Orski, 1987; Poole, 1988), but there does not seem to be any evidence of a strong trend reversal in mode choice or land use planning, and little public pressure exists to demand better transportation options. Kieffer (1985, 230) suggests that this is "... in part because the public and many policy makers perceive that no cost-effective or service-effective options exist to deal with these needs ... In the absence of perceived good options, the public tends to be passive." Still, as the congestion problem worsens and public frustration increases, something will need to be done and there is currently no consensus on what strategies are optimal or even necessary for the near future.

The traditional response to congestion has been to build more infrastructure. But with current budgetary, political and environmental constraints, there is little prospect for a major expansion of our road system. Instead, three complementary types of solutions have been advocated. The first type may be coined "the technological fix". Its advocates are optimistic that the development of intelligent vehicle highway systems (IVHS) will allow for continued reliance on the private automobile, through a more efficient use of existing facilities. IVHS include both "smart streets" or advanced traffic management systems such as computer controlled traffic signals that adapt to changes in traffic patterns, and "smart cars" that contain on-board vehicle navigation systems that provide information and advice on alternate travel routes. Many of the technologies have already been developed and they are relatively low-cost, at least in comparison with the road construction budgets in many urban areas (Willis, 1990). Increasingly, however, transport experts are suggesting that technological innovations on their own may not be enough and that we need to pay more attention to managing demand.

Transportation demand management is the art of modifying travel behaviour in order to reduce auto congestion. It may involve trip cancellation, but more frequently comprises shifts to more efficient transportation modes, to less congested routes and destinations, and to less congested times of the day. A variety of measures have been identified, and evidence to date suggests that many of them have considerable potential for reducing auto travel, especially peak flows (Schonfeld and Chadda, 1985; Dunphy and Lin, 1990; Vlek and Michon, 1992). These measures can be broken into two general categories, labelled the "carrot" and the "stick". "Carrot" options use incentives, such as better transit service or subsidized parking for car poolers, to reduce auto traffic. These measures are generally acceptable to the public and sometimes have strong employer support as well (Angell, 1989; Ferguson, 1990). Their impact to date, however, has been relatively minor as there is an enormous inertia to change. It is widely thought that "stick" options would produce greater results, but they are widely perceived as being "punitive" in nature, providing cost and convenience disincentives for car usage, for example through electronic road pricing or auto-free zones. As such, there are more political and logistical obstacles to their widespread adoption.

The third approach to solving the congestion problem involves changes in land use densities and patterns, so that transit and other alternate forms of transportation can compete with the private auto. Cervero (1986, 1991) argues that Canada is well ahead of the United States in this respect, but even then the modal split in cities like Toronto, Montreal and Vancouver highly favours the private car. In Canada, as in the United States, many of the advocates for land use change have organized themselves into public interest lobby groups, such as Transport 2000, The Transit Advocacy Centre, Environmentalists Plan Transportation and more recently the Better Transportation Coalition. Although they are often perceived by the general public and transport planning community as radicals, their argument is powerful and has been voiced by numerous social critics over the past three decades — unless we are prepared to change land use densities and patterns, North American society will continue to organize its life spaces around the automobile and will by default pay enormous social and environmental costs.

This leads directly to the second major transportation challenge of our times, which is the need to fully address transportation impacts. The concern over impacts has been an evolving concern and, as Hansen (1990) notes, there has been a shift in the prevailing image of transportation from one that emphasizes the economic and personal benefits of transport to one that emphasizes its enormous costs in dollars, energy, pollution and lives. Certainly, the growing awareness of transportation costs has effected changes in transport planning procedures and in the various regulations that deal with safety and environment, but still the incremental, cumulative costs of our transport activities are enormous.

The cry has gone out for "green" or "sustainable" transportation systems, although it is not entirely clear what is meant by these terms. New developments in engine design and fuel composition are likely to reduce vehicle emissions in the near future, and most of the IVHS and demand management options also have positive implications for the environment. But will these be sufficient? Once again, there are those who are advocating change that is much more fundamental — in essence another transportation revolution — that is led by land use policies rather than transport technology:

> "A green urban transport policy would derive from the premise that communal means of movement be favored over those facilitating the excessive usage of owner-operated, low-occupancy vehicles. It would superimpose axes of concentrated development onto currently diffuse patterns of land-use density so as to reduce aggregate metropolitan travel to more tolerable levels. It would exalt (and do its utmost to assist) the popular impulse to resort to pedestrian- and pedal-power instead of piston-power". (Lowe, 1989: 28)

And so the question remains. How do we ensure acceptable levels of mobility and at the same time reduce the negative side effects of transportation. What options should be pursued? The transport research community faces the challenge of examining the feasibility and probable impacts of a wide range of transport alternatives and of effectively communicating their findings to both the public and to policy makers. The challenge is enormous and many disciplines, including geography, have a role to play.

The Development of Transportation Geography

So, where does transportation geography fit in? A number of commentaries and critical reviews on the topic of transport geography have been published over the past two decades, beginning with Wheeler (1971) and including various publications in *Progress in Human Geography* by Alan Hay (1977, 1978, 1979a, 1979b, 1980, 1981), Peter Rimmer (1978, 1985, 1986a, 1988), and others (Leinback, 1976; Muller, 1976; Mackinnon and Barber, 1977; Tinkler, 1979; Taylor, 1980). These reviews provide insight into the development and scope of transportation studies in geography and suggest avenues for new research. Rimmer's (1978) article, which is probably the most provocative and comprehensive overview, provides a useful framework for discussing the evolution of this subfield. He identifies three phases up to the late 1970s — description, quantification and prediction, and repudiation.

The classical treatment of transport topics by geographers prior to the second world war was characterized by description. Early studies provided factual inventories and regional comparisons of transportation facilities and commodity flows. The research process involved gathering information about the visible transport landscape, and interpreting patterns and features within the context of the history and geography of the region. Rimmer (1978, 77) describes such works as providing "grist for the regional geography mill rather than establishing a distinctive transport geography."

In the 1950s, the descriptive approach was usurped by the quantitative-theoretic revolution that swept the social sciences. In geography, transport studies became one of the leading sectors in the re-orientation of the discipline (Hay, 1977). Seminal papers on spatial interaction by Ullman (1954, 1956) and Garrison (1959-60) provided a theoretical bases for the spatial modelling approach that came to dominate geography throughout the 1960s and 1970s. Statistical and mathematical techniques were adopted or adapted from other disciplines and were applied to a variety of transport problems.

By the mid-1970s a sustained and clearly articulated concern over the spatial perspective had emerged. Hay (1977, 313) interprets the centre of the criticism as being that transport geographers had become dehumanized in both academic and applied form and notes that "...the strength of the criticism was reinforced by the fact that the authors (Eliot Hurst, 1974; Wheeler, 1973; Rimmer, 1971) had themselves been contributors to the quantitative theoretical literature and could not be dismissed as ignorant critics." Interpretations of a new transport geography emerged, emphasizing the interrelationships between transport and society (Wheeler, 1974; Stutz, 1976; Taylor, 1980). Rimmer (1978) refers to this era as the repudiation phase. Survey research formed the basis of a number of studies on personal mobility. A variety of conceptual and empirical papers discussed the negative impacts of an auto-based society on both human and natural systems. Still others began to emphasize the political-cultural context in which transport decisions are made.

A quick survey of current geographical journals and membership directories indicates that, while the transportation theme no longer holds the prominence that it once did, a number of transport-related issues continue to be investigated by geographers, and these cut across all three phases as previously described. Investigations occur at a variety of scales, use a variety of analytic approaches, and are motivated by a variety of conceptual frameworks (Hansen, 1986). Often, in fact, individual studies appear to have more in common with the work of engineers, economists, psychologists or political theorists than with research by fellow geographers, and this has been interpreted by some as being problematic. For example, Hay (1978, 324) has noted that "The resulting heterogeneity of transport geography inevitably bemuses students and severely taxes the ingenuity of the teacher who wishes to do justice to all the varied approaches." In a similar vein, Rimmer (1978) has argued that transport geography lacks a unique identity, largely because we have borrowed too much from other disciplines. But I would suggest that both our diversity of approach and our strong linkages with other related disciplines need not detract from our collective contribution, but rather might enhance the role that we play in this extremely complex field.

As a starting point, it is worth noting the similarities between the development of transport geography and that of the broader field of transport planning. In both cases, three broad phases can be identified. Prior to the second world war, both transport planning and transport geography were interested in the development aspect of transport systems. They were localized in their perspective and relatively unsophisticated in their analyses. During the 1950s and 1960s, both activities were revolutionized by computer technology. Transportation research and planning became empirically intensive, analytically sophisticated, and increasingly focused on urban regional systems. Transportation geographers showed the same enthusiasm for spatial modelling and optimization algorithms as did transport engineers and regional scientists. During the 1970s and continuing throughout the 1980s and into the 1990s, the emphasis shifted from one that heralded the benefits of transport developments to one that cautioned against the social and environmental impacts of transport activities. Once again, evidence of this realignment may be found not only in transport planning procedures and policy, but in the academic literature as well. In fact, strong links between transport geography and the broader multi-disciplinary field of transportation planning have always existed and are likely to continue, since the topic of transportation is not easily divided into disciplinary slices, with geographers having their own distinctive piece. Instead transport issues have behavioural, cultural, economic, environmental, political, spatial, and technological dimensions. If we are to have improved understanding and planning in this area, researchers will need to continue to use a variety of analytic approaches in examining transport systems, and academics, planners and policy makers will need to continue to share ideas and methodologies, regardless of disciplinary affiliation.

Deriving a Research Agenda

Over the past couple of decades, two general trends have emerged in geography that provide a starting point for discussing the future of transportation studies within the discipline. The first is a resurgence of interest among human geographers in applied research and planning (Knox, 1984; Rees, 1992). This renewed emphasis on "relevant" issues has also occurred in transport geography (Williams, 1981), as illustrated by a number of recent books (O'Sullivan, 1980; Adams, 1981; Rimmer, 1986b; Whitelegg, 1988), and by the specific research programs of individuals. As examples, Adams (1983, 1985a, 1985b), Andrey (Andrey and Olley, 1990; Andrey and Yagar, 1993) and Whitelegg (1983, 1987) have concentrated mainly on road safety issues; a research group in the U.K. has developed expertise in highway meteorology, providing advice on questions of road design and winter road maintenance (Perry and Symons, 1991; Thornes, 1992); and others are exploring the implications of land use-transportation interactions for energy use and auto emissions (Anderson et al., 1993). As part of this emphasis on pragmatic issues there has been a growing concern with the political aspect of transportation planning.

> "In this respect, transport geographers have taken on board the 'policy variable' as a significant component of transport analysis, finding common ground with researchers in areas such as housing and health care policy and provision ... An increasingly significant aspect of the types of research referred to above has been not merely a recognition of the importance of transport policy inputs to the system being studied ... but also a concern with the outputs of a policy-influenced (or controlled) system. It is then a natural progression for the individual — and hence the conceptual framework of the individual's discipline — to wish to comment on, and then to influence, policy itself". (Farrington, 1985: 109-110)

In fact, the adoption of a policy-based approach is perhaps the most promising aspect of current transportation research by geographers, as it coincides with a time of growing challenges, shrinking budgets, and increased awareness of the need to better understand the regional context of specific transportation problems.

A second trend that has developed in human geography concerns the way in which research is packaged, i.e. the key works that are used in titles and abstracts, the themes around which conferences are organized, and the journals in which research results are released. Increasingly, the emphasis is on the philosophical, conceptual and methodological dimensions of a research project rather than on the specific issue being investigated. For example, topics such as Marxism, post-Fordism, sustainable development, feminism, geographical information systems and choice modelling have replaced the traditional emphases on industrial location, regional economic development, and urban planning. Although this trend may be seen as being progressive, since it reflects a move towards explanation and away from pure description/prescription, it does pose a communication challenge for those geographers who are involved in transport-related studies. This challenge exists because both scholars and practitioners from other disciplines can easily overlook relevant geographical work, because it is no longer clear, based on key words and journal titles, which papers deal with transportation issues. And this communication problem is exacerbated by the fact that geography is often poorly represented at major transportation meetings and in major transportation journals. If we are to be taken seriously by other transportation planners, we must ensure that geographical research is integrated into the mainstream of transportation studies, and that the relevance of our research is articulated to those who make decisions about land use guidelines and transportation investments. Indeed the recent announcement of a new British periodical, *Journal of Transport Geography*, is a positive move in this regard.

In terms of directions for future research, I think that geographers would do well to organize their transportation research around three substantive issues, which cut across the disciplinary boundaries. The first is the need to better understand mobility patterns, especially the linkages between land use planning and travel decision making. In this regard, some geographers will make their contributions through spatial/economic modelling, while others adopt a more humanistic approach. The second is the need to monitor and predict the various impacts of transportation activities. Geographers have shown considerable interest and expertise in various types of impact assessment, and did play an important role in the 1970s in identifying some of the negative spinoffs associated with transportation decisions, but there is much yet to learn about the implications of transportation activities for both society and the natural environment. Finally, we need to take a proactive role in the policy arena, recognizing the fact that all policy options have implications for both mobility and transportation impacts; indeed many policies make explicit tradeoffs between the two.

References

Adams, J.G.U. (1981) *Transport Planning: Vision and Practice*, London: Routledge and Kegan Paul.

_____ (1983) "Public safety legislation and the risk compensation hypothesis: The example of motorcycle helmet legislation," *Environment and Planning C: Government and Policy*, Vol. 1: 193-203,1985a.

_____ (1985a) *Risk and Freedom:The Record of Road Safety Regulation*, Cardiff: Transport Publishing Projects.

_____ (1985b) "Smeed's law, seat belts and the emperor's new clothes," in Evans, L. and Schwing, R.C. (eds.), *Human Behavior and Traffic Safety*, New York: Plenum Press, pp. 194-238.

Anderson, W., Kanaraglou, P., and Miller, E. (1993) "Integrated Land Use and Transportation Model for Energy and Environmental Analysis," presented at the Annual Meeting of the Canadian Association of Geographers, Carleton University, Ottawa.

Andrey, J.C. and Olley, R. (1990) "Relationships between weather and road safety: Past and future research directions," *Climatological Bulletin*, Vol. 24: 123-137.

Andrey, J.C. and Yagar, S. (1993) "A temporal analysis of rain-related crash risk," *Accident Analysis and Prevention*, Vol. 25: 465-472.

Angell, C.D. (1989) "Mobility futures: An overview," *Transportation Quarterly*, Vol. 43: 549-555.

Bardou, J., Chanaron, J., Fridenson, P., and Laux, J. (1982) *The Automobile Revolution: The Impact of an Industry*, Chapel Hill: The University of North Carolina Press.

Cervero, R. (1986) "Urban transit in Canada: Integration and innovation at its best," *Transportation Quarterly*, Vol. 40: 293-316.

_____ (1991) "Land uses and travel at suburban activity centers," *Transportation Quarterly*, Vol. 45: 479-491.

Dunphy, R.T. and Lin, B.C. (1990) *Transportation Management through Partnerships,* Washington, D.C.: The Urban Land Institute.

Eliot Hurst, M.E. (ed.) (1974) *Transportation Geography: Comments and Readings*, New York: McGraw Hill.

Farrington, J. H. (1985) "Transport geography and policy: Deregulation and privatization," *Transactions Institute of British Geographers*, Vol. 10: 109-119.

Ferguson, E. (1990) "Transport demand management - planning, development and implementation," *Journal of the American Planning Association*, Autumn 1990: 442-456.

Garrison, W.L. (1959-60) "Spatial structure of the economy," Parts I, II and III, *Annals of the Association of the American Geographers*, Vol. 49: 232-239, 471-482; Vol. 50: 353-73.

Gillen, D.W. (1990) *Canadian Transportation Policy*, Kingston, Ontario: John Deutsch Institute for the Study of Economic Policy, Queen's University.

Hansen, S. (ed.) (1986) *The Geography of Urban Transportation*, New York: Guilford.

Hansen, M. (1990) "U.S. intercity passenger transportation policy: 1806-1990", in Gillen, D.W. (ed.), *Canadian Transportation Policy*, Kingston, Ontario: John Deutsch Institute for the Study of Economic Policy, Queen's University, pp. 20-34.

Hay, A.M. (1977) "Transport geography," *Progress in Human Geography*, Vol. 1: 313-318.

_____ (1978) "Transport geography," *Progress in Human Geography*, Vol. 2: 324-329.

_____ (1979a) "The geographical explanation of commodity flow," *Progress in Human Geography*, Vol. 3: 1-12.

_____ (1979b) "Transport geography," *Progress in Human Geography*, Vol. 3: 267-272.

_____ (1980) "Transport geography," *Progress in Human Geography*, Vol. 4: 271-275.

_____ (1981) "Transport geography," *Progress in Human Geography,* Vol. 5: 263-267.

Kieffer, J.A. (1985) "The neglected challenge in metropolitan area transportation," *Journal of Advanced Transportation,* Vol. 19: 215-235.

Knox, P. (1984) "Planning and applied geography," *Progress in Human Geography,* Vol. 8: 515-524.

Larson, T.D. (1988) "Metropolitan congestion: Towards a tolerable accommodation," *Transportation Quarterly,* Vol. 42: 489-498.

Leinback, T.R. (1976) "Transportation geography I: Networks and flows," *Progress in Geography,* Vol. 8: 177-207.

Lewis, S., Cook, P., and Minc, M. (1990) "Comprehensive transportation models: Past, present and future," *Transportation Quarterly,* Vol. 44: 249-266.

Lowe, J. (1989) "Green urban transport," *City Magazine,* Vol. 11(1): 28-30.

Mackinnon, R.D. and Barber, G.M. (1977) "Optimization models of transportation network improvement," *Progress in Human Geography,* Vol. 3: 387-412.

Muller, P.O. (1976) "Transportation geography II: Social transportation," *Progress in Geography,* Vol. 8: 208-231.

Orski, C.K. (1987) ""Managing" suburban traffic congestion: A strategy for suburban mobility," *Transportation Quarterly,* Vol. 41: 457-476.

O'Sullivan, P.M. (1980) *Transport policy: An interdisciplinary approach,* London: Batsford.

Perry, A.H. and Symons, L.J. (eds.) (1991) *Highway Meteorology,* London: E&FN Spon.

Poole, R.W. Jr. (1988) "Resolving gridlock in Southern California," *Transportation Quarterly,* Vol. 42: 499-527.

Rees, J. (1992) "Regional development and policy under turbulence", *Progress in Human Geography,* Vol. 16: 223-231.

Rimmer, P.J. (1971) "Government influence on transport decision-making in Thailand", in Linge, G.J.R. and Rimmer, P.J. (eds.), *Government Influence on the Location of Economic Activity, Canberra: The Australian National University*, Research School of Pacific Studies, Department of Human Geography Publication HG/5, pp. 325-358.

_____ (1978) "Redirections in transport geography", *Progress in Human Geography*, Vol. 2: 76-100.

_____ (1985) "Transport geography", *Progress in Human Geography*, Vol. 9: 271-277.

_____ (1986a) "Transport geography", *Progress in Human Geography*, Vol. 10: 397-406.

_____ (1986b) *Rikisha to Rapid Transit : Urban Public Transport Systems and Policy in Southeast Asia*, Sydney: Pergamon.

_____ (1988) "Transport geography", *Progress in Human Geography*, Vol. 11: 270-281.

Schonfeld, P. and Chadda, H. (1985) "An assessment of urban travel reduction options", *Transportation Quarterly*, Vol. 39: 391-406.

Stutz, E.P. (1976) *Social aspects of interaction*, Washington, D.C.: Association of American Geographers Resource Paper.

Taylor, Z. (1980) "Some comments on social transport geography", *Progress in Human Geography*, Vol. 4: 99-104.

Thornes, J.E. (1992) "The impact of weather and climate on transport in the UK", *Progress in Physical Geography*, Vol. 16: 187-208.

Tinkler, K.J. (1979) "Graph theory", *Progress in Human Geography*, Vol. 3: 8-15.

Ullman, E.L. (1954) "Geography as spatial interaction", in Rezvan, D. and Englebert, E.S. (eds.), *Interregional Linkages*, Berkely: University of California, pp. 1-12; Reprinted in Eliot Hurst, M.E. (ed.), Transportation geography: Comments and readings, New York: McGraw-Hill, pp. 29-40.

_____ (1956) "The role of transportation and the bases for interaction", in Thomas, W.L. Jr. (ed.), *Man's Role in Changing the Face of the Earth*, Chicago: University of Chicago Press, pp. 862-880.

Vlek, C. and Michon, J. (1992) "Why we should and how we could decrease the use of motor vehicles in the near future", *IATTS Research*, Vol. 15(2): 82-93.

Weiner, E. (1987) *Urban Transportation Planning in the United States: An Historical Overview*, New York: Praeger.

Wheeler, J.O. (1971) "An overview of research in transportation geography", *East Lakes Geographer*, Vol. 7: 3-12.

_____ (1973) "Transportation geography: Societal and policy perspectives", *Economic Geography*, Vol. 49: 95-184.

_____ (1974) *The Urban Circulation Noose*, North Scituate, Mass.: Duxbury Press.

Whitelegg, J. (1983) "Road safety: Defeat, complicity and the bankruptcy of science", *Accident Analysis and Prevention*, Vol. 15: 153-160.

_____ (1987) "A geography of road traffic crashes", *Transactions Institute of British Geographers*, Vol. 12: 161-176.

_____ (1988) *Transport Policy in the EEC*, London: Routledge.

Williams, A.F. (1981) "Aims and achievements of transport geography", in Whitelegg, J. (ed.), *The Spirit and Purpose of Transport Geography*, Lancaster: IBG Transport Study Group Conference, pp. 5-31.

Willis, D. (1990) "IVHS technologies: Promising palliatives or popular poppycock?", *Transportation Quarterly*, Vol. 44: 73-84.

Chapter 5

From New Town to No Town: Implications of the Increasing Use of Commuting by the Canadian Mining Industry

Keith Storey and Mark Shrimpton
Memorial University

Introduction

"Commuter mining" is a system whereby, because the work place is so isolated from the workers' homes, food and accommodations are provided at the work site and employees spend a fixed number of days working at the site, followed by a fixed number of days at home (Hobart,1979). While the most common method of commuting to and from these mines is by air and the term "fly-in" is widespread in the industry, there are operations which use road and sea transportation. Long-distance commuting (LDC) is an alternative label coined by Hobart (1979), although even it may not be appropriate in the case of some recent mines which use a relatively short commute. However, in the absence of a single comprehensive term, LDC is used here.

This paper is concerned with assessing the geographic implications of this work system. Changing economic, social, political and environmental factors have significantly altered the way in which the mining industry in Canada does business. There is an increasing concentration of mining exploration and development activity in the North and the ways in which new resources are developed have significant implications for patterns of future development in the region. Whether LDC will simply be another means of exploiting northern resources for metropolitan benefit or whether it can be used as a development tool for the benefit of the North and northerners is an important public issue.

This paper uses a place of work - place of residence model to illustrate the centrifugal and centripetal forces which are expected to become increasingly important for resource development and its associated settlement patterns in Canada's North in the future. Within this spatial context, the themes discussed include employment, economic leakage, out-migration and community impacts. The objective is to illustrate the need for a geographic focus on this issue and on related public policy in order to ensure that the differential spatial benefits and costs of these work arrangements are optimized.

This paper draws on a program of research which has been ongoing over the past five years. The primary data sources used are surveys of all LDC mines in Canada, the first of which was undertaken in 1987 and subsequently periodically updated (Storey and Shrimpton, 1988); case studies of three LDC mines; and interviews with miners and spouses in Key Lake, Saskatchewan and Polaris and Lupin, Northwest Territories (NWT), undertaken from 1988-1991 (Storey and Shrimpton, 1989; Shrimpton and Storey, 1992).

The Decline of the Single-Industry Community

Traditionally the community in which miners live and work are one and the same, or sufficiently proximate to allow a daily commute between home and work. Thus the development of remote mineral resources has spawned the single-industry mining town which has become a characteristic feature of the Canadian landscape. However, over the past two decades, this characteristic has been changing and the trend promises to continue. While some existing mining communities may have expanded, a more common event has been the closure of mining operations and the associated downsizing, or elimination of their dependent communities. At the same time, there have been no new mining communities constructed since Tumbler Ridge in British Columbia in the early 1980s.

These changes reflect responses to the economic constraints experienced by the mining industry, together with changes in government policy and society generally, which have had direct impacts on mining development and operational decisions. These include the limitations of single-industry resource towns, changes in the regulatory and policy environment, improvements in transportation and communications technology and infrastructure, and changes in the structure of the mining sector (Storey and Shrimpton, 1988). All of these have seen significant change in recent years, the net result of which has increasingly favoured the use of commuting arrangements for new mining operations at remote locations.

Limitations of Resource Towns

There is a considerable literature on the problems of company or resource towns (see, for example, Robinson, 1984; Robson, 1988). These problems include:

- lack of economic diversity
- lack of alternative employment opportunities, especially for women
- difficulties of recruiting and retaining top quality labour
- vulnerability to "boom and bust" cycles
- seasonal instability in terms of employment and income levels
- a limited and often unpredictable lifespan of the resource
- socio-demographic imbalances
- social problems associated with remote environments, loneliness, alcoholism, etc.
- communities too small to support many urban services, especially in education, entertainment, and retailing
- limitations of the physical, social and political environment
- difficulties of town management
- startup and wind down costs to industry and government
- social and economic problems associated with closure

Many of these problems have been exacerbated over time as Canadian miners and their families have come to expect and demand more recreational, educational and other public facilities, as a higher proportion of children attend post-secondary education institutions, and as demographic, social and economic changes have made two-income families the norm. This is not to suggest that life in small, isolated communities is all bad; in fact many workers and their families express a strong preference for the lifestyle that such communities offer (Shrimpton and Storey, 1992). Still these limitations form part of the rationale for commuter mining.

The Regulatory and Policy Environment

A number of public policy considerations have also affected choices between the resource town and commuting alternatives. Principal among these is the fate of single industry towns when the resource is exhausted or its exploitation becomes uneconomic, thus removing the community's raison d'être. This common Canadian phenomenon has proved costly to the residents of such towns and to the public purse. As an example, the zinc/lead resource base at Nanisivik, NWT is nearing the end of its economic life and within the next few years decisions will have to be made regarding the fate of the community there. A number of suggestions have been made, including using the community and its air and marine infrastructure as a winter military training centre and a base for coastguard activities, but as yet the matter remains unresolved. Accordingly, alternative development options have become more desirable.

At the same time, changes in the regulatory environment have made the construction of resource towns more expensive. The earlier company towns were largely unconstrained by government requirements and controls, leading in many cases to a poor quality urban environment. More recent mining towns, such as Tumbler Ridge in northeast British Columbia, are by contrast conspicuous for the planning efforts and investments that have gone into the design of the community. In the case of Tumbler Ridge the estimated total development cost exceeded $274 million, representing a per capita investment in the order of $45,700 (McGrath,1986). However, recurring problems with coal contracts, in particular, continue to leave the long-term viability of the community in doubt.

Companies contemplating the development of a new town also know they are likely to be subject to the impact assessment process which may require the use of costly management and mitigation measures before the project is allowed to proceed. Developers are now subject to increasingly onerous regulations regarding townsite design, accommodation standards and servicing, which further add to construction costs.

Another constraint to resource town development is that increasing federal-provincial management of resources has tended to transfer much of the decision-making from the private sector context to the political-regulatory context. For example, and as an extreme case, the Alberta Government in the mid-1970s refused to allow any new town development in the Coal Branch area west of Edmonton. In this case developers had no choice but to use a commuting option (Berg,1986). A second example involves affirmative action programs, particularly as they apply to native peoples. The objective of these programs is to encourage native participation in resource development and yet at the same time permit native peoples to maintain elements of their traditional lifestyle. The resource town strategy emphasises working and living within a predominantly "white world," whereas commuting arrangements are thought to allow kinship and community ties to be maintained and traditional pursuits to be followed, while at the same time providing access to income earning opportunities in the industrial economy. This issue is discussed in more detail later in the paper.

Commuting arrangements have also been seen as a means of spreading the economic benefits of resource development to a wide range of communities, native and non-native, rural and urban, and northern and southern.

The effects are the opposite of those of a resource town, insofar as income generated at the mine is spent in a large number of communities. This contributes to the diversification of the economic bases of these communities and serves to spread both the benefits of the mine during its operation and the costs of its closure.

In short, government policy has increasingly encouraged resource developments that address a range of political, economic and social objectives rather than simply economic objectives. As a consequence many of the what, where, when and how questions of development must be evaluated against a wider range of variables, the net result being that in many cases commuting has become the preferred option.

Transportation and Communications Technology

A third element in the new calculus are the changes in movement and communication costs that have occurred in recent years. New technology, particularly with respect to air transportation and telecommunications, has provided resource developers with the basis for the commuting option which simply was not there in the 1950s and 1960s. Air transportation is now fast, dependable and relatively safe and inexpensive and the range in types of aircraft allow operators greater scope in choosing equipment appropriate to their needs. Commuting distances and arrangements vary greatly; for example, the Saskatchewan uranium operations use chartered aircraft from within-province pick-up points while Cominco relies on regularly scheduled commercial flights to bring workers from across Canada to Resolute, NWT and then a small chartered aircraft from Resolute to Little Cornwallis Island.

In addition, satellite communications, computer and fax links now effectively reduce isolation by making communications with corporate offices, suppliers, etc. much easier and for many of these elements there has been, over time, a decline in absolute costs.

The Structure of the Mining Sector

The period 1981 to 1987 saw a crisis in the Canadian mining industry. While it has always been vulnerable to short-term mineral cycles and longer term business cycles, during this recession the cyclical vagaries of international mineral markets coincided with significant structural changes within the industry. This meant that more attention than ever has had to be given to improving productivity, rationalizing operations, and reducing production costs so as to ensure industry competitiveness.

One of the main implications for the Canadian mining industry has been the need for increased extraction efficiency, which implies the likelihood of a smaller workforce — a further incentive to the use of the commuting option. Furthermore, recent mineral price fluctuations have caused attention to focus on development options that are more compatible with variability per se. Commuting offers advantages in that costs of both the start-up and closure of mines, whether temporary or permanent, are reduced. In cases of closure there are no mining town problems, and the saving in commuter transportation costs is immediate. Commuter operations are thus both easier and less costly to open and to close (and possibly subsequently to re-open), as seems to be indicated by the closure of several mines after only two or three years of operation.

Commuter operations also present a number of operational advantages from the company viewpoint. For example, they seem to present fewer difficulties in attracting and retaining workers (Nogas, 1976; Glass and Lazarovich, 1984; Newton, 1986). Thus, the developers of the Rabbit Lake uranium mine in northern Saskatchewan estimated that if they used a mining town they could expect anything from a 35-400 per cent annual turnover rate. In fact turnover started at 28 per cent when it opened as a LDC mine in 1975, and this was down to 5 per cent by 1986 (Nogas,1986).

While low turnover rates at most Canadian commuter mining operations can in part be explained by an absence of alternative mining employment opportunities in the 1980s, there appears, nonetheless, to be a fairly high level of satisfaction with commuting systems. Turnover rates at the Lupin gold mine in the NWT, for example, have declined since operations began. In 1986 the turnover was in the order of 13-14 per cent (Storey and Shrimpton, 1989) and by 1991 it was down to 8.5 per cent (Armstrong, 1991).

Operators of mines using a commute system have also experienced low levels of absenteeism (Newton,1986), primarily because once workers are onsite there is little incentive or opportunity to fail to report for work without good reason. Also it appears that there are fewer industrial disputes. In Canada only six commuter mines have been organized. In 1990, 38 per cent of the commuting mine labour force was unionized. This is in contrast to an overall estimated figure of between 50-60 per cent for the organized mining sector labour force as a whole, as estimated by the federal Department of Energy, Mines and Resources. To date there have been few significant disputes at Canadian LDC mines. In one case, after a short sit-in at Cluff Lake, Saskatchewan in 1980, the issue was rapidly resolved with the intervention of the Saskatchewan government. In another, construction workers, not mine workers, struck over travel conditions to and from the Hope Brook mine in Newfoundland.

The Use of Commuting by the Mining Industry

The use of commuting systems by the mining industry in Canada as a whole has increased rapidly in the last decade. Table 5.1 identifies past and present commuter operations in Canada, and clearly indicates how recent this phenomenon is. The first mine designed to use a fly-in/workcamp system was Asbestos Hill, Quebec, in 1972, (see Figure 5.1 and Table 5.1), 20 of 23 of the operations to date have only been in operation since 1980, and ten have opened since 1987. Gold mines predominate, and may well continue to do so if gold prices recover. However, new LDC mines, at locations close to or north of 60°, are in the planning stages in northern British Columbia (copper), the NWT (uranium), and Quebec (nickel).

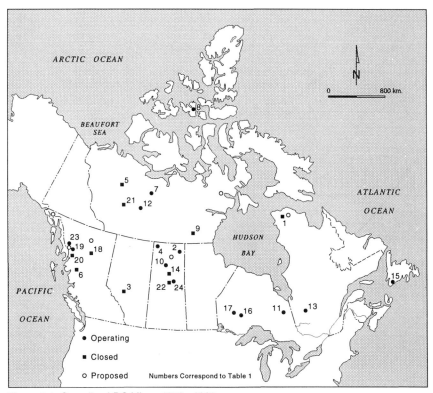

Figure 5.1: Canadian LDC Mines 1972 - 1993

Table 5.1
Characteristics of Current and Former Canadian Commuter Mines

	Mine	Deposit	Province	Opened/ Closed	Employees	Rotation (Days in/out)	Life Expectancy (yrs.)
1	Asbestos Hill	asbestos	Que.	1972-83	c.400	70/14	-
2	Rabbit Lake	uranium	Sask.	1975	350	7/7	>20
3	Coal Valley	coal	Alta.	1978	335	n.a.	n.a.
4	Cluff Lake	uranium	Sask.	1980	260	7/7	>20
5	Camsell River	silver	NWT	1980-85	200	28/28	-
6	Baker River	gold	BC	1981-83	47	14/7	-
7	Lupin	gold	NWT	1982	448	28/14 14/14	15-19
8	Polarios	zinc/lead	NWT	1982	275	63/21 42/28 42/21	15-19
9	Cullaton Lake	gold/silver	NWT	1983-85	130	7/7 42/21	-
10	Key Lake	uranium	Sask.	1983	425	7/7	15-19
11	Detour Lake	gold	Ont.	1983	350	7/7 4/3	10-14
12	Salmita	gold	NWT	1983-87	25	14/14 35/21	-
13	Lac Shortt	gold	Que.	1984-92	183	14/7 7/7 5/2 4/3	-
14	Star Lake	gold	Sask.	1987-89	45	7/7	-
15	Hope Brook	gold	Nfld.	1987-91	273	14/14 4/3	-
				1992	240	14/14	7-9
16	Emerald Lake	gold	Ont.	1988	85	4/4	n.a.
17	Golden Patricia	gold	Ont.	1988	192	14/14	4-6
18	Lawyers'	gold	BC	1988-92	65	14/14 4/4	-
19	Golden Bear	gold	BC	1989	111	28/14 14/14	4-6
20	Johnny Mountain	gold	BC	1989-90	133	28/14 14/14	-
21	Colomac	gold	NWT	1990-91	342	14/14	-
22	Jasper	gold	Sask.	1990-91	80	7/7	-
23	Snip	gold	BC	1991	140	28/14	n.a.
24	Seabee	gold	Sask.	1991	100	7/7	5

While, overall, LDC operations constitute a minority of all Canadian mines, the rate of increase in the use of this system has been rapid. The number of LDC operations as a percentage of all new gold, uranium and lead/zinc mines increased steadily from 9 per cent in 1975-79, to 15 per cent in 1980-84, and to 36 per cent in 1985-87 (derived from Canada,1987). In some regions, notably the NWT, it has become the dominant approach to the development of mineral resources.

Most Canadian LDC mines use relatively short rotation patterns. The most common pattern sees employees spending seven days at work followed by seven at home (7/7), though the 14/14 pattern has shown recent growth, being used at the Colomac and Lupin mines in the NWT among others. Asymmetrical rotations are increasingly uncommon, the most notable exceptions being the Polaris, NWT, and the U.S. Red Dog, Alaska lead/zinc mines. Rotation length and pattern appears to be strongly correlated with location and accessibility. Mines in southern Canada and the near-north have tended to adopt shorter, symmetrical, rotations, while mines at more northerly locations have adopted longer, and often asymmetrical, rotations.

The Spatial Consequences of LDC

Introduction

The use of LDC has a number of potentially significant spatial ramifications with implications for government development policy, community and individual well being. These may be conceptualized in terms of their vertical and horizontal dimensions (Figure 5.2).

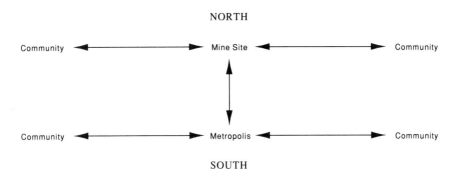

Figure 5.2: Spatial Implications of LDC

The vertical dimension referred to concerns the potential for LDC to rein-force "North-South" centre-periphery relationships by allowing benefits to "fly-over" northern communities. At the simplest level, most mine workers at LDC operations live in the South and commute to the North to work. Incomes generated from the exploitation of northern resources are ex-pended in the south where taxes on those incomes are also collected. Simi-larly, a significant proportion of mine expenditures on supplies and services are made in southern metropolitan centres. All in all, while northern and peripheral regions may have lower initial infrastructure provision, commu-nity and social services and community downsizing costs, they receive only limited infrastructural, industrial, employment and tax benefits from LDC. This calls into question conventional regional development approaches, which seek to influence the location of employment in the vicinity of the resource being exploited.

The horizontal dimension reflects the spatial impacts of LDC within the North and South respectively. With respect to place of residence, LDC al-lows miners and their families a wide choice of residential location, since it minimizes the commute time and associated costs to employees. In spatial terms both centripetal and centrifugal forces are evident.

In the South, data indicate that many workers and their families prefer to live and consequently move to major metropolitan areas, this centripetal clustering giving rise to the phenomenon of the "urban miner" (Shrimpton and Storey, 1989). Centrifugal movements are evident among those who move to rural communities peripheral to major urban centres, where, though there may be few employment opportunities, other quality of life characteristics can be enjoyed.

In the North, the horizontal dimension takes on different characteristics in that native workers, in particular, can continue to live in their home commu-nities and combine traditional lifestyles with waged work, thus maintaining residential patterns. Still, as with many southern workers, there is evidence that some native workers have moved south and now commute from south-ern metropolitan areas.

In terms of the supply of goods and services to the mine site, the absence of an associated mine town, the absence or poor quality of land links to larger communities in the region, and the high quality transportation sys-tems linking the mine to the South, serve to discourage regional purchas-ing. While this tends to be a function of "remoteness" — i.e. as accessibility of the minesite to a regional centre decreases, the more likely purchases are to be made in a distant metropolitan centre — the net effect may be a loss of benefits from regional purchases of goods and services.

In summary, the spatial costs and benefits of LDC operations are quite different from those associated with traditional mining towns and give rise to a set of policy issues that, in Canada, have not been addressed directly. To date, governments have generally welcomed LDC because it avoids the use of single industry towns, and their attendant problems, and because it presents the possibility of spreading employment benefits to the native and non-native residents of small northern communities. Similarly, when the mine closes and jobs are lost, the impacts are not limited to one or two communities in the immediate area of the mine, but are spread over many centres.

Other, indirect, economic benefits to northern residents result from the tax revenues governments receive from LDC mines. Furthermore, commuting permits individuals to live in the communities of their choice and their local expenditures and tax payments may contribute significantly to the continued viability of those communities. Finally, where resource developments are strictly controlled short-term phenomena, the net effect of commuting operations may be to minimize the damage to sensitive environments.

However, there has been increasing recognition that LDC may have negative effects. One of these is the potential for "fly-over", with the labour force and communities close to such mines and even the regions within which they are located, gaining few benefits because labour and other requirements are drawn from larger, more distant, centres. Workers, supplies and services may come not only from distant parts of the region, but from entirely different territories, provinces, states and countries.

Another concern results from the fact that the company usually pays for travel to and from designated "pick-up" points and thus there are minimal costs to individual workers. They are free to move from a small community to a larger one with a greater range of services; alternatively, they may make the reverse move so as to reduce housing costs and live in a community felt to be less stressful and more suitable for raising a family. Even where the company pays only the transportation costs from specific pick-up points, workers may still find it cheaper or otherwise preferable to live at the place of their choice and pay the additional transport costs themselves. If such migration is selective, for example, predominantly the young and skilled workers, this can promote demographic imbalances. The nature and spatial implications of the use of LDC on employment, business and migration is discussed in detail below.

Fly-Over of Employment

While LDC provides considerable scope for distributing employment benefits throughout northern and other peripheral regions, it also has resulted in
a large amount of employment fly-over. While many of the direct and spin-
off employment benefits from a conventional mine may be retained in the
North, there is greater leakage to the South associated with LDC operations, a problem which is exacerbated in the polar regions.

Table 5.2 summarizes data on the places of residence of workers at eleven
commuter mines. Clearly the length of rotation and the transportation policies of companies significantly affect the regional distribution. At one extreme, the gold mine at Detour Lake, Ontario mostly uses a 7/7 day rotation,
and only flies workers to and from two Northern Ontario mining communities: Cochrane and Timmins. Virtually all of its employees live in the region,
with only 4.5 per cent coming from Southern Ontario and 1.5 per cent from
other provinces.

The British Columbian, Saskatchewan and Newfoundland LDC operations
also use relatively short rotations (7/7 and 14/14), only have intra-provincial
pick-up points, and exhibit a considerable concentration of employment.
However, as exemplified by the Saskatchewan mines, there may still be
considerable fly-over of northern communities. This latter group of mines
have both northern and southern pick-up points, and in the case of both the
Key Lake and Rabbit Lake mines about 80 per cent of the labour force live
in the south, mostly around Saskatoon and Prince Albert. Cluff Lake, which
has had a very effective native hiring program, employs a much higher
proportion (approximately 50 per cent) of northern residents (see Figure
5.3).

The Northwest Territories LDC mines also have pick-up points in both the
NWT and the South. Lupin provides, at no expense to the workers, jet service to and from Edmonton and Yellowknife, and turboprop services to selected other pick-up points in the NWT. Polaris, with its long asymmetrical
rotation, provides a free link to Resolute and pays for commercial air transportation between there and any airport in Canada. In the case of both
Lupin and Polaris, workers live throughout the country (Figure 5.4). In the
case of Polaris, there are also employees who live in the Caribbean, Venezuela and United Kingdom. In total, only 10.4 per cent of the employees at
these NWT mines live in the Territories.

The amount of employment leakage from a region also depends on the
location of the mine within it. For example, the Golden Patricia mine in

Table 5.2
Canadian LDC Employees by Mine and Region of Residence

Region	Polaris[1] NWT	Lupin[2] NWT	Johnny Mountain[2] BC	Golden Bear[2] BC	Rabbit Lake[1] Sask.	Cluff Lake[1] Sask.	Key Lake[1] Sask.	Golden Patricia[2] Ont.	Detour Lake[2] Ont.	Lac Shortt[2] Que.	Hope Brooke[2] Nfld.	Total
NWT-Yellowknife	9	12	-	-	-	-	-	-	-	-	-	21
NWT-Other	24	30	-	-	-	-	-	-	-	-	-	54
Yukon	1	-	5	6	-	-	-	4	-	-	-	16
British Columbia	63	80	126	98	2	-	-	12	-	-	-	381
Alberta-Northern	12	78	2	2	-	-	-	6	-	-	-	100
Alberta-Southern	-	200	-	2	3	-	-	-	-	-	-	205
Sask.-Northern	8	5	-	-	70	131	85	-	-	-	-	299
Sask.-Southern	-	15	-	-	297	132	392	10	-	-	-	846
Manitoba-Northern	8	2	-	-	-	-	-	64	-	-	-	74
Manitoba-Southern	-	12	-	-	-	-	-	90	-	-	-	102
Ontario-Northern	59	6	-	-	-	-	-	14	315	-	-	394
Ontario-Southern	-	3	-	-	-	-	-	-	15	5	2	25
Quebec-Northern	27	-	-	-	-	-	-	-	2	142	-	171
Quebec-Southern	-	1	-	-	-	-	-	-	2	32	-	35
Atlantic Provinces	51	4	-	-	-	-	-	1	1	4	271	332
Total	262[3]	448	133	108	372	263	477	201	335	183	273	3055

1. 1987 data
2. 1989 data
3. Does not include catering staff

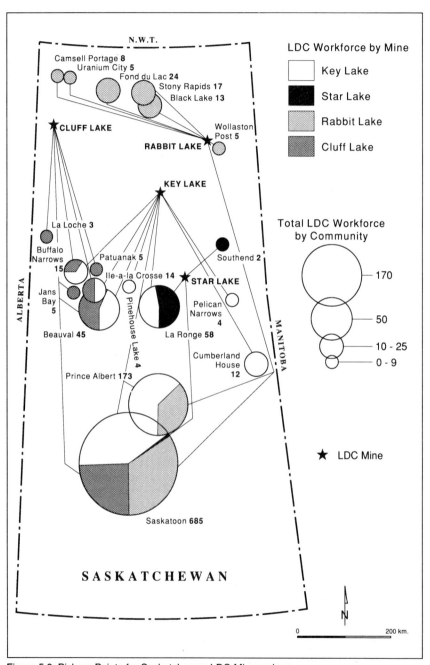

Figure 5.3: Pick-up Points for Saskatchewan LDC Mineworkers

Northwestern Ontario only has pick-up points in that region (Dryden, Sioux Lookout, Pickle Lake, Cat Lake and Slate Falls). However, because of the proximity of the Manitoba border and Winnipeg, the distance to urban centres in Ontario, and the 14/14 rotation, half of the labour force live outside the province. Thirty percent of all workers live in Manitoba, while 8 per cent commute as far as the Yukon and British Columbia.

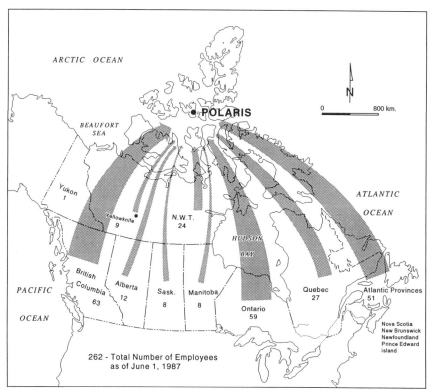

Figure 5.4: Regions of Residence of Polaris Mine Workers

Many of those who choose to live in the South have their homes in major urban centres. A survey of workers at the Key Lake uranium mine in Northern Saskatchewan showed that 57 per cent lived in Saskatoon, Regina, Winnipeg or "a city". Of the respondents to a survey of Polaris miners, 55 per cent lived in major metropolitan areas: Vancouver, Calgary, Edmonton, Winnipeg, Sudbury, St. Catharines, Toronto, Ottawa, Montreal or Halifax.

The commuting of workers to and from the South clearly has both direct and indirect economic impacts. Not only do these miners spend virtually all their payroll in the South, with associated income and employment multipliers, but also they are taxed in a different municipal and, frequently, provincial/ territorial jurisdiction. It is also in the South that their families will live, spend income from other sources, such as spousal employment, and be taxed; albeit these family members are also likely to demand significant social, health and educational services there.

Fly-Over of Business Opportunities

Just as there is a fly-over of employment, many supplies and services may be acquired in the south. Again this is most clearly evident for mining operations in the NWT. Data which contrast the purchasing patterns of western NWT LDC and conventional mines is presented in Table 5.3. The three conventional mines make 35 per cent of their total expenditures on supplies and services within the Territory. By contrast, Lupin, the LDC mine, spends only 23 per cent there.

There is little mining expenditure in the Territory by mines in the east and the same contrast in spending patterns between LDC and conventional mines is not evident. In 1986 there were two mines with total purchases amounting to $26,500,000. Of the $15,000,000 spent by the Polaris LDC operation, only 7 per cent of expenditures were in the Territory, specifically in Yellowknife. By contrast Nanisivik, a hybrid minetown/commute operation on Baffin Island made all of its purchases in Ontario/Quebec and one in the Territory.

A key factor here is clearly the availability of specialist suppliers at a convenient location within the region where the mine is located. In southern Canada, for example, Timmins, Sudbury and Thunder Bay are easily able to meet the needs of the Northern Ontario LDC mines, which are both connected to the provincial highway network (see Table 5.4). Likewise, Golden Bear is near the Yukon border and has good transportation links with it. At the other extreme, the eastern Arctic has a relatively poorly developed mining services industry. The mines ship their ore direct to European and other markets by sea, and most of the equipment and supplies required are brought in the same way with most supplies coming by sea from Montreal. By contrast the Lupin Mine has better air and ground links to Yellowknife, the latter through a seasonal winter road. However, as previously noted, it still makes significantly less of its purchases in the NWT, compared to the non-LDC mines which are located near Yellowknife.

Table 5.3
Purchasing Profiles, LDC and Non-LDC Mines
Northwest Territories, Canada 1986

	LDC Mines[1]	Non-LDC Mines[2]
Total Purchases:	50,219,000	28,271,000
Source (%):		
North West Territories	23.0	34.7
Alberta/British Columbia	39.0	2.8
Saskatchewan/Manitoba	2.0	3.4
Ontario/Quebec	31.0	8.0
United States	5.0	1.0
Other	0.0	0.0
	100.0	100.0

Source: Derived from Stevenson Kellogg Ernst and Whinney, 1987, Exhibit III-3, p.8.

1. Lupin
2. Giant Yellowknife, Nerco Con, Tom

Table 5.4
Purchasing Profiles, Canadian LDC Mines, 1989
(Per Cent Values)

Region	Johnny Mountain BC	Golden Bear BC	Golden Patricia Ont.	Detour Lake Ont.	Lac Short Que.	Hope Brook Nfld.
NWT-Yellowknife	-	-	-	-	-	-
NWT-Other	-	-	-	-	-	-
Yukon	-	20	-	-	-	-
British Columbia	65	55	-	-	-	1
Alberta-Northern	-	-	-	-	-	-
Alberta-Southern	-	-	-	-	-	5
Sask.-Northern	-	-	-	-	-	-
Sask.-Southern	-	-	-	-	-	-
Manitoba-Northern	-	-	-	-	-	-
Manitoba-Southern	-	-	9	-	-	-
Ontario-Northern	-	-	88	75	13	-
Ontario-Southern	-	-	3	15	13	33
Quebec-Northern	-	-	-	5	73	5
Quebec-Southern	-	-	-	5	-	-
Maritimes	-	-	-	-	-	10
Newfoundland	-	-	-	-	-	47
USA	35[1]	25	-	-	-	-

Source: K. Storey and M. Shrimpton, unpublished survey of Canadian LDC Mines, 1989.

1. Alaska

Migration

The fly-over of employment and, to a lesser extent, supplies and services, means that the contribution LDC mines make to the North is more modest than might otherwise be expected. Indeed, LDC operations may have some negative demographic, economic and social effects on the North by removing some of the more skilled and motivated residents. Many companies and governments have actively encouraged the hiring of native and non-native northerners, but when these employees find themselves working alongside employees who live and have families in the South, significant numbers of those hired from the North choose to relocate to the South.

For example, human resources staff at Polaris have reported that as of June 1987 the current number of employees hired from the North was 71, however over the years, 38 (54 per cent) of these had moved South. The main reason attributed to the desire for a change of place of residence, is to allow a family to be closer to friends and family to provide support during the lengthy periods of absence of the spouse. Lupin has also seen some decline in the numbers of workers living in Yellowknife as people choose to move south to take advantage of cheaper living conditions, while a Saskatchewan uranium mine reported that a number of northern employees had moved to the larger centres such as Saskatoon (Storey and Shrimpton, 1989).

The 1988 surveys of Polaris and Key Lake workers confirm this, with 42 per cent and 17 per cent respectively of the respondents stating that they have moved homes because of the LDC work system. While no question specifically sought data on the places they moved from and to, many provided such information. In the case of Key Lake, a majority had moved to be closer to the pick-up points (of which Saskatoon and Prince Albert are the most commonly used), while two of 22 respondents who had moved indicated that they had moved south to get away from "isolated" northern communities. Overall, 74 per cent of all movers stated that their current place of residence was Saskatoon, indicating that one in ten of all Key Lake employees had moved to that city because of the work pattern.

A move closer to a pick-up point is more likely to be important to Key Lake workers, where the 7/7 schedule requires a round trip commute every two weeks, than at Polaris, with its 63/21 rotation and associated round trip every three months. Only one of thirteen Polaris respondents cited a move to a pick-up point as the reason for changing the place of residence, and he saw this as secondary to moving to "a warmer climate and larger city." In total, seven (54 per cent) of the movers said they moved to live in a better climate or a "nice place for R & R," while six (46 per cent) mentioned a desire to be near to their, or their spouse's, family: "so my wife can be closer to parents and sister," etc. Other reasons given included "good schooling for wife and kids," and "Yellowknife — too cold, too expensive."

Those Polaris movers who indicated where they had moved from had lived in the NWT (five respondents), Ontario (three), British Columbia (two), and Yukon, Alberta and Saskatchewan (one each). They had moved to British Columbia (seven), Alberta (two), Ontario (two), and England, while one no longer had a fixed residence. There was also a general move from small to large communities, with two workers mentioning this as a factor in the decision to move. Specific destinations included Vancouver, Calgary and St. Catharines. Another factor which may have fuelled this move is the greater availability of employment opportunities for spouses and children (Shrimpton and Storey, 1989).

As with overall employment fly-over the scope for this migration phenomenon is clearly dependent on both the work schedule and the range and location of pick-up points. The situation at Detour Lake, with a 7/7 pattern and only Northern Ontario pick-up points, presents little potential for out-migration, while Polaris is at the other extreme. Generally speaking, both fly-over and out-migration will be reduced as the rotation becomes shorter and the pick-up points more localized.

Implications for the Future of the "North"

The above analysis suggests that, in the absence of significant economic or policy change, LDC may have major impacts on patterns of development in the Canadian North. These include the following:

No New Mining and Resource Towns

Trends in mineral economics, technology, work schedules and government policy all strongly, and increasingly, favour commuting over the mining town option. No new mining town has been built in the last decade, while during the same period sixteen LDC operations have opened. It is not clear under what circumstances construction of a new mining town would now be deemed feasible and/or desirable by companies or governments.

Closure of Existing Mining Towns

As resource depletion or market forces make existing operations uneconomic, mining towns will, in the absence of other employment and business opportunities, close. Some such communities may be able to survive by providing workers to nearby new mining operations on a daily commute basis, but the growing use of extended workdays limits this by reducing the feasible duration of the daily journey to and from work. While community closure is by no means a new phenomenon, what is different is that these communities are not being replaced by new mining towns elsewhere.

Increasing Concentration of Population

The population of the North will be increasingly concentrated in either the larger administrative and service centres, such as Yellowknife, or in smaller, predominantly native, communities. Some of the residents of both may work at LDC mines, as in the case of the Yellowknife residents at Polaris and Lupin, and the workers at NWT mines who are flown in from small northern villages such as Coppermine.

Fly-Over and Out-Migration

The above evidence suggests that, as conventional mines continue to close, and new commuter mines open, the leakage of mining employment and business from the North associated with the latter development option will increase. Similarly, it seems likely that there will be a continued out-migration of those hired from the North by the operators of existing and new LDC mines. Climate, cost of living, family and other lifestyle factors will continue to promote such movement, as will the fact that the commute schedule allows workers to enjoy the benefits of living in major metropolitan areas while avoiding the congestion peaks and some other disadvantages of living there.

Summary

Clearly, LDC has the potential to cause major changes in the Canadian North, and it seems highly likely that we will see greater use of the system by other industries and in other circumstances. It will be difficult for governments to know whether, and/or how, to respond to these trends. The decision as to whether to respond is dependent on fundamental attitudes towards the North and development; for example, the vexed question of who northern development is for. The question of how to respond is further complicated by the fact that it is not clear what carrots or sticks will be effective in influencing these trends. The experience of LDC to date does, however, suggest some potential that commuting might have as a proactive tool for shaping the North. For example:

1) It may be possible to reduce fly-over and out-migration by the inclusion of greater northern benefits provisions in the terms of development agreements. Northern and/or native hiring requirements are already common in Saskatchewan and, to a lesser extent, the NWT. The use of northern commute networks, limited use or access to southern pick-up points, and shorter rotations, will have some effect in addressing fly-over and out-migration. However, they will also increase industry costs and companies may have problems finding an adequate skilled northern labour force.

2) LDC mines have considerable potential as sources of native employment. Given an appropriate rotation pattern, hiring and training policies, workcamp culture, etc., commuting may be one of the best ways of allowing native northerners to combine industrial employment with a traditional lifestyle (see Hobart, 1989).

The compatibility of the work pattern with native lifestyles may be a limiting factor in the numbers of LDC miners drawn from small northern communities. The high levels of native employment at the Cluff Lake uranium mine suggest the potential of LDC, and it will be interesting to see how successful the Red Dog operation will be in this regard. The work pattern and policies there have been developed jointly by Cominco and the Red Dog Band Council.

Conclusion

LDC is increasingly commonly used by the mining and other resource industries, especially for operations in remote and peripheral regions. The principal advantages of the system from a public policy perspective are that it makes the use of single-industry towns, with their attendant problems, unnecessary, and it allows the economic benefits of the activity — and the costs of closures — to be widely spread.

Patterns of employment and expenditure by LDC mines indicate that they may reinforce North-South dichotomies through the leakage of benefits and skilled labour to the South. This has occurred despite some government and industry initiatives seeking to channel these benefits to native and non-native populations in the North. In some cases, such as the out-migration of northern-hires, these initiatives have proved counter-productive.

Despite this, there is evidence that LDC has potential as a tool for development. However, this potential will only be fulfilled if care is taken to ensure that LDC systems are appropriate to the needs of northern residents, both in facilitating participation *per se,* and ensuring that it complements existing socio-economic structures and relationships. If a satisfactory compromise is to be reached among the competing goals of minimizing industry development and operating costs, minimizing the social and economic costs of non-renewable resource projects, maximizing northern benefits, and achieving other northern development objectives, industry, governments and communities will have to adopt a much more sophisticated approach to the use of LDC.

References

Armstrong, R. (1991) "Lupin Mine, Northwest Territories," in Shrimpton, M. and Storey, K. (eds.), *Long Distance Commuting in the Mining Industry: Conference Summary*, Proceedings No. 24, Kingston, Ontario: Centre for Resource Studies, Queen's University, pp.35-36.

Berg, L. (1986) "From towns to wings to wheels at Sterco," in *Towns, Wheels or Wings for Resource Development?*, Selected Conference Papers from the February 3-4 Conference, Vancouver, B.C: The Institute for Research on Public Policy (IRPP), pp.30-32.

Canada, Department of Energy, Mines and Resources (1987) "Current and past producers in Canada, 07/15/87," Unpublished data, Ottawa: National Mineral Inventory.

Glass, R.D. and Lazarovich, J. (1984) "The government perspective," in *Mining Communities: Hard Lessons for the Future*, Proceedings No.14, Kingston, Ontario: Centre for Resource Studies, Queen's University.

Hobart, C.W. (1979)"Commuting work in the Canadian north: Some effects on native people," Proceedings; Conference on Commuting and Northern Development, Saskatoon: University of Saskatchewan, Institute of Northern Studies, February 15,16, pp.1-38.

Hobart, C.W. (1989) "Company town or commuting: Implications for native people," in Robson, R. (ed.), *The Commuting Alternative: A Contemporary Response to Community Needs in the Resource Sector*, Northern Studies No. 1, Winnipeg, Manitoba: Institute of Urban Studies, University of Winnipeg, pp.25-38.

McGrath, S. (1986) "Tumbler Ridge: An assessment of the local government method of resource community development," *Impact Assessment Bulletin*, Vol.4(1-2): 211-236.

Newton, P.W. (1986) "Settlement options for resource development in Australia," in *Towns, Wheels or Wings for Resource Development?*, Selected Conference Papers from the February 3-4 Conference, Vancouver, B.C.: The Institute for Research on Public Policy (IRPP), pp.54-87.

Nogas, F.R. (1976) "Fly-in Program at Rabbit Lake," *CIM Bulletin*, Vol. 69(774): 125-128.

Nogas, F.R. (1986) "Towns Versus Commuting at the Rabbit Lake Uranium Mine," in *Towns, Wheels or Wings for Resource Development?*, Selected Conference Papers from the February 3-4 Conference, Vancouver, B.C.: The Institute for Research on Public Policy (IRPP), pp.20-24.

Robinson, I.M. (1984) "New resource towns on Canada's frontier: Selected contemporary issues," in Detomasi, D.D. and Gartrell, J.W., *Resource Communities: A Decade of Disruption*, Boulder, Colorado: Westview Press, Inc., pp.1-21.

Robson, R. (1988) "The decline of resource towns," Paper presented to the Canadian Urban and Housing Studies Conference, Winnipeg, Manitoba, February 18-20.

Shrimpton, M. and Storey, K. (1989) "The urban miner: Long distance commuting to work in the mining sector and its implications for the Canadian North," in Robson, R. (ed.), *The Commuting Alternative: A Contemporary Response to Community Needs in the Resource Sector*, Winnipeg, Manitoba: Institute of Urban Studies, University of Winnipeg.

Shrimpton, M. and Storey, K. (1992) *Labour Market Adjustments to Long Distance Commuting Mining*, Report prepared for the Minerals Policy Sector, Energy Mines and Resources Canada, St. John's, Newfoundland: Department of Geography, Memorial University of Newfoundland.

Stevenson Kellog Ernst & Whinney (1987) *Strategies to Improve Northwest Territories Business Opportunities Related to Mining and Exploration*, Report prepared for the Energy, Mines and Resources Secretariat, Government of the Northwest Territories.

Storey, K. and Shrimpton, M. (1988) *Long Distance Commuting in the Canadian Mining Industry*, Working Paper No.43, Kingston, Ontario: Centre for Resource Studies, Queen's University.

Storey, K. and Shrimpton, M. (1989) *Impacts on Labour of Long Distance Labour Commuting in the Canadian Mining Industry*, ISER Report No. 3, St. John's, Newfoundland: Institute for Social and Economic Research, Memorial University of Newfoundland.

Chapter 6

Employment Opportunities of the Urban Poor: An Assessment of Spatial Constraints and the Mismatch Hypothesis

Joseph Mensah and R. G. Ironside
University of Alberta

Introduction

The development of urban spatial systems has been characterized by marked changes in the location and composition of economic activities. Since the 1960s, especially in the United States, despite gentrification and downtown high rise apartments for young singles and retirees, high income families seeking less congestion, safer neighbourhoods, and better amenities have left the inner cities. Some companies, particularly manufacturing and retail trades, have also been drawn to the suburbs and exurbs by homologous advantages: cheaper land, superior environment, improved transport access, and wealthier customers. Remaining in most inner cities are high-skilled jobs and low-skilled workers — a phenomenon referred to as "The Spatial Mismatch Hypothesis" in the geographic literature (Ellwood, 1986: 149; Leonard, 1987: 325; Bourne, 1989: 314; Holloway, 1990: 324).

The kernel of the mismatch hypothesis is that employment opportunities of the urban poor have deteriorated because their job skills no longer satisfy the requirements of the labour market. With the transformation from blue-collar jobs to "knowledge-class employment," the educational and skill requirements of employment in inner cities have risen, yet this is where less educated low-income people are concentrated residentially (Moore and Laramore, 1990; Kasarda, 1990). The bulk of the literature on the spatial mismatch hypothesis has focused on racial minorities in the United States (Kain, 1968; Kasarda, 1980, 1989, 1990), but it is probable that the argument may apply in other places and to other deprived groups such as women, and the urban poor in general.

Difficulties of reaching jobs may impose temporal and monetary costs on the poor, high enough to discourage them from participating fully in the labour market (Ellwood, 1986). Longer distances between home and work locations reduce the extent to which walking and cycling, relative to motorized transportation modes, can be used (White, 1983: 177). The fact that public transportation networks between city centres and suburbs are inadequate compounds the journey to work problems faced by the urban poor. Furthermore, "they [the poor] can afford neither the luxury nor the employment necessity of owning an automobile" (Kasarda, 1983: 46).

There are other factors which make the suburban labour market dysfunctional in meeting the needs of the urban poor. The working poor often depend on second jobs to supplement their household incomes. In a situation where employment locations are widely dispersed, the likelihood of getting a second job within easy reach is restricted and commuting between such widely spaced job sites becomes very demanding (Stanback and Knight, 1976: 168). Even though "the recognition that differential physical access to employment opportunities impacts the life chances of individuals is almost a truism in geography" (Hodge, 1990: 92), very few Canadian geographers have actually addressed the job-related spatial restrictions faced by the urban poor.

This study investigates the impact of spatial constraints upon the employment opportunities of the urban poor, using the city of Edmonton as a case study. The question of whether otherwise "identical" individuals achieve different labour market outcomes in Edmonton because of their respective residential locations is closely examined. Persons living in the city's Community Housing Projects, a subsidized rental accommodation, are considered "poor" for this study. The spatial mismatch hypothesis tested here is that the spatial separation between residence and workplace has had a greater adverse impact on the inner city poor than their suburban counterparts. The spatial mismatch hypothesis is specifically examined by comparing the journey to work distances and times of central Edmonton respondents with those of the suburban residents, using the Chi-Square test.

Previous Research

There has been an ebb and flow in the study of space-related constraints upon employment opportunities. Attempts to trace the origins of the field have suffered from a desire to impose too much order upon a primarily diverse literature. However, some consensus does emerge as to those sources regarded as influential. Kain's (1968) work on spatial constraints on the employment activities of blacks in Detroit and Chicago is considered by many analysts (Mooney, 1969: 299; Ellwood, 1986:149; Leonard, 1987:

325; Hodge, 1990: 87) as the first formal research into the spatial mismatch hypothesis. Kain tested three related hypotheses: First, residential segregation affects the geographic distribution of black employment. Second, residential segregation increases black unemployment. And third, the postwar suburbanization of employment has hindered black employment (Kain, 1968: 176). He found that blacks' share of employment was significantly higher in heavily black neighbourhoods and close to the major ghettos than in suburban areas. Kain made a fundamental policy loaded-observation — that there would be substantially more employment for blacks if neighbourhoods were desegregated.

Several scholars have appraised, disputed, and extended Kain's findings using a variety of methods. Mooney (1969) undertook a similar study using data on the 25 largest Standard Metropolitan Statistical Areas (SMSAs) in the United States. Mooney's results supported those of Kain. He noted that the geographic separation of inner city blacks from burgeoning jobs in the fringe areas reduces their employment opportunities (Mooney, 1969: 309).

Masters (1974), however, criticised Kain's work by arguing that jobs are easier to find in the inner city, and that suburbanization of employment is not the cause of unemployment amongst blacks. It is interesting to note that Kain (1974) responded effectively to this criticism when he observed that:

"If there is a greater demand for labour and higher wages at central city than in the suburbs, white workers may move to convenient central city neighbourhoods and accept these jobs with no transportation cost penalty... In contrast, if jobs are more plentiful and higher paying in the suburbs, black workers, in general, can hold them only by accepting large travel costs" (Kain, 1974: 514).

In a very influential paper, a decade later, Ellwood (1986, 149) concluded that: "Race not space remains the major explanatory factor [for blacks' poor labour force participation]." After an extensive review of Ellwood's work, Kasarda (1989, 36-37) remarked that: "While there is no question that race ... plays a potent role in the relatively poor employment performance of blacks, one should be cautious in using the Ellwood study to dismiss space as a contributing factor."

Although the Canadian literature in this field is modest, there have been some recent studies on the spatial dimension of employment opportunities in urban centres. Bourne (1989) provides the most comprehensive exposition of the spatial mismatch hypothesis, in particular, and the changing properties of Canadian urban areas in general. Among other things, Bourne

(1989) noted that employment has decentralized in urban Canada, and that the relative concentration of jobs downtown has decreased with the need for extensive commuting. Studies by Rutherford and Wekerle (1988) and Dyck (1989, 1990) have included a gender component in the analysis of employment activities and spatial constraints in Canadian cities. However, as rich as these studies are in the insight they provide on the relationships between spatial restrictions and employment activities, they do not address the exclusive case of the urban poor. Geographically disaggregated research relating employment activities of low income people to their places of residence is imperative, if we are to assist the urban poor to participate fully in the job market.

The Study Area

General Overview of Edmonton

The city of Edmonton is situated in the central part of Alberta on both banks of the North Saskatchewan River. It was incorporated as a city in 1904, and a year later designated the capital of Alberta (Edmonton Economic Development Authority, 1991). With a 1991 population of 616,741 (Statistics Canada, 1992), Edmonton is one of the major urban centres in Canada with many shopping malls located throughout the city. The city's West Edmonton Mall, with a total of 1.5 million square meters of retail space and more than 600 shops, is the world's largest commercial development (Jackson and Johnson, 1991). More than one-half of Canada's oil reserves are in Alberta, and over 80 per cent of the current producing wells in Alberta are located in the service area (Edmonton Economic Development Authority, 1991). In 1978, Edmonton became the first North American city with a population of less than one million to have a light rail transit (LRT) (Edmonton Economic Development Authority, 1990). Buses and LRT lines from various neighbourhoods meet at transit centres on a carefully designed timed-transfer basis. As with all major cities, however, Edmonton workers face some basic commuting problems including morning and evening rush hour traffic, limited transit services in newly expanding suburban areas, rising parking fees, and frequent increases in transit fares.

Labour Market Restructuring in Edmonton

The Edmonton labour market is undergoing some changes including a growth of part-time jobs, a transformation from manufacturing to information-based service industries, a general aging of the work force, and a pattern of stagnating inner city and booming suburbs. In this section, we identify the shifts of different employment activities between central and

suburban Edmonton. The initial task, then, is to establish a working definition of what constitutes the inner city or central Edmonton.

Edmonton's inner city is defined as the portion of the city developed prior
to 1971 (Walters and Huang, 1992: 5). For the purposes of addressing the
transportation needs of the city, the Edmonton Transportation Department
has sub-divided the city into 31 traffic districts, out of which eleven are
labelled as the inner city (central) traffic districts (Figure 6.1). These include
the following: Downtown Core, University, Southgate, Jasper Place, North
Central, Calder, Londonderry, Beverly, Capilano, Bonnie Doon and Downtown Fringe (Figure 6.1) and together represent an area of 162 square
kilometres. Both the City of Edmonton's Planning and Transportation Departments use this definition of inner city in their analyses.

Measurements by the City's Transportation Department (1985, 1990) indicate that there were a total of 267,837 jobs in Edmonton in 1984, out of
which 207,095 or 77.3 per cent were in the inner city. By the end of 1990,
the number of inner city jobs had increased by 3.9 per cent to a total of
215,250. During the same period, the total suburban employment bur-
geoned from 60,742 to 85,150. This represents an increase of 40.0 per
cent. In addition, employment in central Edmonton is expected to expand
by only 8.6 per cent between 1984 and 1995, while the corresponding figure for suburban Edmonton is 70.6 per cent (City of Edmonton, Transportation Department 1985, 1990). While the greatest percentage gains in
employment are occurring in suburban Edmonton (Figure 6.1), we must
note, however, that the inner city still contains the bulk of the available jobs
and has shown the greatest absolute gain in employment.

To maximize accessibility to people and firms, companies offering highly
specialized goods and services, such as accounting firms, consulting firms,
luxury goods shops and advertising agencies have traditionally located in
inner city areas. Whether or not this continues to be the case in Edmonton
is hard to establish, due to the dearth of data. Regarding public administrative jobs, Walters and Huang (1992, 9) have argued that recent fiscal restraint by the three levels of government, federal, provincial and municipal,
has resulted in below average job growth in this sector, which has had
adverse consequences on Edmonton's inner city since the majority of public administrative jobs in the province are located here (Walters and Huang,
1992: 9).

The core of the inner city designated as "Downtown" by the City's Planning
and Development Department was a major area of business growth in 1987
and 1988. However, from the beginning of 1989 records show that in that

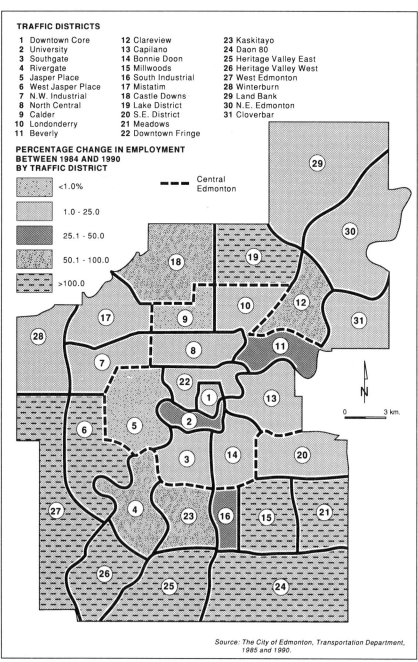

TRAFFIC DISTRICTS

1 Downtown Core	12 Clareview	23 Kaskitayo
2 University	13 Capilano	24 Daon 80
3 Southgate	14 Bonnie Doon	25 Heritage Valley East
4 Rivergate	15 Millwoods	26 Heritage Valley West
5 Jasper Place	16 South Industrial	27 West Edmonton
6 West Jasper Place	17 Mistatim	28 Winterburn
7 N.W. Industrial	18 Castle Downs	29 Land Bank
8 North Central	19 Lake District	30 N.E. Edmonton
9 Calder	20 S.E. District	31 Cloverbar
10 Londonderry	21 Meadows	
11 Beverly	22 Downtown Fringe	

PERCENTAGE CHANGE IN EMPLOYMENT
BETWEEN 1984 AND 1990
BY TRAFFIC DISTRICT

- - - - Central
Edmonton

<1.0%

1.0 - 25.0

25.1 - 50.0

50.1 - 100.0

>100.0

0   3 km.

Source: The City of Edmonton, Transportation Department,
1985 and 1990.

Figure 6.1: Edmonton, Alberta, Canada: Traffic Districts

year Downtown Edmonton lost a total of 51 businesses, concentrated particularly in the retail, construction, and food and beverage sectors (City of Edmonton, Planning and Development Department, 1989, 1990). Broadway (1992, 190) found that manufacturing employment amongst Edmonton's inner city residents has declined by 22 per cent between 1971 and 1986. In contrast, manufacturing employment amongst residents of the rest of Edmonton's CMA grew by as much as 78 per cent during the same period. The shift in manufacturing to the suburbs is clearly a factor in these changes (Broadway, 1992: 190).

Furthermore, structural changes in the manufacturing sector, such as improvements in technology which require less labour per unit of production, have also worsened the employment chances of the urban poor. Changes within the service industry also suggest greater intensity and a demand for higher skills than was the case in the past. Arguably, the employment opportunities of Edmonton's poor are deteriorating because their job skills no longer satisfy the requirements of many jobs in the city.

As with the city's employment, the population of suburban Edmonton has been increasing in recent years. Between 1976 and 1990, the inner city lost 53,735 people. This amounts to a 13 per cent decrease in population in less than one and a half decades. During the same period, the population of suburban Edmonton escalated by a staggering 350 per cent, with an annual growth rate of 25 per cent (City of Edmonton, Planning and Development Department, 1988: 1990). We must note that in addition to experiencing a slow employment growth and a declining population, central Edmonton continues to carry the bulk of the city's low income population. Estimates by the Edmonton Community Trends Working Group (1989) and Broadway (1992) indicate that census tracts in and around central Edmonton contain a disproportionate concentration of social welfare recipients, unemployed individuals, and low income families relative to the rest of the city.

The Survey

Survey Methods

Using the city of Edmonton as a case study, this study explores the impact of spatial constraints upon the employment activities of the urban poor. A survey was conducted among the residents of Edmonton's Community Housing Program to provide data for the study. There are two main low income rental accommodation programmes in Edmonton — The Municipal Non-Profit Housing Programme and the Community Housing Programme. The latter was chosen because it targets far lower income clients, and has about four times the number of housing units than the former. In addition, housing projects in the Community Housing Programme constitute easily identifiable clusters.

The construction of housing units in the Community Housing Programme is financed by the Alberta Mortgage and Housing Corporation with the help of the Canada Mortgage and Housing Corporation. The responsibilities of tenant selection, property management and maintenance are undertaken by the Edmonton Housing Authority — a non-profit organization (Alberta Municipal Affairs, Housing Division, 1990). Housing units provided under the Community Housing Programme are mostly duplexes and townhouses. Rents are set at 25 per cent of a family's income per month. For those on "welfare", rents are based on social assistance rent schedules (Alberta Municipal Affairs, Housing Division, 1990). There are 107 Community Housing Projects throughout Edmonton with a total of over 4,000 housing units (Edmonton Housing Authority, 1990). As a planning policy, the Edmonton Housing Authority avoids the development of very large scale projects that concentrate too many "disadvantaged" people in the same neighbourhood. The authority also tries to limit the geographic polarization by family structure, age, and race as much as possible (Edmonton Housing Authority, 1990).

A multistage cluster sampling technique was adopted for the survey. In the first stage of this procedure, the Community Housing projects were grouped under six main clusters — Northeast, Northwest, West, Central, Southeast, and Southwest (Figure 6.2) — based on their relative location within the city of Edmonton. The second phase entailed the selection of four clusters — Northwest (to represent the entire North), West, Central, and Southwest (to represent the South) — based on the research objective and expert opinion solicited from the Edmonton Housing Authority. Table 6.1 and Figure 6.3 document the housing projects selected for the survey.

A simple random sample dubbed "hit two, miss one" was devised to identify specific housing units to be interviewed for the survey. The technique was simple: Starting from a corner of a housing project (usually, the most accessible and conspicuous area) two housing units were selected consecutively, after which the next house was intentionally avoided. At each of the selected houses, a single questionnaire was administered by personal interview. Telephone interviews were not feasible since the list of residents of the housing projects was not obtainable due to "confidentiality". A total of 286 questionnaires were completed by the end of the survey; the response rate, as a percentage of those approached, was 68 per cent. The breakdown of respondents by clusters is as follows: central, 88 (30.8 per cent);

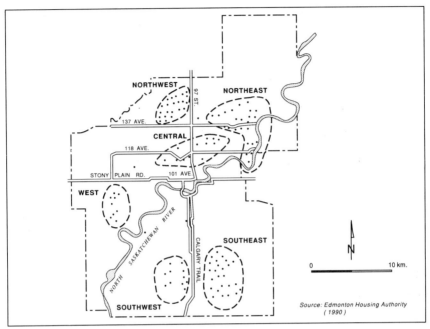

Figure 6.2: Edmonton, Community Housing Project Locations

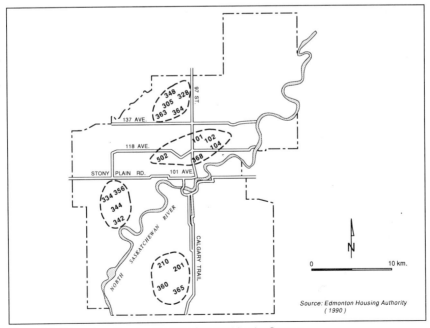

Figure 6.3: Edmonton, Housing Projects Selected for the Survey

west, 70 (24.5 per cent); south, 70 (24.5 per cent); and north, 58 (20.3 per cent).

Table 6.1 The Selected Housing Projects	
Name of Project	**# of Housing Units**
NORTHWEST CLUSTER	
1. Lorelei (VI)	40
2. Dunluce (IV)	52
3. Caernarvon (I)	38
4. Carslisle (I)	39
5. Carslisle (II)	48
WEST CLUSTER	
1. Belmead (III)	55
2. Primmore (I)	69
3. Lymburn (I)	49
4. Ormsby Place (II)	61
CENTRAL CLUSTER	
1. P.M.Q. Kingsway	50
2. McCauley	39
3. New Delton (I)	36
4. New Delton (II)	14
5. Balwin	46
SOUTHWEST CLUSTER	
1. Petrolia	70
2. Yellowbird (III)	47
3. Duggan	108
4. Ermineskin (II)	52

Source: Edmonton Housing Authority, 1990.

Profile of Respondents

The survey produced a sample of 153 women and 133 men. The majority of the respondents were within the age group of 20 to 49 years, although the age structure of the respondents varied across neighbourhoods. Just over one-half (54.5 per cent) of the central city residents were within the age group of 20-34 years, compared with 34.5 per cent in the north; 27.1 per cent in the south; and 20.0 per cent in the west. Conversely, fewer members of the 50-64 years age group lived in central Edmonton. Most of the respondents had low levels of formal education. As many as 24.6 per cent of them had between grade 9 and grade 12 education without certificate, 11.2 per cent had less than grade 9 level of school, and some 2.2 per cent of them had no formal educational background (Table 6.2). According to the 1986 national census, 23.4 per cent the entire Edmonton population (15 years and older) had university education; a comparable figure for the respondents was only 13 per cent. The study found that the female respondents had slightly better levels of schooling than the males.

Table 6.2
Educational Levels of Respondents (n=276)

Educational Level	Frequency	Percent
No formal education	6	2.2
Less than Grade 9	31	11.2
Grade 9 to 12 without certificate	68	24.6
Grade 9 to 12 with certificate	72	26.1
Trade certificate/diploma	52	18.8
Other non-university education	11	4.0
University without degree	10	3.6
University with degree	26	9.4

Forty three percent and 19.2 per cent of the sample were employed full-time and part-time respectively. The rest were not working at the time of the survey. As expected, respondents' levels of education had a significant bearing on their employment status. For instance, more than half of those with grade 9-12 schooling without certificate and those with less than grade 9 education were unemployed compared with only 15 per cent of those with university degrees. The common employment among the respondents included retail, household and child care services, health and social services, and business and clerical services. While the bulk of the construction and manufacturing jobs were held by the men, much of the work that the women did in the labour market mirrored their work in the household and incorporated a significant component of personal services such as child care, food, and accommodation services.

The mean annual household income of the respondents was $14,532; this is less than half of the comparable figure for the city of Edmonton in general. It is not surprising that some 14 per cent of the respondents relied "entirely" on social assistance for their livelihood. The study also found that 29.4 per cent of the respondents were receiving various forms of assistance from community-based social organizations such as the Edmonton Food Bank, the Boyle Street Community Service and the Canadian Native Friendship Centre.

The Mismatch Hypothesis

To gain insight into respondents' journey to work patterns, they were asked to indicate the mode of transportation they used to get to and from work. Sixty one per cent of the applicable respondents (n=166) relied on the public bus/LRT system while 24.7 per cent used their own automobiles. Some 6.0 per cent walked to and from work, and the rest relied on other transportation modes such as car pool, rides and motorbikes. Slightly more women than men relied on the public transit system. More than half of the respondents (62.9 per cent) owned private means of transportation. However, only one-third of the applicable respondents indicated that their automobiles were in either "good" or "very good" condition in terms of road worthiness. Not unexpectedly, one in every three of those who depended on the public transit system for their work trips had no other means of transportation. They represented what Rutherford and Wekerle (1988) termed "captive riders." Others used the transit system primary for convenience and cost considerations.

Several travel-related problems were identified by respondents. Twenty-three per cent cited "fear of being late/destination too far." Other problems mentioned included the severe winter conditions (19.2 per cent), traffic congestion and confusions (11.8 per cent), frequent automobile breakdown (9.6 per cent), and bus/LRT transfer problems (8.1 per cent). Some respondents, albeit a smaller number (3.0 per cent), reported being afraid to walk home at night.

In the preceding section, we have discussed the journey to work characteristics of respondents and the major problems they encounter in their daily journey to work. We now examine the spatial mismatch hypothesis by exploring the work trip patterns of respondents. The analysis involves examination of journey to work distances and times of residents of housing projects in different parts of Edmonton.

Table 6.3 shows the self-reported distance between respondents' homes and workplaces. A considerable proportion of the applicable respondents had short work trip distances. Only 13.4 per cent of them had commuting distances greater than 15 kilometres.

Table 6.3
Approximate Distance from Respondents' Home to Work
(n =119)

Distance	Frequency	Percent
Less than 5 km	32	26.9
5 km to 10 km	38	31.9
11 km to 15 km	33	27.7
16 km to 20 km	16	13.4

Table 6.4 shows the distance to work for respondents of the four different housing areas. The data indicate that those in central and to a lesser extent south Edmonton typically have longer commutes than those from the north or the west. Chi-Square testing shows statistically significant differences in work trip distances on the basis of places of residence. Table 6.5 compares the journey to work distances of central Edmonton respondents with those of the suburban respondents combined. It shows that suburban residents typically have shorter work trip distances. The Chi-Square test confirms the spatial mismatch hypothesis by rejecting the Null hypothesis that there is no significant difference between the journey to work distance of central and suburban Edmonton respondents.

Travel time data show similar trends. Table 6.6 examines the journey to work times of respondents from the four areas of residence. The largest percentage of respondents whose work trip times exceeded 30 minutes resided in central Edmonton, followed by the south, west, and north in that order. The result of the Chi-square test was consistent with a priori expectation. It suggests that respondents' journey to work times are contingent upon residential location within the city. Table 6.7 compares the journey to work times of central city respondents with those of all suburban respondents combined. Again, the Chi-square test confirmed that the journey to work times of central Edmonton respondents were, indeed, longer than those of the suburban residents.

Table 6.4
Chi-square test results: Null Hypothesis that there is no difference in work trip distances by places of residence

	Journey to Work Distance in km			
	< 5 km	5 - 10 km	> 10 km	Total
North	7 (38.9)*	6 (33.3)	5 (27.8)	18
South	7 (17.9)	12 (30.8)	20 (51.3)	39
West	10 (38.5)	12 (46.2)	4 (15.3)	26
Central	8 (22.2)	8 (22.2)	20 (55.6)	36
Column Total	32	38	49	119

*Row percentages in parenthesis; x^2 = 14.19; df = 6; p < 0.05.

Table 6.5
Chi-square test results: Null Hypothesis that the work trip distances of central Edmonton respondents are not different from those of suburban respondents

	Journey to Work Distance in km			
	< 5 km	5 - 10 km	> 10 km	Total
Suburbs	24 (28.9)*	30 (36.1)	29 (34.9)	83
Central	8 (22.2)	8 (22.2)	20 (55.6)	36
Column Total	32	38	49	119

*Row percentages in parenthesis; x^2 = 22.92; df = 3; p < 0.05.

Table 6.6
Chi-square test results: Null Hypothesis that the amount of time spent on the journey to work is not different amongst respondents from different neighbourhoods

	Journey to Work Time (Minutes)			
	< 16	16 - 30	> 30	Total
North	9 (32.1)*	14 (50.0)	5 (17.9)	28
South	14 (35.9)	11 (28.2)	14 (35.9)	39
West	18 (46.2)	8 (20.5)	13 (33.3)	39
Central	14 (25.5)	11 (20.0)	30 (54.5)	55
Column Total	55	44	62	161

*Row percentages in parenthesis; x^2 = 17.00; df = 6; p < 0.05.

Table 6.7
Chi-square test results: Null Hypothesis that the amount of time spent on the journey to work by central Edmonton respondents is not different from that spent by suburban residents

	Journey to Work Time (Minutes)			
	< 16 min.	16 - 30	> 30	Total
Suburbs	41 (38.7)*	33 (31.1)	32 (30.2)	106
Central	14 (25.5)	11 (20.0)	30 (54.5)	55
Column Total	55	44	62	161

*Row percentages in parenthesis; x^2 = 9.06; df = 2; p < 0.05.

These empirical tests clearly support the spatial mismatch hypothesis. The results show that journey to work distance and time are dependent upon respondents' places of residence, and that typically low income residents in central Edmonton travel longer distances and take more time to get to work than their suburban counterparts.

What is the impact of spatial constraints upon the job search activities of the respondents? To the question, "Are you currently looking for work?," 64.5 per cent of the unemployed respondents answered in the affirmative, while the rest responded negatively. Respondents' usual sources of job information included newspapers, employment and placement centres and social contacts. Approximately two in every three of the job seekers had some relatives, friends or social organizations which were assisting them in their job search activities.

As with the employed respondents, many of those looking for work, 43.6 per cent, relied primarily on the public transit system for their job search trips. Their own cars/trucks were used by 30.9 per cent while 19.7 per cent and 5.6 per cent relied on "rides" and motorbikes respectively. Overall 70 per cent of those looking for work were ready to accept job offers in all parts of the city and this proportion was even higher in Central Edmonton. The study found that the most worrisome problem faced by the unemployed respondents in their job search activities was "the high cost of searching for jobs." Other pressing problems mentioned included: "difficulties in finding good-paying jobs," "difficulties in finding a job in their fields"; "transportation problems" ranked third.

Policy Implications

This study has attempted to provide insights into some of the space-related problems faced by the urban poor. The empirical findings of the study support the spatial mismatch hypothesis: Low-income residents of central Edmonton had significantly more severe job-related spatial constraints than their suburban counterparts. This has a major policy implication — providing more public housing in the inner-city will only exacerbate the problem. Nonetheless, there has been an increasing proclivity, on the part of many suburban residents, towards the "Not In My Back Yard Syndrome" (NIMBY) (Bourne, 1991: 39; Gans, 1990: 275) in finding sites for low-income housing projects in Edmonton. In addition there is mounting pressure from private developers who insist that the city is distorting the building market by competing directly with them.

In addition to stigmatizing neighbourhoods, large concentrations of the poor tend to increase the risk of new capital investment. We, therefore, advocate the continued building of small scale housing projects which do not concentrate too many disadvantaged people into the same neighbourhood. As a long-term approach, the three levels of government — federal, provincial and municipal — should team up to provide the poor with sufficient funding to enable them to make their own decision on where and how they want to house themselves. Alternatively, low-income housing residents could be allowed and encouraged to purchase their housing units if they can obtain a very small downpayment and pay a portion of their salary in monthly mortgage, as is done in many Australian cities (Goldsmith and Blakely, 1991: 295).

The study found that the majority of the sample relied on the public transit system for their job-related journeys, reflecting the low ownership of reliable private automobiles amongst the respondents. This indicates that any sustainable anti-poverty or anti-unemployment policy package should include some transportation elements. An additional impetus for transportation policy for the city's poor emanates from a recent study by the Edmonton Food Policy Council. Among other things, the study revealed that: "Low income Edmontonians are much more likely to walk or take a bus to buy groceries, compared to the general population" (Edmonton Food Policy Council, 1991: 6). Clearly, income levels influence who uses what mode of transportation, where and when. The need to restructure the city's transportation system to cater for the shopping and employment needs of the city's poor cannot be over-emphasized.

Consulting with the low-income people who experience these transportation problems is a crucial first step in developing sustainable solutions. The transportation restructuring process might also include modifying schedules and fares within the city's transit system to reflect the needs of low-income people, and poor neighbourhoods. Presently, the city's bus and light rail transits run at far longer time intervals during weekends. Also, the current peak-hour bus/LRT fare of $1.60 per ride, which may be very cheap for some people, is apparently too high for the city's poor. Any improvement in these directions will certainly enhance the mobility of the "captive riders."

Without the necessary bus routes, shopping and support programs, suburban life for the poor can turn out to be a "...jail without walls, where 'errant' behaviour is met with ostracism...." (Murphy, 1987: 5). As Herbert Gans aptly puts it:

"The dysfunctions of dispersal may be as bad as those of over-concentration, not because the latter has any virtue, but because, until an effective jobs-and-income-grants program has gone into operation, requiring very poor people to move away from the neighbourly support structures they do have deprive them of their only resources" (Gans, 1990: 275).

Without question, some of the policy guidelines offered may not be cost-effective, at least, in the short-run. Nonetheless, long-term gains are inevitable through increased productivity on the part of the urban poor, and through less public spending on social problems which are associated with massive unemployment and poverty. Evidently, space is not a mute variable in explaining the straitened employment outcomes of the urban poor. Interconnections between homes and employment locations can generate differences in the employment opportunities of urban residents. There is, therefore, a need to develop better spatial models and concepts that recognize the requirements of the urban poor in their attempts to undertake activities tied to the urban labour market.

References

Alberta Municipal Affairs, Housing Division (1990) *Housing Programs*, Edmonton: Department of Municipal Affairs.

Bourne, L.S. (1989) "Are new urban forms emerging? Empirical tests for Canadian urban areas," *The Canadian Geographer*, Vol. 33(4): 312-328.

_____ (1991) "Addressing the Canadian city: Contemporary perspectives, trends and issues," in Bunting, T. and Filion, P. (eds.), *Canadian Cities in Transition*, Toronto: Oxford University Press, pp.25-44.

Broadway, M. (1992) "Differences in inner-city deprivation: An analysis of seven Canadian cities," *Geographica, The Canadian Geographer*, Vol. 36(2): 189-196.

City of Edmonton, Planning and Development Department (1988) *Population forecasts by traffic districts, 1988-2008*, Research Paper # 25, Edmonton: Planning and Development Department.

_____ (1989) *Business growth in Edmonton-1988*, Research Paper #29, Edmonton: Planning and Development Department.

_____ (1990) *Business growth in Edmonton-1989*, Research Paper # 35, Edmonton: Planning and Development Department.

City of Edmonton, Transportation Department (1985) *Employment Study: Final Report*, Edmonton: Transportation Department.

_____ (1990) *Recalibration of the city of Edmonton regional travel model to 1989 base condition and development of travel forecast, 1989-long term*, Edmonton: Transportation Department.

Dyck, I. (1989) "Integrating home and wage workplace: Women's family lives in a Canadian suburb," *The Canadian Geographer*, Vol. 33(4): 329-341.

_____ (1990) "Space, time, and renegotiating motherhood: An exploration of the domestic workplace," *Environment and Planning D: Society and Space*, Vol. 8: 459-483.

Edmonton Community Trends Working Group (1989) *Tracking the trends*, Edmonton: Edmonton Social Planning Council.

Edmonton Economic Development Authority (1991) *Edmonton Report*, (Spring), Edmonton: Economic Development Authority.

_____ (1990) *Welcome to Edmonton: Helpful facts*, Edmonton: Economic Development Authority.

Edmonton Food Policy Council (1991) *Community food needs assessment project: Preliminary findings*, Edmonton.

Edmonton Housing Authority (1990) *Housing projects by housing numbers*, Edmonton: Edmonton Housing Authority.

Ellwood, D.T. (1986) "The spatial mismatch hypothesis: Are there teenage jobs missing in the Ghetto?," in Freeman and Holzer (eds.), *The black youth employment crisis*, Chicago: The University of Chicago Press, pp. 147-190.

Gans, H.J. (1990) "Deconstructing the underclass: The term's dangers as a Planning concept," *Journal of the American Planning Association*, Vol. 56: 271-277.

Goldsmith, W. and Blakely, J.E. (1991) *Generations of Poverty: America's Underclass as an Economic and Political Dilemma,* Berkeley: Institute of Urban Development, University of California at Berkeley.

Hodge, D.C. (1990) "Geography and the political economy of urban transportation," *Urban Geography,* Vol. 11(1): 87-100.

Holloway, S.R. (1990) "Urban economic structure and the urban underclass: An explanation of two problematic social phenomenon," *Urban Geography,* Vol. 11(4): 319-346.

Jackson, L.E. and Johnson, D.B. (1991) "Geographic implication of megamalls with special reference to West Edmonton Mall," *The Canadian Geographer,* Vol. 35(3): 226-232.

Kain, J.F. (1968) "Housing segregation, Negro employment, and metropolitan decentralization," *The Quarterly Journal of Economics,* Vol. LXXXII(2): 175-197.

_____ (1974) "Reply to Stanley Masters' comment on housing segregation, Negro employment, and metropolitan decentralization," *The Quarterly Journal of Economics,* Vol. 88: 513-519.

Kasarda, J.D. (1980) "The implications of contemporary redistribution trends for national urban policy," *Social Science Quarterly,* Vol. 61(3): 373-400.

_____ (1983) "Entry-level jobs, mobility, and urban minority unemployment," *Urban Affairs Quarterly,* Vol. 19(1): 21-47.

_____ (1989) "Urban industrial transition and the underclass," *Annals of the American Association of Political and Social Sciences,* Vol. 501: 26-47.

_____ (1990) "Structural factors affecting the location and timing of urban underclass growth," *Urban Geography,* Vol. 11(3): 234-264.

Leonard, J.S. (1987) "The interaction of residential segregation and employment discrimination," *Journal of Urban Economics,* Vol. 21: 323-346.

Mooney, D.J. (1969) "Housing segregation, Negro employment, and metropolitan decentralization: An alternative perspective," *The Quarterly Journal of Economics,* Vol. 83: 299-311.

Moore, T.S. and Laramore, A. (1990) "Industrial change and urban jobless-ness: An assessment of the mismatch hypothesis," *Urban Affairs Quarterly,* Vol. 25(2): 640-658.

Murphy, J. (1987) *Social housing or social engineering: How will the poor be housed?,* Paper Presented to the Canadian National Conference on the International Year of Shelter for the Homeless, Ottawa.

Rutherford, M. B. and Wekerle, R.G. (1988) "Captive rider, captive labour: Spatial constraints and women's employment," *Urban Geography,* Vol. 9(2): 116-137.

Stanback, M.T., and Knight, R. (1976) *Suburbanization and the city,* New York: Allanheld Osmun.

Statistics Canada (1992) *Profile of Census Divisions and Subdivisions, Alberta, Part A,* Ottawa: Statistics Canada.

Walters, P.O. and Huang, T.J. (1992) *An Analysis of Transit Demand Changing City Structure in Edmonton, 1965-1991,* Edmonton: The City of Edmonton, Planning and Development Department.

White, R.P. (1983) "Transport," in Pacione, M. (ed.), *Progress in Urban Geography,* London: Canberra, pp.168-192.

Part II

Assessing Response to Change

Chapter 7

Community Futures in Ontario: Geography and the Organization of Local Economic Development

Bob Sharpe
Wilfrid Laurier University

Introduction

Government involvement in regional development has changed rapidly and dramatically since the 1980s in Canada and other western nations. There has been a de-emphasis on regional planning and a growing emphasis on bottom-up, community-directed, local economic development (LED). Governments at all levels throughout North America and Europe now advocate local initiative as a remedy to the difficulties of restructuring and decline within local economies (Economic Council of Canada, 1990; OECD, 1984, 1985). Yet, the locality-based approach to economic development can be problematic.

One problem is that there are relatively few reports of localities which have successfully implemented locally based initiatives (Young and Charland, 1991). More importantly, there are several fundamental questions about the potential for localities to effectively respond to global forces of change. The very meaning and importance of the locality concept has been debated in a recent literature (Pickvance, 1990). A key question concerns how a local development policy can be implemented, particularly by senior governments (Freshwater and Ehrensaft, 1992). Underlying this question is a geographic concern for the appropriate scale and spatial unit for implementing LED policy. Is the locality a viable spatial unit for economic development? What are the appropriate boundaries for a locality?

These questions are considered in this paper by examining the Community Futures Program, the Canadian government's major LED policy mechanism. Particular attention is paid to the problems the Community Futures Program faces bringing clusters of communities together into new spatial units to create new institutions at the subregional level. A central challenge for the Community Futures Program is to organize and integrate the divergent and often conflicting interests of municipalities, government agencies, service clubs and business coalitions within a single subregional administrative unit.

The approach taken in this paper is to focus on the implementation of this national program within Ontario. The first section discusses the meaning and scope of the local economic development process. Then the institutional context for implementing LED within Ontario is outlined. Within the range of national, provincial and municipal programs, the Community Futures Program is shown to be an innovative program for promoting locally based initiatives. The intention of this paper is to evaluate or assess the program, drawing on previous work (Canada, 1989, 1990c; Freshwater and Ehrensaft, 1992) and personal research and in doing so to focus on the geographical problem of defining localities evident in the implementation of the Community Futures Program. Evidence is presented from two very different Community Futures areas in Ontario to help illustrate the objectives and problems in delineating an appropriate spatial unit for stimulating the process of LED.

The Institutional Context for LED in Canada

Local economic development can be broadly defined as those processes involved in sustaining and generating meaningful work, wealth, and a satisfactory quality of life within a locality. It is apparent from the disparate literature, however, that there are important differences in the LED processes among and within western nations. No doubt these differences arise from the wide variety of political and institutional contexts in which LED initiatives are embedded.

A fundamental distinction among models of LED process is the degree of emphasis put on economic development, as opposed to community economic development. Economic development is typically equated to industrial development and is primarily concerned with the number of jobs created, infrastructure built, taxes collected or investment raised. On the other hand, community economic development refers to longer-term processes of empowering local residents in the use of indigenous resources in order to sustain their communities (Coffey and Polese, 1984a, 1984b; Bryant and Preston, 1987; Perry, 1989; Douglas, 1989; Shaffer, 1990; Sharpe, 1991a). These processes commonly include local capacity building, resource mobilization, and strategic planning. This latter, broader definition of LED which encompasses the full range of locality-based processes is the concept of LED intended by the Community Futures Program.

The LED process also varies with the size and structure of communities, and with the particular set of concerns that exist in a place (Canada, 1990b). Hence there are programs for single industry towns, small agricultural towns, large cities undergoing industrial restructuring, settlements in the rural-urban fringe, and native communities. The LED processes considered in this paper are those active in the non-metropolitan localities targeted by the Community Futures Program.

With all these variations in the LED process it is not surprising that the institutional framework in Canada is characterized by a pluralism of actors, organizations and experiences (Brodhead et al., 1990). Among the organizations involved are government agencies at all levels, business coalitions, and networks of training agencies, economic development corporations, service clubs, chambers of commerce, non-governmental organizations and individuals (Douglas, 1989). Table 7.1 provides a more complete list of the types of enabling vehicles and organizations which may be involved in the LED process. The roles and relative importance of these various agencies differ from place to place and over time as the LED process emerges.

Within Ontario the LED process between 1989 and 1992 was very active, promoted by a number of municipal, provincial and federal agencies and programs. Typically several of these agencies were active in a locality at one time. At the municipal level, local governments with sufficient budgets could hire Economic Development Officers, and establish Economic Development Committees and Corporations. Through these agencies, municipalities would typically attempt to retain, attract and generate industry by marketing and promoting the community, and by offering various non-financial bonuses such as land below market value, tax deferrals, and the provision of infrastructure.

At the provincial level, Ontario promoted LED between 1989 and 1992 through many departments and agencies. However, these efforts were not geographically-based but instead sectoral and provincial in scope. Those with a clearly local orientation to development were the following:

• Ministry of Economic Development and Trade: Eastern Ontario Community Economic Development Program; Ontario Development Corporation

• Ministry of Treasury and Economics: Community Economic Transformation Agreement Program

Table 7.1
Local Development
Enabling Vehicles and Organizations

1. GOVERNMENT
   A. Federal: (Legislation, Funding, Advisory Services)
   B. Provincial (Legislation, Funding, Advisory Services)
   C. Military Bases
   D. Government Purchasing Programmes
   E. Direct Government Employment

2. REGIONAL DEVELOPMENT SCHEMES
   A. Free Enterprise Zones
   B. Special Economic Zones
   C. Capital and Labour Subsidies

3. LARGE BUSINESS INCUBATION
   A. Intrapreneurship
   B. Employee Hive-Off

4. NEW BUSINESS DEVELOPMENT INITIATIVES
   A. Community Advisory Services
   B. Entrepreneurial Groups

5. FINANCIAL INSTITUTIONS
   A. Credit Unions
   B. Non-traditional Credit Unions
   C. Venture Capital Programmes

6. CO-OPERATIVES
   A. Worker-Owned
   B. Member-Owned
   C. Mixture

7. MUNICIPALITIES
   A. Industrial Development Commission
   B. Local Economic Development Commission
   C. Chamber of Commerce
   D. Business Improvement Association
   E. Business Incubators
   F. Native Band Corporations

8. LOCAL DEVELOPMENT ORGANIZATIONS
   A. Non-profit Corporations
   B. Non-Governmental Organizations
   C. Voluntary Associations
   D. Developmental Advocacy Movements/Networks

- Ministry of Northern Development and Mines: Municipal Economic Development Agency

- Ministry of Agriculture and Food: Rural Community Development Program

Some of these programs, like those administered by the Ontario Development Corporation, emphasized industrial development and offered assistance to individual companies. Other programs, like the recently implemented Rural Community Development Planning Pilot Project (Ontario, 1993), stressed community economic development.

Several federal agencies were active in development in 1989-92. Similar to the provincial level, most of their activities were aspatial and thus sectoral and national in scope. Nonetheless, there were a few important federal programs active in Ontario with a clear locality orientation. These were the following:

- Employment and Immigration Canada (EIC): Canada Jobs Strategy, Community Futures Program (CFP)

- Department of Indian Affairs and Northern Development (DIAND): Canadian Aboriginal Economic Development Strategy

- Federal Economic Development Initiative in Northern Ontario (FED-NOR)

Overall, the Community Futures Program was unique within this complex institutional framework as the only major program intended to promote community-based LED. The next section describes the CFP in detail.

The Community Futures Program (CFP)

The CFP was created by the Progressive Conservative government in 1985 as one of six programs in the Canada Jobs Strategy. The Canada Jobs Strategy is a component of a more general neo-conservative shift in government policy towards supply side economics (Prince and Rice, 1989). This has been characterized by an increased reliance on free market forces, entrepreneurship, and training. It has also been accompanied by the de-emphasis of direct job creation and regional planning, along with a growing emphasis on decentralisation, selective programming for certain employment disadvantaged groups, and local economic development (Hansen, et al., 1990). This shift occurred when the new government came to power in 1984 and dismantled the Department of Regional Economic Expansion (DREE). The regional development function was decentralized to four regionally based development agencies, the Atlantic Canada Opportunities Agency, the Western Diversification Office, the Federal Economic Development Initiative in Northern Ontario, and the Federal Office of Regional Development (Quebec) (Savoie, 1992). Along with decentralisation measures, the very pressing needs of nonmetropolitan communities across the country were to be met at the local level by the Community Futures Program.

Employment and Immigration Canada (EIC) is the federal administrative agency for the Canada Jobs Strategy and the CFP. The broader context for the CFP is summarized by Freshwater and Ehrensaft (1992:7) as follows:

"The Community Futures Program fits into both broader federal government and EIC strategies of focusing on equalization and labor force development. The distinguishing feature of CF has been its focus on nonmetro areas, which marks new ground. Historically, federal programs have been either generally available, or have adopted a "growth pole" approach that has keyed on major urban places within provinces or sub-provincial areas. At the same time CF follows the tradition of a number of earlier development programs. The focus on multi-year agreements, strategic planning and technical assistance is a logical extension of the DREE experience over the previous twenty years. Most importantly Community Futures has to be assessed in terms of a formal agreement to equalization, embedded within the Canadian Constitution, that includes considerable pressure to maintain communities."

The Conservative government's commitment to the CFP has grown since 1986. Funding grew from $71.5 million in 1987/88 to $150 million in 1990/91 (Canada, 1990a). In addition, another $50 million was added to the program with the creation of the Labour Force Development Strategy in 1991 (Canada, 1991b). Also in 1990/91, after five years of operation the CFP was positively reviewed and renewed with only a few alterations (Canada, 1990c, 1990d). It is not yet clear, however, to what degree the program has changed, or what communities will be re-selected or de-selected in the second generation of funding.

The CFP evolved out of several previous local employment development programs offered by EIC. These began with the Local Initiatives Program in 1969-70 and can be traced through the Local Employment Assistance Program (1973), Community Employment Strategy (1975), Local Economic Development Assistance (1980), Local Employment Assistance and Development (LEAD) (1983), Industrial Adjustment Services/Modified Industry and Labour Adjustment Program (1984). These early programs provided assistance to specific projects and offered few mechanisms for community-based development. It wasn't until the early 1980s, however, that community-based development became central to EIC thinking (Brodhead et al., 1981). In 1983 the LEAD program established local development corporations in 100 communities. These LEAD corporations provided project assistance with the requirement that projects be justified in a community development plan. Without the organizational resources necessary to develop such plans, however, many non-metropolitan communities failed to benefit from this program. From this experience emerged the CFP which has placed more emphasis on strategic planning by the community, added resources, provided funding over a longer term, increased local flexibility in project funding, and focused on non-metropolitan communities.

The CFP serves a large population and has wide geographic coverage. By 1989, 214 Community Futures areas had been created. These areas represent 2,200 individual communities with an estimated population of 6.5 million, about 2/3 of Canada's non-metropolitan population (Canada, 1990a). The national distribution of Community Futures (CF) areas is roughly proportionate to provincial population size, although there are higher proportions of selected areas in the east, particularly Newfoundland, Nova Scotia, and Quebec (see Table 7.2). Within Ontario, 48 CF areas were designated by 1989. These include rural areas of southwestern and southeastern Ontario such as Sarnia-Lambton and Ottawa Valley; single industry towns from northern Ontario such as Atikokan; and native communities from across the province including the Six Nations reserve near Brantford.

The selection and delineation of CF areas are critical aspects of the program. Communities eligible for selection tend to be those that are:

> "...experiencing acute and chronic levels of unemployment over time, single industry dependent communities facing mass layoffs or closures, communities experiencing or anticipating significant employment declines, or occupational shifts, due to structural adjustments in their economic base" (Canada, 1991a:1).

Eligible communities are normally outside metropolitan areas and outside reasonable daily commuting distances from buoyant labour markets. This

criteria alone, however, defines more communities than there are resources available so that it is necessary to prioritize communities. Communities are prioritized at the regional level according to a number of additional
factors such as the nature, severity and/or immediacy of economic problems, the potential for success, the capacity to organize resources and
interest groups, and the likely degree of local cooperation.

Table 7.2
Regional Distribution of Community Futures
Areas in Canada - 1989

Region	CF Areas[1]	Population[2]
Newfoundland	16	564,425
Nova Scotia	13	870,650
P.E.I.	3	125,175
New Brunswick	8	714,300
Quebec	51	6,566,025
Ontario	48	9,538,400
Manitoba	11	1,088,425
Saskatchewan	8	965,050
Alberta/NWT	26	2,439,775
B.C./Yukon	30	3,036,450
TOTAL	214	25,908,675

Sources: 1 - Canada, 1990a; 2 - Canada, 1992.

Several objectives are evident in the way CF areas are delineated. CF
areas typically include several communities clustered together. This objective is based in part on the previous experiences of LEAD corporations,
which needed a minimum threshold population in order to sustain effective
local operations. In practice there are wide variations in CF areas. For example, in terms of population, these areas in Ontario range from 1,750 in
Atikokan to 40,425 in Peterborough (Canada, 1992).

Another objective is for CF areas to delineate local labour markets. Local
labour markets are difficult to define, however, so that often consumer markets or even school district boundaries are adopted. In only some cases are
administrative boundaries the basis for clustering communities. Further,
Native CF areas, because of their small size, are typically comprised of
several non-contiguous reserves. This is the case with the Seven Bands

CF area from southwestern Ontario. These differences in boundary definition result in difficult problems for data collection and area comparison.

Current thinking in LED supports the objective of community clustering as
a means of stimulating multicommunity collaboration. Subregional spatial
units are thought to encourage efficient and cooperative interactions
among several social, economic and political systems. The coordination
and mobilization of resources is expected to enhance local capacity and
comparative advantage, and to reduce competition among neighbouring
communities (Cox and Mair, 1988). Furthermore, the locality is seen as a
basis for promoting territorial identity, a sense of belonging, and community
ownership of the LED process. These are thought to be necessary in establishing new and effective locality-based institutions.

Another critical element of the CFP is the Community Futures Committee
(CFC). According to the Operational Procedures of Employment and Immigration Canada (Canada, 1991a, p.9) a 12-person committee is appointed
in each CF area. The membership is to be representative of local business,
government, unions, training institutions, and interest groups.   They are
described as follows:

> "The CFC is a decision-making community committee which
> groups together major players in the community. The CFC can
> best assess possibilities for development and mobilize commu-
> nity resources to work toward the common goal of community
> development. The role of the CFC is to develop a plan or strategy
> for economic development and adjustment; secure and maintain
> the cooperation and coordinated participation of necessary re-
> sources and expertise in the implementation of the plan; ensure
> the appropriateness of the strategy over time to local needs; and
> promote the equitable participation of employment disadvan-
> taged individuals in the design and benefits of development."

The CFC is one of the most innovative elements of the Program. It is a new
local institution formed from partnerships among local government, business and volunteer groups. It intends to broaden the base of local resident
participation in LED, and to empower local residents, including interest
groups and individuals previously marginalized from local decision-making
processes.

CFCs receive a typical budget of $400,000 over five years to hire perma-
nent staff and consultants. They are able to establish, under Ministerial

approval, four program options. The two most important options are the Business Development Centres and the Community Initiatives Fund.

Business Development Centres in many cases are extensions of the LEAD Corporations that existed prior to the Canada Jobs Strategy:

> "Business Development Centres assist in the establishment, expansion and stabilization of small businesses through the provision of technical/advisory services. It may also administer an investment fund to assist small businesses to become established or to expand" (Canada, 1991a, p.11).

The Business Development Centre receives a $1.5 million capital grant plus an annual operating budget to hire professional staff. In addition, selected centres are able to offer a Self Employment Assistance option in order to provide persons, otherwise eligible for Unemployment Insurance or Social Assistance, with a threshold income while pursuing opportunities for self-employment. Business Development Centres can be more or less separate from the CFCs according to the local circumstances.

Another major option of the CFC is to establish a Community Initiatives Fund (CIF):

> "The Community Initiatives Fund (CIF) is a special option, the purpose of which is to support innovative and particularly worthwhile initiatives that have been identified by CFCs as integral to the implementation of their strategies for employment growth and recovery. All proposals for support from the CIF will be assessed against clear evidence that they would increase the long term level of employment in the community" (Canada, 1991a, p.11).

The CIF is also intended to attract non-federal investors by matching funds on a 50/50 basis. Potentially the CIF is a major source of funding for creating innovative employment initiatives, although it is not yet clear how this option has been deployed.

In some localities a fourth and final program option is available, Purchase Training:

> "This option provides occupational training for individuals in Community Futures communities to acquire the skills needed in a changing economy and to increase their earnings and employment potential" (Canada, 1991a, p.11).

In Ontario the Purchase Training option has recently been discontinued with the creation of a tripartite program between Employment and Immigration Canada, the Canadian Labour Force Development Board, and the Ontario Government (Ontario et al., 1991). This new program establishes 22 local labour boards across Ontario that operate independently of the CFP. It is interesting to note that one of the central controversies with this new program has been the delineation of boundaries for the local boards. Several localities oppose the program as it proposes boundaries that effectively reduce their local autonomy by grouping localities together into larger regional units.

With these four options the CFC are able, in principle, to customize the LED process to local needs and conditions. It is somewhat paradoxical, however, that local initiatives are constrained by the policy priorities of the central government. Indeed, the Federal Minister of EIC has final approval over the selection of CF areas, the appointment of members to these committees, and the implementation of program options (Canada, 1991a: 7). The Minister, however, acts on advice from a EIC Regional/Territorial Review process that purportedly ensures "that the interests and expertise of relevant stakeholders, internal and external...are represented" (Canada, 1991a: 7). Furthermore, integral to the review process, and a key link between the CFCs and EIC bureaucracy, are the CF consultants. In Ontario there are 15 CF consultants, each of whom is responsible for between two and five CF areas. These consultants have a key role in the CF Program, acting as resource persons, identifying and solving problems, and ensuring the CFP is implemented within the guidelines set by the EIC. Thus the CF consultants can have a critical role in customizing the CFP to local needs and conditions.

It is difficult to generalize about the experience with the CFP among the various CF areas across Canada. Employment and Immigration Canada does not maintain centralized records on individual CF areas. Nonetheless, a basic overview of the Program is provided by a 1991 survey of CF managers undertaken by Ray Funk (1991) who is the Federal Member of Parliament for Prince Albert/Churchill River, as well as the New Democratic Party critic for cooperatives and community development. He received 88 responses or 41 per cent of all CF areas across Canada.

Respondents were asked to evaluate the CFP in general as well as its program options based on the experience in their localities. They were also asked to comment on a number of specific issues relating to the program. The responses reflect a consensus of belief that emphasized:

"...the positive characteristics of the program: its flexibility, innovative approach, nominal cost to the government, how it can trigger cooperation between the interest groups and the fact that it
is community based and controlled" (Funk, 1991, p.4).

The various program options were also viewed to have a positive impact
on local development leading to an increase in the employment rate. A
commonly mentioned weakness of the different program options was insufficient funding. The most critical comments focused on the CIF.

"Some have not accessed this option yet and those who have
tried feel there are no clear guidelines and that requirements tend
to change, that the administrative procedure is very heavy, that
the approval process is very slow, that funding is far too low and
that the process has become too political. The overall feeling is
that although this option could be very useful (and in some cases,
it has been), it generally has not met the needs of the communities and is too difficult to access" (Funk, 1991, p.6).

Other responses to various specific issues were much more divided. These
focused on the degree of central government control and cooperation, the
red tape of administrative processes, the inadequacy of funding. Notably,
some respondents questioned the appropriateness of the geographic sizes
of localities. Overall, these responses reflected great variations in the operation and perception of the program across Canada.

Further insight into the organization and process of LED as implemented
through the CFP can be gained from case studies of specific localities. This
approach has been used fruitfully by previous reviews of the CFP (Freshwater and Ehrensaft, 1992; Canada, 1989). For this analysis Norfolk District in southwestern Ontario, and the Superior East area of northcentral
Ontario were selected for more detailed examination. A wide range of developmental experiences were expected to emerge given the dissimilarities
between these two localities in terms of their industrial structures, demographic compositions, and relative locations.

The research method for these case studies was to collect a combination
of primary and secondary data for each area. Previous studies, local newspaper accounts, and reports from the CFCs were first gathered in each
locality. From these sources the key developmental issues and actors were
identified. Interviews were then conducted with the key actors, including the
CF chairpersons, various committee members, and staff. In the case of the

Norfolk District these methods were then followed up with a small survey of local agencies involved in the LED process. The two cases are summarized in the following sections beginning with brief descriptions of the CF areas. The committees are then examined along with their progress towards multicommunity collaboration, innovation, and broad-based forms of community participation. Further detail can be found in a thesis on LED in the Superior East area (Sadler, 1992), and another on the Norfolk District (Bader, 1992).

The Norfolk District Community Futures Area

The Norfolk District Community Futures Area is in southwestern Ontario approximately 70 kilometres south of Kitchener-Waterloo. The area is comprised of two major municipalities, namely Simcoe and Nanticoke, two townships, and 63 unincorporated settlements. The area population in 1991 was 65,922 which is a 9.4 per cent increase from 1986. This is compared to a 10.8 per cent increase for Ontario as a whole.

In at least two respects the Norfolk District is an integrated local labour market. In terms of geography, the District is relatively small at about 1,900 square kilometres and the communities are close together. Although many local residents commute outside the locality to work and shop, they express a strong recognition of, and attachment to the Norfolk District. In terms of local economies, industrial activity varies little across the District being based primarily on agriculture, tobacco in particular, and its related processing activities (see Figure 7.1). Similarly, the economic problems leading up to the creation of the CF area are shared across the District. These problems stem from the gradual shift of the economic base from agriculture to services. This shift accelerated abruptly after 1982 with the decline in the tobacco industry and the loss of agricultural processing from the area.

Previous attempts have been made to promote industrial development in this area. A top-down initiative was taken in the early 1970s with the construction of an Ontario Hydro electrical generating facility, an oil refinery, and a Stelco steel mill. To accommodate the expected population influx associated with these developments a new town, the City of Nanticoke, was planned. In addition, in 1974 Norfolk and Haldimand Counties were amalgamated to form the Regional Municipality of Haldimand-Norfolk. These developments were intended to accommodate an expected population influx estimated at 320,000 persons. This growth, however, has not materialized, and the population has grown at a rate less than the provincial average.

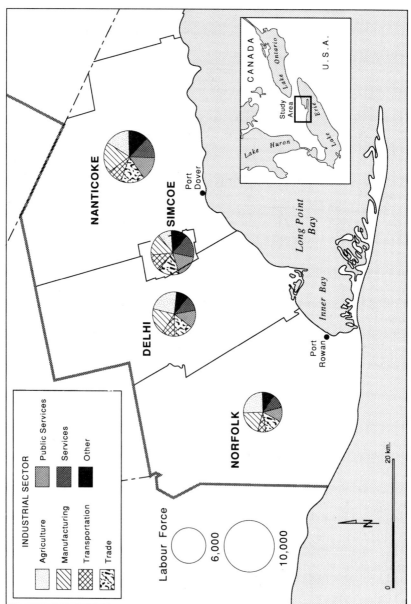

Figure 7.1: Norfolk Community Futures Area, Labour Force by Industrial Sector

Even though the local economy has been expanding, employment growth has been too slow to accommodate the small population increase and rising participation of women in the work force. The result is a persistent out migration of young people, relatively low participation rates compared to the rest of the province, and a relatively large elderly population.

In response to these problems a bottom-up approach was encouraged with the designation of the Norfolk District as a CF area in 1988. Initially a temporary Options Analysis Committee of about 20 members was appointed to devise program options under the CFP. On the advice of this Committee a Norfolk District Community Futures Committee (ND-CFC) was incorporated. A Norfolk District Business Development Centre (ND-BDC) was also relatively quickly incorporated as it basically flowed from its predecessor, the Simcoe LEAD Corporation.

Between the ND-CFC and ND-BDC there were eighteen central actors in this Community Futures area. The ND-BDC had a board of seven, one of whom also sat on the twelve-member ND-CFC committee. The membership of these boards consisted primarily of local, older, male professionals working in the areas of agricultural, business, municipal economic development, and education. Among the eighteen board members were two retired executives from local industries, a proprietor of a local retail store, and the owner/operator of a local resort. Three board members were women.

In addition to the direct involvement of the ND-CFC and the ND-BDC in developmental activities, other local and external agencies were brought into the process. Indeed, a network of agencies and individuals was formed through the personal contacts and overlapping affiliations that committee members had with other agencies. An analysis of the organizational memberships of nine committee members revealed a network of strong ties to locally-based business associations, agricultural agencies, town councils and educational institutions. These members, however, were weakly tied outside the area with only four memberships in external agencies. Overall, this network generally reflected the local biases of the ND-CFC and ND-BDC with their specialisations in agriculture, business, and training.

The composition of the ND-CFC and the ND-BDC and their associated networks have both advantages and disadvantages. The network clearly had the strength of specialised knowledge and experience in the areas of agriculture, training and business. Nevertheless, the committee membership was less representative of the concerns of women, young adults, and financially distressed persons in the district. Thus, although the committee membership helped to integrate various sectors within the locality, it may have been less effective bringing marginalized individuals and groups into the decision-making process. It is interesting to note, however, that this was not seen as a problem by a small number of network members who responded to a survey-questionnaire. Respondents were rather more concerned about the potential for volunteer burnout arising from the over-reliance on a few key individuals, and the relatively small and stable pool of participants. These are indications that the particular cluster of communities in the Norfolk District may not comprise a critical mass of volunteers.

Although the ND-CFC has had some success in building a network of individuals and agencies throughout the locality, this network building may have reached a limit. In an effort to expand the network of participants, the ND-CFC has recently become involved in an initiative to create a South-Central Ontario Community Futures Association. The proposed association would bring together the ND-CFC with like committees in Dunnville-Haldimand, Brant, Port Colborne/Wainfleet, Welland and the Six Nations areas. Such an association would incorporate over 8,300 square kilometres and 400,000 people. The proposed collaboration is expected to benefit the existing localities by broadening the network of individuals, resources, and skills that might become involved in LED process. It also, however, potentially threatens the uniqueness and autonomy of individual localities. This tension illustrates an inherent dynamism in the LED process and hence the difficulty of delineating static boundaries for localities.

The ND-CFC reported success in implementing the CF options (Norfolk District, 1992). Over the first five years of operation the NF-CFC and ND-BDC administered a total budget of almost $11 million and helped create the equivalent of 443 full-time jobs. More than half of these jobs were created through the expansion of locally owned businesses. They were funded directly by the ND-BDC at a cost similar to that of other programs under the Canada Jobs Strategy such as the Job Development Program. Under the Training Option, another 100 workers were placed in paid retraining positions, while 55 jobs represented new ventures under the Self-employment Option. The Training and Self-employment Options involved a larger investment, but approximately 25 per cent of this investment was non-federal money.

The largest single expenditure came from the CIF. It supported five main projects, the most ambitious and costly of which was a Central Marketing and Storage Facility. Other projects included the Lighthouse Festival Theatre, an Incubator Mall, the Port Dover Harbour Museum, and the Backus

Heritage Conservation Area. Although these community initiatives directly created only 40.5 jobs, they represent an investment in the longer term diversification of the local economic base. Their value to the community is evident in that over 50 per cent of the investment required came from local and non-federal investors, with the balance originating from Canada Employment and Immigration.

Overall, the ND-CFP has made a good start contributing to job creation, training, raising local investment, and diversifying the economic base in the Norfolk District. In this sense the Community area has proven to be an effective subregional entity, although it has yet to initiate innovative and broad-based forms of community organization.

The Superior East Community Futures Area

The Superior East Community Futures Area is in north central Ontario approximately 75 kilometres north of Sault Ste. Marie. The area is centred around the Township of Michipicoten, but it is more commonly known as the Wawa/Chapleau area. There are four major municipalities; Michipicoten, White River, Chapleau, and Dubreuilville as well as six unincorporated settlements. Although the area, at about 91,000 square kilometres, is much larger than the Norfolk District, the population in 1991 was only 9,162. Furthermore, in contrast to Norfolk, the population here declined by 12.7 per cent from 1986.

This grouping of dispersed communities does not comprise an integrated local labour market as does the Norfolk District. Not only are the major centres over an hour's drive apart but their local economies are very dissimilar. The economic base of the locality is resource dependent, but this varies among communities. Wawa, for example, is reliant on mining whereas Chapleau and the other two communities are heavily dependent on logging (see Figure 7.2). Industries of secondary importance include transportation, tourism and public services.

With their dependency on extractive industries, these communities are vulnerable to boom and bust cycles and a gradual decline in population. Central to this process of decline has been the downsizing and threatened closures of the Algoma Steel mill in Sault Ste. Marie and the associated Algoma Ore mine in Wawa. From a peak of 1029 workers in 1957, the number of employees at the Wawa mine dropped to 280 in 1991. In addition, employment in the neighbouring forestry-based communities has suffered with the declining demand for Canadian wood products.

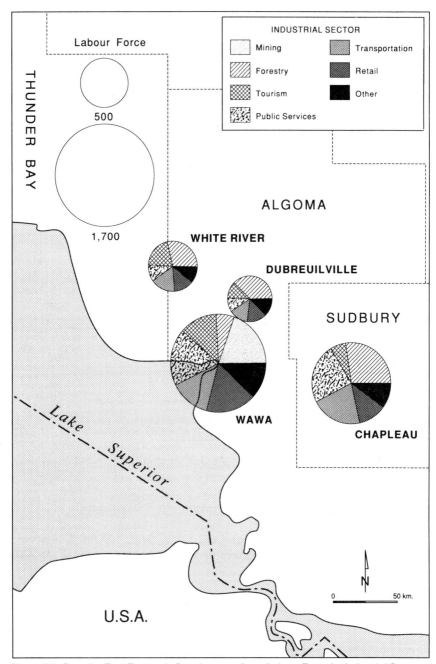

Figure 7.2: Superior East Economic Development Area, Labour Force by Industrial Sector

The current LED process was initiated in the Wawa/Chapleau area in 1986 when Algoma Ore cut back production and reduced their workforce from 550 to 350 employees. In response to this crisis the municipal council of the Township of Michipicoten hired an economic development officer. Later, with the financial support of the Ontario Ministry of Northern Development and Mines, the municipal council formed the Wawa Economic Development Corporation (WEDC). The LED process that emerged from this partnership was largely defined by the province which provided immediate financial assistance for local economic stabilization support and assistance in initiating short-term economic diversification projects (Sewell, 1991). It is doubtful, however, if such rapid deployment of prescriptive measures could be effective in empowering local residents to take charge of their local economy. This approach was not the long-term, mixed-search process associated with community economic development.

Federal involvement in the Wawa/Chapleau area also began in 1986 with the designation of a CFC and the formation of the Superior East Economic Development (SEED) Corporation. SEED has made progress in the preparation of community profiles and a strategic economic plan (Superior East, 1991). There has been much less success, however, in achieving demonstrable results from the various options of the CFP. The Superior East Business Development Centre (SE-BDC), for example, has been operational only since 1989 and personnel problems have hindered concrete action since that time. The Self Employment Assistance option only assisted 6 individuals in 1991. Finally, both the Training and Community Initiative Options have been instrumental in developing sub-committees but have not progressed much beyond the initial planning stages.

A number of obstacles have blocked the progress of the LED initiatives in this area. One obstacle is the small size and skewed demographic structure of the area's population. This limits the potential base of those volunteers who have the necessary political, technical and organizational skills. Membership on the SEED Corporation and the WEDC represent the main developmental sectors of the locality, namely tourism, small business, and education. But this membership appears to have only a few ties to a limited number of other agencies within the area. Consequently, the developmental network is small and fragmented with few links to external resources. The large distances between communities and their dissimilarities in industrial structure are further obstacles to the identification of shared interests and to the promotion of a subregional identity.

A second and related set of obstacles is the apparent lack of coordination and the conflicting interests between the provincial and federal governments. From the outset the LED initiative was uncoordinated, emerging simultaneously from two levels of government. Furthermore, the municipal development corporation (WEDC) acted primarily in the municipality's interest, whereas SEED was attempting to support all communities within the area.

Another obstacle to mobilizing local residents are the largely negative and divergent attitudes to LED in the SEED area. As in other small resource-dependent communities, the Superior East area is particularly vulnerable to attitudes and interpersonal relations that might block development (Sharpe, 1991b; Esman and Uphoff, 1984). For example, some local participants in Wawa refered to LED as a limited process of job creation. They were resistant to a broader conception of community economic development. Furthermore, there was a resident attitude of dependency and subordination to the major employer which is also characteristic of single-industry towns. An associated lack of self-esteem stymies local initiative and discourages the entrepreneurial spirit.

Overall, as a result of these obstacles, it is not surprising that the objectives of multicommunity collaboration, broader local participation, and work generation have been frustrated in this locality.

Conclusions

The experiences of these two localities operating under the same nationwide program point to the difference that geography makes in the organization and process of LED. In both localities an objective of the CFP was attempted to encourage multicommunity collaboration and spatial integration at the subregional level. Norfolk has been faster and more successful than Superior East in establishing a viable subregional unit and in generating effective subregional institutions. Several factors account for the different experiences between these areas. Some differences were due to local particularities such as leadership experience and interpersonal relations. Other differences, however, illustrate how the geographic definition and delineation of the locality can influence the LED process. The case studies suggest that several of the conditions present in a locality which influence the effectiveness of the LED process are largely a function of how the locality is geographically defined and delineated. These conditions include:

1) a population and area of sufficient size to sustain a market as well as to provide a critical mass of resources, entrepreneurs, volunteers, and local capital;

2) an existing field of community interaction, such as the local labour market, to serve as a basis for further multicommunity collaboration;

3) shared geographic boundaries among local, provincial and federal administrations to facilitate data collection as well as the coordination and cooperation of different programs;

4) a place of meaningful social identity and attachment sufficient to engender a sense of community ownership and the volunteer commitment needed to sustain the LED process; and

5) a socio-spatial web of interpersonal networks that are both rooted in the locality and include the external ties needed to mobilize necessary resources.

The case studies begin to illustrate how these geographically delimited conditions act as catalysts and obstacles to LED. Further analysis of the case studies would reveal the underlying mechanisms in more detail. An alternative approach would be to collect systematic data from numerous localities and assess the relative contribution of these conditions to the LED process. Both intensive and extensive approaches are appropriate in the analysis of the relationship between locality characteristics and various LED experiences. Further knowledge of these relationships will be of practical benefit in helping identify and promote the necessary and optimal conditions for the implementation of LED. In this way a geographical perspective can contribute to the assessment and refinement of local economic development as public policy.

References

Bader, S. (1992) "Local initiatives in action: A case study of the Norfolk Community Futures Committee," Honours Geography Thesis, Wilfrid Laurier University.

Brodhead, D., Lamontagne, F. and Peirce, J. (1990) *The Local Development Organization: A Canadian Perspective*, Local Development Paper No. 19, Ottawa: Economic Council of Canada.

Brodhead, P. D., Decter, M. and Weisskopf, T. E. (1981) *Community-Based Development: A Development System for the 1980s*, Technical Study No. 3, Task Force on Labour Market Development, Ottawa: Employment and Immigration Canada.

Bryant, C.R. and Preston, R.E. (1987) *A Framework for Local Initiatives in Economic Development*, Economic Development Bulletin, No. 1, Waterloo, Ontario: University of Waterloo Economic Development Program.

Canada (1989) *Community Based Strategic Planning as an Approach to Local Economic Development and Capacity Building in Rural Canada*, Community Futures Policy, Employment and Immigration Canada, Mimeographed paper.

_____ (1990a) *Report of the Community Futures Review*, Community Development Employment Policies, Employment and Immigration Canada.

_____ (1990b) *Report of the Federal/Provincial Committee on Rural Community Development*, Mimeographed paper.

_____ (1990c) *Evaluation of the Community Futures Program: Overview Report*, Strategic Policy and Planning, Employment and Immigration Canada.

_____ (1990d) *Final Report: Role Review and Community Impact Analysis of the Community Futures Program*, prepared by Price Waterhouse, Employment and Immigration Canada.

_____ (1991a) *Canada Jobs Strategy: Operational Procedures*, Chapter 6: Community Futures Program, Employment and Immigration Canada.

_____ (1991b) *Partnerships for the Future - Implementing the Labour Force Development Strategy*, Employment and Immigration Canada.

_____ (1992) *1989 Taxfiler Data*, Community Programs and Services, Employment and Immigration Canada.

Coffey, W. J. and Polese, M. (1984a) "Local development: Conceptual bases and policy implications," *Regional Studies*, Vol. 19: 85-93.

Coffey, W. J. and Polese, M. (1984b) "The concept of local development: A stages model of endogenous regional growth," *Papers of the Regional Science Association*, Vol. 55: 1-12.

Cox, K. R. and Mair, A. (1988) "Locality and community in the politics of local economic development," *Annals of the American Association of Geographers*, Vol 78: 307-325.

Douglas, D. J. A. (1989) "Community economic development in rural Canada," *Plan Canada*, Vol. 29(2): 28-46.

Economic Council of Canada (1990) *From the Bottom Up: The Community Economic Development Approach*, Ottawa: Ministry of Supply and Services.

Esman, M. J. and Uphoff, N. T. (1984) *Local Organizations - Intermediaries in Rural Development*, London: Cornell University Press.

Freshwater, D. and Ehrensaft, P. (1992) *Initial Results from the Implementation of Canada's Community Futures Program*, Mimeographed paper.

Funk, R. (1991) *Results of the Community Futures Survey*, Mimeographed paper.

Hansen, N., Higgins, B. and Savoie, D.J. (1990) *Regional Policy in a Changing World*, New York: Plenum Press.

Norfolk District Community Futures Committee (1992) *Funding Proposal for Year Five*, Simcoe.

OECD (1984) *Community Business Ventures and Job Creation: Local Initiatives for Employment Creation*, Paris: OECD.

OECD (1985) *Creating Jobs at the Local Level*, Paris: OECD.

Ontario (1993) *OMAF Community Planning Pilot Projects*, Ontario Ministry of Agriculture and Food, Mimeographed paper.

Ontario, Canadian Labour Force Development Board, Employment and Immigration Canada (1991) *Local Boards: A Partnership For Training*, Toronto: Local Boards Secretariat.

Perry, S. (1989) *The Community as a Base for Regional Development*, Papers in Local Development No. 12, Ottawa: Economic Council of Canada.

Pickvance, C. (1990) "Introduction: The institutional context of local economic development: Central controls, spatial policies and local economic policies," in Harloe, M., Pickvance, C.G. and Urry, J. (eds.), *Place, Policies and Publics: Do Localities Matter?*, Boston: Unwin Hyman, pp. 1-41.

Prince, M.J. and Rice, J.J. (1989) "The Canadian jobs strategy: Supply side economics," in Graham, K.A. (ed.), *How Ottawa Spends 1989-90*, Ottawa: Carleton University Press, pp. 247-87.

Sadler, K. (1992) "Local and regional economic development: A case study of the Town of Wawa, Ontario," Honours Geography Thesis, Wilfrid Laurier University.

Shaffer, R. (1990) "Building economically viable communities: A role for community developers", *Journal of the Community Development Society*, Vol. 21(2): 74-87.

Savoie, D. J. (1992) *Regional Economic Development: Canada's Search for Solutions*, 2nd edition, Toronto: University of Toronto Press.

Sewell, J. A. (1991) The Resource Dependency Situation Within the Township of Michipicoten in Northeastern Ontario, and an Examination of the Provincial/Municipal Response, M.A.E.S. Research Paper.

Sharpe, B. (1991a) "Social movements in the local economic development process," *Environments*, Vol. 21(2): 56-8.

_____ (1991b) *Beliefs Regarding Local Development: A Conceptual Framework*, Paper presented at the Annual Meeting of the Canadian Association of Geographers, Kingston, Ontario.

Superior East Economic Development Corporation (1991) *1992 Renewal Submission , Annual Report.*

Young, D. and Charland, J. (1991) *Successful Local Development Initiatives*, Toronto: Intergovernmental Committee on Urban and Regional Research.

Chapter 8

Assessing Urban Renewal: The Changing Geography of Main Street and The Public Sector Connection

Trudi E. Bunting and Pierre Filion
University of Waterloo

Introduction

The purpose of this chapter is to understand the course of events that led to the very limited success of the grandiose plans for urban renewal that were cast in the early sixties for the City of Kitchener, Ontario. The paper deals with change in the Central Business District (CBD) in Kitchener over the period 1961-1991. Our chronology begins in 1961 because the early years of the sixties mark the beginning of an organized form of municipal intervention in CBD improvement in Kitchener as in many other Canadian cities. This chapter is particularly concerned with the political economy of the built environment, a perspective that has been somewhat overlooked in mainstream research in urban geography as compared, for example, to geographic subfields such as resources management or regional economic development, a point well illustrated in many of the other papers in this collection. From a political-economic perspective, the public sector is seen to have a significant impact on all types of urban development — some more so than others. In the post-World War II years core area improvement was a particular concern of many public sector agencies. Here, in the absence of strong or comprehensive initiatives on the part of the private sector, the role of the public sector has tended to predominate.

The Case of Kitchener Ontario: The Geographic and Public Sector Context

Four sets of key actors are seen to be directly involved in Kitchener's downtown renewal efforts. These include elected public officials (i.e. city council) who are ultimately responsible for plan approval and implementation. Also important are municipal civil servants, planners and others responsible for developing plans to be proposed to council. Particularly important too are active supporters of core area renewal, most obviously downtown business people. In the Kitchener case the latter two groups, that is the public servants and entrepreneurs, were to a large extent responsible for maintaining active support for CBD revitalization among the local citizenry, and for ensuring that a renewal agenda was put regularly before council. Lobbying by local interest groups was another feature of CBD change, though on the whole the role of such groups tended to be somewhat sporadic and overall less influential.

The three decades 1961-1991 mark a period of fast growth in the Kitchener metropolitan area. Throughout this era we are able to see the impact on the CBD of growth that is primarily suburban. We can then trace the evolution of municipal renewal interventions designed to counteract some of these growth trends and redirect new development to the core area. Our concern focuses on the relative lack of success of these initiatives and on the highly suburbanized form that characterizes the spatial geography of present-day Kitchener (Bunting, 1984; Burton, 1963; English and McLaughlin, 1983).

Over the period 1961-1991, Kitchener was a rapidly expanding medium-size metropolitan centre with its economic base firmly entrenched in manufacturing. In 1961 it posted a population of 74,485 within a larger urbanized region of 176,754 residents (Dominion Bureau of Statistics, 1961). By 1991, the respective populations of the city and metropolitan region were 150,604 and 356,421 (Statistics Canada, 1992). Kitchener has been selected for analysis here because its growth has been accompanied by a sprawling form of development as well as a serious decline in CBD retail activity. While Kitchener reflects the Canadian situation as regards urban sprawl and public sector central area interventions, the sharp decline of its CBD retail activity is considered somewhat atypical of most Canadian core areas. Kitchener's CBD retail sales have dropped by approximately 45 per cent from 55 per cent of the overall market share in 1965 to about 10 per cent at present! Today, CBD-type retail functions are effectively housed in a large and ever-expanding regional shopping mall, Fairview Park Mall, located in the south-east area of the city. King Street, the former "main street", has a derelict, dilapidated look (See Figures 8.1 and 8.2). It suffers from high rates of vacancies and reported problems with "street people", vagrants of all types and, for Kitchener, relatively high rates of incidents requiring police intervention. The overall picture is not unlike that said to characterize so many U.S. core areas (Goldberg and Mercer, 1983).

Figure 8.1: Downtown Kitchener Clearance Centres on King Street

Figure 8.2: High Vacancy Rates throughout the Core Area

The Chronology of CBD Development

The following discussion outlines the evolution of downtown Kitchener and the steps taken toward downtown revitalization (Table 8.1), decade by decade, from 1961 to 1991. It demonstrates the importance of geographic and political-economic factors that were largely responsible for continued CBD decline in the face of uninterrupted attempts to bring about core area revitalization on the part of the public sector.[1]

The First Formal Plans in the 1960s[2]

In the early to mid 1960s a new concern with the declining state of Kitchener's downtown sprang up. This concern came in response to several events. To begin with, Frederick Street Shopping Centre (a community-sized centre) opened in 1961 as Kitchener's first large-scale suburban retail outlet. Quickly following, in 1962, was the announcement of the development of a regional-level centre anchored by a Sears store, Sears being a major department-store type merchandising corporation that was beginning to spread throughout most of Canada from the United States. A closely related phenomenon saw significant numbers of middle and upper-middle class residents relocating in the large, new tracts of planned communities located in what were becoming referred to as the "suburbs" at the edge of the rural-urban fringe. In geographic terms, the new housing was distant from downtown and suffered poor transit access but, being located near suburban shopping centres, it afforded a ready market to new, planned retail centres. As well, modern post-war industry was favouring large, flat, and relatively low-cost sites that were to be found only in the suburbs. As a result of these suburbanization trends, key interests in downtown — the Chamber of Commerce, the majority of local merchants, and the Kitchener Planning Board — became alerted to significant competition in the fastest growing residential zones of the city. Counteractive responses were urged on public officials in the form of more low-cost parking, improved appearances, greater public and private transportation access and the like (Sikora, 1988).

In 1962, the Kitchener Planning Department was created and quickly became the foremost public-sector agency poised to deal with the development and cultivation of central-city renewal. These various groups became immediately connected together in July 1962 when the deteriorating character of the downtown was commented on severely by the city's newly-appointed Director of Planning (Kitchener-Waterloo Record, 1962). A publicly-initiated renewal program for the CBD and inner-city zones was one of the Director's major initiatives which continued throughout the

Table 8.1
Chronological Sequencing
Kitchener Downtown Revitalization

1954	Frederick Street Mall opens (first suburban shopping centre).	1967	City of Kitchener, Ontario, Downtown Urban Renewal Scheme.	1980	Approval from council to hire consultants to make recommendations further for revitalization of the downtown core; King Centre constructed.
1961	Kitchener Planning Department established.	1968	Phase One of the "Urban Renewal Scheme" approved by council and submitted to Central Mortgage & Housing Corp. and the province for renewal funds. November Federal Government freezes funding on all new urban renewal projects.		
1962	Confirmation of the construction of Fairview Park Mall.			1981	Kitchener Downtown Study presented by Woods Gordon Management Consultants.
1963	Planning Director criticizes state of down town. Urban Renewal Committee established.			1984-1986	Two major transit proposals turned down.
1964	Public meeting to address downtown deterioration. Three studies completed: *Downtown Kitchener, Ontario Economic Analysis for Redevelopment Planning. *Downtown Kitchener: A Land Use Analysis. *Kitchener 2000...A Regional Concept. Central Mortgage and Housing Corporation offers renewal grants.	1970	A revised scheme was prepared; funds were used for the perimeter route (ring road), total renewal of underground services, some money for land assembly; Valhalla Inn constructed.	1987	Downtown Revitalization Plan Volumes 1-3.
				1988	Major King Street department store closes.
				1989	King Centre downgraded to "bargain mall."
		1971	Council approves $1,000,000 sale of City Hall Land. December, referendum vote in favour of Oxlea redevelopment project.	1991	Canada Trust Tower (Phase 1) begins construction. Toronto Dominion Centre under construction. Kitchener City Centre (City Hall) under construction.
1965	The Plan...Downtown Kitchener receives approval for financial urban renewal assistance from the federal government.	1973	Market Square built.		
		1975	Work for which the renewal funds were provided was completed.		

1960s. In 1963 his role was further supported with the inauguration of a 50-member Urban Renewal Committee that was primarily comprised of local business persons, among whom CBD merchants predominated. As well, a newly-released report predicted a 55 per cent growth in retailing over the next 20-year period. Those with core area interests assumed that downtown would retain its primary position in the retail hierarchy (Smith, 1964).

In 1965, the early renewal initiatives were brought together in the form of a major public document, The Plan...Downtown Kitchener (City of Kitchener, 1965). The rationale for this public commitment was that major redevelopment initiatives by public sector agencies would create a rebound or "spin off" effect on private development. To aid in this, the city planned to expropriate tracts of CBD land which were to be made available to private development interests.

It is important to note that municipal institutions and government were not the only public-sector agents involved in the process of downtown renewal. Most of the funding necessary for planning and implementation required the support of higher level agencies. To this end, a co-operative alignment was established with a 50-25-25 per cent balance taken up respectively by the federal, provincial and municipal governments. However, lack of available municipal funds held up any immediate initiatives. (A rapid completion of the first stages in the renewal plans were prerequisite to the granting of federal moneys. Yet the city's annual budget was insufficient to meet the demand due to its limited holdings and prior commitments.) It is ironic that the major prior commitment of municipal funds was for a cross-town expressway by-passing the congested downtown core. From the outset the 1965 plan was flawed by the two very different, indeed, contradictory spatial geographies, i.e. suburban vs. core, set out in this municipal agenda!

A revision of the first plan was completed by the end of 1967 (City of Kitchener Planning Department and Project Planning Associates Ltd., 1967). It consisted of seven phases that were to span a 20-year period. The first stage for renewal incorporated two major projects. It was to include upgrading of public utility services and the acquisition and clearance of run-down properties affronting a six-block span along Kitchener's main street, King Street. Given hindsight, the latter project proved to be a second major blunder, and, again, a fundamentally geographic one. The Plan had designated downtown as a pedestrian environment. However the delineation of the CBD retail core was a linear one spanning six long blocks (see Figure 8.3). This was to become highly problematic due to the fact that the area encompassed (81 acres) was too large for the size of the consumer population in the Kitchener metropolitan region. Even if one discounted increasing retail

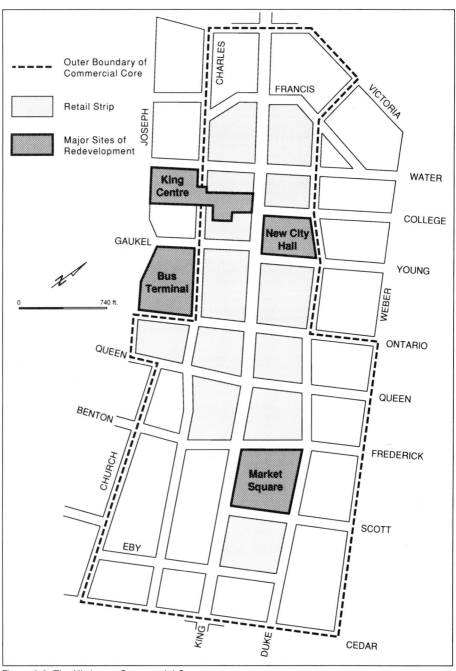

Figure 8.3: The Kitchener Commercial Core

competition from the suburbs, the long-distance walk between one end of the CBD and the other, often in inclement weather conditions, was too challenging physically for the average consumer — the majority of whom were automobile-oriented, or captive clients forced to shop at the closest possible place (i.e. the relatively poor, the elderly and the disabled who are predominant in residential areas closest to the CBD).

In public funds the cost of these two projects, infrastructure and property clearance, was estimated at $16.3 million (figures are quoted in constant dollars throughout the text) of which the federal government agreed to provide $8 million. However, most components of the two projects were prematurely aborted just as they were about to commence in November 1968 when Ottawa froze its budget for urban renewal.[3] Although the municipal government lobbied strongly in Ottawa, the federal government relented only slightly in providing $1.2 million towards the first phase of Kitchener's renewal projects.

In sum, the 1960s marked a decade when the City received broad local support for its urban renewal schemes. This support originated from major actors involved in the downtown scene: the Chamber of Commerce; the Downtown Business Association; local media; and, most actively of all, planners and city council members. Little opposition was incurred except from a small taxpayers' association. However, while the city made some effort by increasing parking and improving arterial roads, none of the major goals for the decade were realized. At the end of the 1960s downtown was in much worse condition than it had been 10 years earlier due to lack of upkeep — in anticipation of impending redevelopment (i.e. the so-called "slum landlord" phenomenon), continually increasing suburban competition and inconsistent actions taken up by public agencies at the municipal and federal levels.

Revision and Implementation of Plans in the 1970s

In January 1970, city council approved a $4.3 million urban renewal plan with a $1.2 million federal contribution, a $1.4 million provincial contribution, and a $1.7 million city share. The relative order of cost sharing had moved between various levels of the public sector with the federal government now contributing the least funding and the city the most. The combined public funds were directed towards land purchases needed to accommodate a ring road system around King Street, the upgrading and/or replacement of underground services, and the purchase of a deteriorated block of land behind city hall, as was planned earlier for the 1960s. After demolition of the buildings along the city block, the municipality planned on selling the land to a developer willing to undertake a major project. It was proposed that proceeds would be used as a rolling fund that would serve to purchase other run-down properties in the core area. However, as it turned out, there were insufficient funds for property purchase as a result of high underground service costs and inflating property values. Nonetheless, in 1970 the first significant (albeit relatively small) private-sector development was completed when local business persons constructed a hotel which was quickly bought up by the Toronto-based Valhalla chain.

In June 1971, city council approved the $1 million sale of the city hall site and adjacent municipal properties, a small square and the regionally-famed farmers' market. The purchaser, a major development company, Oxlea, planned to construct a $15 million, multiuse complex combining an enclosed shopping mall, an office tower and a multi-story parking garage which would also provide space for the relocation of the farmers' market. The project depended on a $2.5 million municipal contribution to the garage and market, a relatively low return to the public coffers for the land being sold, and a move of municipal offices from the city hall that was to be demolished to Oxlea's privately-developed office tower for a minimum rental period of 15 years.

Until its announcement in June 1971, the work of the urban renewal subcommittee and negotiations with the developer were kept confidential. Later when this policy or private "dealing" incurred outcry from anti-development lobbyists, the city's public administrators rationalized that it was a term set by the private developer who wanted an opportunity to gain options on nearby, privately-owned sites at an uninflated price. The municipal administration hoped that this initial large-scale private reinvestment in the CBD would trigger further, spin-off redevelopment projects. From an urban renewal point of view, another benefit of the Oxlea scheme was that the municipal land sale would at last allow the purchase of the dilapidated block east of city hall that had been targeted for demolition since the early 1960s. Finally, the municipal administration looked forward to increased tax revenues from the project which it believed, in the long run, would more that compensate for the initial outlay of municipal funds.

The Oxlea project aroused quite widespread opposition. This opposition was dominated by one member of city council plus a citizen group primarily led by university professors and students. The Oxlea camp, on the other hand, consisted of all but one member of city council, municipal planners, most local business people, business associations, Kitchener's media (radio, T.V., newspaper), the local labour association and the city's public and private sector elite. This ensured that the pro-development camp was very well endowed with both financial and human resources.

The ensuing conflict within the factionalized community provoked the Ontario Municipal Board (OMB) to call for a public referendum that would decide for or against core area redevelopment. The referendum took place about six months later in December with the pro-development camp winning by a relatively slim 57.6 per cent majority.

Upon completion however, the project proved not at all successful in generating spin-off retail development. Once again the problem was fundamentally a geographic one because the Oxlea development like most retail malls of the era was basically inward centred, i.e. not conducive to moving people out of the mall onto the "main street" retail strip. Notwithstanding, a few significant private sector investments were realized from 1976 onwards including two large office buildings (one of 150,000, the other of 300,000 square feet), and a new $30 million shopping centre — the King Centre — on King Street West. The King Centre, too, located at the far western end of downtown (see earlier, Figure 8.3) proved a mistake. Once again the problem was inherently geographic. Neither the public officials nor the private developer (Marathon) had grasped the spatial impracticability of a pedestrian-oriented six-block downtown. Customers, especially those driving, patronized one or the other of the two centres, both advertising subsidized rates in attached high-rise parking garages.

Summing up, through the initiatives of the coalition forces of public administrators and local interest groups the 1970s witnessed a few significant private developments in the CBD, though the overall spatial form was flawed as would appear more and more evident in the forthcoming decade.

Renewal in the 1980s: Some Success and Continuing Failure

By the mid 1980s progress towards a major goal of the 1965 Plan was partially realized with the drafting of a proposal for two different transit terminals, one in 1984 and one in 1986, both intended to provide efficient public access to downtown, for shoppers and workers particularly. Both were rejected for various reasons, a primary one being land cost. Ultimately the city opted for a geographically poor site — a block south of King Street affording no view of the main street (See Figure 8.3), located, in fact, in a rather derelict area that urban geographers refer to as the "zone of transition."

Retail decline continued: a locally-owned junior department store went bankrupt and the newly built King Centre at the western end of the core was downgraded to a 'bargain' mall status.[4] Table 8.2 shows that downtown retail vacancies continued on the increase and Table 8.3 shows a total employment drop from 18,394 to 13,899 between 1980 and 1989. In this period significant municipal initiative in the provision of new (historically-designed) street furniture was made affordable through a provincial funding program. The major public revitalization scheme of the entire 30 year period came with the 1988 decision to develop a new city hall complex in the northwestern sector of the CBD (1990 cost estimate, $65 million). As with previous decisions this further accentuated the polarized spatial form of redevelopment at either end of the six-block core of the CBD.

Table 8.2
Downtown Kitchener Retail Development Change

Year	Number of Outlets	Vacancy	Total Retail Sq. Ft.
1961	N/A	N/A	525,293
1971	201	14	528,000
1976	211	22	N/A
1982	231	51	1,217,816

Source: Sikora, (1988).

Table 8.3
Downtown Kitchener Employment Profile - 1980, 1989

Employment Sector	1980	1989
Resource Production	0	0
Resource Extraction	0	0
Manufacturing	4,858	1,501
Storage/Transport	269	336
Retail Repair & Service	3,694	1,830
Business and Community	8,953	9,951
Recreational	532	179
Construction	88	50
Total	18,394	13,899

Source: Regional Municipality of Waterloo, Summary of Employment and Office Space Survey (1990).

In the 1980s new opposition to core area revitalization and expansion came from inner-city neighbourhoods at that time undergoing the first in Kitchener's proposed sequence of secondary planning exercises. The neighbourhoods' goal of retaining low density housing was largely upheld by OMB with the notable exceptions of those deteriorated sites held by "slum landlords" in anticipation of intensive private-sector redevelopment projects. This further both delayed and discarded many of the plans brought forward in earlier years.

CBD Revitalization: The Public Sector Connection

At this point we pull together the 30 year chronology of attempts at CBD revitalization in downtown Kitchener. Our aim is to understand how the powerful pro-redevelopment camp suffered so much difficulty in achieving its original goals as evidenced by compromised transit facilities, lack of private-sector spin-off activity, a near collapse of core-area retailing and other flawed projects.

The major chronology of events impinging on the revitalization of downtown Kitchener have been described in the previous pages. In the first decade, the sixties, plans were laid but virtually no development ensued. The most insurmountable obstacle at the time was the curtailment of federal funding support for new urban renewal programs. Throughout, the 1960s can be characterized as one of high expectations and ambitious plans. In the next decade some of these plans were to come to fruition, most notably the Market Square project. Readjustment of earlier aspirations and implementation of revised renewal projects were characteristic of Kitchener's response to issues of urban renewal over the seventies. The last decade, the 1980s was one of ongoing renewal efforts with many compromises.

All of the decisions dealt with in this paper were political decisions, which were strongly supported by both civil service professionals and key members of the local community, especially those who had economic interests at stake. It was however, elected members of Kitchener's City Council who were the ones responsible for approving those plans and proposals that were put forward.

The Coalition of Renewal Forces

The renewal camp's strength in local political circles was centered on the major roles taken on by the professional (planners and others) and political-economic elite. The continued promise of "spin-off" effects made the economic argument of a recoup of initial outlays by the public sector, of

increasing ridership on the heavily subsidized transit system and of increasing the diminutive coffers of the local parking authority a powerful one.
Credence was lent to these beliefs by the avowed intention of many local
businesses to invest in the renewed CBD. Support of the local media was
another major influence on public opinion, especially during the referendum
period. The coalition also had direct access to important and varied resource persons skillful in local politics and legal matters and capable of
quickly accessing needed information and commissioning background
studies. Notables supporting the revitalization forces included the local
member of parliament who had working relations with the federal government as well as the president of the Urban Renewal Committee who was a
personal friend of Oxlea's president. Finally, and rather obviously, it needs
to be reiterated that elected council members were strong "city boosters".
For them downtown was quintessentially the symbol of a strong and vibrant
city.

Obstacles to Urban Renewal

As shown earlier in this discussion, despite all its resources and influence
the pro-renewal camp failed to meet the grandiose goals which had
seemed so attractive in the sixties viz. pedestrian malls, low-rise retail,
high-rise commercial and residential projects and the like. Widespread suburbanization of housing, industry and most importantly high-order retailing
and services had made it impossible to lure people back to downtown.
Fairview Mall, the new CBD in all but name, underwent successive expan-
sions. CBD retail sales for non-food items dropped from almost 60 per cent
in 1961 to less than 10 per cent in the late 1980s. Vacancies, disrepair and
vandalism produced a run-down derelict look, much worse than the unat-
tractive image that had spurred on renewal efforts in the 1960s.

Our analysis produces several factors as particularly important in understanding this rather limited success in the urban renewal exercise: 1) the
geography of the city and in particular suburbanization and related shifts in
political and economic power at the municipal level; 2) the vulnerability of
municipal administrations to senior governments' priority changes; 3) tensions and altercations within the coalition itself; 4) and design flaws.

The foremost obstacle with which CBD interests were faced was geographical — like many of the problems found within the CBD itself, only in
this instance on a city-wide geographic scale. As in most large and medium
size Canadian cities, extensive suburbanization of the Kitchener metropolitan region occurred in the decades following World War II (Bunting, 1984).
This form of urban development provoked the emergence of planned retail

activity poles that first competed with, and later overtook, the CBD. The city's foremost retail node moved from the core to Fairview Park Mall which has been continually expanded in response to population and income growth within the Kitchener-Waterloo Region. Anticipated suburban competition gave rise to the first concerns for CBD renewal in 1961 when the core area predominated the retail hierarchy with some 60 per cent of total sales. Despite many beautification schemes, as sales plummeted to about 10 per cent of the metro total.

Suburbanization also served to diminish the renewal coalition's ability to influence the municipal administration. Municipalities' fiscal dependence on property taxes creates a strong incentive for the public sector to support and promote lucrative forms of urban development in almost any location. As a result Kitchener's administration directed much of its capital expenditure towards the periphery where development potential was strong. Often this occurred at the expense of its own downtown renewal initiatives. The simultaneous planning for CBD renewal and a by-pass expressway is a good example of this type of conflict. In the same vein, Council turned down, in 1981, a request from CBD merchants to freeze new retail development across the metropolitan region. The negative municipal decision can largely be attributed to an interest in fiscal and economic rewards. Throughout the post-war decades the municipal administration was in the contradictory position of supporting both core and newer forms of development which were widely recognized as the underlying cause of downtown's decline.

Over time, suburbanization further served to diminish the influence of the CBD on municipal administrators. In part, this can be attributed to the continued decrease in the core area's share of the total municipal tax base. In the early 1960s pressure groups stressed dire consequences for municipal finances accruing from significant decline in CBD assessment values. The argument lost much weight when the CBD's share of the overall municipal assessment base fell appreciably. Similarly, lobbyists for the CBD had increasingly to contend with other pressure groups defending the interests of newer parts of the city.

Another factor significantly inhibiting CBD renewal in Kitchener as in most other Canadian cities is municipalities' vulnerability to priority changes from the more fiscally powerful higher levels of provincial and federal governments. For Kitchener, this effectively stymied the development of a comprehensive and consistent renewall strategy in Kitchener.[5] This is most obvious in the 1968 cutback in federal grants for urban renewal which stymied Kitchener's first strategy plans.[6] Another example would include the provincial funding of the 1970s which was targeted at street furnishing and other sorts of outdoor beautification schemes. Throughout the seventies and the eighties the increasing influence of inner-city neighbourhoods was a direct result of provincial and federal agencies' retargeting of funds away from the business core towards central-city neighbourhoods.

The third important factor was the development of inner tensions associated with disagreements over the means of achieving CBD renewal occurred increasingly over time within the renewal coalition. Not surprising this had a disabling effect on their efficiency. The tensions, which may, in part, have been responsible for a lack of consistency in renewal measures, were largely the outcome of clashes between the two professional groups, planners and merchants, whose fundamental coalition had allowed the renewal plans to be put forward in the first place. There were, however, great differences in the constraints and rewards inherent in the respective costs and returns associated with the two groups. Planners tended to take up the currently dominant and fashionable views of the profession at large regarding urban development and redevelopment models. These were people whose professional status depends to a great extent on up-to-date knowledge of these models.[7] Their status is also closely tied to their ability to implement programs that are consistent with planning models that are currently in vogue within the profession. Also, planners adopted a long-term perspective on CBD renewal by defining interventions as steps towards the actualization of an overall concept. For example, planners viewed King Street pedestrianisation experiments as early measures towards the implementation of the overall CBD renewal concept as defined in the 1965 plan.

By contrast, merchants' interest in renewal was largely driven by the short-term impact on sales levels of different types of interventions. The difference in perspective became particularly manifest when merchants opposed pedestrianisation schemes because of adverse business consequences associated with parking and traffic difficulties. A similar problem arose when the municipal administration came up with a proposal to close King Street to private circulation and transform it in to a transit mall. Again merchants opposed the idea on the grounds of a possible loss of car-driving customers.

Finally, a variety of problems associated with Kitchener renewal initiatives come under the umbrella of design flaws within various plans and projects. Examples abound: building a by-pass expressway with no efficient hook up to the CBD; locating the new public transit terminal in an off-King St. location; increasing parking but to a large extent through a fragmented series of small lots that drivers found difficult to locate; and site plans for Market

Square which effectively cut this unit off from the rest of the retail strip. Planners had little control over many of these projects due to lack of funds, unavailability of property that could be acquired (often a major problem for redevelopment projects in the inner city) and the inability or disinclination to act in opposition to a variety of pressure groups, particularly developers.

The fundamental design flaw is probably simply one of historic accident whereby local residents had over time come to think of downtown (see Figure 8.3) as running from Water St. where the main department store, Eaton's, was located in pre-renewal times to the site of the old city hall on Frederick St. However, in earlier times the major retail outlets were concentrated at the western end of the "strip". The renewal projects spread retail functions along King St. with concentrations at either end of the "strip". The six block long linear strip was simply not a viable concept for a pedestrian downtown in the post-World War II period. (In marketing theory it was also too large for the number of consumers patronizing downtown.) Hard and unpopular decisions would have had to be made to limit CBD retailing to an efficient and effective core in the Market Square area while redefining the remainder of the area for some appropriate alternative use. This type of decision would have been particularly unpopular with the downtown merchants especially those located in the declining western end of the strip. Thus instead of proposing reasonable geographic limits to the CBD, the municipal administration actively attempted to accentuate its lengthy linear delineation. King Centre was approved as a new "anchor" mall at the far western end of the strip, and, when faced with choices for a new city hall site the administration chose a block directly across from the already declining King Centre. The result of this commitment to a long "strip" as we have seen has been high vacancy rates and run-down, poorly kept-up store fronts. This pattern is particularly marked in the middle of the strip, the no-man's land between the nodes at either end of King St. CBD.

All the above circumstances explain variations in financial capacity, political support and design criteria which accounted for difficulties in pursuing effective long-term strategies in a consistent fashion. The rapid succession of varying plans and interventions that developed over the three decades can be attributed to the combination of factors hindering CBD renewal possibilities despite ongoing pressures for renewal efforts. Over the period, the municipal administration would launch interventions in response to pressures from the pro-renewal forces. Long-term interventions ran into difficulties and were continually interrupted. Subjected to further pressures, the municipal administration would then initiate other interventions of a short or long-term nature, would again face problems and be halted, which would provoke further requests for municipal intervention.

The Political Economy of Urban Renewal

Turning to the broader concern of the political economy of renewal, it is important to realize in the first place that public sector interventions are an integral part of urban development. Indeed successful urban development depends on three prerequisites. First, the public sector provides infrastructures and a legislative framework that enables development. Second, private investors take advantage of these conditions to build commercial, industrial or housing projects. And finally, the success of these projects depends on consumer support. Each stage is essential and can either prevent the realization of a project or cause its financial failure.

Urban renewal represents a particular case of public sector intervention in matters of urban development. The three conditions for the success of urban developments remain valid, but public sector involvement becomes more prominent in the case of renewal. Since the purpose is to transform an area and achieve outcomes that would be impossible through prevailing market trends alone, public sector agencies will redefine infrastructure networks and zoning regulation so as to accommodate anticipated projects, and will become involved in the market process. This involvement will attempt to address the obstacles that deter private investment in a given sector. Typically in a central business district these obstacles consist in the high cost of land, the presence of buildings on this land, and fragmented property ownership. It is interesting to note that in its original urban plans, the City of Kitchener intended to make available to prospective developers large tracts of land that had been cleared and assembled.

There is an irony in urban renewal efforts. It resides in the public sector's simultaneous efforts to reorient and support prevalent market trends. Fiscal dependence and sensitivity to pressures from developers explain why local governments tend to sustain market trends. We have seen in the case of Kitchener that the municipal government supported peripheral development including that of a regional shopping mall, Fairview Park Mall, while it was attempting to stimulate redevelopment in the core. These circumstances make for uncertain and costly urban renewal attempts. In Kitchener, despite a succession of renewal programs and some private sector investments in the core, shoppers by and large are still attracted to suburban outlets which were themselves enabled by public sector infrastructures and regulations. Thus, the third prerequisite for successful urban development (or redevelopment), consumer support, eludes Kitchener's CBD.

Conclusion

The chronology produced here has revealed the discrepancy between the presence of a locally powerful coalition promoting CBD renewal, and its inability to effectively mount a long-term strategy or prevent the decline of the CBD. While some of the case study's observations are specific to Kitchener CBD renewal, others can be extended to the role of the municipal public sector. On the one hand, Kitchener's geographic form, its linear multipolar nature, and its overall low density and transit use give rise to a state of CBD decline and deterioration that has been atypical in the Canadian context. Thus difficulties in achieving core revitalization that were associated with the geographic magnitude of the suburbanization process and the long linear configuration of "main street" were to some extent specific to Kitchener. Similarly the sequence and timing of events and their consequence for renewal initiatives were also usually unique to Kitchener. The most adverse consequence stemming from these factors was the incapacity to take advantage of the federal urban renewal program because Kitchener, being one of the last major cities in Canada to apply for funding, found that the funds had in fact "dried up".

On the other hand, different observations pertain to the more general matter of local power. Through its examination of the urban renewal issue area, the case study has suggested a number of obstacles to the capacity of municipal administrations and influential local interest coalitions to pursue long-term policies. We have witnessed difficulties associated with municipal reliance on conditional grants which makes municipalities vulnerable to senior governments' priority changes. We have also noticed the impact of OMB decisions on the municipal planning process which at the provincial level can force departures from municipally-defined priorities. Another major obstacle is municipal fiscal dependence which accounts for development support in areas that are most appealing to private investors. This dependence seriously impairs the capacity to pursue municipally-defined development options.

Other factors limit the maintenance of broad and stable interest bases that are required for the achievement of long-term objectives of local importance. This case study has raised the issue of contrasts in planners' and merchants' professional interests, in their particular time horizons and in their respective evaluation of renewal interventions. In a similar vein, the entry on the local political scene of a plurality of interest groups makes it more difficult for municipal administrations to concentrate their resources on a limited number of large-scale strategies.

Endnotes

[1] In methodological terms, three different avenues of investigation have been pursued. First, a content analysis of newspaper reporting yields a clear picture of the changes that took place in downtown Kitchener over the period under review. Second, an analysis of planning reports and related documents provides background information on the public sector's strategies. Finally interviews with a number of key public sector actors offer more detailed understanding of how and why some initiatives were undertaken and others abandoned.

[2] For further details on the 1961-1991 renewal processes see, Filion and Bunting (forthcoming). This paper also includes a complete listing of the documentary materials that provided a background to this study.

[3] This freeze was put in place pending review of a major report from a federal Housing Task Force which was set up in response to widespread disapproval of then current urban renewal policies, primarily on the part of the larger metropolitan areas. The task force concluded that renewal schemes which incorporated massive redevelopment of the existing urban environment should be abandoned in place of more people-oriented styles of renewal (Federal Task Force on Housing and Urban Development, 1969).

[4] See for example: "K-W Retailers Call for Freeze on New Stores," *Kitchener-Waterloo Record*, November 20, 1981.

[5] The Kitchener case suggests that this vulnerability was greater for medium than for large-size cities. We have seen that in freezing and later abandoning its urban renewal program, the federal government was, broadly, responding to protest in two large cities, Toronto and Vancouver. Meanwhile medium-size cities had little influence on this particular aspect of federal policy making. Local interests effectively failed in their pressures for reconsideration of the federal government's decision to cut financial support for the Kitchener CBD program. The best that the municipality achieved was a mere $1.2 million federal concession.

[6] On the influence of professionalism on bureaucrats' attitudes, see Bennis (1970); Chackerian and Abecarian (1984) and with more direct reference to planners, Baum (1983); Vasu (1979).

[7] On municipal governments' reduced autonomy resulting from their dependence on conditional grants from senior governments, see Cameron

(1980); Canadian Federation of Mayors and Municipalities (1976); Higgins (1986); Magnusson (1983).

References

Baum, H.S. (1983) *Planners and Public Expectations*, Cambridge, Mass.: Schenkman.

Bennis, W.G. (1970) *American Bureaucracy*, San Francisco: Aldine.

Bunting, T.E. (1984) *Kitchener - Waterloo: The Geography of Mainstreet*, Waterloo: Department of Geography Publication Series, Occasional Paper No. 3, University of Waterloo.

Burton, I. (1963) "A restatement of the dispersed city hypothesis," *Annals, Association of American Geographers*, Vol. 53: 285-289.

Cameron, K. (1980) "Municipal government in the intergovernmental maze," *Canadian Public Administration 23*, 195-217.

Canadian Federation of Mayors and Municipalities (1976) *Puppets on a Shoestring*, Ottawa: The Federation.

Chackerian, R. and Abecarian, G. (1984) *Bureaucratic Power in Society*, Chicago: Nelson-Hall, 63-4.

City of Kitchener (1965) "Kitchener urban renewal committee and planning department," *The Plan ... Downtown Kitchener*, Kitchener, Ontario: City of Kitchener.

City of Kitchener Planning Department and Project Planning Associates Ltd. (1967) *City of Kitchener Ontario: Central Kitchener Urban Renewal Scheme, Phase 1*, Kitchener, Ontario: City of Kitchener.

Dominion Bureau of Statistics (1961) *Census of Canada: Population, Historical 1901-1961*, Ottawa: Queen's Printer, 1963, Catalogue 92-539.

English, J. and McLaughlin, K. (1983) *Kitchener: An Illustrated History*, Waterloo: University of Waterloo.

Federal Task Force On Housing and Urban Development (1969) *Report*, Ottawa, Ontario: Queen's Printer.

Filion, P. and Bunting, T. (Forthcoming) "Local power and its limits: Three decades of attempts to revitalize Kitchener's CBD", *Journal of Urban History*.

Goldberg, M. and Mercer, J. (1983) *The Myth of the North American City*, Vancouver: University of British Columbia Press.

Higgins, D.J.H. (1986) *Local and Urban Politics in Canada*, Toronto: Gage, 66-120.

Kitchener-Waterloo Record (1962) "Planner Blasts Kitchener Apathy to Development", July 24.

Magnusson, W. (1983) "Introduction: The development of Canadian urban government," in Magnusson, W. and Sancton, A. (eds.), *City Politics in Canada*, Toronto: University of Toronto Press, 24-25.

Sikora, J.P. (1988) "Central business district revitalization in Kitchener: The issue of public response," in Bunting, T. E. and Filion, P. (eds.), *The Changing Canadian Inner City*, Waterloo, Ontario: University of Waterloo, Department of Geography Publication Series, 121-136.

Smith, Larry and Company (1964) *Downtown Kitchener, Ontario: Economic Analysis for Redevelopment Planning*, Toronto: Larry Smith and Company.

Statistics Canada, (1992) *Profile of census metropolitan areas and census agglomerations, Part A*, Ottawa: Ministry of Industry, Science and Technology, Cat. 93-337.

Vasu, M.L. (1979) *Politics and Planning*, Chapel Hill: University of North Carolina Press.

Chapter 9

Ports: Public Policy Issues

Brian Slack
Concordia University

Introduction

Ports lie largely under federal jurisdiction in Canada. They represent important, although frequently under-appreciated, elements of national policy. They facilitate international and domestic trade, and because they are instruments by which direct federal spending can be made in many parts of the country, they can serve as agents of regional economic development. One of the reasons why ports have been placed under public administration in Canada is that historically they have been spatial monopolies. Each port has been the outlet for its own discrete hinterland. Public control is a means of ensuring that all shippers in the hinterland have access to the facility.

As public bodies, most port authorities in Canada have evolved as landlords. They provide the superstructures, such as the docks and storage sheds, and frequently the infrastructures such as the handling gear. Actual port operations are carried out by private companies and by the shipping lines themselves. As monopolies, the port authorities do not get directly involved in commercial operations, and have seen their function primarily as providers of transfer facilities for others to exploit.

Over time some of these characteristics have changed. Other types of port authority have been allowed to develop. Private companies have established their own terminals, and the provinces have become more involved in port operations. The result is that presently, in Canada, there exists a patchwork quilt of port administrations (McCalla, 1982).

This administrative complexity is being brought to the fore as a problem because of recent changes in maritime transportation in general. Competition has largely destroyed the comfortable monopolistic position formerly enjoyed by ports. Improvements in land transport systems and the emergence of mega-ocean carriers have completely transformed the situation. No longer can many ports depend on the exclusive traffic of their own hinterlands, and the hinterland concept itself is in doubt. How can landlord ports survive in such an environment?

These developments have some considerable relevance for public policy in Canada. While ports do not enjoy a high profile in general policy debates, their economic importance requires that there must be a careful assessment of changes that limit their effectiveness. The two developments discussed here — administrative complexity and growing competition — are extremely relevant policy issues, since the problems engendered can be mitigated by carefully considered policy responses. Geographers have an important role to play both in the analysis of the problems and in the discussion of policy solutions. Geography has a long tradition of contributing to port studies, and geographical concepts such as port systems and hierarchies, as well as the detailed knowledge of individual cases, including land use relations, are important considerations for the issues discussed here. As will be demonstrated, many of the problems are spatial, and how they are resolved will shape the pattern of port development in Canada for many years to come.

Port Administration in Canada

Although the federal government has constitutional authority over ports in Canada, it does not exert its jurisdiction over all the more than 300 ports and harbours that are maintained in the country. Nevertheless, the tradition of public ownership and control of ports is very strong in the country. A problem is that the form of this public ownership is very diverse.

The present pattern is one that has evolved out of various attempts to legislate port administration in Canada. The first major reform came out of the Great Depression. Sir Alexander Gibb's recommendations of the early 1930s led to the establishment of the National Harbours Board (1936), under whose control were placed all the major "national" ports such as Montreal, Vancouver and Halifax. This resulted in a very centralized pattern of port administration. The exceptions were the Harbour Commission ports, such as Toronto and Hamilton, that had been established by local interests, which were allowed to continue under their largely local administrations.

By the 1960s this system was beginning to break down. The National Harbours Board was seen as too autocratic and rigid, some Harbour Commission Ports were implicated in dubious local political scandals, and the vast majority of small ports lay outside these structures. In 1977, after several studies, the Canada Ports Act was introduced into Parliament. It proposed that all ports be administered by a Canadian Ports Commission, with 20 of the larger ports being allowed more local autonomy through the creation of local ports commissions. This proposed act generated a great deal of opposition, mainly because it was seen as an attempt to politicise port policy, with the power vested in the Civil Service. The act died on the order paper.

In 1983 a new act was adopted, the Canada Ports Corporation Act. This act established a new crown corporation to administer the 15 former National Harbours Board ports. The debts and obligations of its predecessor were absorbed, but the new body had to be financially self-sufficient. The act enabled those ports that had the financial resources to be established as local port commissions. Significantly, it left the Harbour Commissions alone. They had lobbied vigorously to retain their independence, and the government acceded to the pressures brought to bear.

In 1985, all the diverse smaller ports under direct federal control were placed under Transport Canada's Ports Directorate as a result of the Public Harbour's and Port Facilities Act. These ports, which do not generate sufficient revenues to cover expenses, were grouped into five regional administrations: Newfoundland, Maritimes, Laurentide, Central, and Western.

The result of all these "rationalisations" is that Canada does not have a unified port administrative structure. To a certain degree the structure is hierarchical (see Table 9.1). At the top of the ladder, as it were, are the ports nominally under the control of the Canada Ports Corporation (CPC). There are two types of CPC ports: the seven that have been granted Local Ports Corporation (LPC) status, St John's, Halifax, Saint John, Montreal, Quebec, Vancouver and Prince Rupert, and seven other ports such as Sept Iles, Trois Rivières, Chicoutimi, which are administered from Ottawa. The local corporation ports have been given a great deal of autonomy although they must still report to the CPC, and have their capital and corporate plans approved by the Minister and the Treasury Board. They set their own charges and finance capital development out of revenues. The CPC itself must be financially independent of the State, but can allocate revenues from one port in its system to cover investments in another.

The Harbour Commission ports, such as Toronto, Thunder Bay, Fraser River, operate largely outside federal control, although they nominally report to either the Minister of Transport or the federal cabinet. They represent local interests to a great degree, and must be financially self-sufficient.

Three hundred and twenty four public ports are administered by the Harbours and Ports Directorate of Transport Canada. As mentioned above, Transport Canada has responsibility for operating and maintaining the smaller facilities whose traffic is usually insufficient to be able to sustain their financial independence. A local harbour master ensures day to day operations, but the ports are administered regionally.

Table 9.1
Typology of Port Administrations in Canada

Administrative Control	# of Ports	Examples
Federal Canada Ports Corp. Local Ports Corps.	7	St. John , Halifax, Montreal, Vancouver
Canada Ports Corp. Ottawa administered	7	Trois Rivières, Chicoutimi, Belledune
Harbour Commissions	8	Toronto, Thunder Bay, Fraser River, Nanaimo
Transport Canada	324	Bayside, Gros Cacouna, Goderich, Victoria
Provincial ministère de l'industrie et du commerce (Québec)	1	Bécancour
Municipal	1	Valleyfield
Mixed Private-Public	n.a.	Baie Comeau, Havre St.-Pierre, Cornerbrook
Private	n.a.	Forestville, New Richmond, Nanticoke

There are two other kinds of public ports in Canada. Bécancour is a port administered by the province of Quebec. As the terminal adjacent to an industrial park, it is responsible to the Quebec Ministry of Trade and Industry. Quebec also has a municipal port, Valleyfield, which operates on land leased from the St. Lawrence Seaway Authority. It serves local industrial users, but is under the management of the municipality.

As if this structure is not complicated enough, there exist various degrees of private involvement in ports in Canada. Some of the largest ports involve private operations. However, it is important to distinguish between a "port" and a "terminal". Some public ports are in fact mixed as to ownership and operation. Large ports, such as Baie Comeau, comprise small public facilities adjacent to much larger private terminals, and thus these ports are really "mixed" as to ownership. Other "ports" are purely private facilities. Examples in Quebec include Forestville, New Richmond and Port Alfred that are operated and controlled by local industries for their own use.

Issues of Port Administration

There is a growing debate in the academic literature over appropriate administrative structures for port systems (Goss, 1979, 1990; Herschman, 1988). At issue are questions of the level of jurisdiction under which should port administration be placed. The British economist Goss (1990) has recently surveyed some of the main systems in place around the world. He identifies two main types: one where the national government administers ports, the other where a local body controls port development.

The national government model is one found in many countries where there are many ports, such as France and Mexico. Britain, which used to maintain a great deal of national control over ports has progressively slipped from this group, as it is moving towards a privatised system (Ircha, 1992). The strongest argument for national control over ports is that it permits national policies to be implemented. Ports represent very significant investments and frequently play important roles in national economic development. Investments can be made to fulfil national goals, and can be allocated in ways that reduce duplication. In France, state involvement in port development has been consistent and considerable. Beginning with the Vth National Plan, ports have figured very significantly in economic and regional development in France. Certain ports were selected for major infrastructural investments, and the result has been the success of Le Havre and Marseille. Other ports chosen for development, Dunkirque and Bordeaux, have not fared as well (Slack, 1980).

The decentralised port model is one found in many countries such as Germany, Holland, Belgium and the U.S. Here jurisdiction lies at the municipal level, such as in Holland and the U.S., or at the regional level as in Germany and in some U.S. states. The advantage ascribed to local control is that the ports can be responsive to local conditions. The local community can be involved, and the port may be able to respond more rapidly to changes, because they do not have to go through a state bureaucracy in order to get financing. This model has worked well in Holland where Rotterdam has enjoyed great success as a municipal port. In the U.S. the growing competitiveness of the port system vis-a-vis Canada is partly due to the dynamism of some of its locally administered ports, such as Seattle and Tacoma (Pisiani, 1989).

There are of course drawbacks to each of these models. The centralised system requires that a strong national policy be enunciated. This policy may well be unpopular, since it has to prioritize investments, and this invariably leads to local and regional resentments that may manifest themselves at election time. Britain attempted such a strong national ports policy in the early 1960s but it collapsed when exceptions were made to the policy for political reasons, as in the Portbury decision, where the decision of the National Ports Council not to support Bristol's request for expansion was overturned by the government (Bird, 1971). In France, successive governments have withstood the complaints from ports that were not prioritized, although it may be noted that increasing state funds have been made available to ports such as Rouen and Nantes over time. Herein lies another weakness of the centralized system. Economic conditions are evolving at a very rapid rate, and ports have to adjust very rapidly to these developments. If the system is tied to a policy that is not capable of being easily or rapidly modified, the ports may find themselves in unworkable situations. These difficulties are not faced by ports administered by local bodies. On the other hand, there are several specific problems associated with the decentralized model. Of major concern is the question of duplication and the waste of public capital investments. Where ports are free to make their own investment decisions there is an inevitable tendency to over build. Each port has to offer comparable infrastructures, even if they are not immediately usable. U.S. ports have invested huge sums in container facilities, because no port wants to be left out of the game (Herschman, 1988). It should be noted that many of the most successful locally administered port systems are where there is little or no national competition. Rotterdam occupies a supremely dominant position in Holland, and in Germany there are only two major seaports, Hamburg and Bremerhaven.

A further problem for local authority ports is that they may not have access to sufficient capital in order to make the necessary investments. This may appear paradoxical in light of the previous points, but port infrastructures are exceedingly costly, especially where dredging and land reclamation are involved. If forced to finance capital projects out of current revenues, potentially serious constraints may be encountered.

The actual system of port administration in Canada clearly does not correspond to either of the models discussed above (McCalla, 1982). Although there is some public control over the vast majority of commercial ports, there is considerable autonomy in the system. Unfortunately, many of the disadvantages of both ideal models are in evidence, while few, if any, of their advantages are present.

One of the perceived advantages of national port administrations is that national policies can be implemented. This has not occurred in Canada, and a basic question must be: could Canada develop a national ports policy? I think that this is very unlikely for several reasons. The needs of ports differ, and their roles vary regionally and functionally, so that a national plan would be very difficult to design. Despite the fact that most ports in Canada are under some form of public control, the inconsistencies between federal, provincial and municipal administrations, make it highly unlikely that national goals or national policies could be agreed upon. Even if such policies were defined, it is doubtful that they could be implemented under present conditions. It would be very difficult, for example, for the federal government to control many of the activities at ports that are operated privately.

The closest Canada comes to the development of a ports policy is with regards to the public harbours administered by Transport Canada. Administering the commercial ports that cannot sustain themselves, Transport Canada has developed a regional approach to management. It undertakes periodic reviews of the needs of the ports in each system, and allocates its capital budget on the basis of this survey. Unfortunately, these investments have been subject to political pressures, and local federal deputies have been known to influence decisions. In addition, they have been used for the purpose of promoting regional economic development, which may not coincide with the transport needs of the ports. For example, the expansion of Matane and the establishment of a deepwater facility at Gros Cacouna were major features of regional development initiatives in Quebec in the 1970s and early 1980s. While these investments did provide both locations with excellent marine terminals, it was done at the expense of Rimouski. There have been subsequent diversions of timber shipments from Rimouski to Gros Cacouna, and a present function of Rimouski, serving as the supply port for the Lower North Shore, is threatened by possible relocation to Matane.

As a de facto decentralised system, the Canadian port scene provides numerous examples of duplication. In New Brunswick, the Transport Canada Bayside facility is diverting traffic from the CPC port of Saint John. Similarly, the provincially owned port of Bécancour in Quebec is diverting timber exports from the CPC port of Trois Rivières, just across the St. Lawrence River. In western Canada there is controversy over the existence of three separate ports in the Vancouver region, one the LPC port of Vancouver, and the two independent Harbour Commission ports of Fraser River and North Fraser River. In all these cases, issues are raised concerning the allocation of resources, the duplication of facilities, and unfair competition.

Similar issues also arise at private ports. Some industries that depend on maritime transport either for raw material imports or exports of finished products have made significant investments in their own terminals. Other similar industries use public wharves. Given the fact that at the Transport Canada public wharves the rates charged do represent the full capital cost of the facilities, firms that use these ports are in effect receiving a hidden subsidy. To take one example, at Pointe au Pic, a small Transport Canada port, there is considerable pressure from the Donoghue mill, the major user, for additional storage and warehouse space. If this is provided, it will be paid for by public monies, an investment that will not likely be fully recovered by the rates charged by Transport Canada.

Canadian ports are not equal in terms of financial resources, obligations to the local community, or legal standing. The Transport Canada ports are subsidised, since it is claimed that they are too small to be able to be self-sufficient. On the other hand, Canada's largest ports have been given a great deal of financial independence, which entails them covering capital expenditures out of operating income and accrued profits. While there is no evidence at present to suggest that Canada's largest ports lack the resources to undertake expansion projects, fears have been raised that they cannot compete with their U.S. competitors that can issue tax-free bonds to pay for capital projects (Containerisation International, 1990). Many U.S. ports, such as New York and Tacoma, are in the process of undertaking very large expansion schemes, that may influence the competitiveness of the Canadian system (Slack, 1991).

Canadian ports act with varying degrees of independence from the local milieu. A common complaint about the federal ports is that they rarely involve the municipal and regional governments in their planning and development. Numerous locational conflicts have arisen as a result. This has been particularly evident over issues relating to the conversion of former port land and expansion projects (McCalla, 1978). Paradoxically, perhaps the most independent port is one that is administered by a province. Bécancour operates with absolute independence from its locality, and has powers of expropriation, rights granted under its own special provincial charter.

There exist, therefore, numerous inconsistencies in the role and mandate of Canadian ports. How can they serve in the national interest and yet respond faithfully to local needs? Why should some ports be subsidised, while others are required to be self-supporting? How can such a patchwork of administrations be expected to confront the commercial and planning challenges that confront the ports?

Issues of the Landlord Ports

Most of Canada's ports are owned and maintained by public authorities, while the facilities are leased out to private firms. The landlord port model is dominant in all types of public ports. It has worked relatively well, ensuring that users have good cargo handling facilities. Two problems have arisen recently for the landlord ports, however.

The first is that most general cargo ports are no longer in a monopolistic situation. Containerization, and the recent developments in multi-modal transport systems have provided technological opportunities that have worked with deregulation to greatly free trade flows. Ports can no longer be guaranteed to handle the traffic of even their local markets. This fact has been reinforced by the emergence of mega-carriers. A feature of contemporary transportation is the dominance of large transportation companies, frequently shipping lines, that operate world-wide, across all major modes. They operate networks that are global in scale, and hence select their itineraries and chose their ports of call based less and less on purely local considerations. Individual ports are finding that their traffic, which is after all their raison d'être, is at the mercy of decisions made thousands of kilometres away by corporations with little local commitment. Ports around the world are finding that facilities, provided at considerable public expense, are made idle by shipping lines that relocate elsewhere. All major Canadian ports have experienced this, and in the case of Saint John and potentially in Halifax, it can be crippling.

A second problem is that port operations have become significantly less labour intensive. Mechanisation of cargo handling has drastically cut the needs for manpower. Containerisation has also led to losses in other traditional port activities such as storage, warehousing, and recent developments in electronic data interchange are reducing the manpower needs of service occupations such as forwarding and customs clearance. The result is that ports are finding that they are losing much of their economic importance (Slack, 1992).

There is a close relationship between the globalisation of trade and the mechanisation and automation of traditional port functions. Landlord ports find themselves particularly vulnerable to both. They are frequently called upon to make significant investments to attract carriers, only to see those facilities vacated as the result of some decision made well beyond the control of the individual port. It may take more than five years for a port to plan and construct a new facility; a shipping line may vacate it overnight.

Towards Solutions

It is clearly beyond the scope of a chapter such as this to provide answers to the serious problems alluded to. Rather, it is hoped that by raising the issues, a public debate can be enjoined, because part of the problem at the moment is that few people are aware of the difficulties.

Of the two issues raised, the former, that of the complexity of port administration, is one that is well within the power of the federal government to resolve, while the problems facing the landlord ports are based on challenges that lie beyond the control of the government. Nevertheless, it is perhaps best to deal with the problems of the landlord ports first, since their resolution may impact on the nature of the administrative structure that is eventually put in place.

Ports around the world are trying to cope with the issues raised by the globalisation of the economy and by the fact that they have been relegated to serve as but one link in an intermodal chain. There are some ports that have made successful adaptations and thus we must learn from their experience, even though the conditions may not be analogous.

In order to reduce the likelihood of lines skipping from one port to another, there must be incentives for carriers to become more deeply attached to the ports they use. Several U.S. ports are granting users very favourable terms, such as reduced fees and harbour dues, for long term leases of terminals, in which the carriers pay a substantial part of the development costs and equipment purchases. By encouraging the carriers to commit themselves through investments, the likelihood of a shift will be reduced. There are many problems with this possible solution. Canadian ports cannot offer the same economies of scale with regards to containers that their U.S. competitors provide, and hence the carriers might be less interested in making the same degree of investment in Canadian ports. However, one of the important aspects in this question is the extent to which Canadian ports are willing to allocate space to individual lines. Most Canadian ports operate multi-user terminals, that achieve enviable throughputs, but do not permit one line to have exclusive rights. In order to entice private investment Canadian ports will have to re-think their policies, and consider single user occupancy as an alternative.

In order to recoup some of the losses in manpower and other economic impacts and to attract new trades, port authorities must become more pro-active. They can no longer maintain their landlord position of sitting back and letting the users come to them. Recent improvements in marketing have been made, but Canadian ports must become more directly involved in port economic activities. In an attempt to retain its pre-eminence as a motor of the Dutch economy, the port of Rotterdam is actively involved with private industries in developing distribution and logistic services adjacent to the port. In these "distriparks", imported goods are stored, packaged and supplied to users all over Europe on a just-in-time basis (van Horsen, 1991). The goal is to maintain traffic through the port, and also to develop new value added functions. The port is enhancing its traditional role by adapting to new technologies and business practices. Canadian ports need to pursue similar or parallel schemes in order to adapt to the new forms of business logistics.

Both these suggestions imply that Canadian ports should become less and less landlords and more and more pro-active in their operations. They require a complete re-assessment of the role and function of port authorities. In turn, this indicates that the much needed reorganisation of port administration in Canada cannot pursue a solution calling for more centralised control (Ircha, 1992). Commercial ports must be made more independent, but the ambiguities and inequalities in structure that are present today must be removed. CPC ports, the Harbour Commission Ports, and the viable Transport Canada ports must be given local autonomy and placed on an equal footing. The precise form of this autonomy must be subject to much further analysis, discussion and consultation. However, it must reflect the actual operating conditions in the area, and difficult though it may be to achieve, separate entities in the same geographical region should be fused. These autonomous ports must be made financially independent, and free to negotiate with private users. By entering into private partnerships, the ports should be able to secure additional sources of funds for future capital projects.

The ports that are not capable of being self sustaining (of all previous jurisdictions) cannot be independent, by definition, have to be administered differently. The concept of the present system of the Transport Canada Ports and Harbours Directorate, appears to have certain advantages. This implies that the smaller commercial ports should be administered on a regional basis. However, there must be a careful evaluation of the merits of leaving the administration under a federal department as against a more independent set of regional crown corporations. The latter might ensure a greater degree of independence of action. Whatever form these regional commissions take, a priority must be a rationalisation of the system. At present there are too many ports being supported by state funds. Certain facilities are being maintained that handle minimal traffic volumes. A careful assessment of these ports, involving analysis of their traffic and regional functions, must be carried out.

Conclusions

This paper has highlighted some of the public policy issues arising out of two contemporary problems confronting Canadian ports. Although the complexity of administrations is a domestic problem, and the difficulties wrought by the globalization of trade are international, both converge in relation to issues that confront the status of ports. Competition between ports has increased and yet Canada's port system is administered with inequality. Its ports still operate with a landlord mentality, when the economic environment produces conditions in which traffic can no longer be taken for granted.

While the solutions to these problems will require a great deal more analysis and evaluation, certain broad suggestions are presented. Port administration has to be simplified, the multiplicity of types have to be re-ordered, and it would appear that a wider autonomous system has advantages in the present economic climate. Port authorities have to become more actively involved in operations, marketing, and the promotion of new functions, which is another reason for the preference for a decentralised model. On the other hand, many ports that serve vital local or regional functions will likely never be self-sufficient, and hence will require continued state support.

Acknowledgements

The author wishes to thank John MacDonald and Mark Ziegler of Transport Canada for their helpful comments on an earlier draft of the paper. The views expressed within are those of the author.

References

Bird J. (1971) *Seaports and Seaport Terminals*, London: Hutchison.

Containerisation International (1990) "Annual survey of North American ports," *Containerisation International*.

Goss R.O. (1979) *Comparative Study of Seaport Management and Administration*, London: Government Economic Service.

_____ (1990) "Economic policies and seaports," *Maritime Policy and Management*, Vol 17: 231-244.

Herschman M.J. (ed.) (1988) *Urban Ports and Harbor Management*, New York: Taylor Francis.

Ircha M.C. (1992) "Canadian ports: A commercial approach," *Portus*, Vol 7: 6-12.

McCalla R.J. (1978) "Waterfront land uses changes in Halifax," in McCalla, R.J. (eds.), *Marine Studies and Coastal Zone Management in Canada*, Halifax: Saint Mary's University Occasional Papers in Geography, No. 2, pp. 81-102.

_____ (1982) "A study of harbour administration in Canada," *Maritime Policy and Management*, Vol. 9: 279-293.

Pisiani J.M. (1989) *Port Development in the U.S.*, Tokyo: IAPH.

Slack B. (1980) "French and British ports policy contrasts," *Canadian Shipping and Marine Engineering*, Vol 52: 26-29.

_____ (1991) *Intermodal Monitor*, Transport Canada, Ottawa: TP 10495E.

_____ (1992) "Port planning in a competitive environment," *Portus*, Vol. 7: 12-15.

van Horsen W. (1991) "The port of Rotterdam's distriparks," *Port of Rotterdam*, Vol. 91(6): 4-10.

Chapter 10

The Role of the Port Authority in Urban Coastal Zone Management: The Case of Vancouver, B.C.

J. Paul Georgison and J.C. Day
Simon Fraser University

Introduction

The urban harbour is the focal point for much of the human activity, commerce, and habitation in the coastal zone. Its geographic features enable marine vessels to moor and exchange people, cargo, and provisions. Consequently, it is in and around these sheltered coastal environments that the great industrial and transportation networks have been concentrated to serve the delivery systems of surrounding regional and national economies.

The governmental institution usually placed in charge of administering and developing these marine commercial facilities in North America is the public port authority. Traditionally, a public port's sole responsibility has been to manage waterfront developments and harbor improvements to ensure efficient, cost-effective movements of goods and persons through its jurisdiction to maximize business for the economic benefit of its constituency.

However, port authorities have begun to face broader public pressures over the past two decades. Increasingly, people are valuing the harbour for reasons that extend beyond its usefulness as a transportation utility or a commercial service center. To port city residents, an urban harbour is also a natural and cultural maritime resource, providing scenic and experiential pleasures which improve their quality of life. Because of the public port's jurisdiction over harbour-front land and water, it is expected by neighboring communities, either directly or indirectly, to preserve and enhance local quality of life, to make the harbour cleaner and quieter, to provide recreational amenities, and to support cultural and historic projects (Hershman, 1988).

Value changes in the port community have coincided with general societal and public policy trends toward increased environmental protection. Public interest groups and government agencies now actively promote the protection and enhancement of water quality, the remaining natural habitat, fish and wildlife, and recreational opportunities along coastlines. Consequently, it is no longer deemed acceptable for port authorities to pursue their commercial mandates without subjecting their developments to environmental regulation, impact assessment, and public review.

Fortunately, most of these modern management issues can be resolved by a port authority through modified institutional arrangements which account for all relevant stakeholder objectives. Public ports operate under a broad mandate with considerable harbour land, financial resources, governmental powers, and autonomy that enable them to engage in a wide range of activities. They also have a stable corp of professional managers and an ability to respond rapidly to changing economic, political, and social demands. For these reasons, accountable port authorities can make profound contributions to improved harbour management (Hershman, 1988).

The public port authority can support urban harbour management objectives in two ways. First, a port authority can act as a leader by bringing together the multitude of stakeholders to assist in decision making and to form management plans or development strategies. It can also ensure that development proposals are located and designed so that they fulfill their intended purposes without causing unnecessary degradation to the harbour environment. Second, a port authority can cooperate in designing and implementing portions of broader harbour environmental goals. In this participatory capacity, the degree and adequacy of port authority commitment depends largely on the quality of the environmental planning and public review procedures controlling its developments and operations.

These themes are all relevant in the Port of Vancouver, British Columbia. Vancouver is one of the world's largest ports in terms of volume of goods moved, and its importance to the Canadian economy is reflected in strong federal government investment. Indeed, Ottawa has allocated a huge expanse of harbour foreshore and seabed to the Vancouver port authority so it may accommodate national trade objectives. However, the harbour is surrounded by a large urban community with cultural and economic roots that are set in the same maritime resources from which port industry has thrived. Burrard Inlet and Indian Arm, which constitute the focal point of the Vancouver Harbour and federal port jurisdiction, possess myriad nonport amenities such as coastal habitat, recreation opportunities, and superb aesthetics. These resources may be lost or impaired by port projects, thereby posing the potential for conflicts between federal trade and local interests. This situation clearly underscores the need for port administration within a balanced decision-making framework.

This paper assesses the adequacy of existing Port of Vancouver planning, assessment, and regulatory frameworks for accommodating, addressing, and supporting modern harbour management pressures and responsibilities. This evaluation of decision-making accountability is aided by comparison with the approaches used to confront similar challenges in the Port of Seattle, Washington State. Both ports must contend with comparable circumstances that extend beyond the basic competitive relations between such shipping centers. Vancouver and Seattle are marine coastal ports situated within 200 kilometers of each other on the central west coast of North America (Figure 10.1). Although they emphasize different types of cargo handling, both ports serve as gateways for North American trade with Pacific Rim nations, particularly the Asian community. Vancouver and Seattle share the same natural environment, which includes spectacular water and mountain vistas, world renown salmon fisheries, and coastal forests. Furthermore, the urban communities surrounding these harbours have similar cultural profiles and support similar lifestyle objectives. Comparative analysis is used to reveal strengths and weaknesses in the current Port of Vancouver administration for attending to broader harbour management issues while continuing to honour its national commercial trade mandate.

Port Management: Vancouver

The Port

The Port of Vancouver comprises the federally owned seabed and foreshore of Burrard Inlet and Indian Arm, adjacent to the southwest mainland of British Columbia (Figure 10.2). Any landfill into the inlet is deemed a Port of Vancouver development (Jordan, 1991). A parcel of federal seabed near the mouth of the Fraser River on Roberts Bank is also port property. These port lands are surrounded by the Vancouver Harbour, over which the Vancouver port authority has the right to regulate navigation. The physical and strategic attributes of Burrard Inlet and Roberts Bank have made Vancouver the largest and most important port in Canada. Resource extractive industries across Canada, particularly in the western Canadian provinces, rely heavily on the movement of their goods through Vancouver for economic success. Consequently, bulk movements of grain, forest products, minerals, and fossil fuels dominate the Port of Vancouver cargo profile. Because of its size, importance, and the types of materials it moves, Vancouver consistently ranks among the top three foreign tonnage ports in

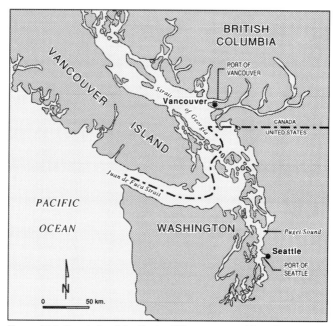

Figure 10.1: Proximity of the Ports of Vancouver and Seattle

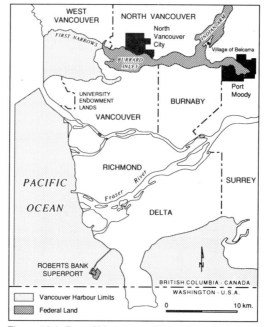

Figure 10.2: Port of Vancouver, British Columbia

North America (Vancouver Port Corporation, 1992). Over 70-million tonnes were moved in its peak year of 1988 (Vancouver Port Corporation, 1989).

Institutional Structure and Mandate

There has been an overwhelming federal presence in the administration of Canada's port systems since British Columbia entered confederation in 1871 (Transmode Consultants Inc., 1988). In Canada, ports have always been considered control points for national security, trade, immigration, and customs. Government policy, legislation, and the courts have clarified the dominant federal role. Presently, Canada's commercial ports are organized to support the National Ports Policy, which outlines federal objectives for a port system that efficiently achieves Canadian trade objectives.

The Canada Ports Corporation Act (CPCA) regulates Canada's largest ports in support of the National Ports Policy (Canada, 1985). CPCA enables establishment of local port corporations (LPCs) to govern affairs of each port of national significance. LPCs are self-standing federal crown corporations given the authority to acquire, sell, and lease property, develop port facilities and infrastructure, and manage port uses in its harbour. Those ports administered under CPCA comprise Ports Canada, which is coordinated by the Canada Ports Corporation (CPC) in Ottawa.

The Vancouver Port Corporation (VPC) was established in 1983 to administer, manage, and control federal lands within the Port of Vancouver in accordance with the National Ports Policy. VPC jurisdiction also encompasses Port of Vancouver cargo terminals and related marine installations. Vancouver functions as a landlord port, with all port-owned facilities operated by others under contract. All development and use proposals on Port of Vancouver lands must be approved by the port corporation. VPC is governed by a seven-member board of directors appointed by federal cabinet. The board is responsible for final approval of corporate polices and development proposals according to VPC's superordinate goal. It is: " . . . to facilitate the efficient movement of maritime imports and exports through the Port of Vancouver in the best interests of Canadian trade objectives" (Vancouver Port Corporation, 1990a: 1).

Port Management: Seattle

The Port

The Port of Seattle comprises waterfront terminal areas and marine cargo and related facilities owned, managed, and financed by the Seattle Port District. Port of Seattle property is concentrated around the Duwamish Waterway and adjacent Elliot Bay, along the southeastern shore of Puget Sound (Figure 10.3). All port district property is either operated by the port authority itself, or it is leased to and utilized by various marine businesses. This capital, totalling nearly 500-hectares of harbor-front space, is owned exclusively by King County taxpayers (Blomberg, 1990).

Seattle ranks among the largest U.S. ports, and it is one of the busiest container ports in the world (Port of Seattle, 1990a). Annual trade is approximately 12-million tonnes, far less than Vancouver's throughput (Port of Seattle, 1990b). However, high-value containerized manufactured and specialty goods constitute the bulk of marine shipments passing through Seattle (Port of Seattle, 1990b). Indeed, Seattle recently ranked fourth among U.S. ports in value of total trade (Port of Seattle, 1990a).

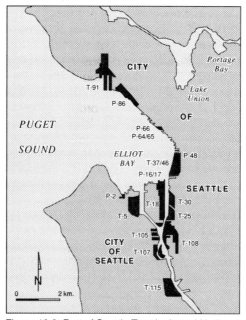

Figure 10.3: Port of Seattle Terminals and Harbour

Institutional Structure and Mandate

The approaches adopted to administer the ports of Vancouver and Seattle are strikingly different. In contrast to the strong national institutional framework adopted in Canada, the U.S. has no central federal agency with any direct administrative or financial review functions over port organizations

(Hershman and Kory, 1988). Moreover, there is no U.S. national port administration law or national port development policy. Instead, state and local governments are principally responsible for port administration. In Seattle, such governing power rests with King County voters, who have mandated the Port of Seattle to function as a means to foster economic development and to preserve and enhance the quality of life in the local community.

In Washington State, a grassroots populist movement coerced the state legislature in 1911 to pass the Port District Act (Washington, 1989a; Historical Society of Seattle and King County, 1986). This legislation enabled the creation of locally controlled public port districts, an entirely new political division independent of state, county, or city organization, devoted to the sole purpose of port development and administration.

Port districts may be established in various counties of the state. The power to form a port district rests solely with local county governments and their constituencies through the electoral process. A simple majority in favor of such a proposition results in port district formation. Port districts may vary in size from as small as a city to an entire county (Washington, 1990).

Port districts have the power of eminent domain and the authority to acquire, develop, and regulate port lands, facilities, and services within their boundaries (Washington, 1989a). Other important provisions include the right to levy a yearly property tax on citizens of port districts to finance property acquisition and capital improvements which benefit the community.

The legislative framework in Washington State has created a unique form of governance among ports along the North American west coast. The powers of the port district are exercised through a board of elected port commissioners, with port district elections held in conjunction with county elections. Consequently, local taxpayers control the port decision-making process, as they elect port policy makers and form the port development financial base.

Established in 1911, the Port of Seattle carries out the responsibilities of the Seattle Port District municipal corporation as outlined in the Port District Act. Unlike Vancouver, the Port of Seattle has not been accorded a large area of government-owned land. Instead, it must compete with private interests in purchasing waterfront property with public funds (Historical Society of Seattle and King County, 1986).

The Port of Seattle is governed for King County citizens by five locally elected commissioners (Port of Seattle, 1990a). Port commissioners are responsible for ratifying port policy, and they have final approval authority over development proposals (Washington, 1990). The port's mandate is: " . . . to be a leader providing services and facilities to accommodate the transportation of cargo and passengers . . . to foster regional economic vitality and a quality life for King County citizens" (Port of Seattle, 1990c: 1).

Assessing Port Authority Accountability

Accountability for public port authorities is a controversial subject. At the heart of this controversy is the fact that these agencies have both public characteristics and commercial enterprise features. As publicly owned agencies, ports require measures to ensure they account for constituent objectives; as business enterprises, they require flexibility and degrees of autonomy unlike regular government agencies. Balanced decision-making accountability is a difficult proposition for a public port authority. This is particularly true for Vancouver, because its administrative policy is based on the preeminent federal obligation to serve nation-wide trade interests.

However, the public port authority can no longer base decisions solely on the interests of its clientele. Popular control measures must require that all stakeholders are accounted for before decisions which affect harbor resources are made. Accommodating these needs is tenable through institutions which ensure: consideration of all stakeholder objectives; empowering of planning or decision-making authority to representatives of these interest groups; facilitation of public consultation in planning and decision-making processes; and, access to information for all interested parties prior to decision making.

Any assessment of port authority accountability must consider this institution's ultimate reference point: the port's market base and economic profile (Olson, 1988). Retrenched federal port policy and diverse, highly developed, regional economies in many U.S. areas make ports such as Seattle more attuned to local governance (Hershman and Kory, 1988). In contrast, Vancouver's economic basis and responsibility as an exporter of bulk raw materials from across Canada necessitate strong federal government representation.

In light of these principles, the organizational and policy approach adopted for Port of Vancouver administration is assessed according to the degree to which it is accountable to all relevant stakeholders, including adjacent communities. Evaluation includes comparison with Port of Seattle administration to pinpoint institutional strengths and weaknesses.

Port of Vancouver Policy Issues

The juxtaposition of federally and locally administered land is the basis for most of the public issues evolving from the VPC decision-making process. While the Port of Vancouver has grown, and administrative policy has developed, urban communities governed by several municipal corporations have been established on the surrounding lands. The port is, in fact, an "island" of federal territory surrounded by eight municipal jurisdictions and the Greater Vancouver Regional District (GVRD). This patchwork of contiguous federal and local jurisdictions poses the potential for conflict and disorganization among resource management policies for the harbor, as priorities, goals, and objectives may differ considerably between the two government levels.

Many of the encroaching communities' resource-use objectives focus on the myriad nonport amenities of Burrard Inlet and Indian Arm, such as recreation opportunities and superb esthetics, which contribute substantially to living quality for local residents. However, port development may foreclose opportunities for the public to enjoy these attributes, and port-related activities may degrade the living environment of nearby residents. Detrimental impacts on the surrounding community include: noise from operations; air and water pollution from terminal, shipping, and other marine activities; aesthetic impairment such as view blockage; dredging and landfill in ecologically sensitive areas; and hazardous cargo spill risks.

The residential and human needs of the city dweller on one side, and the space and access requirements of commercial seaport users on the other, form the essential resource-use conflict that constrains effective harbour management. Public port authorities such as VPC have an important role to play in working to improve this relationship because of their preeminent administrative authority and substantial land and financial resources that can directly affect the harbour and its uses. Pressure for VPC to resolve waterfront issues has intensified in recent years as a result of the high visibility of port operations, increased media attention, and stronger environmental concerns.

This predicament necessitates a port administrative arrangement which promotes the identification and resolution of disputes among stakeholders. The institution must be accountable to all groups with a vested interest in the port's affairs and jurisdiction. This includes the governments and residents of the lands abutting Port of Vancouver property, as port functions may have direct economic and environmental impacts on these communities (Greater Vancouver Regional District, 1990). Consequently, VPC has an inherent responsibility to account for the concerns of, and impacts on, these stakeholders. Furthermore, a management structure which denies opportunities for involvement by all stakeholders can lead to decision-making uncertainty for VPC, thus inhibiting the attainment of long-term, port-development goals.

The conflict and controversy surrounding several Port of Vancouver developments in the late-1980s indicate that VPC has been slow to embrace an open, accountable approach toward local publics. Many government representatives and residents of surrounding communities are of the opinion that Port of Vancouver administration has failed to acknowledge local and regional objectives in decision-making (Greater Vancouver Regional District, 1990). They cite the incidents of the previous decade in which VPC precluded local publics and governments from decision-making functions, refused to disclose information, and rejected local concerns without due process during development planning and approval.

Three widely publicized development disputes in the late-1980s were largely responsible for damaging relations between federal port and local community interests. In early-1989, lobbying residents persuaded Vancouver city council to oppose a Port of Vancouver development proposal because of anticipated aesthetic, noise, and air quality impacts. Regardless, VPC approved the project without subjecting the proposal to public review or a public impact assessment process. Second, North Vancouver residents' complaints of dust and noise compelled that city's government to reject a facility expansion proposal on nearby port land a few months later. The city of North Vancouver asked the proponent to enter into an agreement to comply with provincial environmental regulations. However, VPC prohibited such an agreement and replaced it with an internal corporate pact. Last, considerable public interest and opposition to hazardous cargo, particularly oil, movements were focused on the Port of Vancouver in the late-1980s. Interested publics and local governments had no opportunity to review or discuss traffic policy or plans with port officials, despite the fact that oil shipments and related spill risks were increasing significantly at the time.

Analysis: Port of Vancouver

For the most part, the potential for unilateral and apparently insensitive decision making continues to exist, as it is entrenched in the Port of Vancouver institutional structure. As a federal authority, VPC has preeminent decision-making power over provincial, regional, and municipal policy. Canadian courts have granted federal landowners such as VPC the authority to override municipal and provincial land-use regulations for the purpose of accommodating national trade interests (Jordan, 1991). In fact, the port corporation has the freedom in most instances to ignore conflicting objectives put forward by these so-called "inferior" governments (Wright, 1990). Granted, VPC is ultimately responsible to Canadian trade objectives. However, this obligation should not be exploited as a rationale for bluntly overriding concerned local governments. Such an approach should only be justified through a process which ensures all stakeholders are heard and which clearly and judiciously concludes that the national interest outweighs regional interests.

The National Ports Policy and CPCA establish a decision-making framework which ensures federal trade objectives take precedence over provincial, regional, and local interests without providing consistently appropriate means for these stakeholders to be heard. All VPC directors are federally appointed to ensure national trade strategies are supported in Port of Vancouver policy. Consequently, nonfederal objectives are not represented. In addition, this secretive appointment process means that stakeholders outside of federal cabinet and Ports Canada have no opportunity to influence the selection of those empowered to make final decisions on corporate jurisdiction.

The enabling legislation contains one clause that could maintain some decision-making equity in Port of Vancouver management. According to the National Ports Policy, CPCA states that LPCs should support local economic and social objectives (Canada, 1985). Unfortunately, this broad and ambiguous term can be interpreted in many ways. VPC has traditionally claimed fulfillment of this responsibility through its direct employment of over 9000 workers (Duggan, 1990). This point is largely valid, as the port is a major contributor to the regional economy. However, VPC can limit its interpretation of this clause to this specific economic benefit. Consequently, the support of nonfederal harbor management objectives is under the complete discretion of VPC.

CPCA also recognizes the need for stakeholder consultation in port administration, but it fails to specify explicitly how this need should be fulfilled. Section 3(2)(b) requires LPCs to establish consultative bodies to assist in port policy making, planning, and operation. VPC established the Port Economic Development Advisory Council in 1983 to provide occasional consultation in the planning of its port. Membership includes delegates from lower mainland municipal governments, labour, waterfront employers, business, carriers, and terminal operators (Vancouver Port Corporation, 1991a). However, this council is not involved directly in port planning or administration, it excludes the provincial government, and its mandate is restricted to transport issues (Transmode Consultants Inc., 1988).

Recent development disputes compelled VPC to form the Port Municipal Liaison Committee in 1990 as a direct line of contact between the port corporation and its eight neighbouring municipalities. This committee is considered a consistently reliable forum for communication between member municipalities and the port (Reichelt, 1991). However, local government officials are skeptical as to whether the committee can provide leverage to the municipalities when contentious development issues arise (Droettboom, 1990; White, 1991). Consequently, VPC interprets and fulfills the CPCA requirement for consultative bodies in a manner which suits corporate objectives but fails to effectively represent all stakeholders in decision-making.

VPC's legal foundations and administrative policy also enable the corporation to conduct its business in a secretive manner. It is not legally required to hold board meetings in open public forums or to allow for public participation in any of its planning and decision-making processes (Kimpton, 1990). Consequently, all VPC board meetings are held in camera, and publics outside of the national port administrative structure have no reliable means for contacting corporate directors. As a competitive crown corporation, VPC can withhold documents from public consumption (Jordan, 1991). This proprietary right is not justifiable for port corporations, because its actions can have sustained, multiple, and region-wide impacts on adjacent communities. Moreover, VPC is exempt from the federal Environmental Assessment and Review Process (EARP) guidelines and the major requirements of the forthcoming Canadian Environmental Assessment Act (Canada, 1984; 1992). Consequently, developers on Port of Vancouver lands are not legally obliged to submit their proposals to public environmental review.

Progressive Initiatives at the Port of Vancouver

Although it is not legally required to ensure open, responsible, decision making, VPC has undertaken several progressive initiatives in recent years to enhance its relations with nonfederal government and local public interests. The corporation has established a corporate communications department so that citizens may discuss issues with public affairs staff. In addition, it has established an informal arrangement whereby one VPC director or upper level manager is assigned to monitor the status of port-related issues or concerns in a specific municipality abutting the port (White, 1991). VPC has also made some of its internal documents more readily available to interested publics, albeit on a selective basis.

The port corporation has significantly improved its approach to environmental review in recent years. VPC hired an environmental services manager to assist in the formulation and implementation of environmental policy, which includes a corporate environmental appraisal procedure (Vancouver Port Corporation, 1990b). VPC was the first LPC in Canada to adopt such measures. Development proponents on VPC land are required to submit their proposals to an internal environmental appraisal committee, which reviews all proposals for impact significance and consults with VPC directors regarding projected public concerns. In the event that the board determines it desirable to communicate with the public, consultation may be accomplished by: public input through written submissions; public input in camera; or public input through an open forum. These public involvement options are flexible and optional, and their application is subject to the discretion of VPC officials.

Under its new, more open, administration, VPC has occasionally provided opportunities for more extensive stakeholder involvement in decision making. For instance, open-house meetings have been held for environmental review of development proposals, dangerous cargo spill risk assessment, and land-use planning. However, VPC retains full discretion as to whether stakeholders may participate, if at all, in these processes. In essence, VPC's open-house initiatives have been isolated reactions, rather than components of a consistent program, for stakeholder participation. Some effort may be made to forewarn publics about impending projects, but local interest groups have little opportunity to effect change.

VPC has made significant advancements in strategic planning since 1990. Despite no legal obligation to plan comprehensively, VPC initiated a process in 1990 to formulate long-term, land-management policies for its property. Port 2010 is intended to be a 20-year comprehensive land-use and land-management plan for guiding Port of Vancouver development. Port 2010 is a response to corporate perceptions that it is increasingly obliged to confront environmental, urban growth, and public process issues associated with Port of Vancouver land-use competition and controversies (Vancouver Port Corporation, 1991b). Sensitivity to municipal objectives is apparently given high priority, largely because VPC does not want to be neutralized by local municipal opposition (Vancouver Port Corporation, 1990a). Consequently, VPC conducted a process that provided stakeholders, including all government levels and publics, the opportunity to comment on draft plan proposals. The port corporation is using this input in creating its final plan, which is targeted for completion in 1992 (Vancouver Port Corporation, 1992).

Continued VPC commitment to broadly based consultations during, and widespread endorsement of, Port 2010 formulation and implementation should contribute substantially to improved integration of stakeholder objectives in Port of Vancouver decision making and long-term policy. However, no mechanism guarantees continued interest group consultations over the evolution of this admittedly dynamic blueprint. This inadequacy is underscored by VPC's failure to establish an external, broadly based, advisory committee for direct involvement in Port 2010 formulation, implementation, and amendment. In addition, VPC proposes no Port 2010 public review and update program, despite the fact that development priorities and issues change over time.

Coordinated regional planning in the Port of Vancouver has also extended into the environmental management realm in the past two years. VPC signed onto the Burrard Inlet Environmental Action Program (BIEAP), with Environment Canada, Fisheries and Oceans Canada, the British Columbia Ministry of Environment, and GVRD in June 1991. BIEAP is a five-year strategy intended to coordinate agency responsibilities and improve protection and remediation programs for water, habitat, and sediment quality in the inlet and Indian Arm (Burrard Inlet Environmental Action Program, 1992). Initiation of this program is a political acknowledgement that the harbor has serious environmental problems and that concerted governmental commitment, including VPC action, is needed to clean it up. In response to initial funding, primarily from federal Green Plan sources, the program has initiated preliminary programs, which included a public meeting held in June 1992 and circulation of a newsletter. BIEAP may have a major effect on the way VPC approaches environmental planning and decision making. Program administration by a multiagency steering committee, and heightened public disclosure and subsequent awareness of port activities, may oblige VPC to further open up its decision-making process and integrate community and environmental interests more effectively.

In summary the legal and institutional basis for Port of Vancouver management impedes the adoption of measures to ensure VPC adequately and consistently accounts for all stakeholders in decision making. Instead, recent attempts by VPC to establish a more responsible decision-making process have been piecemeal, discretionary reactions to historical events rather than the result of analyses to make the basic management structure the most effective long-term administrative arrangement possible (Droettboom 1990; White 1991). Consequently, Port of Vancouver administration lacks balanced accountability, as local publics and municipal, regional, and provincial stakeholders are not provided with consistent and effective opportunities to participate in decision making.

Analysis: Port of Seattle

Despite recent VPC initiatives, the discretionary and generally sporadic provisions for stakeholder involvement in Port of Vancouver decision making contrast sharply with Port of Seattle administration. Indeed, the legal and institutional framework for Port of Seattle governance requires broadly based participation in virtually all phases of its decision-making process.

The Port of Seattle is mandated to foster both regional economic vitality and a quality life for King County citizens, and the institutional structure is organized to provide these taxpayers with the power to ensure that these goals are fulfilled. First, King County taxpayers elect port district commissioners, so local citizens have direct control over who establishes port policy. Second, port commissioners can be contacted directly by any member of the public. Third, the port must comply with local land-use regulations (Port of Seattle, 1989).

The Washington State Open Public Meetings Act requires that all official commission meetings, including all development decisions, be held in open public forums (Washington, 1989b). In addition, all commission decisions are subject to public review and comment prior to adoption (Port of Seattle, 1989). Citizens can become involved in every major decision-making step by attending meetings, serving on committees, or submitting written comments. Public disclosure laws require that all port district records be made available to interested publics upon request, except in rare cases when disclosure violates privacy or commercial rights (Washington, 1990). The Port of Seattle encourages port district constituents to join a mailing list to receive information on impending projects. The port has also published a brochure which describes the opportunities available to publics for becoming involved in Port of Seattle decision making (Port of Seattle, 1989).

Extensive obligations to open and responsible administration compel the port authority to establish external advisory committees to aid stakeholder consultations during major development planning and construction. These committees ensure broad representation and are involved directly in port planning. For example, the Neighbors' Advisory Council (NAC) was established to monitor proponent compliance to a redevelopment agreement between the developer and two nearby residential districts (Port of Seattle, 1989). Monthly NAC meetings promote information exchange and dispute resolution, and a quarterly newspaper provides updates to the affected communities. Port of Seattle development programs are based on policies designed during a year-long collaboration among port staff, consultants, and the broadly represented Harbor Development Advisory Committee (HDAC)(Port of Seattle, 1986).

The Port of Seattle is subject to applicable environmental impact assessment (EIA) and review legislation. All development policies, plans, and projects are subject to a rigorous set of codified rules for implementing and enforcing the State Environmental Policy Act (SEPA)(Washington, 1983). The City of Seattle is empowered to administer the SEPA review process for Port of Seattle development proposals. This legislation requires public review of all proposals, with the level of public involvement relating to project size.

Externally administered land and water use policies play a major role in the planning and management of developments undertaken by the Port of Seattle. A systematic regulatory framework based on coordinated federal, state, and local government legislation controls virtually all uses along the Washington State coast. Indeed, every port shoreline development must comply with zoning ordinances administered according to this coastal zone management system.

The U.S. Coastal Zone Management Act encourages coastal states to develop and administer comprehensive management programs in exchange for federal funding, technical assistance, and consistency (United States, 1972). To qualify for federal assistance, states must implement and enforce policies for protecting natural resources, managing coastal developments, preserving and enhancing coastal public access and recreation, and involving citizens in decision making.

Washington State developed a federally approved coastal management program through its Shoreline Management Act (SMA)(Washington, 1976, 1989c). SMA regulates development on all of the state's marine waters and associated wetlands, including at a minimum all upland area 200 feet, or 60 meters, from ordinary high water. Local governments must prepare and administer comprehensive shoreline master programs (SMPs) under state supervision.

After numerous public consultations, the Seattle SMP was ratified in 1977 (Hildreth and Johnson, 1985). It establishes overlay districts which specify uses to: protect shoreline ecosystems; encourage water-dependent uses; provide for maximum public use and enjoyment of the city's shoreline; and, preserve, enhance, and increase views of the water and access to the water (Seattle, 1988). Furthermore, developers are required to provide publics with sufficient notice and opportunity for input during the permit approval process.

All Port of Seattle coastal projects must meet Seattle SMP zoning requirements and receive state approval (Port of Seattle, 1989). Proposals must conform to city land-use regulations if situated outside SMP jurisdiction. Port development proponents must follow specific, legally binding, SMP construction standards for impact mitigation and procedural requirements for decision-making fairness. Port development is forbidden on areas designated for conservation and public enjoyment. Consequently, the US coastal zone management program establishes a legally binding, rational, land and water use regulatory framework that ensures the Port of Seattle, other developers, regulators, and publics clearly understand where and how marine industrial projects may be undertaken and where sensitive and valued coastal amenities merit protection.

Summary and Conclusions

The Ports of Vancouver and Seattle are administered according to strikingly different mandates and institutional structures. Vancouver is federally controlled to support national trade objectives while Seattle is governed by a local special purpose district to foster regional economic vitality and a quality life for King County citizens. These basic differences, combined with sharply contrasting approaches to environmental and land-use regulation, have profound implications to the effectiveness with which the two public port authorities integrate urban coastal zone management objectives into decision-making (Table 10.1).

VPC: An Improved Approach in the 1990s

Three years ago, VPC initiated administrative modifications to reduce mounting tensions between the port authority and surrounding communities caused by interjurisdictional development disputes. Since then, VPC has made significant advances in support of its inherent coastal management responsibilities. Official liaison was established with adjacent municipalities. A environmental manager was hired to administer corporate environmental policy, including an EIA process for all Port of Vancouver proposals. Provisions for stakeholder involvement were incorporated into these guidelines, so public participation opportunities in VPC administration became a distinct possibility for the first time. Port 2010 was initiated to facilitate open discussions among all stakeholders regarding the long-term fate of Port of Vancouver development. Furthermore, VPC signed onto BIEAP, a multiagency strategy committed to protection and enhancement of Burrard Inlet.

Table 10.1
Port Authority Accountability: Comparative Evaluation

Vancouver	Seattle
• can override local land-use policies	• must comply with local land-use policies
• decision makers secretly appointed by federal cabinet	• decision makers elected by local taxpayers
• support of nonfederal objectives discretionary	• mandated to support local objectives
• advisory and liaison committees have no direct role in planning	• advisory committees broadly represented, involved directly in planning
• administration more secretive	• administration more open
• public access to information discretionary, selective	• public access to information required, more consistent
• public meetings discretionary, occasional	• public meetings required, frequent
• VPC exempt from federal environmental assessment and public review regulations; enforces own internal procedure; public involvement discretionary	• legally required to submit proposals to externally enforced environmental impact assessment and public review process; public involvement mandatory
• land and harbor uses controlled by VPC; discretionary	• land and harbor uses locally administered according to coordinated federal, state, and local coastal zone management regulations; legally binding

Institutional and Policy Limitations

Despite these commendable initiatives, this analysis reveals that continued reliance to the secretive and unilateral decision-making structures comprising Port of Vancouver management and regulation is inhibiting the effectiveness of VPC's new policy directions. Comparison to the Port of Seattle approach clearly indicates that superior arrangements are available to accommodate local and regional stakeholders in the decision-making process. These institutional mechanisms include: establishment of decision-making power at the local level; requirements for holding all official meetings and development decisions in open public forums; ensuring opportunities for public review and comment of all development decisions and initiatives; public correspondence and information programs; subjection to an externally enforced environmental assessment and public review process; establishment of broadly based, advisory committees for major plans and projects; and coordination of federal, state, and local land and water use objectives. To varying degrees, all such programs are feasible, regardless of the government level at which a public port is administered.

Examination of Port of Seattle administration also underscores that effective and pervasive local accountability measures are not detrimental to the basic commercial motive of such an enterprise. Indeed, Seattle has adopted innovative marketing strategies that have contributed to its strong growth in the lucrative and highly prized container trade market (Nicolai, 1990).

In Vancouver, nation-wide trade responsibilities should not be exploited as a rationale to avoid providing reliable and effective opportunities for publics and nonfederal governments to include their objectives in the port's decision-making process. The port corporation should follow the example of port authorities such as Seattle by opening its administrative process to the publics and adopting formal measures for broadly based consultation. Institutional reform, whereby municipal and provincial government representation is established at the policy level without removing the federal government's majority power, should also be investigated. Furthermore, additional effort should be directed to ensuring long-term commitment to open, integrated port planning through Port 2010 and BIEAP. These initiatives provide the means to enforce VPC's local, regional, and environmental obligations through coordinated government suasion and increased public disclosure and awareness.

Recommendations

Analysis reveals that improvements are necessary to the Port of Vancouver institutional design in order to promote modern urban harbor management principles. Balanced decision-making accountability is becoming more of a policy issue with port and community tensions increasing and with greater public attention being directed toward waterfront activities. It is necessary for VPC and the federal government to intensify and expedite their shifts toward more responsible management of the Port of Vancouver. More importantly, adopting the following measures could improve overall efficiency and reduce long-term decision-making uncertainty, as the full range of factors and interests could be more appropriately assessed before conflicts or unnecessary adverse impacts are experienced. Adopting the measures proposed below could contribute to establishment of an effective, long-term, solution to existing institutional inadequacies without unduly disturbing the administrative structures for supporting national trade objectives.

Board Reconstitution

The VPC Board of Directors should be restructured so that two of the seven seats are occupied by municipally elected representatives and one seat is held by a member of the BC legislative assembly (MLA). The local government representatives should be appointed by the councils of their respective municipalities, with the two applicable municipalities to be determined on a rotating basis by agreement among the eight municipal councils abutting the port. The MLA should be appointed by provincial cabinet. The four other directors, including the chair and the vice-chair, should continue to be appointed by the federal government.

Corporate Policy Package

VPC should adopt a policy package to broaden and strengthen its accountability to local stakeholders. The following measures should be taken:

- VPC Should Establish a Port Development Advisory Committee. This committee should replace the existing Port Economic Development Advisory Council. The 20 to 30 member committee should include representatives from provincial, regional, and municipal government, business, industry, labor, regional universities, and environmental and civic organizations. This committee should be appointed and funded by VPC in place of the previous council. It should convene and consult directly with the VPC Board of Directors and senior staff regarding any port-related issues on a quarterly basis, particularly long-term development options.

  Initially, this committee should work closely with and assist port staff in the formulation of VPC's Port 2010 development and management plan. After the completion of this initiative, the committee should remain intact as a consultative body to VPC regarding plan implementation and other port-related issues which may arise.

- VPC Should be Subject to Federal EARP Guidelines. Federal environmental assessment legislation should be amended so that crown corporations such as VPC are subject to the same environmental assessment and public review guidelines as other federal authorities. This would remove VPC's discretionary power in this context and establish more objectivity in the determination of impact significance and the need for public involvement.

- VPC Should Adopt Stricter and More Consistent Public Notification Guidelines. VPC should discard its flexible, discretionary policy and replace it with guidelines that state explicitly the measures to be taken to ensure that all potentially affected parties have sufficient notice regarding all development projects on VPC property. Measures should include: a corporate communications program whereby publics can be included on a mailing list to receive information on impending projects; and a one-month prior notice policy or immediate public notification of all development proposals with newspaper advertisements and conspicuous signage at potential construction sites.

- VPC Should Adopt a Public Access to Information Policy. This initiative should require disclosure of all VPC board decisions, by-laws, policies, guidelines, resolutions, and revisions upon public request. All VPC records should be made available to the public at an in-house library, or by mail, except for those few exceptions when disclosure would violate privacy or commercial rights.

- VPC Should Adopt an "Open Door" Policy. This policy should require VPC to provide prior notification of all official board meetings, and all such meetings should be held in open public forums. VPC should also ensure that all major corporate planning initiatives, development programs, and studies are subject to public review and are accompanied by public meetings prior to VPC approval and implementation. Public meetings could be held in the open house format adopted for the recreation and tanker traffic risk studies, in which meetings were held at different locales in the affected region. However, future programs should focus more on providing effective prior notification and information to the surrounding community so that concerned citizens do not feel left out of the process.

- VPC Should Adopt a Port 2010 Public Outreach Program. As part of its planning program, VPC should adopt and implement a program whereby the public can gain information regarding Port 2010 progress. Mechanisms could include telephone and mailing list services which provide interested publics with planning updates and future times and locations of open house or other VPC public discussion forums. A regional network of information displays could be set up to present citizens with general information and pamphlets containing Port 2010 background material and phone numbers and addresses.

- VPC Should Adopt a Plan Review and Update Program. Upon completion and adoption of the Port 2010 blueprint, VPC should establish an annual program of plan review and revision by port staff, the advisory committee, and the board of directors. Opportunities for involvement by the general public should be made available during this annual exercise.

BIEAP Funding

The federal and provincial governments, as well as partner agencies, should ensure that all Burrard Inlet Environmental Action Program requirements are met to the maximum extent possible. Initiatives should focus on harmonizing regional coastal and environmental management policies with the assistance of such potentially effective tools as VPC's Port 2010 program. BIEAP success depends on solid financial commitment and cooperation by the signatories. Adequate economic investment would ensure BIEAP has sufficient administrative capabilities to compel VPC to make the necessary commitments to Burrard Inlet environmental management.

References

Blomberg, G. (1990) Personal communications with senior manager, Environmental Planning Section, Port of Seattle, WA: Engineering Department.

Burrard Inlet Environmental Action Program (1992) *Annual Report: 1991/1992*, Vancouver, BC: Burrard Inlet Environmental Action Program.

Canada (1984) *Environmental Assessment and Review Process Guidelines Order*, Canada Gazette SOR/84-467.

_____ (1985) *Canada Ports Corporation Act*, RSC C-9.

Canada, House of Commons (1992) *Bill C-13: Canadian Environmental Assessment Act*, Third session, 34th Parliament, 40-41 Elizabeth II, Ottawa, Ont: Supply and Services Canada.

Droettboom, T. (1990) *The Port of Vancouver and the Greater Vancouver Community: An Agenda for Improvement,* Burnaby, BC: Greater Vancouver Regional District.

Duggan, B. (1990) Personal communication with director, Corporate Communications, Vancouver, BC: Vancouver Port Corporation.

Greater Vancouver Regional District (1990) Memorandum from GVRD Development Services to Port (VPC)/Municipal Liaison Committee: "Consolidated list of municipal issues," Burnaby, BC: Greater Vancouver Regional District.

Hershman, M.J. (1988) "Harbor management: A new role for the public port," in Hershman, M.J. (ed.), *Urban Ports and Harbor Management,* Washington, DC: Taylor & Francis.

Hershman, M.J., and Kory, M (1988) "Federal port policy: Retrenchment in the 1980s," in Hershman, M.J. (ed.), *Urban Ports and Harbor Management,* Washington, DC: Taylor & Francis.

Hildreth, R.G. and Johnson, R.W. (1985) "CZM in California, Oregon, and Washington," *Natural Resources Journal,* Vol. 25(Jan): 103-65.

Historical Society of Seattle and King County (1986) *Portage: The Port of Seattle Celebrates 75 Years of Service,* Seattle, WA: Historical Society of Seattle and King County.

Jordan, A.J. (1991) Personal communications with manager, Environmental Services, Port Development Department, Vancouver, B.C.: Vancouver Port Corporation.

Kimpton, R. (1990) Personal communications with internal legal counsel, November, Vancouver, BC: Vancouver Port Corporation.

Nicolai, P. (1990) Personal communication with senior property and acquisition manager, August, Port of Seattle, WA: Marine Terminals Department.

Olson, D.J. (1988) "Public port accountability: A framework for evaluation," in Hershman, M.J. (ed.), *Urban Ports and Harbor Management,* Washington, DC: Taylor & Francis.

Port of Seattle (1986) *Harbor Development Strategy*, Seattle, WA: Port of Seattle.

_____ (1989) *Our Doors are Open: A Citizen's Guide to Public Participation in Port of Seattle Development*, Seattle, WA: Port of Seattle.

_____ (1990a) *The Seattle Harbor*, Seattle, WA: Port of Seattle.

_____ (1990b) *1989 Annual Report*, Seattle, WA: Port of Seattle.

_____ (1990c) *Port of Seattle Mission and Goals Statement*, Seattle, WA: Port of Seattle.

Reichelt, R. (1991) Personal communication with director, October 30, City of Port Moody, BC: Parks and Recreation Department.

Seattle (1988) *Seattle Shoreline Master Program*, SMC Ch. 23.56, 23.60.

Transmode Consultants Inc. (1988) *Ports Policy in British Columbia*, Victoria, BC: BC Ministry of Transportation and Highways.

United States (1972) *Coastal Zone Management Act*, USPL 92-583.

Vancouver Port Corporation (1989) *1988 Statistics*, Vancouver BC: Vancouver Port Corporation.

_____ (1990a) *Port 2010: Phase I: A Framework for Consultation*, Vancouver, BC: Vancouver Port Corporation.

_____ (1990b) *Environmental Appraisal Procedures*, Vancouver, BC: Vancouver Port Corporation.

_____ (1991a) *Fact Sheets 1-10*, Vancouver, BC: Vancouver Port Corporation.

_____ (1991b) *Port of Vancouver International Port Handbook 1991-92*, Norfolk, UK: Charter International.

_____ (1992) *The Port and You*, Vancouver, BC: Vancouver Port Corporation.

Washington, Washington Department of Ecology (1976) *Washington State Coastal Zone Management Program*, Olympia, WA: Washington Department of Ecology.

Washington (1983) *State Environmental Policy Act,* RCW Ch. 43.21C.

_____ (1989a) *Port District Act,* RCW Ch. 53.04 et seq.

_____ (1989b) *Open Public Meetings Act,* RCW Ch. 42.30.

_____ (1989c) *Shoreline Management Act,* RCW Ch. 90.58.

Washington, Washington Research Council (1990) *Washington's Public Ports,* Olympia, WA: Washington Research Council.

White, R. (1991) Personal communication with assistant planning director, October 30, City of North Vancouver: BC: Development Services Department.

Wright, R. (1990) Personal communication with director, Property Administration, February 9, Vancouver, BC: Vancouver Port Corporation.

Chapter 11

Oldman River Dam

M. Sundstrom
University of Lethbridge

Overview

This study deals with the continuing effort of provincial and federal governments to define their respective jurisprudence and roles in the field of environmental issues, with special reference to the case of the Oldman Dam,
southern Alberta. The case involves the use of institutional arrangements,
such as environmental impact assessment, and appeals to the Supreme
Court of Canada by citizen groups concerned about the need for and effects of the construction of the dam as well as the adequacy of its pre-pro-
ject and other studies and procedures. Fundamentally the study provides
insight into the politics of resource development and the environmental
challenges associated with mega-projects of wide governmental and public
interest, such as the Oldman Dam. In the context of the foregoing objectives, five topics are covered.

1) A summary of the regional significance of irrigated agriculture and the
history of irrigation development in Alberta;

2) A chronology of events associated with the debate, decision, and construction of the dam;

3) A review of the highlights of the January 1992 Supreme Court of Canada
decision on the dam;

4) The highlights of the relations between the Oldman River Dam and the
new federal EIA legislation; and

5) Some considerations notably about the applicability of the "Corporatism
model" to the interpretation of the case and associated events.

Introduction

The Supreme Court decision on January 23, 1992 represents an important step in the continuing effort of provincial and federal governments to define their respective jurisprudence and roles in the field of environmental issues. As a result of an appeal by a citizens group [Friends of the Oldman River V. Canada (Minister of Transport et al.)], the Court ruled that the federal government has responsibility for conducting environmental reviews and is required to adhere to its own Guidelines Order as part of the Environmental Assessment and Review process to address environmental concerns prior to the approval of provincial mega-projects. The Supreme Court decision established an important precedent which environmental groups interpreted as a successful effort in clarifying the federal role in conducting environmental assessment reviews. This, however, puts additional pressure on provincial and federal governments to work out a cooperative strategy for resolving environmental issues, since unilateral action by the federal government would certainly result in a strong response from the provinces. In fact, throughout the 1980s, changes in the legislative framework and societal attitudes towards the environment have required all levels of government to approach development issues differently.

The new framework for the appeal by a citizens group was put in place with the passage of the Charter of Rights and the Constitutional Act of 1982 (Cairns, 1992). Societal implications of the Charter of Rights are continually being defined by the courts. Rising awareness of environmental issues by Canadians has led to increased use of the Charter of Rights and the courts to contest a wide range of environmental concerns, such as those involved in the construction of the Oldman Dam for irrigation purposes (Skogstad and Kopas, 1992).

Regional Importance of Irrigated Agriculture and History of Irrigation Development in Southern Alberta

The first large irrigation projects in southern Alberta were undertaken early in the twentieth century, and by the 1950s Alberta had emerged as a Canadian leader in irrigated agriculture with a variety of specialty crops, livestock feeding enterprises, dairying and a domestic sugar beet industry built around the availability of irrigation. The situation described by Raby (1965) in a paper on irrigation development in Alberta in the early 1960s has remained largely unchanged over the past thirty years. Much of the acreage currently devoted to irrigation is utilized for feedgrains and livestock feed production, since markets and processing facilities for large volumes of specialty crops are lacking. The feedlot finishing industry supports a meat packing industry in the region and contributes to diversity, stable farm incomes and agricultural prosperity for southern Alberta. Only four per cent of Alberta's arable land is irrigated, but it accounts for 12 per cent of the gross value of agricultural production in the province (Sanderson, 1982). Since agriculture is the dominant element in the regional economy, the multiplier effect of agricultural investment is evident throughout southern Alberta. Prosperity in southern Alberta is thus closely linked to and dependent upon the performance of the region's agricultural industries, including that which is irrigation-based.

The city of Lethbridge, the regional supply and marketing center for the industry, advertises itself as the "Irrigation Capital of Canada." The 1991 census of Canada statistics indicate that, in 1990, Alberta accounted for 63.8 per cent of irrigated land in the nation (458,000 out of 718,000 hectares). However, the amount of land under irrigation in any given year can vary considerably due to weather variations and market conditions (Raby, 1965; Sanderson, 1982). Most of Alberta's irrigated agriculture is located in 13 operating irrigation districts in southern Alberta, where a long growing season and abundant sunshine make irrigation attractive for crop and livestock production. Although all census divisions in Alberta recorded some land under irrigation, census division two in which Lethbridge is located (Figure 11.1) accounted for the largest provincial share with 280,219 hectares (71.1 per cent) in 1980. In the same year, census division one in southeastern Alberta had almost 53,000 hectares in irrigated agriculture (13.5 per cent) and census division three in southwestern Alberta, where the Oldman River dam is located, claimed a further 18,200 hectares (4.6 per cent). However, only a small percentage of farmers in the province utilize irrigation. In 1980 there were 4,159 farms with irrigation representing 7.2 per cent of the total number of Alberta farms (58,056). Thus a small number of farmers account for the intensive specialty crop and livestock agriculture associated with irrigated farming in Alberta.

The present significance and characteristics of irrigated agriculture is best understood in an historical context. Small scale irrigation schemes were undertaken in southern Alberta in the 1880s. By the beginning of the twentieth century the Canadian Pacific Railroad and the Mormon Church were engaged in more ambitious projects. As larger scale projects were developed, the necessity for new legislation and additional capital became apparent, resulting in more provincial government involvement, and enactment of the Alberta Irrigation Districts Act in 1915. Under this legislation irrigation districts were granted quasi-municipal powers which allowed them to issue debentures to raise capital, thereby making a transition from the commercial to the district phase of irrigation development in the pro-

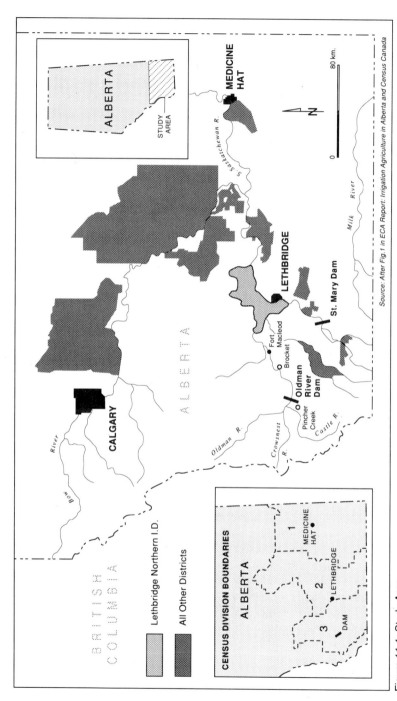

Figure 11.1: Study Area

vince (Smith, 1978). In 1919 the Lethbridge Northern Irrigation District was formed, financed by a bond issue guaranteed by the Alberta Government. When the headworks construction for the district had been completed four years later, the distribution system for the Lethbridge Northern Irrigation District was in place, remaining largely unchanged until rehabilitation occurred in the 1980s.

The government-district phase of irrigation development in Alberta began in 1942 with the Meek Report recommending construction of the St. Mary project in order to establish rights to the Canadian share of international waters and to accommodate the return of war veterans (Smith, 1978). In the 1940s and 1950s major irrigation projects, such as the St. Mary river dam and the South Saskatchewan river dam, were planned and built with provincial and federal government financial support. Negotiations between the federal and provincial government resulted in an agreement in 1973 that transferred all responsibility for planning, management and construction of irrigation works to the province. Previously, responsibility for some projects had remained under federal jurisdiction or were shared with the province. Following this agreement, the Alberta government acquired all responsibility for irrigation works in the province, and after 1974 all irrigation districts in Alberta came under the 1968 Irrigation Act.

In the decades following construction of the St. Mary and South Saskatchewan river dams, numerous benefits flowed from the expansion of irrigated agriculture, notably near the headwaters of a number of tributaries of the South Saskatchewan River and where the growing season is suitable for a wide range of irrigated crops. The importance of agriculture to the economy and periodic droughts in the 1970s and 1980s reinforced the case for irrigation expansion to stabilize this important sector of southern Alberta's economy. With new powers over irrigation, new sources of natural resource income, and a willingness by the Alberta government to undertake additional irrigation projects and underwrite construction costs, it was only a matter of time before further irrigation development occurred. The Oldman River Dam at the Three Rivers site (Oldman, Castle and Crowsnest rivers) provided the opportunity to undertake a major water development project in southern Alberta as part of water resource planning in the Oldman River Basin. A lengthy period of debate followed the initial announcement of plans for onstream storage. The exchange intensified when the final decision to proceed with construction was made, and continued with legal and other challenges during construction of the dam.

Debate, Decision and Construction

The chronology of events related to the Oldman River Dam is summarized in Table 11.1. The initial provincial planning studies of the Oldman River Basin, known as Phase I studies, were undertaken with the purpose of determining current and estimated future water use requirements, available sources of supply and the best manner in which to ensure that supply could satisfy demand (Environment Council of Alberta, 1979). Phase I studies were undertaken in 1974 by the Planning Division of Alberta Environment through its creation of a Technical Advisory Committee, which gathered information from federal and provincial departments, planning commissions, industries and municipalities in the region.

Three major conclusions resulted from Phase I studies: (i) flow regulation reservoirs or onstream sites are economical if they provide ample water supply for irrigation purposes; (ii) the current water shortages which were inhibiting the expansion of irrigation in the basin were mainly due to the deterioration of distribution facilities in the irrigation districts; and (iii) based on existing water requirements, the current water management systems did not provide an assured water supply (Environment Council of Alberta, 1979).

These three conclusions became the focal point for public discussions and debate. Onstream storage for the Oldman river proved to be the most difficult issue, with opponents pointing out that if rehabilitation and better management were undertaken there would be no need for onstream storage. Supporters of onstream storage argued that even if the other problems were addressed, there would still be insufficient water to ensure security of supply in drought years and to allow for expansion of irrigated land base.

In response to initial public reaction and numerous questions about the cost and feasibility of various sites, the Government of Alberta established the Oldman River Basin Management Committee to undertake Phase II studies. A number of consulting firms were hired to do comprehensive research, address social impacts, answer specific questions related to reservoir sedimentation and irrigation efficiencies, and provide an economic analysis on the construction of onstream storage. Nine reservoir sites were evaluated by the Oldman River Basin Management Committee for the purpose of selecting the most suitable sites for onstream storage. The Brocket site, the Fort MacLeod site and the Three Rivers site were identified as the most suitable of the nine sites, with the Three Rivers site being preferred because it had the lowest estimated storage costs (Environment Council of Alberta, 1979).

Table 11.1
Chronology of Events: The Oldman River Dam

1974	Federal-provincial agreement transferring responsibility for planning, management and construction of irrigation facilities to the Province of Alberta. Phase I Studies commence.
1976	Development plans for the Oldman River announced by the Province with a number of onstream storage options being presented. Oldman River Basin Management Committee undertakes Phase II studies.
1978	Report of the Oldman River Basin Management Committee presented. Environment Council of Alberta given responsibility to inquire into water management in the Oldman River basin and make recommendations to the Province, Public hearings conducted at eight centers in Southern Alberta.
1978	Environment Council of Alberta report is presented with recommendation against onstream storage on the Oldman River but gives priority to rehabilitation of the Lethbridge Northern Irrigation District.
1980	Province announces intention to building a dam on the Oldman River, but does not make a decision about a particular site, pending negotiations with the Peigan Indian Band about a possible reserve (Brocket) site.
1984	Premier Lougheed announces decision to build a dam at the Three Rivers site near Pincer Creek.
1986	Construction of the service roads and infrastructure for the dam begins.
1987	Friends of the Oldman River Society incorporated.
1988	Construction of the Oldman River dam at the Three Rivers site commences.
1991	Oldman River dam filling begins. Federal Environment Assessment Panel provides a report on the safety of the dam, indicating that the structure will withstand a catastrophic flood or major earthquake.
1992	Supreme Court of Canada finds in favour of the Friends of the Oldman River Society. Federal Environmental Assessment Panel completes its report recommending decommissioning of the dam, and Bill C-13 the Canadian Environmental Assessment Act is passed.

Source: *Various newspaper reports, government documents and Alberta Wilderness Newsletter.*

Just as the Oldman River Basin Management Committee was reporting in the summer of 1978, the Environment Council of Alberta (ECA) was given a mandate to hold public hearings in southern Alberta and to inquire into conservation, management and utilization of water resources within the Oldman River Basin. Throughout the fall of 1978 the four member ECA panel held public hearings at eight locations in southern Alberta. When their report was submitted in 1979 it contained 74 recommendations. The most controversial recommendation related to the issue of onstream storage:

> "The Environment Council is convinced that an onstream dam is not required at this time, nor in the foreseeable future. All the suitable and economically irrigable acres north of the Oldman River can be serviced by offstream facilities."
> (Environment Council of Alberta, 1979, p.196.)

Instead of recommending onstream storage, the Council recommended that:

> "The district rehabilitation program be the first priority for water management in the Oldman River Basin and be designed to reach completion no later than 1995."
> (Environment Council of Alberta, 1979, p.192)

Additional recommendations of the ECA covered many aspects of irrigation in the Oldman River basin from water allocation and quality to market development and watershed management especially those with financial implications. These include the cost-sharing formula for rehabilitation projects, which normally allocates 86 per cent of the benefits (and costs) to the province and the nation, and 14 per cent to the irrigation district. The Council recommended that this be gradually changed to a 75/25 ratio (Recommendations 46 and 47). The second controversial recommendation (Number 50) was that a wholesale price for water be charged to some of the irrigation districts in order to emphasize the value of water and ensure conservation efforts. The issue of pricing water resources is currently a part of the debate in the proposed new provincial water act (Duckworth, 1992). In terms of infrastructure, additional offstream storage to serve the Lethbridge Northern Irrigation district was planned and funded by the province. The need for these expenditures was widely recognized and the province proceeded with these improvements, while postponing the decision of onstream storage. The province, however, did indicate in 1980 that construction of a dam on the Oldman River would probably proceed over the next decade, with the Three River site being the most likely choice for a dam (Morton, 1980).

Closure of the Lethbridge Northern Irrigation system during critical growing periods in the summer of 1977, 1979, 1983 and 1984 due to low water levels at an offstream storage site contributed significantly to the argument of supporters of onstream storage. In early August, 1984, following reports that the region was experiencing its worst drought since 1910, the Premier of the province, Peter Lougheed, toured southern Alberta and announced plans for the construction of a 200 million dollar earth filled dam at the Three Rivers site on the Oldman River (Cernetig, 1992). Reaction from farmers and ranchers who would be displaced by flooding for the reservoir was understandably negative. On the other hand, farmers in the Lethbridge Northern Irrigation District and the municipalities dependent upon the river for their water supplies were delighted at the prospects of onstream storage and a more reliable water supply.

Following this announcement, early conflicts over irrigation development were reignited (Rood and Jankunis, 1988). Many of the arguments of participants were similar to those presented at ECA hearings but there were new issues and new participants. A native group called the Lonefighters, and a coalition of environmental opponents to onstream storage, known as the Friends of the Oldman River Society (FOR), became outspoken critics of the decision to build the Oldman River dam. While membership in both groups was limited, the involvement of Andy Russell, a nationally known naturalist and author with FOR, contributed to a growing national awareness of adverse environmental consequences of the project. Each group pursued different directions in their opposition to the dam, with some liaison between the two organizations. The Lonefighters attempted to construct a diversion ditch on the Oldman River, which if completed, would have cut off water supply to the Lethbridge Northern Irrigation District's weir. FOR actively pursued their opposition through the courts and eventually took their case to the Supreme Court of Canada. The province stalled these legal maneuvers and continued with the dam construction program in the course of the controversy.

As construction neared completion, questions about safety of the structure were raised. However, in November, 1990, a Federal Environment Assessment Panel was established: (i) to review safety aspects; and, (ii) to make an environmental assessment of the project. An interim report was issued in the summer of 1991 in which the panel concluded that the design and construction of the dam met high standards which took account of the possibility of a catastrophic flood and a severe earthquake (Wilson, 1991). The final report dealing with the environmental assessment was released in 1992.

In summary, the need for onstream storage on the Oldman River was one of the key questions during the prolonged debate. Environmental issues and related socio-economic impacts were also raised by participants at public meetings. In the background were such questions as the need for meeting the annual delivery volume at the Saskatchewan border under an apportionment agreement with that province, and the potential export of water to the United States. The decision to build the Oldman River dam became an emotionally charged issue, dividing communities such as Pincher Creek and giving rise to frustration for all those who took a position either for or against the construction of the dam (Alberta, 1987).

The Supreme Court Decision

The Supreme Court decision on January 23, 1992 [Friends of the Oldman River Society v. Canada (Minister of Transport)] represented a landmark in the development of Canadian environmental law (Hanebury, 1992). The judgement supported the position of environmentalists that the federal government had a responsibility to conduct an environmental assessment and that the Oldman River dam project fell under mandatory Guideline Orders since its construction would interfere with navigation, thus making the Minister of Transport responsible for initiating a review of the project

Provinces have historically had jurisdiction in the field of resource development and had been unchallenged in projects until the 1980s. Although the province of Alberta felt it had legally complied with both provincial and federal requirements for environmental assessment in the Oldman River dam case, the province may not have been fully aware of the importance of the new rules of operation in a post-Charter legal setting. The Charter allows individuals to ask the courts for interpretations of cases in which the rights of individuals are involved. Success in courts over the Oldman River dam case in Alberta added to the perception that courts offer the best option for environmental groups wishing to challenge provincial megaprojects. Furthermore, the Guideline Orders provided a powerful tool for opponents as it outlines in great detail the steps and procedures required in the Environmental Assessment and Review Process (EARP). Under the Act there is a legislatively entrenched regulatory scheme requiring approval of the initiating department which in this case was the Department of Transport. Only one of the judges dissented from the decision, thereby adding to the importance of this precedent.

The court ruling helped clarify to provinces and the federal government the preeminent role of the latter in environmental matters and the importance of following procedures of the Guideline Orders. Responsibility of the federal government for assessment of environmental impacts arising when megaprojects infringe on any one of a number of areas of federal jurisdiction was clearly stated. This means there is potential for conflict with virtually every province when environmental concerns are pitted against resource development projects. The Rafferty-Alameda dam project in Saskatchewan, the Great Whale development in northern Quebec and the Kenamo diversion in British Columbia have all made the national news as a result of court action over environmental issues. In fact, legal challenges threaten the ability of provinces to undertake many resource development projects (Day and Quinn, 1992). It is almost certain that legal challenges will continue until some co-operative arrangement between the two senior levels of government is made which addresses this dilemma.

Similarly, conflicts can also emerge between provinces over river basin jurisdiction. Provincial water development projects may pit provinces against other jurisdictions when development in one province may have adverse impacts in another province or in a foreign country. This may occur over river basin developments or apportionment agreements between provinces where projects in one province may alter flow levels or affect water quality or flood control in another jurisdiction. Proposals for the export of large volumes of water from one of the western provinces could also trigger a series of legal maneuvers which might involve the federal government.

Another issue arising from the court decision was the broad interpretation that the Supreme Court placed on the environment. The Supreme Court decision noted that the environment involves more than the biophysical sphere, and includes all that is around us, meaning that socio-economic issues associated with development must be taken into account. In addition, the federal government has responsibilities in a number of fields that cannot be entrusted to the provincial government. This includes such things as transportation and navigation, fisheries, Indians and Indian lands. This increases the range of issues over which environmental challenges can be made. In such cases of overlapping jurisdiction the two senior levels of government must resolve the problem through co-operation and negotiations. This will require a delicate balancing of the positions of both parties as well as the willingness to compromise. Failing this, the ultimate decision is likely to be a court decision, which may be interpreted as a failure in the political process.

Final Report of the Environmental Assessment Panel

As noted previously, a six member panel was appointed in November, 1990 under the federal EARP with a mandate to make recommendations on the design and safety of the Oldman River dam, the significance of potential environmental and socio-economic effects of the dam and its operation and options for mitigating these effects. An interim report in the spring of 1991 concluded that the dam met safety standards and could withstand earthquakes and catastrophic floods.

The final May, 1992 report concluded that the construction and operation of the dam would result in substantial environmental social and economic costs. This provided the rationale for 24 recommendations. The first recommended the decommissioning of the dam by opening the low level diversion tunnels to allow unimpeded flow of this river (FEARO, 1992: 5).

A second alternative was presented if this recommendation was not acceptable. This alternative recommended conditional approval with stringent conditions; an environment management committee for mitigating major environmental impacts, and, an agreement between the proponent (Alberta) and the Peigan Indian; lack of adherence to any of the foregoing recommendations would lead to decommissioning the dam.

The panel's first recommendation brought a negative response from both the province and the federal government. Clearly the federal government does not want to get involved in an inter-jurisdictional conflict with Alberta, or any other province over resource issues. Thus, it is likely that negotiations with the Alberta government will occur to ensure that the alternative recommendations involving mitigation of the detrimental environmental effects, an environmental management committee, and negotiating an agreement with the Peigan are pursued.

Recommendation 20, dealing with the economic assessment of the project, also proved contentious. The panel examined this particular point in detail and noted:

> "As far as the Panel understands, the Province based its economic conclusions on an application of benefit cost analysis which was explicitly contrary to Treasury Board and other accepted guidelines" (FEARO, 1992: 28).

The panel had two major criticisms of the benefit cost analysis. They questioned the inclusion of secondary and spin-off benefits, which the panel maintains should not be included in the benefit category. The panels argued that these benefits would occur from any regional investment of this magnitude and should therefore not be included in the calculations of benefits. It was also noted that the discount rate used for justifying the project had a major bearing on the outcome of the analysis. Veeman (1988) had previously criticized the benefit cost analysis used by the province at several public forums, maintaining that inclusion of secondary benefits was not appropriate. In addition, Veeman observed that some of the crop return scenarios were based on very optimistic outlooks for future crop prices.

Economic issues were central to arguments presented by the Alberta government during the prolonged debate on benefits of further irrigation development. Ministers from Agriculture and Environment involved in the decision for construction of the dam and onstream storage have consistently used benefit cost analysis of the Oldman River Dam project to justify the expenditures. Ken Kowalski, Alberta's Minister of Public Works, restated that position in a recent news story on the Environmental Review Panel Report. Criticism of the technical approach to the province's economic case only increased the suspicion that the economic justification of the megaproject was flawed.

The Oldman River Dam and the Canadian Environmental Assessment Act (Bill C-13)

The history of the Canadian Environmental Assessment Act reflects difficulties such legislation presents for federal-provincial relations. Initially this bill was proposed in order to correct what was perceived by the federal government as some serious flaws in the federal Guidelines Order and began its life as Bill C-78. It was reintroduced as C-13 in May, 1991, passed third reading in Parliament in March, 1992 and received Senate approval in June, 1992. When Bill C-13 is proclaimed it will become the law of the land on environmental issues and the legislative framework for environmentalists and development proponents. Several sections of the legislation represent important efforts at clarifying procedures to ensure that the problems arising in previous court challenges are addressed prior to project approvals.

The Canadian Environmental Assessment Act makes a concerted attempt at ensuring the assessment is completed prior to undertaking any work [section 50 (1)]. The assessment should be undertaken as early as practical in the planning stage [section 54 (1)] of the proposal. Had this legislation been in place and been adhered to by provincial government, the Oldman River Dam might have never been approved.

Section 61 of the Act makes provision for the establishment of an agency to be known as the Canadian Environmental Assessment Agency to advise and assist the Minister in performing the duties and functions of the legislation. This could play an important and constructive role given some of the responsibilities listed in section 62 of the Act.

The five functions of the Agency are:

> "(a) to administer the environment assessment process and any other requirements and procedures established by this Act and the regulations; (b) to promote uniformity and harmonization in the assessment of environmental effects across Canada at all levels of government; (c) to promote or conduct research in matters of environmental assessment and to encourage the development of environmental assessment techniques and practices, including testing programs, alone or in cooperation with other agencies or organizations; (d) to promote environmental assessment in a manner that is consistent with the purposes of this Act; and (e) to ensure an opportunity for public participation in the environmental assessment process."

Implementation of this agency function could help avoid some of the criticism the Oldman River Dam Assessment Panel raised about environmental impacts and the benefit cost analysis employed by the Alberta government.

On the other hand, sections of the legislation could weaken the scope for environmental opponents or require legal action to establish precedents. The provision for ministerial discretion [section 43 (1)] allows for substituting another body for a review panel, which could be a federal authority or the government of a province. This is a major departure from the Guidelines Order which does not allow this alternative. While this will reduce duplication of efforts, the problem in reviews conducted in Alberta and Saskatchewan was that the assessment process was not viewed as an open impartial inquiry. While it may have been necessary to include these provisions in the legislation in order to facilitate passage and reduce federal-provincial conflict, it weakens the position of environmental organizations which increasingly depend upon access to the courts and the power of the Guideline Orders to make provinces more environmentally accountable for their megaprojects. The application of the Act will require interpretations, and possibly some legal challenges to clarify under what circumstances substitution will be possible.

The thrust of the legislation is to provide a co-operative arrangement between the federal and provincial governments over issues that clearly affect both jurisdictions. This assumes that the model of co-operative federalism becomes the standard for resolving interjurisdictional conflicts rather than the use of the courts. However, since the Charter was passed, Canadians have increasingly become accustomed to utilizing the courts to assert their claims against governments. This strategy has been successfully adopted by individuals and groups concerned with environmental issues. The environment assessment process has been given considerable weight by the courts in attempts to address environmental concerns. It remains to be seen therefore whether the co-operative federalism approach can accommodate the pressures exerted by an increasingly aware public that places high priority on environmental assessment impacts arising from megaproject developments.

The Corporatism model, which maintains that there is a limited elite group with access to the decision-making process, may closely describe how decisions relating to the Oldman River Dam were perceived. Under this model certain groups and individuals become marginalized or largely ignored in the decision-making process. This fits into the "business as usual" approach that is increasingly being challenged as a result of greater societal concern for the broad range of environmental issues. Redress through environmental assessment and the legal system appear to have been an effective means for environmental groups to challenge conventional ways of doing business. In the Oldman River case the efforts of these challenges remain to be demonstrated.

There will obviously be a testing period associated with the Canadian Environmental Assessment Act, as provinces, the federal government and interested third parties become familiar with the new rules of the game, and attempt to utilize those rules in ways that address their particular agendas. Some politically contentious cases still must be resolved under the rules that existed prior to the implementation of the Canadian Environmental Assessment Act. Environmental reviews can no longer be treated as public relation exercises in provincial megaprojects planned for the 1990s. The history of the Oldman River Dam project showed that both provincial and federal laws can be ignored and/or subverted to give the appearance that proper evaluation has occurred. Such may not be the case in the future. The case for a stronger environmental review process is supported by the fact that public funding is typically involved either for supporting infrastructure or actual construction. Accountability requires a more open, forthcoming approach to resource development projects in a Canadian society that places high value on environmental issues.

References

Canadian Environmental Assessment Act (1992) Bill C-13, Third Session, Thirty-fourth Parliament, March 19.

Cairns, A.C. (1992) *Charter Versus Federalism: The Dilemmas of Constitutional Reform*, Montreal: McGill-Queens University Press.

Cernetig, M. (1992) "The high cost of making a prairie bloom," *The Globe and Mail,* June 5.

Day, J.C. and Quinn, F. (1992) *Water Diversion and Export: Learning from Canadian Experience,* Canadian Association of Geographers, Public Issues Committee, Number 1, Waterloo, Ontario: Department of Geography Publication Series Number 36, University of Waterloo.

Duckworth, B. (1992) "Making the water last," *The Western Producer,* April 6.

Environment Council of Alberta (1979) *Management of Water Resources within the Oldman River Basin: Report and Recommendations,* Edmonton: Environment Council of Alberta.

Federal Environmental Assessment Review Office (1992) *Oldman River Dam: Report of the Environmental Assessment Panel,* Ottawa: Minister of Environment.

Hanebury, J. (1992) "The Supreme Court Decision in Oldman River Dam: More pieces in the puzzle of jurisdiction over the environment," *Resources,* The Newsletter of the Canadian Institute of Resource Law, No. 37 (Winter), p.6.

Morton, P. (1980) "Oldman dam still uncertain says Cookson," *The Calgary Herald,* Aug. 12.

Raby, S. (1965) "Irrigation development in Alberta," *The Canadian Geographer,* Vol. 9: 31-40.

Rood, S. and Jankunis, F. (eds.) (1988) *Economic, Environmental and Social Aspects of the Oldman River Dam Project,* Proceedings of the Oldman River Dam Forum, Lethbridge, Alberta: University of Lethbridge, March 4 and 5.

Sanderson, K. (1982) *Irrigation Agriculture in Alberta: Summary*, ECA81/B9, Edmonton: Environment Council of Alberta, p.1.

Skogstad, G. and Kopas, P. (1992) "Environmental Policy in a Federal System," in Boardman, R. (ed.), *Canadian Environmental Policy: Ecosystems, Politics and Process*, Toronto: Oxford University Press, pp. 43-59.

Smith, R.F. (1978) "History and current status of irrigation in Alberta," *Canadian Water Resources Journal*, Vol. 3: 1 -14.

Supreme Court of Canada (1992) Friends of the Oldman River Society v. Canada (Minister of Transport et al.) 1991: February 19, 20; 1992: January 23.

Veeman, T.S. (1988) "The Oldman River Dam: The economics of onstream storage and irrigation expansion revisited," in Rood, S. and Jankunis, F. (eds.), *Economic, Environmental and Social Aspects of the Oldman River Dam Project*, Proceedings of the Oldman River Dam Forum, University of Lethbridge, March 4 & 5, pp. 37-44.

Wilson, B. (1991) "Panel says Oldman dam safe enough," *The Western Producer*, July 25, p.16.

Chapter 12

First Nations' Strategies for Reintegrating People, Land Resources and Government

Jackie Wolfe
University of Guelph

"...indigenous peoples are reminding us that for them 1492 was not the end of history" (Berger, 1991, p. xiv).

Introduction

During the heated and often bitter debates prior to the patriation of the Canadian constitution in 1982, then Prime Minister Pierre Trudeau demanded of aboriginal leaders "just tell us what you want." Since the making of the land treaties (the so-called named and numbered treaties) in the late nineteenth and early twentieth century, the aboriginal peoples of Canada have not ceased telling the people and politicians what they want. What they were saying was scarcely heard and little heeded until 1990-92. Then Indian MLA Elijah Harper said "No" to the Meech Lake Accord in the Manitoba legislature; Mohawks and the military confronted each other in an armed standoff over land held as sacred by the Mohawks at Oka, Quebec; and the justice inquiries in Nova Scotia and Manitoba revealed the extent of civil and legal injustice experienced by Canada's aboriginal people. These events, the national constitutional debate, and the re-evaluation of post-Columbian history (Berger, 1991; Knudtson and Suzuki, 1992), compelled Canadians to relearn their own history.

For more than two hundred years, First Peoples' traditional forms of government were forbidden by successive federal and provincial "settler" governments. Their ancestral lands were appropriated for European settlement and resource development. Elected councils with very limited powers and authority were imposed, replacing elaborate participatory, consensus-building, and often gender-egalitarian forms of governance. Treaties established small parcels of land reserved for Indian residence in southern and central Canada and sometimes brought peoples from different groups together into a single settlement. Across much of the northwest, northeast and north, land treaties were not signed. Nevertheless, lands and traditional resources were alienated. People were coerced into living in permanent centralized settlement, and again, traditional governments were ignored.

First Peoples have in common a tradition of autonomous, participatory, consensus-based, and, with some notable exceptions along the coast of the Pacific northwest, egalitarian government (Little Bear et al., 1984). They also have in common a belongingness to the land. They understand themselves as part of a "sacred geography" and sacred ecology (Knudtson and Suzuki, 1992, p. 140). As First Peoples have been pointing out for several centuries, and as numerous studies have documented, separation of peoples who derive their food, their economic support, their social and cultural construction, and their spiritual well-being from intimacy with the land, has been catastrophic for their economic viability, and social, cultural and spiritual vitality (Hawthorne, 1966; Indian and Northern Affairs Canada, 1980; Indian and Northern Affairs Canada, 1989a; Ponting, 1986; Richardson, 1989).

When First Peoples "tell us what they want," the message is consistent. They seek reintegration of their people with their ancestral lands under their own governments. However, they do not speak with one voice on the details. The distinct cultural tradition of each nation precludes this. The culture of each group of First Peoples was distinct, and continues to be, despite the impacts of contact with non-native society. Plains Indians differ in language, custom and means of livelihood from the Indians of the Eastern Woodlands, and from the peoples of the West Coast, and from the Inuit of the Arctic. Further, the impact of colonization has created deep divisions between those who have treaty title to land, however small, and those who have none — between the status Indians and Inuit for whom the federal government has formal primary jurisdiction, and the Metis and non-status Indians for whom it does not.

Where they have a land base, First Peoples' priority is to re-establish forms of government over their lands and peoples which are not only recognized by other governments but which are legitimate in the eyes of their own people. Whether or not they have a land base now, First Peoples are also seeking ways to exercise their responsibility for traditional lands and resources over which they presently do not have formally recognised jurisdiction. These, they contend, are necessary conditions to rebuild economic vitality and greater self-reliance. Further, they regard them as essential if they are to regain individual, family and community health and well-being.

Cultural and spiritual revitalisation are dependent, they argue, upon reintegration of people with land and with government.

The First Peoples have applied pressure at the negotiating table, in the courts, and at the barricades for responsibility and authority for social and economic programs, a voice in decision-making for ancestral lands and resources, and self-determined self-government. In the last fifteen years the federal and provincial governments have begun, slowly and reluctantly, to respond. But, this paper argues that upper tier governments have consistently sought to separate policies and programs concerning greater native self-government from those dealing with land and resources, thereby de-coupling economic development and social, cultural and spiritual revitalization from those matters most critical to their success: people, land and resources, and government.

Consequently, First Peoples have had to develop their own strategies for reintegration. The strategies which First Peoples have adopted are adaptations to their particular circumstances. For those who form the majority population in their ancestral lands, such as the Inuit of Nunavut in the eastern Northwest Territories (NWT), establishment of majority aboriginal public government is a feasible strategy. The Council of Yukon Indians, learning from the experience of groups which have already completed the comprehensive claims negotiation, has found a way to incorporate self-government into their land claims process. Comprehensive claims signatories, who have limited legally recognized jurisdiction over much of their ancestral lands, or peoples like the Nishnawbe-Aski of northwestern Ontario, who have no formally recognized jurisdiction over most of their traditional lands, are negotiating for joint authority and responsibility for lands and resources. Co-management is their strategy. Those with no formal jurisdiction over ancestral land have to be especially innovative. The Algonquins of Barriere Lake in Quebec have made the link between traditional principles and methods of nurturing the land and maintaining its fruitfulness, and the notions of sustainable development proposed in the Brundtland Report (1987), and have challenged the Quebec government to enter into responsible joint management for sustainable development of forest lands and wildlife in the vicinity of La Verendrye park. Finally, when they have exhausted other options, First Peoples have used litigation as a means to gain legal recognition and implementation of their rights to use land and resources and exercise their own forms of government.

This paper examines the shared visions and different strategies of several First Peoples in Canada for reintegration of people, land, resources and government, and some of the internal and external problems First Peoples confront in pioneering approaches to regaining control over land and government. The paper is presented in three major sections. The first offers a brief discussion on rights and responsibilities to provide a framework for examination of the policies of upper tier governments and the strategies particular First Peoples have adopted in their efforts to link land and government. The framework illuminates both the external barriers and internal difficulties which they encounter. The second section reviews the policies and programs which the federal government has developed to deal with aboriginal land and government issues, and illustrates how these have kept self-government issues separated from land claims. The third and major section presents key strategies adopted by groups of First Peoples across Canada.

Rights to Land and Government or Responsibilities for Land and Government

Much has been written in the last decade on the strength of the rights of First Peoples relative to the rights of the Canadian state and the provinces. Canada presumes that it has overriding rights, as a sovereign state, over its residents and lands. Aboriginal people maintain that, as First Peoples, they have persistent and unextinguished rights, including but not restricted to rights to their ancestral lands. Outright ownership, by individuals or the Crown, was alien to the thinking and systems of the First Peoples. Land and its resources were to be used for the common good, with no individual ownership. Nevertheless one clan, house, or nation's traditional lands were recognized as their's by their neighbours. Also, land-holding groups accepted that they had custodial responsibilities to sustain land and wildlife (Sanders, 1991, p. 187).

But as Slattery observes:

> "It is commonly assumed that indigenous American nations had neither sovereignty in international law nor title to their territories when Europeans first arrived; North America was legally vacant and European powers could gain title to it simply by discovery, symbolic acts, occupation, or treaties among themselves" (Slattery, 1991, p. 197).

However, Slattery goes on to support his argument that:

> "...indigenous American nations had exclusive title to their territories at the time of European contact, and participated actively in

the formation of Canada and the United States" (Slattery, 1991, p. 197).

With few exceptions, successive federal and provincial governments, and many citizens, hold to the first position: that the rights of the state override any residual rights that native peoples might still have. Some do, however, acknowledge that the state has certain responsibilities with respect to native peoples. The legal interpretation on responsibilities is that the state is in a fiduciary or trust relationship to native people (see R v Sparrow, 1990). First Nations criticize the state for its negligence in carrying out its fiduciary responsibilities to their people. They likewise criticize the state for its negligence towards the land and its renewable resources, arguing that, far from properly regulating and controlling development so that it is sustainable, the state has at worst promoted and at best overlooked exploitation, pollution, and destruction of land and wildlife.

Two sets of rights, and the responsibilities of governments and aboriginal people with respect to those rights, are particularly contentious: aboriginal assertion of their inherent right to self-government; and aboriginal claim of aboriginal and treaty rights to land and resources. Several recent books and articles (Isaac, 1991a, 1991b, 1992a, 1992b; Assembly of First Nations, 1991; Bartlett, 1991; Sanders, 1991; Slattery, 1991; Clarke, 1990;) throw light on aboriginal interpretation of rights and responsibilities on the one hand, and federal and provincial government interpretations, on the other, and on the judgements of the courts.

Rights and Responsibilities of Governments

Many First Peoples share a goal; constitutional affirmation and guarantees of their inherent right of self-government (Erasmus, 1988; Erasmus, 1989; Cassidy, 1991). This, those leaders argue, will be their only guaranteed protection from unilateral repeal or amendment by later federal governments. Constitutional recognition would symbolise a significant shift in power in favour of the First Peoples, and guarantee their right to determine for themselves their forms of government without having it dictated by other governments. They do not ask that this right be bestowed. They assert that they were self-governing before European settlement. They demand that their inherent right be affirmed in the constitution. Further, they resist the demands being placed on them to spell out how, within the framework of the Canadian state, their governments would be structured, what powers they would exercise, or what functions they would perform. They argue that this is a contradiction in terms: if they are forced to detail what self-government is, it clearly cannot be self-determined self-government (for a discussion on inherent and contingent rights to self-government, see Isaac, 1992a).

> "Self-government means making one's own laws, laws that can have precedence over the laws of outside law-makers when the laws conflict" (Clarke, 1990, pp. 6-7).

As the 1991/2 constitutional debate revealed there are, however, some groups, particularly native women's organisations, whose experiences make them wary of this interpretation of self-government. They continue to press for the application of national and international constraints on abo- riginal governments. The Native Women's Association of Canada's state- ment on the 1992 Referendum, for example, called for the application of the Canadian Charter of Rights and Freedoms to aboriginal governments, with the exception of section 33 of the Charter, which gives a government the right to pass a law even if it violates Charter rights (Native Women's Association of Canada, 1992).

In the decade since the patriation of the Canadian Constitution in 1982, aboriginal organizations have gradually forced aboriginal self-government to the forefront of the Canadian political agenda. Despite the 1984 federal all-party report favouring Indian self-government (Penner, 1983), federal and provincial governments have long clung to the position that the only appropriate form of aboriginal government is modified and expanded mu- nicipal-style government, with limited powers and functions devolved from upper tier government, and no constitutionally guaranteed existence (De- partment of Indian Affairs and Northern Development, 1982a). Four consti- tutional conferences held between 1983 and 1987 failed to reach agreement on the issue. Nevertheless, a broad base of public support for aboriginal self-government became evident in the Spicer hearings on the constitution in 1991, and was sustained during the four major conferences on the constitution in late 1991 and early 1992.

Some legal and constitutional experts have argued that the right of aborigi- nal self-government already exists in the constitution by virtue of the Con- stitution Act, 1982, Section 35, which recognizes and affirms existing aboriginal and treaty rights of the aboriginal peoples of Canada, namely Indian, Inuit and Metis (Clarke, 1990; Isaac, 1991a, 1992a). Controversy swirls around how broad or narrow a definition is given to existing aboriginal rights. In the words of Doris Ronnenberg, President of the Native Council of Canada, the First Peoples:

"...assert that Section 35 is a full box of existing rights, which provides the constitutional mechanism needed to validate or empower aboriginal self-government. The question remains, however, whether the political will exists in Canada to adopt that position" (Ronnenberg, 1991, pp. 39-40).

The Supreme Court of Canada's 1990 ruling in the case of R v Sparrow, that an existing Aboriginal right may be exercised in a form which reflects the community's evolution, provides a strong legal basis for a broad definition of aboriginal rights. According to the Sparrow judgement, "the notion of 'frozen rights', that is the right to live using only pre-contact technologies, is rejected." Clarke (1990) maintains that the key issue is, therefore, how to apply a right that already exists, specifically the right of self-government, not how to define it. The papers by Isaac (1991b, 1992b) on Sparrow and the Constitution explore many legal interpretations of aboriginal rights and discuss both definitions and applications.

By early 1992, the principle of constitutional recognition of the aboriginal inherent right of self-government gained further acceptance. The Royal Commission on Aboriginal Peoples stated that the right of self-government should be "inherent in nature, circumscribed in extent, and sovereign within its sphere" (Royal Commission on Aboriginal Peoples, 1992, p. 23).

Debate and dispute now focus on what that right entails, and on the responsibilities of the federal, provincial and aboriginal governments to each other and to aboriginal people. Of particular concern is the effect of affirmation of self-government on the fiduciary or trust relationship between the federal government and aboriginal people, which requires that the federal government use its powers to protect and promote the interests of aboriginal people. The government has, to date, been inconsistent and often negligent in its fiduciary responsibilities.

The issues still to be resolved concerning the application of aboriginal self-government are numerous, and are increasing rather than diminishing (for a thorough review and comprehensive bibliography see Cassidy, 1991). Among them are: financing aboriginal governments; intergovernmental transfer payments to enable the governments to carry out existing programs and address unmet and emerging new needs; application of federal, provincial and aboriginal laws to aboriginal lands, to non-aboriginals on aboriginal lands, and to aboriginals away from their aboriginal land base; and the relationship between individual and communal rights, particularly protection for the rights of women.

Rights and Responsibilities for Land and Resources

At a recent conference on Indigenous Land Rights (Department of Geography, University of Canterbury and Ngai Tahu, New Zealand, 1992), a Sekani from British Columbia challenged participants by arguing that they should not be talking about rights; they should be focusing on responsibilities. Responses from participants indicated that they presumed he was criticizing central governments for not carrying out their responsibilities to First Peoples, and that he was calling for stronger aboriginal rights. They were wrong. It soon became clear that he was referring to the responsibilities that native people have for their land, not the rights claimed by them or the responsibilities of governments to respond to those rights. When asked to explain further, the Sekani talked about his peoples' understanding of their responsibilities to nurture the land and its wildlife and other resources, and maintain them in a healthy and productive condition.

First Peoples argue that their rights to land were bestowed by the Creator "from time immemorial," that they have continued to occupy and use their lands, and that their rights have not been extinguished by European occupancy and British or Canadian law (Slattery, 1991). The record of occupancy and land and resource use by each group, and the record of agreements with their neighbours has been passed on through oral history and physical record. For example, the Algonquins of Barriere Lake, in the vicinity of La Verendrye, Quebec, kept knowledge of their traditional lands through public retelling at regular public assemblies at which decisions were made for the coming year (Matchewan, 1989, p. 143).

In his judgement in the case of Delgamuukw v R., 1991, B.C. Chief Justice Allan McEachern held the position that he was "unable to accept adaawk, kungax, and oral histories as reliable bases for detailed history but they could confirm findings based on other admissible evidence" (McEachern, 1991, p. 75).

Oral history was, in many cases, supplemented by a physical record of events, in the manner of a written record. The wampum belts cherished by many aboriginal groups of the eastern forests provide a record of agreements and laws. For example, the Gus-Wen-Tah or Two Row Wampum records the treaty of peace and friendship made between the Haudenosaunee, the Iroquois Confederation, and Europeans. There are two rows of purple wampum beads separated by three beads of white symbolizing peace, friendship and respect. The two purple rows symbolize two paths or two vessels, travelling down the same river together (Penner, 1983, back cover).

The Royal Proclamation of 1763 put in writing the Crown's policy on land, by recognizing that lands possessed by First Peoples anywhere in what was then British North America are reserved for them unless or until they cede land to the Crown. The policy has never been revoked (Sanders, 1991, p. 187). Indeed, the rights recognized in the Royal Proclamation are protected in the Canadian Charter of Rights and Freedoms, Section 25, and the protection of the Charter is extended in Section 25 (b) to "any rights or freedoms that now exist by way of land claims agreements or may so be acquired." Section 25 also guarantees that other Charter rights and freedoms "shall not be construed so as to abrogate or derogate from any aboriginal rights or freedoms that pertain to the aboriginal peoples in Canada."

Since Calder v Attorney General of British Columbia, in 1973, First Nations have argued, in a series of landmark cases, that they have an aboriginal right to occupy land, use its resources, and/or prevent occupancy and use by others (see Guerin v R., 1985; Martin v British Columbia and MacMillan Bloedel - known also as Meares Island; Simon v R., 1986; Sioui v R., 1990). Judgements in these cases have gradually put in place stronger legal interpretation of aboriginal rights to occupancy of lands and to use of resources (Bartlett, 1991). The strongest judgements in favour of aboriginal rights are found in Sparrow v R., 1990, a case dealing with aboriginal fishing rights and the constitutional protection afforded them.

The Sparrow judgement contains several significant elements, which have the potential to alter the way in which aboriginal land and resource rights are dealt with in Canada. Among other things, the Canadian Supreme Court found that an aboriginal right exists, and is therefore protected by Section 35 of the Canadian Constitution, unless the Crown can show that it has been extinguished. Extinguishment may not be implied. There must be "a clear and plain intent to extinguish."

The Supreme Court made reference to provincial law, saying that a provincial law, also, will not apply, to the extent that it interferes with an Aboriginal right, unless there is a "compelling" reason for it to do so. As an example, a compelling justification would be the need to conserve and manage the fisheries resource. Laws and regulations must be drafted and implemented in such a way that aboriginal rights are "recognized and affirmed." Tests for justifying limitation of aboriginal rights include the following. Is fair compensation available in a situation of expropriation? And, has the aboriginal group in question been consulted with respect to the conservation measures being implemented (Usher, 1991, p. 20)?

As Bartlett comments:

> "Invariably, local courts are unsympathetic to aboriginal claims. It requires the decision of the highest court in the land to require the local courts to give effect to aboriginal rights" (Bartlett, 1991, p. 112).

The Sparrow judgement states that an existing aboriginal right may be exercised in a form which reflects the community's evolution. Existing aboriginal rights must be interpreted in a large, generous and liberal way, and are to be understood in their contemporary form. The notion of "frozen rights," that is, the right to live using only pre-contact technologies, is rejected. According to Sparrow, existing aboriginal rights are constitutionally protected by Section 35 of the Constitution, and are to be interpreted as evolving, changing, and adapting with a community's evolution. This substantially opens up the legal interpretation of aboriginal rights in Canada. Again, though, the lower court judgement of Chief Justice McEachern in Delgamuukw v R., 1991 is not consistent with the Supreme Court judgement in Sparrow, in that he does not offer a liberal interpretation of aboriginal rights. He observes that:

> "the evidence satisfies me that most Gitksan and Wet'suet'en people do not now live an aboriginal life...there is practically no one trapping and hunting full time, although fishing has remained an important part of their culture and economy (McEachern, 1991, p. 56).

Potential implications of Sparrow are wide ranging for aboriginal rights and responsibilities with respect to land and resources. For example, Sparrow implies that, after the requirement of conservation, any surplus of wildlife shall be allocated first to meet Indian requirements for food (Usher, 1991, p. 21). It also implies that aboriginal rights include involvement of aboriginal people in the conservation and management of the resource, and include their direct involvement in regulation of resource use. Increasingly, First Peoples are arguing that settler governments and organisations have not exercised their rights to land and resource ownership in a responsible fashion, and that the First Peoples should play a greater, even dominant role in exercising responsibility for land and resources. The Sparrow judgement lends weight and credibility to their position.

Commentary

The link between land and resource rights and responsibilities and self-government is clear. Rights without mechanisms to exercise those rights are hollow and meaningless. Rights require institutions of government to fulfil the promise of the rights. The instruments of government, in turn, cannot be imposed, foreign constructions. A most significant right is the right to occupy and use land. This requires instruments for allocation, regulation, management, and enforcement; it requires government. Because of the variation in the level of rights and responsibilities presently exercised by First Nations over ancestral lands, forms of government range through varying degrees of formally recognized self-government (much as that is in itself a contradiction in terms) from Nations who hold treaty or aboriginal title to land, to co-jurisdiction and co-management.

Government Programs for Self-Government and Land Claims

Self-Government Programs

While a right to self-government has not yet been explicitly entrenched in the constitution, the federal government has been promoting several lesser pathways to self-government (Little Bear et al., 1984; Penner, 1983; Cassidy and Bish, 1989) for status Indians with a land base. They form something of a hierarchy, from new legislation to increased options within the existing Indian Act.

Federal Acts of self-government provide First Nations with powers which go well beyond those possible under the Indian Act. The Cree-Naskapi (of Quebec) Act 1984 is one example of special federal legislation, as is the Sechelt Indian Band Government Act 1986. The 1984 Cree-Naskapi Act set up governments which are similar to conventional municipal governments, with "some extraordinary powers (for example over hunting and fishing rights, and over the environment)" (Moss, 1985). A form of regional government operates over a huge area of northwestern Quebec, through the Cree Regional Authority and special purpose regional bodies for health and social services and education. These regional bodies exercise delegated provincial functions for the Cree and Naskapi communities (Cassidy and Bish, 1989, pp. 144-145).

The Sechelt Band, in southern British Columbia, pioneered special legislation which greatly expands the degree to which it is self-managing and self-administrative (Etkin, 1988; Taylor and Paget, 1989). The Sechelt Act provides the band with powers beyond those in the Indian Act. The band has, for example, fee simple title to all of its reserve lands, with powers, under the terms of the band government constitution, to make disposition of those lands. The band can make laws across twenty-one classes of matters, including access to, and residency, building, zoning, and planning, on Sechelt lands. It also has responsibility for education, health, social and welfare services; public order and safety; management of natural resources including fish and other wildlife; and regulation of commerce. However, the powers set out in the act are not inherent rights. The Sechelt Act is specific to the Sechelt Band. Band Council operates concurrently under authority delegated from the federal government, and under provincial municipal legislation. By some, therefore, it is regarded as little more than an extension of the municipal model.

Through the INAC program for greater self-government, called Community Self-Government Negotiations, bands and tribal councils can negotiate terms of special federal legislation through which their councils assume responsibilities and exercise authority beyond the existing Indian Act (Wolfe, 1992). However,

> "self-government negotiations will not alter the division of powers between the federal and provincial governments but will, through practical measures, attempt to accommodate Indian government within the existing constitutional framework" (Indian and Northern Affairs Canada, 1989b, p. 1).

Minimum matters to be negotiated include institutions of government, membership, land title and land management, and political and fiscal accountability. The full range of powers and functions may also include administration of justice, taxation for local purposes, community services, education, health, social development, renewable resources, business and trades, and protection of the environment (Indian and Northern Affairs Canada, 1990). While nearly 150 Nations have made self-government proposals to INAC only a handful are working on so-called Framework Negotiations, and fewer still have progressed to the level of substantive negotiations. To date none have been finalized under the Community Self-Government Negotiations program.

INAC, together with Indian leaders, is also examining legislative alternatives to the Indian Act. The Chiefs involved in the review concluded, as have many others before them, that the Indian Act is totally inadequate as the legislative foundation for Indian government. They also concluded that the community-based self-government legislation, which requires developing and enacting separate federal legislation for each First Nation is slow, costly, and not national in its scope.

Another INAC program, Alternative Funding Arrangements, allows band and tribal councils greater program delivery flexibility within existing legislation. The program has four main features: greater accountability of chief and council to the membership; optional multi-year funding; flexibility to transfer funds between programs; and local authority to modify or re-design federally funded programs. This enables councils to establish their own priorities and redesign programs. However, councils do not receive any more funding, and are still accountable to INAC for their expenditures. Eligibility of First Nations to enter the program is determined by senior regional departmental staff (Wolfe, 1992). Again, this is but a modest modification of the municipal model of government.

INAC maintains that its greater self-government programs provide for the varied needs of aboriginal groups. However, these programs are specific to First Nations with a legally recognized land base. INAC determines the "readiness" of a First Nation to enter a particular program. Only a limited number of nations can be accommodated in the most elaborate of the programs, Community Self-Government Negotiations. Nations may only negotiate matters that fall within the scope of the program. Further, the programs delegate rights and responsibilities — some extensive, as in special federal legislation, some still narrow and within the confines of the Indian Act, as in the case of band councils, which continue to be ultimately responsible to and accountable to the federal government rather than its own constituents. Nevertheless, the programs do begin the complex process of transferring of rights and shifting in responsibilities from the federal government to First Nations governments. In the words of the former chief negotiator for the Nishnawbe-Aski Nations:

> "Even if we got constitutional self-government tomorrow all of these things would still have to be worked out (Bill Nothing, personal communication, 1991, quoted in Wolfe, 1992, p. 300).

Land Claims

> "The First Nations of Canada do not view their rights in terms of 'claims'." We more properly view the claims process as one of the few mechanisms available for implementing our constitutionally protected rights" (Assembly of First Nations, 1991, p. 244).

Throughout the 1980s, the federal government has recognised two types of aboriginal claims with respect to land: comprehensive claims arising from unsurrendered aboriginal lands and resources, and specific claims to address breaches of federal obligations, usually with respect to treaties. It has established two policies and accompanying programs to address land issues. Through these, the federal government seeks to establish "certainty" of land title. The First Nations, for their part, seek to have their rights both recognized and implemented. First Nations interpret government policy as an instrument to extinguish the governments's "burden" of aboriginal rights. They accuse the federal government of being in a conflict of interest between its fiduciary responsibility to act in the best interests of aboriginal peoples, and its responsibility to protect the interests of the Canadian state and its citizens. Further, First Nations object to the whole notion of being claimants. Rather, they view the claims process as one of the few mechanisms available to them for implementing their constitutionally protected rights (Assembly of First Nations, 1991, p. 244).

Under a policy revised in 1981 (Department of Indian Affairs and Northern Development, 1981) and again in 1986, Aboriginal groups in those parts of Canada where no treaties were signed, mainly the north, northwest and northeast, may enter a process of negotiation of claims arising from unsurrendered aboriginal ownership of lands and resources.

Groups which have entered negotiations include the Inuvialuit of the western coast of the NWT, the Tungavik Federation of Nunavut in the eastern Arctic, the Dene and Metis of the Mackenzie Valley, and the Council of Yukon Indians, among others (Crowe, 1990). Although now changed, it was initially federal policy that only six claims can be negotiated at any one time. Final Agreements generally guarantee outright ownership of part of the land covered by the agreement, usually village lands, areas adjacent, and lands of special value to the traditional economy; cash compensation for loss of land and past damages; a voice in the management of land, wildlife and renewable resources in the claim area through participation in and membership on management boards; and preferential or exclusive hunting, fishing and trapping over specified lands.

Two aspects of the federal comprehensive claims policy are particularly contentious: extinguishment of aboriginal rights, and exclusion of self-government from the claim agreements (Coolican, 1985; Assembly of First Nations, 1991). Federal comprehensive claims policy requires that claimants "cede, release, surrender and convey all their aboriginal claims, rights, title and interests" (Department of Indian Affairs and Northern Development, 1984, clause 3 (4), p. 3).

For example, in the 1984 Inuvialuit Agreement:

"Canada recognizes and gives, grants and provides to the Inuvialuit the rights, privileges and benefits specified in this Agreement" (Department of Indian Affairs and Northern Development, 1984, clause 3 (11), p. 3).

In other words, claimants are required to surrender their aboriginal rights and title in return for specified rights. In the case of the Inuvialuit, they surrendered claim to the equivalent of 30,000 sq. mls. per capita in return for 2.0 sq. mls. per capita in fee simple absolute title with both surface and sub-surface rights. This land, however, can only be conveyed within the Inuvialuit community or to the government of Canada (Crowe, 1990). The federal government regards this surrender of aboriginal title as essential to achieve its priority of:

"obtaining 'finality' through settlement agreements, thereby providing the 'certainty' required for resource development to proceed" (Assembly of First Nations, 1991, p. 134).

The Coolican Report on Comprehensive Claims Policy (1985) criticised the policy of extinguishment, finding that:

"To many aboriginals, aboriginal rights are intimately tied to culture and lifestyle and are integral to their self-identity. The blanket surrender and extinguishment of these rights suggests assimilation and cultural destruction" (Coolican, 1985, p. 40).

Equally contentious is the exclusion of self-government from comprehensive claims agreements. First Nations argue that they need recognized self-government to take full advantage of such benefits as the claims agreements afford. With secure title to land, albeit less land than their ancestral territories, they expect to be self-governing over their lands, resources, and peoples. The federal government has consistently refused, since the comprehensive claims agreements, like the treaties, are given constitutional protection in Section 35 (3). Inclusion of a self-government clause in the final claims agreement would, the federal government maintains, set precedents of constitutionally recognized native self-government not agreed upon by the country's First Ministers. Consequently, the 1986 revisions to the claims policy did not provide for self-government.

Despite many shortcomings, the comprehensive claims policy has produced agreements on claims (Crowe, 1990), even though each one has taken eight to ten years to finalize, and some claims have had to be re-opened or completely re-worked because of the reluctance of individual communities and nations to ratify specific terms in the agreement (see for example, the CYI claim and the Dene-Metis claim).

The same cannot be said for the specific claims policy (Department of Indian Affairs and Northern Development, 1982b). Federal policy is to accept only claims regarding breaches of rigorously defined legal obligations and then to negotiate compensation. The strict criteria mean that the program cannot be used to resolve the majority of claims.

First Peoples' Strategies for Reintegrating People Land Resources and Government

Aboriginal Majority Public Government

"Governments, territorial and federal, have made continual attempts to separate our political rights from our rights to land, and Inuit have had to drag these governments, kicking and screaming, to the negotiating table..." (Amagoalik, 1992).

For aboriginal peoples who continue to be in the majority across their ancestral lands, aboriginal public government offers a means of extending their legislative authority beyond those lands which they hold in fee simple title, as in the case of Inuit claimants who have completed a comprehensive land claim, or in treaty title, as in the case of the Nishnawbe-Aski of northern Ontario.

The Inuit Tapirisat of Canada, representing the Inuit of the eastern and northern NWT, proposed creation of Nunavut in the late 1970s. A constitutional conference which brought together "all the elected community, Inuit organization, regional council and NWT legislature Inuit throughout the region" (Jull, 1991, p. 18) gave unanimous support to a comprehensive proposal, Building Nunavut (Nunavut Constitutional Forum, 1985). The proposal is designed to establish Inuit majority public government in the eastern part of the NWT, and provide a jurisdiction in which Inuit tradition and culture would thrive (Weller, 1990).

Inuit of the eastern Arctic consider establishment of Nunavut territory and government, and the settlement of their comprehensive land claim as two aspects of a single process.

> "Wildlife harvesting rights and economic rights to the land contained in our land claim must go hand-in-hand with political authority over those ancestral lands. The land claim, on its own, deals with some of our immediate needs, such as job creation and economic development, but for long-term solutions, we must have self-government" (Amagoalik, 1992, p. 20).

Again, because comprehensive claims settlements are constitutionally protected, the federal government refuses to entertain direct discussion of either aboriginal self-government or aboriginal majority public government. The Nunavut Settlement Area Agreement-in-Principle, 1990, offers the Inuit $580 ml. and fee simple title to about 18 per cent of the 800,000 sq. mls. claimed as traditional lands. However, Article 4 of the 1992 Final Agreement for Ratification makes the link between land and Nunavut government stating that the government of Canada "will recommend to parliament...legislation to...establish a new Nunavut Territory" and that the federal and territorial governments "shall negotiate a political accord to deal with the establishment of Nunavut." While it does not require establishment of Nunavut, the signing of the Nunavut political Accord in April 1992 and the "yes" vote on the proposed boundary between the eastern and western parts of the NWT in May 1992 prepare the way for establishment of Nunavut before the year 2000. The position of the Tungavik Federation of Nunavut, comprising the Inuit regional associations of Baffin, Keewatin and Kitikmeot, which negotiated the land claim, has always been "no Nunavut, no land claim" (Bell, 1992, p. 17).

The forty-six First Nations which comprise the Nishnawbe-Aski First Nation (NAN) in northwestern Ontario are engaged in a tripartite negotiation, with the federal and provincial governments, for greater self-government. Nishnawbe-Aski constitute the overwhelming majority of the population of northern Ontario. Most of the constituent nations have externally recognized title to only that small part of their ancestral lands which are in reserves.

Consequently, NAN is proposing to the provincial government, which has responsibility for creating lower tier municipal government, that a northern Ontario public regional government be established under provincial legislation. Such a government would have provincially delegated authority to pass by-laws, administer programs, and control and regulate aspects of land use for the whole area (Nishnawbe-Aski Nation, 1991, p. 36).

The draft response from the Ontario government is noncommittal (Ontario Native Affairs Secretariat, 1991). It raises a number of critical issues, such as protection for the rights of non-Indian residents; the nature of powers for the different levels of the proposed regional government, and the process through which the public can give consideration to the proposal. Both the province and the government of Canada will need to be assured that no fundamental objection exists within the wider public.

Self-Government as Part of Comprehensive Claims

As discussed earlier, the federal government will not include self-government within comprehensive claims agreements because the agreements have constitutional protection. Each group of claimants has argued strenuously that they need the full and recognized powers of autonomous aboriginal government to implement the terms of the agreement. In 1990 the Council of Yukon Indians (CYI) achieved a breakthrough when it initialled the Umbrella Final Agreement for its comprehensive claim. The Agreement included a clause which committed both the government of Canada and the Yukon government to negotiate self-government agreement with those Yukon First nations that request such arrangements. Self-government negotiations will be conducted within the Community Self-Government Negotiations program of INAC.

Although this is a compromise between the position of the federal government and the demand of claimants, its importance should not be underestimated. Powers conferred through the constitutionally recognized claims agreement can be exercised by an aboriginal government. Consequently, each member nation of the CYI with an established government has the opportunity to administer rights conferred by the claim. In previous claims agreement, such as that of the Inuvialuit, rights bestowed by the claim settlement have been exercised by a specially constituted corporation, not by a government. In some cases, notably the Makivik corporation and the Kativik Regional Government in northern Quebec, the corporation has commanded considerable power through its control over compensation funds, and its role in land and resource management, while the local government has had to operate from a relatively weak base. Aboriginal people do not wish to separate land and resource management, which they view as critical to their economic and cultural survival, from their exercise of government.

The community-level CYI self-government agreements currently being ne-gotiated, allow for the creation of First Nations governments under federal statute (in much the same manner as the Sechelt Act). There may also be need for Government of Yukon statutes where First Nations communities are located adjacent to hamlet boundaries. Negotiations will have to involve the existing level of municipal government, and necessitate the develop-ment of cooperative arrangements between the two adjacent or overlap-ping sets of governments. The Yukon territorial government has publicly supported establishment of strong aboriginal government (Penneket, 1991, pp. 143-150).

Co-Jurisdiction and Co-Management

First Peoples across Canada are seeking to extend their participation in planning and management of those parts of their ancestral lands which lie outside of areas which they hold in exclusive aboriginal title or fee simple. A number of possibilities exist: areas of exclusive jurisdiction with appropri-ate linkages and support systems; co-jurisdiction with shared and equal partnership; First Peoples management control over areas or matters under the jurisdiction of another government; or, shared and equal partner-ship (Johnson, 1991, p. 79).

The advantages for First Peoples are considerable. Co-jurisdiction and co-management, in addition to giving First Peoples the decision-making power over land and resource use which they seek, also provides a way to im-prove their management capabilities. It demands that care be taken to make constructive links between state level scientifically-based research and management regimes and local level indigenous knowledge and man-agement systems (Freeman and Carbyn, 1988; Osherenko, 1988; Berkes et al., 1991; Usher, 1987; Usher, 1991).

As Berkes et al. (1991) have succinctly summarised, there are a number of barriers to effective co-jurisdiction and co-management. Indigenous sys-tems have been disrupted or disregarded, and to a considerable extent rendered ineffective by the interference of the state regimes. State manag-ers and wildlife biologists, with few exceptions, consider management to be their exclusive responsibility and do not give credence to local knowledge systems, and even less to the effectiveness of local management systems. Also, state planning and management regimes have been put in place largely to meet the needs and protect the interests of non-native third party interests in land and resources, such as mining companies, sports hunters and fishers, and naturalists. Indeed Usher (1993) maintains that depletion of lands and resources is most likely a result of delocalization of markets and reduced security of tenure and access. He argues that communal property systems do not result in resource depletion, contrary to prevailing economic and biological theories of common property systems, because communal property users can be expected to maintain their own system of conservation locally in relatively stable, non-competitive situations even where commerce is involved (Usher, 1993). Problems arise, however, when communal property users are confined to an increasingly restricted land and resource base, or when the area is penetrated by non-local users, and de-localization of decision-making persists.

Nevertheless, a number of co-jurisdiction and co-management systems are being put in place. For example, all the comprehensive claims settlements have provisions for joint management of wildlife. The roles of joint government-aboriginal management boards are being clarified and more strongly defined with each agreement. From being token members of management boards, aboriginal representatives now have formally recognized responsibility for joint decision-making. Joint decision-making is institutionalized in a partnership of equals (Berkes et al., 1991, p. 12); now the partners have to make the partnership work.

Another route to co-jurisdiction and co-management is through land use planning arrangements. A partnership agreement between the Dene, Metis, Inuit, Inuvialuit and federal and territorial governments established a land use planning program in the NWT in 1983. This evolved from the much criticized planning system in which local and regional planning was to be undertaken by specialists who were to present planning options to the Minister of Indian and Northern Affairs. The Minister would make the final decision and disband the planning agencies (Rees, 1985; Fenge, 1987). The NWT planning program eventually provided for joint planning at both the regional and the local level through aboriginal representation on the regional Commissions and broad-based community participation in local-level planning teams. The community planning team represented key community groups such as hunters and trappers, elders, political organisations and local government. The process was designed to be participatory and consensus-building. However, both the NWT and Yukon programs are being wound down following a Fall 1991 federal government budget decision to curtail financial assistance. Some form of joint land use planning is expected to continue through land claim agreements.

In the territories, both joint land use planning and renewable resource co-management are being institutionalised as land claim settlements put the concept and reality of shared jurisdiction more firmly in place. In most of the provinces co-management remains elusive. For example, the Nishnawbe-

Aski Nations (NAN) in northwestern Ontario have been engaged in tripartite negotiations for greater self-government with the federal and provincial governments since 1986 (Nothing and Wolfe, 1993).

To strengthen its influence on land use and resource management NAN is proposing a three-fold system of land classification and administration similar to that used in the James Bay and Northern Quebec Agreement and several of the Comprehensive Claims Agreements (Nishnawbe-Aski Nation, 1991, pp. 55-59). Zone A would consist of reserve lands in Indian title fully controlled by each First Nation. Zones B and C involve provincial crownland. Zone B would provide a land use area for each First Nation over which it would exercise unique and specified powers and authority. Proposed powers include First Nation control of land use planning; exclusive right to harvest wildlife and trees for individual and community traditional and non-commercial uses; restricted public access requiring First Nation's consent; and no development by outside interests without a joint participation agreement. These proposals represent a considerable extension of First Nation's control beyond reserve lands.

The Teme-Augama Anishnabai, in northeastern Ontario, have been trying for over a century to affirm its rights to its traditional lands in and around Lake Temagami. As far back as 1884 the federal government surveyed a 260 sq. km. reserve at the southern end of the lake, but the Ontario government refused to release its control of the crownlands on the grounds that there was too much valuable timber on the proposed reserve lands. Since then the Teme-Augama Anishnabai have employed every means available to them, including formal claims procedures, blockades, and litigation, to gain some degree of control over their lands (Potts, 1989). In 1991 the Supreme Court of Canada dismissed the appeal of the Teme-Augama, ruling that the title was surrendered through arrangements made subsequent to the treaty in which the Indians accepted treaty annuities and a reserve. However, it did follow the Sparrow ruling when it stated that the Crown had failed to meet some of its obligations and had breached its fiduciary obligations to the Indians (Bartlett, 1991).

In April 1990, the province of Ontario and the Teme-Augama Anishnabai signed a memorandum of understanding that included a clause calling for the participation of the Teme-Augama Anishnabai in the timber management of their ancestral homeland, n'Daki Menan. The role of the Teme-Augama Anishnabai is purely advisory. In the first year, the Teme-Augama Anishnabai undertook field inspections based on the Ministry of Natural Resources' (M.N.R.) cutting plans and presented many specific recommendations to management unit foresters, and did follow-up work on their recommendations. Also, the Teme-Augama Anishnabai have developed two principles that guide their approach to timber management: stewardship, which means that human uses must respect forest life and use it only in ways which ensure forest continuity; and sustained life, which refers to the self-renewal of the forest ecosystem.

The Teme-Augama Anishnabai undertook a simple evaluation of the participation in management process (Heather Ross, Researcher for the Teme-Augama Anishnabai, personal communication, 1992). The evaluation found that of 125 recommendations made to M.N.R., half were rejected, about one third were accepted in principle and not acted on or not responded to, while about 15 per cent were accepted by the Ministry. M.N.R. has been most responsive to those recommendations which reflect the cultural heritage of n'Daki Menan. Few recommendations aimed at improving the management of timber operations or preserving habitat were accepted. In the second year of the agreement, however, the Teme-Augama Anishnabai shifted from making primarily site specific recommendations to more general and policy-oriented recommendations. The Ministry was more inclined to answer the recommendations and provide reasons for rejection. The Teme-Augama concluded that participation in resource management in an advisory role does not amount to co-management. That requires major institutional changes in roles and relationships between First Nations, the state and significant third party interests.

The Native People's Circle on Environment and Development (1991, p. 30) in Ontario has grasped at the initiatives opened up by the Teme-Augama Anishnabai and other First Peoples, and has recommended in its report on environment and economy that "the Province enter into arrangement with the Aboriginal people for the co-management of natural resources on Crown land." The Circle states that the province of Ontario should develop allocation agreements with Aboriginal people which ensure fair access to resources; a share in economic benefits from the use of resources; and decision-making power over the resource base. The Circle argues the need for "proprietary rights, not just access rights." The concept of private ownership is foreign to aboriginal people, who more commonly think in terms of community use of lands and resources, and territorial boundaries which shift from season to season as patterns of resources change. Nevertheless, to build healthy economies and to protect environments from further damage, aboriginal people are looking for ownership of a greater part of the land base, and increased control over resources.

Linking Traditional Models and Sustainability Concepts

A number of First Nations are challenging non-native governments' commitment to environmental quality and habitat and wildlife sustainability by making the link between traditional principles and the concepts of sustainability promoted in the Brundtland Report (1987). The Algonquins of Barriere Lake live in an area designated by the province of Quebec presently known as La Verendrye Wildlife Reserve. After considerable Indian pressure, the Quebec government established a 16,6000 sq. km. area as an Indian hunting reserve in 1928. In the 1940s, the provincial government cut a highway through the reserve, withdrew a 32 km. by 16 km. corridor either side of the highway from the reserve, and sought to attract tourists to the area by promoting non-native hunting and fishing. The province has given private outfitters exclusive rights for their clients to hunt, trap and fish in specified "underexploited" areas. Since the 1960s, large parts of the reserve has been clear cut.

The Algonquins of Barriere Lake argue that the provincial wildlife and forest management policies and practices are "designed for extinction" (Matchewan, 1989, p. 160). They blockaded the road through La Verendrye Park, blockaded new logging roads to prevent contractors from spraying the forests with herbicides, and established a protest camp on Parliament Hill in Ottawa. They are not entering a land claim, though they claim the lands are traditionally theirs and have not been ceded to the Crown. They say that they are not intending to totally exclude logging companies, sports hunters and fishers and other interests; rather, they remind the federal and provincial governments that each has endorsed the Bruntland Report on Environment and Development, and demand that the time has come "to put principles into action" (Matchewan, 1989, p. 161). They have invited the Quebec government to enter into joint management of forests and wildlife in the vicinity of La Verendreye Park, based on concepts of sustainable development.

Somewhat similarly, the Mohawks of Akwesasne, near Cornwall, Ontario, have adopted a comprehensive wildlife conservation law, which provides for penalties for both aboriginal and non-aboriginal offenders who pollute the environment and harm fish and wildlife (Native Peoples Circle on Environment and Development, 1991, p. 18).

Specific Claims and Land and Resource Issues

Cassidy has recently proposed a nine point program to improve relationships between the First Nations and the Canadian state. One of his key recommendations is establishment of a modern treaty process which does not detach self-government from matters that relate to land and resources, and is not based on extinguishment of aboriginal rights and aboriginal title (Cassidy, 1991). Neither the comprehensive claims nor the specific claims programs of the federal government adequately address the land and resource concerns of the First Peoples.

Specific claims refer to claims made by Indians against the federal government which relate to the fulfilment of Indian treaties and to the administration of land and other Indian assets (Department of Indian Affairs and Northern Development, 1982a, p. 19). The specific claims process restricts itself to the federal government's negligence in fulfilling per capita reserve acreage to which a First Nation is entitled under treaty, and to removal of land from reserves without consent or compensation (for example, for roads, hydro corridors, and military bases).

The Department applies strict legal criteria, thereby rejecting many claims, and reducing others (Assembly of First Nations, 1991, p. 240). When a claim is accepted for negotiation the process is usually lengthy (Wagner, 1991, p. 25). The specific claims process is generally regarded as failing to settle the outstanding business of land issues (Wagner, 1991). Also, it is not designed to deal with aboriginal treaty rights of hunting, fishing, and trapping beyond designated reserves. It is not surprising, therefore, that many First Nations have turned to the provincial and federal courts for resolution of aboriginal and treaty rights.

Litigation and Land and Resource Issues

Litigation is the option of last resort for many First Peoples. Some, such as the Teme-Augama Anishnabai (A.G. Ontario v. Bear Island Foundation, 1985, A.G. Ontario v. Bear Island Foundation, 1986 and Bear Island Foundation v. A.G. Ontario, 1991), Gitksan Wet'suet'en (Delgamuukw v. R, 1991) and Lubicon (Ominayak v. Norcen Energy Resources Ltd, 1984 and Lubicon Band case, 1985), turn to litigation to assert unextinguished aboriginal title to lands threatened by external resource development, or when comprehensive or specific claims are rejected, or negotiations within the specific claims process fail to reach an agreement satisfactory to the First Nation. Many others regard litigation as the only way to force governments to recognize aboriginal and treaty rights and act accordingly.

First Peoples continue to exercise what they regard as their treaty or aboriginal rights, and have regularly been taken to court for infractions of federal and provincial wildlife laws. As Wagner (1991, p. 26) explains, the Migratory Birds Convention Act (MBCA) contradicts the intent of the treaties and Section 35 of the Constitution Act, 1982, which recognizes and affirms existing aboriginal and treaty rights. Canadian lower and higher courts have held that the statute, being a federal law, overrides treaties. Consequently, Indians have been regarded by resource managers and by the courts as subject to the same bag limits and game seasons as sports hunters.

The Supreme Court of Canada 1990 rulings in the Sparrow case referred to earlier have the potential to significantly alter the way in which provincial governments and the courts respond to cases concerning the exercise of aboriginal and treaty rights to hunt, trap and fish beyond lands in aboriginal title or aboriginal fee simple title, by upholding the Indian right to fish, subject only to the needs of good conservation. For example, the province of Manitoba has stopped all charges against Indians for violations of the MBCA and the federal Fisheries Act. The province of Ontario, similarly, is no longer charging Indians for hunting or fishing out of season.

Many non-native people, including sports hunters and fishers, have responded negatively to First Peoples exercise of their rights. Many are not aware of the Sparrow decision. Many others are misinformed or do not understand its implications. Still others refuse to accept that aboriginal peoples have particular rights which courts and governments are now obligated to recognize. The consequences of the Sparrow decision further highlight the need for effective, cooperative co-management of natural resources by First Peoples and provincial governments (and in the case of the coastal fishery, the federal government).

Commentary

Extraordinary legal, institutional and political obstacles restrict the ability of First Peoples to realize their vision of reintegration of people, lands, resources and government. The obstacles are a compound of the monumental ignorance of the Canadian public about First Peoples culture, and traditions; public misinformation on the history of relationships between First Peoples and the Canadian state; public indifference to contemporary conditions and enduring injustices; and public attitudes unsympathetic to the reality that the First Peoples of Canada occupy a special position within the Canadian state.

Because of the obstacles in their way, they have had to be resourceful and persistent in finding and carrying through new strategies when previous ones were blocked by systemic refusal to recognize rights and share power. From this have emerged new and creative strategies, such as public regional government, co-jurisdiction, and co-management. Co-management incorporating indigenous knowledge and management practices, and sustainable development strategies, reflect First Nations' conviction that the rights they seek to have affirmed or recognized carry substantial responsibilities for re-establishing and sustaining environmental quality.

The successes of the past two years, reflected in the Sparrow decision, the "yes" vote on the Nunavut boundary, and the growing acceptance of both the principle and reality of self-government have come at a high price. The manoeuvring that First Peoples have had to do to compel the Canadian state and Canadian public to respond to their rights and their needs, are a huge drain on their human energy and financial resources. First Peoples have been drawn into developing leaders who are politicians and lawyers, at the expense of doctors, engineers, computer scientists, biologists, geographers, and planners. Slowly, thanks to those politicians, lawyers and an array of researchers, they are winning back some control of their governments and greater say in decision-making for their lands and resources. But the issues remain far from being resolved. Self-government, of itself, will not resolve the issues, nor will co-jurisdiction or co-management. The root problems lie deep within both non-native society and First Peoples themselves, and are a product of post-Columbian history. Political will, financial support, and institutional and attitudinal changes on the part of Canadian society, and, equally importantly, commitment by First Peoples, are all required to transform the painfully won gains of the last few years into lasting reintegration of people, land and government.

References

Amagoalik, J. (1992) "The land claim and Nunavut: One without the other isn't enough," *Arctic Circle*, Vol. 2(4): 20.

Assembly of First Nations (1991) "A critique of the Federal Government's land claims policies," in Cassidy, F. (ed.), *Aboriginal Self-Determination,* Lantzville, B.C.: Oolichan Books and the Institute for Research on Public Policy, pp. 232-249.

Bartlett, R. H. (1991) *Resource Development and Aboriginal Land Rights,* Calgary: Canadian Institute of Resources Law, University of Calgary.

Bell, J. (1992) "Nunavut: The quiet revolution," *Arctic Circle*, Vol. 2(4): 12-21.

Berger, T. (1991) *A Long and Terrible Shadow: White Values, Native Rights in the Americas*, Toronto: Douglas and McIntyre.

Berkes, F., George, P. and Preston, R. (1991) "Co-Management: The evolution in theory and practice of the joint administration of living resources," *Alternatives*, Vol. 8(2): 12-17.

Cassidy, F. (1991) "Aboriginal governments in Canada: An emerging field of study," in Cassidy, F. (ed.), *Aboriginal Self-Determination*, Lantzville, B.C.: Oolichan Books and the Institute for Research on Public Policy, pp. 252-282.

Cassidy, F. and Bish, R. (1989) *Indian Government: Its Meaning in Practice*, Victoria: Oolichan Books and the Institute for Research on Public Policy.

Clarke, B. (1990) *Native Liberty, Native Sovereignty: The Existing Rights of Aboriginal Self-government in Canada*, Montreal and Kingston: McGill-Queens University Press.

Coolican, M. (1985) *Living Treaties; Lasting Agreements*, *Report of the Task Force to Review Comprehensive Claims Policy*, Ottawa: DIAND.

Crowe, K. (1990) "Claims on the land, (Part 1)," *Arctic Circle*, Vol. 1(3): 14-23.

Department of Indian Affairs and Northern Development (1981) *In All Fairness: A Native Claims Policy, Comprehensive Claims*, Ottawa: DIAND.

Department of Indian Affairs and Northern Development (1982a) *The Alternative of Indian Band Government Legislation*, Ottawa: DIAND.

Department of Indian Affairs and Northern Development (1982b) *Outstanding Business, A Native Claims Policy* (Specific Claims), Ottawa: Ministry of Supply and Services Canada.

Department of Indian Affairs and Northern Development (1984) *The Western Arctic Claim: The Inuvialuit Final Agreement*, Ottawa: DIAND.

Erasmus, G. in CARC (Canadian Arctic Resources Committee) (1988) *1987 Conference on Aboriginal Self-Government and Constitutional Reform*, Ottawa: Canadian Arctic Resources Committee, p. 51.

Erasmus, G. (1989) "Introduction" and "Epilogue," in Richardson, B. (ed.), *Drumbeat: Anger and Renewal in Indian Country*, Toronto: Summerhill Press and Assembly of First Nations, pp. 1-42 and pp. 295-302.

Etkin, C. (1988) "The Sechelt Band: An Analysis of a New Form of Native Self-Government," *Canadian Journal of Native Studies*, Vol. 8(1): 173-105.

Fenge, T. (1987) "Land-Use Planning in Canada's North: A Wind of Change or a Bag of Wind?," in Fenge, T. and Rees, W. (eds.), *Hinterland or Homeland: Land-Use Planning in Northern Canada*, Ottawa: Canadian Arctic Resources Committee, pp. 21-53.

Freeman, M.M.R. and Carbyn, L.N. (eds.) (1988) *Traditional Knowledge and Renewable Resource Management in Northern Regions*, Edmonton: Boreal Institute.

Hawthorne, H.B. (1966) *A Survey of the Contemporary Indians of Canada*, 2 vols., Ottawa: The Queen's Printer.

Indian and Northern Affairs Canada (1980) *Indian Conditions: A Survey,* Ottawa: Indian Affairs and Northern Development.

_____ (1989a) *Highlights of Aboriginal Conditions 1981-2001*, Parts I, II and III, Quantitative Analysis and Socio-Demographic Research Working Paper, Series 89-1,2,3, Ottawa: INAC.

_____ (1989b) *Indian Self-Government Community Negotiations: Guidelines*, Ottawa: INAC.

_____ (1990) *Self-Government on Essential and Optional Subject Matters*, Policy Directorate, Self-Government Sector, Ottawa: INAC.

Isaac, T. (1991a) "The Constitution Act, 1982 and the constitutionalization of aboriginal self-government in Canada: Cree-Naskapi (of Quebec) Act," *Canadian Native Law Review*, Vol. 1: 1-13.

Isaac, T. (1991b) "Understanding the Sparrow Decision: Just the beginning," *Queen's Law Journal*, pp. 377-379.

_____ (1992a) "The storm over aboriginal self-government: Section 35 of the Constitution Act, 1982 and the redefinition of the inherent right of aboriginal self-government," *Canadian Native Law Review*, Vol. 2: 7-24.

_____ (1992b) "The B.C. court and aboriginal rights," *Policy Options*, March, pp. 16-18.

Johnson, I.V.B. (1991) "Sharing power: How can First Nations Government work?," in Cassidy, F. (ed.), *Aboriginal Self-Determination*, Lantzville, B.C.: Oolichan Books and the Institute for Research on Public Policy, pp. 78-80.

Jull, P. (1991) "Canada's Northwest Territories: Constitutional development and aboriginal rights," in Jull, P. and Roberts, S. (eds.), *The Challenge of Northern Regions*, Darwin, Australia: Australian National University North Australia Research Unit.

Knudtson, P. and Suzuki, D. (1992) *Wisdom of the Elders*, Toronto: Stoddart Publishing Co.

Little Bear, L, Boldt, M. and Long, A. (eds.) (1984) *Pathways to Self-Determination: Canadian Indians and the Canadian State*, Toronto: University of Toronto Press.

Matchewan, Chief J.M. (1989) "Algonquins of Barriere Lake: Our long battle to create a sustainable future," in Richardson, B. (ed.), *Drumbeat: Anger and Renewal in Indian Country*, Toronto; Summerhill Press for the Assembly of First Nations, pp. 139-166.

McEachern, A. (1991) *Reasons for the Judgement of the Honourable Chief Justice Allan McEachern*, in the case of Delgamuukw v R., Smithers Registry No. 0843, March.

Moss, W. (1985) "The implementation of the James Bay and Northern Quebec agreement," in Morse, B. (ed.), *Aboriginal Peoples and the Law: Indian, Metis and Inuit Rights in Canada*, Ottawa: Carleton University Press, pp. 684-694.

Native People's Circle on Environment and Development (1991) *Native People's Circle on Environment and Development: Draft Report*, Toronto: Ontario Round Table on Environment and Economy.

Native Women's Association of Canada (1992) "The future will live with the choices we make today," Statement on the Charlottetown Accord, Referendum '92, Ottawa: Native Women's Association of Canada.

Nishnawbe-Aski Nation (1991) *The Federation: M.O.U.*, Sioux Lookout, Ontario.

Nothing, B. and Wolfe, J. (1993) "Reintegrating land and government through federation: Visions and strategies of the Nishnawbe-Aski Nations in Northern Ontario," in Cant, G. et al., *Indigenous Land Rights in Commonwealth Countries: Dispossession, Negotiation and Community Action*, Christchurch, New Zealand: Ngai Tahu Maori Trust Board and the Department of Geography, University of Canterbury, pp. 121-131.

Nunavut Constitutional Forum (1985) *Building Nunavut: Today and Tomorrow*, Ottawa: Nunavut Constitutional Forum.

Ontario Native Affairs Secretariat (1991) *Issues Arising from The Nishnawbe-Aski Nation Model of Governance*, Ontario Draft Paper, in Nishnawbe-Aski Nation, Sioux Lookout.

Osherenko, G. (1988) *Sharing Power with Native Users: Co-Management for Arctic Wildlife*, Ottawa: Canadian Arctic Resources Committee.

Penneket, T. (1991) "The Road to Self-Determination," in Cassidy, F. (ed.), *Aboriginal Self-Determination, Lantzville*, B.C.: Oolichan Books and the Institute for Research on Public Policy, pp. 143-150.

Penner, K. (1983) *Indian Self-government in Canada: Report of the All-Party Committee* (Penner Report), Ottawa: Ministry of Supply and Services.

Ponting, R. (ed.), (1986) *Arduous Journey: Canadian Indians and Decolonization*, Toronto: McClelland and Stewart.

Potts, Chief G. (1989) "Last-ditch defence of a priceless homeland," in Richardson, B. (ed.), *Drumbeat: Anger and Renewal in Indian Country*, Toronto: Summerhill Press for the Assembly of First Nations, pp. 203-228.

Rees, W. (1985) "Northern land use planning: Genesis of a program," *Plan Canada*, Vol. 24: 88-96.

Richardson, B. (1989) *Drumbeat: Anger and Renewal in Indian Country,* Toronto: Summerhill Press for the Assembly of First Nations.

Ronnenberg, D. (1991) in Cassidy, F. (ed.), *Aboriginal Self-Determination,* Lantzville, BC: Oolichan Books and the Institute for Research on Public Policy, pp. 39-40.

Royal Commission on Aboriginal Peoples (1992) *The Right of Aboriginal Self-Government and the Constitution: A Commentary,* Ottawa: Royal Commission on Aboriginal Peoples.

Sanders, J. (1991) "First Nations sovereignty and self-determination," in Cassidy, F. (ed.), *Aboriginal Self-Determination,* Lantzville, B.C.: Oolichan Books and the Institute for Research on Public Policy, pp. 186-196.

Slattery, B. (1991) "Aboriginal sovereignty and imperial claims: Reconstructing North American history," in Cassidy, F. (ed.), *Aboriginal Self-Determination,* Lantzville, B.C.: Oolichan Books and the Institute for Research on Public Policy, pp. 197-218.

Taylor, J.P. and Paget, G. (1989) "Federal and provincial responsibility and the Sechelt," in Hawkes, D.C. (ed.), *Aboriginal Peoples and Government Responsibility,* Ottawa: Carleton University Press, pp. 297-344.

Usher, P. (1987) "Indigenous management systems and the conservation of wildlife in the Canadian North," *Alternatives,* Vol. 14(1): 3-9.

Usher, P. (1991) "Some implications of the Sparrow Judgement for resource conservation and management," *Alternatives,* Vol. 18(2): 20-21.

Usher, P. (1993) "Aboriginal property systems in land and resources," in Cant G. et al., *Indigenous Land Rights in Commonwealth Countries: Dispossession, Negotiation and Community Action,* Christchurch, New Zealand: Ngai Tahu Maori Trust Board and the Department of Geography, University of Canterbury, pp. 38-55.

Wagner, M.W. (1991) "Footsteps along the road: Indian land claims and access to natural resources," *Alternatives,* Vol. 18(2): 23-27.

Weller, G.R. (1990) "Devolution, regionalism and division of the Northwest Territories," in Dacks, G. (ed.), *Devolution and Constitutional Develop-*

ment in the Canadian North, Ottawa: Carleton University Press, pp. 317-314.

Wolfe, J. (1992) "Changing the pattern of aboriginal self-government in Canada," in Bowler, I.R., Bryant, C.R. and Nellis, M.O. (eds.), *Contemporary Rural Systems in Transition,* Vol. 2, Economy and Society, Oxford: C.A.B. International, pp. 294-306.

World Commission on Environment and Development (1987) *Our Common Future,* Oxford and New York: Oxford University Press.

Chapter 13

The Politics of Interest Groups in Environmental Decision Making

Bryn Greer-Wootten
York University

Geographical research on environmental decision making has benefited greatly from using conflict theories as conceptual frameworks in the last twenty years, even if a full exploration of such theories has not been developed. The large number of studies evaluating environmental policy from a political process-oriented perspective might appear to have usurped the discipline's traditional concerns with providing information inputs to decision-making processes. The latter approach has been strongly criticized by Torgerson (1986) as technocratic: "knowledge is more important than politics." It is contended in this paper, however, that positivist orientations continue to pervade much geographical research on environmental decision making, a situation not uncommon in most social scientific research on policy questions (Bradshaw-Camball and Murray, 1991). Two sets of factors could be discussed to support such a contention. The first is a methodological analysis, based on the research products themselves (i.e., internal to the research process: see Greer-Wootten, 1988). The second is an epistemological critique, which would contextualize the research outputs in a broader fashion (Fischer, 1990). In this paper, the second approach is emphasized.

Environmental decision-making processes can be contextualized in a number of ways, but one feature would emerge regardless of approach: the evolution of a multi-stakeholder process that threatens to replace the traditional three parties or actor groups common to most conflict theories: i.e., "proponents" (industry/private sector interests), "opponents" (organized public interest groups), and "regulator" (government public sector interests). Multiple stakeholders have developed partly in relation to the nature of many environmental disputes, especially as they become more localized, and partly in the context of changing attitudes of regulatory authorities. It is often thought that decision situations today required consensual approaches, almost as if there is some sort of "natural" progression at work, opening up the process for greater public participation. The trend to public consultations or debates that could potentially affect policy in Canada in the last ten years, appears to support this idea. Indeed, some observers (e.g., Doern, 1991) have suggested that there has been a significant change in Canadian political processes since the mid-1980s, so that environmental decision making must be placed in this larger public arena. On the other hand, in this paper, I emphasize the changing roles of non-governmental organizations (NGOs), in particular, and their new relationships with both public and private sector actors, especially large multinational corporations, as key components of the politics of environmental decision making in the 1990s.

Information Sources: The Opinion Leader Research Program

The information used in this analysis is drawn from the data base of the Opinion Leader Research Program (OLRP), which was established in 1982 to determine short-term (five year) trends in Canadian economic, social, political and technological issues. The program is executed by The Hay Group, Toronto, with annual membership fees from both public and private sector organizations in approximately equal proportions. The data base is developed from in-depth qualitative interviews, which are tape-recorded and average about 90 minutes in duration, with more than 200 "opinion leaders" on an annual, continuing basis. In addition to interviews carried out by the two professional social scientists who direct the Program, the remaining six interviewers are all university faculty persons. As in my own case, an attempt is made to match the expertise of opinion leaders with the research interests of faculty. The resulting information, then, is of very high quality. The interview protocol is structured quite broadly in comparison to the typical questionnaire format: (i) the general protocol asks for identification and in-depth analysis of the major issues facing Canada, and this line of questions is repeated for the informant's home province; (ii) the "special issue topics" protocol covers similar ground for the area(s) of expertise of the opinion leader, but tends to be more specific as certain topical issues are monitored over the years. There are approximately 25 special issue areas, ranging from economic policy topics to women's and native issues, for example. In many ways, the opinion leader constructs the interview in his or her own terms.

Opinion leaders are defined as leading thinkers and decision makers in Canada, who play a crucial role in defining the issues and responses for major organizations. Each respondent is further defined as an "expert" in one or more fields on the basis of peer recognition or reputation. The annual sample is made up of about 70 per cent repeat interviews, while the remaining 30 per cent consists of individuals suggested by respondents in the previous year. Elected officials are excluded from the sample. The sectoral and geographical coverage of the sample, are illustrated by the following data for 1990:

By Institutional Affiliation

Federal Government 24
Provincial Governments 44
Industry & Business Associations 61
Interest Groups.. 23
Research/Teaching Organizations 52
Labour Unions... 14
Media... 11

TOTAL...**229**

By Location of Interview

Maritimes... 18
Quebec... 44
Ontario... 66
Manitoba/Saskatchewan 22
Alberta 17
British Columbia 23
Ottawa 39

TOTAL...**229**

In this chapter, "opinion leader(s)" refers to the total set of respondents in general, and "experts" or "environment experts" are opinion leaders who are recognized as such by their peers. For the present purposes, I have decided to outline some major components of the OLRP information with respect to environmental decision making, with an emphasis on locality issues. The data are drawn from interviews with 25-35 environment experts, over the period 1988-1991, so that some appreciation of the dynamics of the relationships between public and private sectors and non-governmental organizations can be gained. Note that experts are affiliated with any one of these groups: each of the institutions and all of the regions are represented. A fuller analysis of these data can be found in the published version (Greer-Wootten, 1990): it is based on a qualitative interpretation of the interview transcripts.

The design of the Opinion Leader Research Program responds well to Brint's (1990) proposition that "general elite" studies should be abandoned, because of the structural variations and differences between members of various elites. The research design also reflects the need to incorporate different voices (Bradshaw-Camball and Murray, 1991) into social science research on organizational politics and decision making. Indeed, Hooker (1992) has demonstrated the epistemological necessity of incorporating and understanding the relevant actors' values, as well as their roles, in environmental policy analysis. Such values are implicated in positions taken with respect to substantive issues.

As a final note on the information basis for this chapter, the nature of elite perceptions and their role in policy formation should be emphasized. The typical cycle of policy analysis (Portney, 1992; Marcus, 1992) usually commences with the identification of issues that may find their place on the public agenda. The OLRP is concerned not only with identifying the issues, but also with understanding why the relevant actors and groups promote some issue areas rather than others, and particularly how they frame the problem itself (Vári, 1991). This initial representation of the issue, then, is structured primarily by elites, and it is this structuring that is subject to public debate. In assessing public issues by means of a study of elite discourse, we are able to trace one of the sources of the policy debate itself.

The Major Players in Environmental Decision Making

While environment experts emphasize the importance of local issues for the political centralization-decentralization debate, opinion leaders from many areas agree that the nature of the relationships between the major actors in environmental decision making is a central concern. Although there are variations within each group of actors, as much as between them, most opinion leaders identify industry/private sector, government/public sector, and non-governmental organizations (NGOs)/environment interest groups, as the three major players in the set of stakeholders.

The public, in general, is not left out of this discussion, however. Rather, it is regarded as a key force, as in public pressure, public awareness, or public support, which affects the roles played by each stakeholder.

All environment experts agree that the relationships between the three major groups of actors have changed remarkably in the last five years, and that this change has been towards more cooperation, replacing traditional conflict models (Mitchell, 1991). Some trace this evolution to several large-scale public consultation enquiries that paralleled the work of the 1986 National Task Force on Environment and the Economy (Lecuyer and Aitken, 1987), such as the 1987 National Forest Strategy (National Forest Strategy Steering Committee, 1992) or the Energy Options process (Kierans, 1988). These task forces were quite different from earlier consultation exercises: they had very broad terms of reference, allowing greater room for discussion, accommodation and consensus among various concerned groups.

All of these enquiries, then, are examples of the evolution of a multi-stakeholder consultative process that is unique to Canada, and most can trace their stimulus to the debate on sustainable development (MacNeill, 1988; Greer-Wootten, 1989). The fact that consensus reports were published is itself indicative of changed perceptions of environmental issues, and the desire for cooperative action.

It would be tempting to attribute this ongoing process to an opening-up of decision making by central government, but environment experts point to the greater importance of multi-stakeholder agreements as evidenced in the Round Table meetings and reports (e.g., Ontario Round Table on Environment and Economy, 1992). In fact, as enquiries/consultations become more localized, the specifics of particular environmental questions also force participants to deal with the issues in a more concrete way. The end result is a more open, better-defined decision-making process that has a higher potential for cooperation or consensual outputs.

For most experts, local multi-stakeholder agreements would ideally feed forward into larger arenas of discussion, but to date this remains a desired end-product with many hurdles to be cleared before such a level of cooperation is commonplace (Greer-Wootten, 1993). Most geographical research in this area has given a strong role to regulatory frameworks — the government as "prime movers" in environmental decision making. In fact, the dynamics of the relationships between the three major players would indicate a new and much reduced role for government at the local level, particularly in contrast to the demands for increased responsibilities at the federal level which are due to global environmental issues (Doern, 1993).

The Changing Role of Government

Historically, government held the reins in all aspects of environmental decision making. In the case of provinces, of course, these were legislated powers. Both the role of "leader" and "enforcer" of regulations have come under scrutiny in the last five years, however, as these functions of government are increasingly viewed as responses to unsustainable development. Under sustainable development objectives, a proactive outlook is required, but this tends to run counter to normal structural inertia in most bureaucracies (Tuohy, 1992). Opinion leaders who criticize the pace of government change say the continuing status quo is caused by a mind-set that is reactive and regulation-oriented, rather than one that is proactive and strategy-oriented.

These same opinion leaders view government as slipping even further behind public demands for action in the next five years. They feel that government will continue to flounder, with a lack of consistent direction in policy terms and some poorly-conceived, designed and executed programs (Rea, 1992). In terms of environmental regulations, they think there will be an increased level of enforcement and monitoring, but the overall picture will be quite spotty. A few are more optimistic, believing that regulatory controls will be improved on average, perhaps as an unanticipated outcome of closer links with the United States following the Free Trade Agreement. This is in contrast to Wilson's (1989) view that the agreement reflects a "retreat from governance" on the part of the federal government.

The situation in Ontario may be a useful indicator for the future of environmental regulations at a provincial level. Ontario is highly regarded by all opinion leaders commenting on this issue, with the Municipal/Industrial Strategy for Abatement (MISA) program for commercial water pollution often singled out as an excellent example of the design of regulatory standards. These standards were a result of a negotiated decision-making process, i.e., derived from multiple sectoral and locality-based actor groups, rather than being imposed "from above".

But the overall increased levels of regulation in Ontario have brought their own problems, in terms of the bureaucracy itself. For example, according to experts in the public sector, workloads have increased threefold and there is an urgent problem of meeting staffing needs — of an agency being unable, therefore, to fulfil its own self-defined mandate. There are fewer problems for monitoring existing programs such as MISA, apart from time delays in implementation, but when attention in the future is given to air quality or solid waste disposal, the situation is quite bleak. Even the movement to incorporate economic instruments in these areas, as proposed by the Green Plan (Government of Canada, 1992), is regarded as problematic by most opinion leaders (Greer-Wootten, 1993).

In brief, the lessons of Ontario for provincial governments responding to public pressures for increased environmental protection are clear: the mission has changed, but it is not evident that structural change within governments will be sufficient to meet the demands of sustainable development (i.e., to become proactive).

The Legitimacy Question for Governments

It is in their relations with the public, however, that governments have their most difficult task (Varette, 1993). Environment experts see the imprint of reactive mindsets in crisis management episodes, of which the Hagersville tire fire is only one example. Governments are currently in a "no-win" situation with respect to such environmental crises: they cannot win by simply throwing money at the problem, and not only do they fail to gain public confidence in their abilities to deal with crises, but their actions only serve to increase public concern. Such episodes are cumulative and feed into a process of accelerating public awareness that is evident in every NIMBY situation. Thus, crisis management is not only counter-productive in terms of sustainable development objectives, but it also works more broadly against the legitimacy of public consultation.

Many opinion leaders believe that if governments continue to lack any real leadership or consistent policy to placate public concerns, they will lose power to the public in decision-making terms (Taylor and Muller, 1992). The typical government response to environmental concerns — increase regulations, define stricter thresholds for emissions, build up enforcement mechanisms for a stronger monitoring effort, or, more recently, to incorporate market mechanisms into environmental policy — is a minimum answer to the continuing demands from the public. But these pressures may reflect an out-moded appreciation of the power of government to handle these questions effectively (Paehlke, 1990).

A significant minority of environment experts, as well a number of other opinion leaders, think there is an urgent need for governments to reassert their legitimacy in environmental protection. The experts argue that what is at risk is the real value of public participation in Environmental Impact Assessment (EIA). Other experts, however, expect governments to gain legitimacy in environmental decision making by enhancing the role of public participation in impact assessment procedures.

For opinion leaders commenting on the role of government in environmental decision making, the loss of power to the public is a broad concern. More specifically, they note that increased linkages between industry and NGOs — a "wary coalition" — have effectively reduced the power of government. They believe this is an important trend because the bureaucracy feels threatened by these changed relationships. Unlike industry and

NGOs, who have demonstrated a learning capacity for rapid response, government has been very slow to define its ground rules for environmental protection (Currie, 1992).

The disruption in normal power relationships within governments is a major cause of their inaction. Ministries fight to retain their position and find it difficult to function. Opinion leaders state that this scenario is maximized in Ottawa, but it is present to varying degrees in most jurisdictions.

The traditional guardianship role for government, then, is now seriously questioned by many environment experts, and a legitimate place for government in the multi-stakeholder decision-making processes necessary for sustainable development is at risk. Environmental impact assessment procedures might again provide a possible way out of this "no-win" situation, although in their more legalistic context, government acts as a facilitator of decisions rather than as the leader of others.

The issue of government as a lost leader has its strongest impact at the local level, where specific parameters force the decision-making process into its most conflictual or its most consensual mode. Since all local jurisdictions (municipalities, cities, regional governments...) are the "children of the province" in Canada, the powers of localities are quite restricted. At the weakest level of government, then, the demands for environmental protection will be greatest. Such demands will emanate from residents of potentially impacted communities and regions, feeding into the dynamics of localism. For all these reasons, current discussions concerning the future of environmental impact assessment are viewed as crucially important by environment experts.

Private Sector Responses to Environmental Issues

Traditionally, as the proponent of economic development, industry has been cast as the villain in the play. Most experts agree that there are some encouraging signs of changes in attitudes, and industry itself has definitely recognized that the environment is not limitless. Recognizing only that the costs of environmental clean-ups are enormous, however, is a short-term and very limited view, since even a still-reactive mind-set is forced to see the real costs (Main, 1988). A more significant change would be proactive in terms of long-term planning (Sadler and Hull, 1990), maximally with the costs of waste treatment/management built into the total project costs, in order to minimize environmental harm.

The industrial/private sector group contains the highest variability of the three major sets of actors. The "scorecard" on those corporations that are really committed to environmental protection, is "fair" at best. In addition, they might account only for about 5 per cent of the sector, according to most experts. But they believe it is significant that some companies have established a strong lead in environmental strategies, and that the proponents within these companies are often young (the next generation of leaders) and that they will help to diffuse the message to others (Hooper and Rocca, 1991).

There appear to be two major impediments to change, apart from organizational inertia. Firstly, companies are greatly conditioned by their sectoral affiliation, with its correlates of size and location (especially in peripheral regions). Some industrial sectors contain very few companies that are attempting to take steps towards becoming more environmentally responsible, so there is little pressure for any company to change (Mitchell, 1989). Sectoral inertia is a factor along with an individual company's individual inertia. The forest products industry is a good example of sectoral inertia.

On the other hand, for some manufacturing industries, survival itself can be in question if companies do not demonstrate environmental responsibility. The economic burden of cleaning up spills or emissions beyond the regulated limits is well recognized, but crises are cumulative in their impact on public awareness. There have already been examples of calls for boycotting certain products, and cumulative impacts could lead to negative consumer reactions. Some observers feel that one type of industry could thus be tarred with the poor records of a few firms. Conversely, a "clean" company within a "dirty" sector might use their environmentally responsible practices to advantage in the market place (Enslow, 1992).

The second, more important factor affecting industry's response to sustainable development initiatives is size. Clearly, larger corporations have a much stronger resource base, both financial and human, as well as organizational systems that can be modified for new strategies (Collison, 1989). Unlike the majority of small companies which are serving the Canadian market, environment experts think, in general, that these larger corporations are more responsive to environmental questions because they are operating in international markets.

In the U.S., for example, there are stronger laws that might be used in legal proceedings against a company. In the European Community, environmental issues are more politicized in any case, with the advent of the Green Party, so that environmentally responsible behaviours are expected to a greater extent than in Canada (Tully, 1989). Often, these larger companies operate on a corporate-wide basis in more or less the same way, at least in the developed world, so that their activities in Canada reflect this external experience.

What are the chances of diffusion of new strategies to smaller companies, more oriented to the Canadian market? The outlook for this change is of the order of five to ten years, according to experts in environmental issues, i.e., relatively short-term because of the increasing role of industrial associations. Some of these groups are specific sectoral associations, as in the case of oil and gas, so that change might be more rapid than for more general associations. Experts point to the environment task forces established by the Business Council on National Issues or the Canadian Chamber of Commerce as significant first steps. The general aim is to create environmental codes of practice that can be adopted by all industries, as well as to promulgate the idea of incorporating market mechanisms into environmental policy (Hull and St.-Pierre, 1990).

Opinion leaders from industry see these changes as "normal" responses to a new set of initiatives, in that once strategic directions have been established, a number of more explicit policy directions can be issued "from the top". At the same time, the success of these changes is strongly influenced by the response from the shop floor and from localities in which production facilities are sited. The case of Noranda, with its decentralized system of environmental controls, is instructive in this context.

Noranda introduced the idea of an "Environment Committee" as a management tool, modelled along the lines of Health and Safety Committees (i.e., wide representation from all levels of employees, local autonomy in fleshing out the details of remedial responses to particular risk conditions, etc.). The Health and Safety Committees, common in all larger organizations, worked because of their strong local roots and responsibilities generated from shared endeavours. If "health and safety is every employee's business", can "environmental care and protection is every employee's business" be far behind?

Redefining the Role of Industry

Between larger and smaller companies there will have to be more cooperation if environmental protection strategies are to have major impact. Technology will have to be shared to a greater extent, in order to aid in the diffusion of environmentally responsible behaviours. It is a fair question, then, to ask if such cooperative endeavours will emerge in the competitive private sector ... will the environmental imperative be strong enough to effect such a change?

By itself, concern for the environment might not be sufficient, but it is driven by public awareness (Henriques, 1993). A majority of opinion leaders feel that it is the public that is ahead of all other actors in setting the agenda for change, and that this represents a permanent shift in values. Most Canadian governments, and especially the federal government, do not understand this value shift and continue to interpret environmental activism as a "trend", implying that it will pass.

Environment experts contend that industry will respond to a shift in power from government to the public by assuming a new leadership role in environmental issues. To achieve credibility in this respect, industry must have ethical behaviour as a first principle (Sadler and Hull, 1990). Many opinion leaders other than environment experts also think industry will likely respond to the environmental ethics question, as a way of rebuilding some of the reputation lost in the "unethical '80s".

Ethical responsibilities imply that new management styles are needed to avoid NIMBY problems in potentially impacted communities. The oil and gas industry in Alberta has demonstrated this principle in its developments recently: project planning and community approaches are integrated from the outset, and citizen coalition groups are proactively involved in the process. The objective is to avoid legal or quasi-legal hold-ups which could occur at each stage of a project, with considerable cost implications. The benefits from this proactive, multi-stakeholder approach, then, are both economic and social. Clearly, it demonstrates a new format for localized decision-making processes.

In redefining its role and relationship to the environment, industry has generally become more active, recognizing that it needs to work with both government and NGOs. One example of such fruitful partnerships is the New Directions Group (1991). NGOs are now widely regarded by industry opinion leaders as representing legitimate public interests, staffed by knowledgeable persons, etc. There are signs of "an increasing though tentative and appropriately wary coalition" between industry and NGOs, versus government — in the words of one environment expert. Some NGOs have received financial support from the private sector, but the cooptation question is always raised. According to some experts, it could be seen as a very positive sign if more general support for environment NGOs came from the private sector, rather than monies tied to specific projects. Certainly this approach would influence public opinion, which remains fairly sceptical on industry's motives.

With respect to government, industry used to think it had a privileged access, but it now realizes it must share this with NGOs. There is also some confusion about the direction that government is headed with its environmental policy, except for the general agreement that regulations will increase in the future and there will be some experiments with economic instruments (Greer-Wootten, 1993). It is clear that most companies will respond to new regulations, but the expectations are that they will do so at a minimum level only: there is no credit for exceeding the thresholds under regulatory regimes.

From industry's viewpoint, incentives are as necessary for solving environmental problems as shorter-term increased controls. In fact, there is a strong trend toward market-based solutions endorsed by many environment experts, including those from NGOs (Paehlke, 1990). At the same time, the environment NGOs contain some of the strongest voices against market solutions. One can expect this debate to achieve prominence in the resolution of legitimacy among the various actors in environmental decision making in the 1990s.

The Emergence of Environment NGOs

The role of environmental NGOs as "the voice of the public" has been augmented in the last few years by an alliance with the media. In part, this is due to media response to environmental crises, but it is equally due to the maturing of the interest groups themselves. NGOs are no longer regarded as "idealistic fringe players" by most opinion leaders, but rather as legitimate professional groups, with good management skills and a solid record of research-based knowledge and expertise (Doern, 1990). Part of the maturing process has been in gaining political skills, including ways of handling the media in their best interests. Certainly, most experts agree that NGOs are now more realistic than in the past, less likely to suggest policies or solutions to problems from a purely ideological basis.

Internally, NGOs are much stronger than in the past. They are likely to contain persons who have spent part of their careers in industry and/or government. This means that NGOs often have the ability to argue environmental issues on technical grounds. As organizations, they tend to be relatively informal. Ties between NGOs also tend to be informal networks. Such flexibility and the recognized need to communicate and share information widely, provide the foundation for the strength of NGOs.

Of all the actors involved in environmental decision making, NGOs have probably experienced the greatest change recently (Wilson, 1992). In some areas, such as wildlife, conservation and heritage planning, they are widely recognized as the most powerful actor. In other aspects of their work, such as endorsement of "environmentally friendly" products or "green" investments, the power of NGOs is quite evident. In supporting a policy initiative or conservation program, for example, their impact may be more indirect. In the longer term, however, these endorsements are indicative of an important trend: the politicization of environmental concerns at a local level.

Although there are very few murmurings about the rise of a Green Party in Canada, environment experts agree that interactions in the decision-making process by NGOs have taken a new turn. In part, this has evolved from the experiences of NGOs themselves. They now realize to a much greater extent than in the past, that they must work together in those areas where they can achieve consensus — in order to become more effective politically. The areas themselves are becoming more clearly linked as knowledge of the interconnections among components of the ecosystem is augmented by research on global change. Formerly separate groups concerned with wildlife/species conservation, or naturalists, or heritage preservation NGOs, for example, are finding that they have much in common with anti-pollution groups or energy conservation advocates.

Besides the informal networking that characterizes their contacts, NGOs are regularly called upon to serve on advisory committees or public consultation bodies, by either industry or government. Such advisory and administrative work, with its 'outside' contacts, augments the legitimation process for NGOs. Interestingly, all of these groups at one time started as locality-based public interest spokespersons, so that although many of them now have re-defined their mandates beyond locality, the importance of community ties and relationships is not forgotten. This is evident whenever there is a local crisis situation, when the permanent organizations will provide resources for local ad hoc groups. These interactions feed further into the legitimation process.

There is a tendency in discussions of this trend to regard the increased power of NGOs as reflecting a departure from their local roots. But the criticisms that NGOs do not represent the public do not themselves bear examination in the context of increased public consultation over the last four or five years. Most experts believe that this trend will continue to gain pace, and not only in environmental areas.

Experts note that, ironically, the apparent loss of power by government, in relation to other actors, is probably due to increased government intervention in the past. As this resulted in many more contacts between public and government, people realized the extent to which government decisions affected their lives. In turn, this led to the desire for some degree of control, obtainable only through organized opposition.

The fact that, today, the organizations seek a role in decision making as one of a number of stakeholders in the decision process, does not mean that the general circumstances that led to organized opposition in the first place have disappeared. Rather, the arena in which decisions are made has changed its structure, allowing a greater role for more organizations. It is likely to change even more in the future, given the further evolution of sustainable development initiatives in Canada.

As indicated above, relationships between NGOs and industry have started to change to a more cooperative standing, although the degree of change is not as extensive as that brought about from NGOs' linkages with government. Many NGOs have realized that their interests are increasingly similar to those of industry, and that they "no longer corner the market in virtue," in the words of one expert. Moreover, both sides of this relationship tend to be relatively flexible, open to new avenues of decision making. As a result, the changes have been quite rapid and both actor groups comment favourably on this aspect of their new linkages, in comparison to the slow bureaucratic responses of government.

Yet, it is still with government that NGOs have stronger linkages because of an emerging trend of "trading" leadership. A significant number of persons who worked for many years in NGOs, now work for government — and vice versa. The impact of these interchanges is that NGOs now tend to be more aware of the constraints faced by policy-makers, and although they may continue to berate them as inefficient and out-moded, there is an increased recognition of the legitimacy of political constraints. The same argument can be made for the trading of leadership between NGOs and industry (although with much less vice versa trade): the legitimacy of the economic interests of industry is more realistically evaluated by NGOs today (Tucker, 1991).

There is, then, a noticeable trend towards a greater understanding of legitimate concerns between the actors. Yet, this dynamic is not endorsed by all environment experts. For a significant minority, from all three actor groups, the traditional attributes of NGOs are still evident, as the "polarizers" of environmental disputes (Downey, 1991). Such NGOs tend to be single-issue groups and stand in contrast to the "consensus-builders", seen as multiple-issue groups working more closely within sustainable development objectives.

The Power Bases of Environment NGOs

Most experts believe that the latter orientation will emerge as a stronger force in the future, bolstering the position of NGOs as the new power brokers. But whether or not this happens depends on two interrelated sets of conditions:

1) changes in the economic context within which environmental decision making operates; and

2) changes in the dynamics of the decision-making process itself.

The economic argument is based on the observation that Canadian industry itself no longer has assured control over its own product, in isolation from global economic change. For example, control can be bought out and changed over a short period of time by mergers, acquisitions, etc. The potential for change in such circumstances can lead to the development of a broader base of technical and financial expertise in order to assure relative stability in company operations.

In government, as well, there has been an increase in "general purpose" management and expertise, as it is recognized that many environmental problems do not rest neatly in specific specialist agencies. These trends have resulted in a new set of accommodations between industry, government and NGOs and some experts believe the NGO community is the most disadvantaged in this respect.

Now that problems of environmental protection have moved to central areas of Cabinet, for example, they are discussed in the context of larger issues such as education, national defence, crime prevention, etc. Thus, the budgeting and resource allocation questions dealt with by a multi-purpose government present a set of issues for NGOs which are beyond their control and expertise, as their power base lies in more focused questions. Some experts, however, counter this argument by observing that no one can escape environmental issues, and that environmentalists have already demonstrated their great learning capacities in evolving from single to multiple environmental issues, via coalitions.

These changes, in the form of debates on resource management conflicts, hold the danger of re-alienating interest groups. As well, the second set of factors concerning the nature of decision-making processes themselves, could add to this danger. The danger to NGOs' new roles as power brokers is seen in the challenge that, as public consultation increases, their freedom of action becomes lessened (Wilson, 1992). This is the constant concern with cooptation, voiced by many NGO opinion leaders: how to be part of the solution (rather than as traditionally cast, as part of the problem) yet to maintain an independent role as critic.

This problem has not been resolved and it has led to some divisions between environmental NGOs. Most experts feel that NGOs will have to position themselves very carefully on this question, and they may have to do this by issue rather than by philosophy (Eder, 1990). Again, counter arguments are readily forthcoming from other experts, who point to the rise of coalition groups of NGOs, with a greater political power base to respond to the challenges.

The problems of locality issues have always triggered responses by opposition groups, and the linkages with grass-roots organizations continue to be a vital force for NGOs. The danger of a widening gap between local groups and more broadly-based NGOs is rejected by most environment experts, because of the two sides of the "locality coin":

1) locality as backdrop — the arena in which many issues can be meaningfully related to each other because the questions or problems are specific. Locality issues, by their very nature, involve multiple issues for which general-purpose strategies must be negotiated between concerned actors; and

2) localism (i.e., local activism) as a positive force for change in environmental decision making.

A vital addition to both components of locality is the nature of NGO organization and composition: flexibility, inter-connections, networking. The power base is built on these relatively informal networks, so that NGOs and their evolving role in environmental decision-making processes have become a distinct voice in comparison to both industry and government.

Concluding Remarks

Discussions of environmental decision-making processes often refer to the role of "the general public" as a factor influencing the behaviours of the major actors. In fact, the recent Ontario review of EIA has made a significant contribution in disaggregating the "general public" into constituencies of publics potentially impacted by development proposals. Nonetheless, it is likely that the common usage — general public — will continue. In reality, however, a number of publics are involved in environmental conflicts, and their actions effectively set the stage in which the three major actors operate.

Environmental conflicts present a new set of problems, so that the rules for mediation, for example, are not established or accepted by all parties (Hooker, 1992). The problems tend to be relatively well defined, but not the solutions: the staging is dynamic and ambiguous.

The necessity of changing decision-making processes with respect to the environment is one of the more important lessons learned from the National Task Force on Economy and the Environment in its public consultations. The call for more stakeholders to play their parts in cooperative mechanisms has resulted in a multitude of voices, but little clarification at present (Lane, 1993). Thus, in addition to the three major actors, environmental discussions can attract contributions from consumer groups (strongest in Quebec), some churches, professional groups (e.g., doctors concerned with public health issues), and the labour movement.

In this sense, the arena for consultations with a larger number of concerned publics has changed since the mid-1980s. The research on "new social movements" or the "new politics" has attempted to capture this evolution. For example, Miller (1991) and MacDermid and Stevenson (1991) have interpreted survey research findings on public attitudes to the environment in this framework. From a more aggregate perspective, Tuohy's (1992) institutional analysis of the complex ways in which Canadian public policy is formulated is instructive. She demonstrates that the stimulus, in particular sectors, for policy change is conditioned by the shifting alignments of various interest groups. The "ambivalence" in the intriguing title of her book is due to the fact that allegiances, relationships and coalitions among interest groups (including departments of the government bureaucracy) are constantly changing in relation to the policy problem under discussion. The "new social groups" attempt to insert themselves into this ambiguous arena, often with little power and legitimacy (Eder, 1990). The task is made more difficult because they have to grapple with the "politics of expertise" (Fischer, 1990), but it is clear that in Canada, environment NGOs have progressed remarkably since the early 1980s.

At one time, the environment community in Canada was labelled "a small, self-selecting elite," according to one opinion leader, and some members of this group now feel threatened by the emergence of so many "new faces". This "loss of control" for some observers is matched by "new opportunities to contribute to environmental decision making" for others. One constant for all actors is that the environment is politically attractive, of course. Similar factors operate in the emergence of coalitions of environment NGOs.

Sustainable development initiatives strongly imply, by their emphasis on proactive strategies, that all concerned publics should be more involved at the "front end" of any project or development proposal. According to some environment experts, this trend is already in place in the oil and gas industry in Alberta, where the decision-making process has been described as "much flatter" than in the past. It is expected to flatten further in future, as local communities become more involved at the front end. In this sense, localities can positively affect the evolution of sustainable development in Canada.

The fact that local issues are specific in nature is a valuable asset. In comparison, the broader public consultation process designed as input to policy development, as in the Energy Options process, has its drawbacks. While it was widely accepted as a positive step, it has since been criticized because of the lack of any visible signs of actions based on the consultations. If the purpose of the process is not clear to participants, the value of participation itself will be questioned (Shepherd, 1993). Such broad, "non-locality" consultation processes, then, can be counter-productive in the trend toward more cooperative, consensual decision making, although the social learning that they engender is important (Voluntary Planning, 1991).

The more common image of local response to development proposals is the negative reactions implied by the "not in my backyard" (NIMBY) syndrome. For a minority of experts, NIMBY reactions are emotional and not based on an understanding of the issues involved. A more significant number of environment experts, however, evaluate the NIMBY situations in a positive sense because they demonstrate the vitality of locality issues for potentially impacted residents. Local demands for representation and participation in the decision-making process — if fulfilled — allow a public airing of views and ordinary people to feel that they do have a part to play in their own future. An excellent example in the Toronto region is the work of the Crombie Commission (Royal Commission on the Future of the Toronto Waterfront, 1992). As a result, most experts feel that institutional responses to NIMBY situations must be sympathetic to these concerns — in effect, to grant them legitimacy. It is in this local context that environment NGOs return to their grass-roots power bases, and, with their new status in relation to both industry and government, they will be crucial in structuring local responses to environmental problems.

References

Bradshaw-Camball, P. and Murray, V.V. (1991) "Illusions and other games: A trifocal view of organizational politics," *Organizational Science*, Vol. 2: 379-398.

Brint, S. (1990) "Rethinking the policy influence of experts: From general characterizations to analysis of variation," *Sociological Forum*, Vol. 5: 361-385.

Collison, R. (1989) "The greening of the boardroom," *Report on Business Magazine (The Globe and Mail)*, July, pp. 42-55.

Currie, J. (1992) "An approach to assessing the management of environmental responsibilities in federal departments and agencies," *Optimum, The Journal of Public Sector Management*, Vol. 23(3): 69-77.

Doern, G.B. (1990) "Getting it green: Canadian environmental policy in the 1990s," in Doern, G.B. (ed.), *The Environmental Imperative: Market Approaches to the Greening of Canada*, Toronto: C.D. Howe Institute Policy Study 9, pp. 1-18.

Doern, G.B. (1991) "Social regulation and environmental-economic reconciliation," in Doern, G.B. and Purchase, B.B. (eds.), *Canada at Risk? Canadian Public Policy in the 1990s*, Toronto: C.D. Howe Institute Policy Study 13, pp. 100-115.

Doern, G.B. (1993) *Green Diplomacy: How Environmental Policy Decisions Are Made*, Toronto: C.D. Howe Institute Policy Study 16.

Downey, T.J. (1991) "And the real challenge for environmentalists," *Policy Options*, April, pp. 27-30.

Eder, K. (1990) "The rise of counter-culture movements against modernity: Nature as a new field of class struggle," *Theory, Culture and Society*, Vol. 7: 21-47.

Enslow, B. (1992) "The green advantage," *Across The Board*, June, pp. 21-25.

Fischer, F.A. (1990) *Technocracy and the Politics of Expertise*, Newbury Park, California: Sage.

Government of Canada (1992) *Canada's Greenplan: Economic Instruments for Environmental Protection*, Ottawa: Minister of Supply and Services Canada.

Greer-Wootten, B. (1988) "The science of locational risk or the risk of locational science?," in Massam, B.H. (ed.), *Complex Location Problems: Some Interdisciplinary Approaches*, North York, Ontario: York University Institute for Social Research Monograph Series, pp. 98-132.

Greer-Wootten, B. (1989) *Sustainable Development in Canada: Promise or Paradox?*, Toronto: Hay Opinion Leader Research Program.

Greer-Wootten, B. (1990) *Canadian Environmental Issues and Localities: "Not In My Back Yard,"* Toronto: Hay Opinion Leader Research Program.

Greer-Wootten, B. (1993) *Canadian Environmental Issues at the Regional Scale: "Not In Our Back Yard,"* Toronto: Hay Opinion Leader Research Program, 38 pp.

Henriques, I. (1993) *Business and the Environment: 1992 Corporate Survey,* North York, Ontario: York University Faculty of Administrative Studies (Erivan K. Haub Program in Business and the Environment).

Hooker, C.A. (1992) "Responsibility, ethnics and nature," in Cooper, D.E. and Palmer, J.A. (eds.), *The Environment in Question: Ethics and Global Issues*, London: Routledge, pp. 147-164.

Hooper, T. L. and Rocca, B.T. (1991) "Environmental affairs now on the strategic agenda," *The Journal of Business Strategy,* May/June, pp. 26-30.

Hull, B. and St.-Pierre, A. (1990) *The Market and the Environment, Market-Based Approaches to Achieve Environmental Goals,* Ottawa: Conference Board of Canada (Report 62-90), 26 pp.

Kierans, T. (1988) *Energy and Canadians into the 21st Century: A Report on the Energy Options Process,* Ottawa: Minister of Supply and Services, Canada, 127 pp.

Lane, P. (1993) "Ontario's fair tax commission: An innovative approach to public consultation," *Optimum, The Journal of Public Sector Management*, Vol. 23(4): 7-17.

Lecuyer, G. and Aitken, R. (1987) *Report of the National Task Force on Environment and Economy*, Downsview, Ontario: Canadian Council of Resource and Environment Ministers, 18 pp.

MacDermid, R. and Stevenson, M. (1991) *Identification with New Social Movements: The Structure of Public Opinion on Environmental Issues*, North York, Ontario: York University Institute for Social Research Working Paper, 29 pp.

MacNeill, J. (1988) "Sustainable growth," *Policy Options*, March, pp. 22-25.

Main, J. (1988) "Here comes the big new cleanup," *Fortune*, November 21, pp. 102-118.

Marcus, A.A. (1992) *Controversial Issues in Energy Policy*, Newbury Park, California: Sage, 155 pp.

Miller, D. (1991) "What the polls tell us," *Women and Environments*, Vol. 13: 68-69.

Mitchell, B. (1991) "'BEATing' conflict and uncertainty in resource management and development," in Mitchell, B. (ed.), *Resource Management and Development: Addressing Conflict and Uncertainty*, Toronto: Oxford University Press, pp. 268-285.

Mitchell, J. (1989) "Ecologies of scale," *Financial Post Moneywise*, June, pp. 38-43.

National Forest Strategy Steering Committee (1992) *Sustainable Forests: A Canadian Commitment*, Congress Version for the National Forest Congress, Ottawa, March 2-4, 34 pp.

New Directions Group (1991) *Reducing and Eliminating Toxic Substances Emissions: An Action Plan for Canada*, Toronto: New Directions Group, 12 pp.

Ontario Round Table on Environment and Economy (1992) *Restructuring for Sustainability*, Toronto: Ontario Round Table, 75 pp.

Paehlke, R. (1990) "Environmental policy in the 1990s," in Doern, G.B. and Purchase, B.B. (eds.), *Canada at Risk: Canadian Public Policy in the 1990s,* Toronto: C.D. Howe Institute Policy Study 13, pp. 214-223.

Portney, K.E. (1992) *Controversial Issues in Environmental Policy: Science vs. Economics vs. Politics,* Newbury Park, California: Sage, 180 pp.

Rea, J.C. (1992) "Product stewardship - A basis for an industry/government partnership," *Optimum, The Journal of Public Sector Management,* Vol. 23(3): 17-23.

Royal Commission on the Future of the Toronto Waterfront (1992) *Regeneration: Toronto's Waterfront and The Sustainable City, Final Report,* Toronto: Queen's Printer for Ontario/Ottawa: Minister of Supply and Services Canada.

Sadler, B. and Hull, B. (1990) *In Business for Tomorrow: The Transition to Sustainable Development,* Ottawa: The Conference Board of Canada (Globe '90 Highlights), 31 pp.

Shepherd, R.P. (1993) "The citizens forum: A case study in public consultation," *Optimum, The Journal of Public Sector Management,* Vol. 23(4): 18-27.

Taylor, D.W. and Muller, T.E. (1992) "Eco-literacy and environmental citizenship: A social marketing challenge for public sector management," *Optimum, The Journal of Public Sector Management,* Vol. 23(3): 6-16.

Torgerson, D. (1986) "Between knowledge and politics: Three faces of policy analysis," *Policy Sciences,* Vol. 19: 33-59.

Tucker, W. (1991) "Shaking the invisible hand," *Forbes,* April 1, pp. 64-65.

Tully, S. (1989) "What the 'Greens' mean for business," *Fortune,* October 23, pp. 159-164.

Tuohy, C.J. (1992) *Policy and Politics in Canada: Institutionalized Ambivalence,* Philadelphia: Temple University Press.

Varette, S. (1993) "Consultation in the public service: A question of skills," *Optimum, The Journal of Public Sector Management,* Vol. 23(4): 28-39.

Vári, A. (1991) "Argumatics: A text analysis procedure for supporting problem formulation," *Quality and Quantity*, Vol. 25, pp. 1-17.

Voluntary Planning (1991) *Report on the Public Consultation Process: Encounter on the Nova Scotia Economy, May 22 - May 30, 1991*, Halifax, N.S.: Voluntary Planning.

Wilson, H.T. (1989) *Retreat From Governance: Canada and the Continental-International Challenge*, Hull, Quebec: Voyageur.

Wilson, J. (1992) "Green lobbies: Pressure groups and environmental policy," in Boardman, R. (ed.), *Canadian Environmental Policy: Ecosystems, Politics, and Process*, Toronto: Oxford University Press, pp. 109-125.

Acknowledgements

I would like to thank the Director, Tom Atkinson, and the Associate Director, Gillian Gilmour, of the Hay Opinion Leader Research Program for their continuing support and encouragement.

Part III

Working for Improvement

Chapter 14

Geographers in Post-Secondary Education Planning in British Columbia

John D. Chapman and Walter G. Hardwick
The University of British Columbia

Introduction

In almost 50 years, British Columbia (BC) has developed a large, comprehensive, and partially articulated public post-secondary education and training system. In l945 post-secondary academic programs were offered at the University of British Columbia (UBC) in Vancouver and some 30 schools with Grade 13, for a total enrollment of less than 10,000. In l993 there are 25 public institutions (4 universities, 17 colleges, and 4 institutes) providing academic, career-technical, and vocational programs to more than 130,000 enrollees in every part of the province (Figure 14.1). This paper will describe the extent and pace of change, explore the processes involved in the emergence of the system focusing especially on the provision of information, policy formulation, strategic program planning and governance. Then it explores the roles of geographers and the insights of their discipline in planning for the expansion. This paper describes the evolution of the system over four time periods: 1945-62, 63-75, 76-87, and 88-present.

Emergence of the Post Secondary Education System

Rising Expectations: 1945-62

By the end of the Second World War, the demand for post-secondary education in BC started to rise rapidly. The increase was fueled by a wave of returning veterans, a rising number of school leavers, and increasing recognition for formal education and training after high school. The demand for academic programs was met by a dramatic expansion of UBC and Grade 13 classes at approved high schools throughout the province (Figure 14.2). Vocational training programs continued in high schools, and later in adult vocational schools funded in part with federal funds. Programs continued at the two normal schools in Vancouver and Victoria. Degree programs were concentrated in Vancouver, and, by contrast, vocational training was more dispersed.

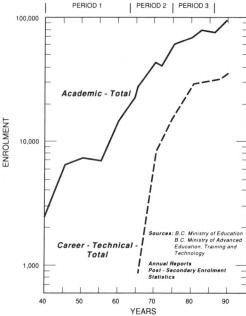

Figure 14.1: Enrolment in British Columbia
Post - Secondary Education

As early as 1957 attention was drawn to the need for a comprehensive, planned province-wide system of institutions (Hardwick, I957). In I958 the Public School Act was amended to enable School Boards to establish district colleges in affiliation with UBC, and later that year, a Royal Commission on Education was established which reported in 1960 (B.C. Royal Commission on Education, I960). It recommended in part the expansion of Grade 13 and the creation of "Collegiate Academies" offering Grades 11-12-13. Except for a feasibility study carried out for the Kelowna School District (Dawe, 1959) no action was taken. At UBC, however, the administration recognized the need for a comprehensive post-secondary data bank and enrollment forecasting, and in 1959 J.D. Chapman was seconded to the President's office to undertake the empirical studies. Later the UBC Senate was presented with a case for more equitable access for students outside the metropolitan areas and a forecast and recommendations as to the location of universities and colleges (Hardwick, I960). As the decade concluded the stage was set for change.

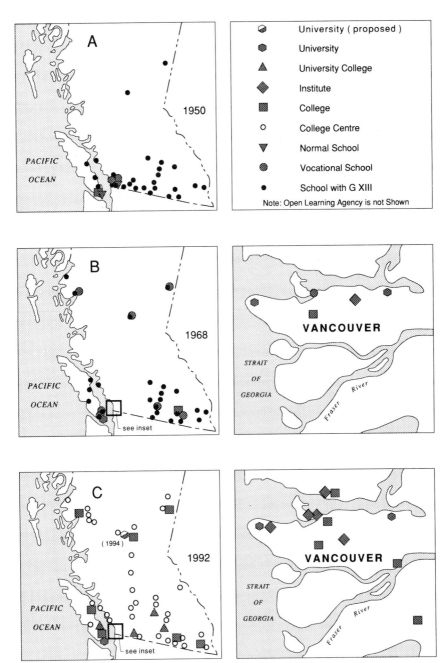

Figure 14.2: British Columbia, Post Secondary Education Facilities

Macdonald Report and Emergence of a Post-Secondary System: 1962-75.

The agent of change came in the person of the newly appointed President of UBC, Dr. John B. Macdonald. With a team of advisors, which included the two authors, both then members of the Geography Department, the President prepared a report on higher education (Macdonald, 1962). For the first time, post-secondary education was considered as a comprehensive system (Figure 14.3). This resulted in the establishment of two additional universities and, within a decade, nine community colleges. Indirectly it lead to the appointment of an academic, Dr. Neil Perry, formerly Dean of Commerce and Business Administration at UBC, as the first Deputy Minister of Education. Dr. Perry introduced modern management to the Ministry and established a Division of University and College Affairs. The first Acting Director of the division, assigned to develop a management information system, was geographer J.D. Chapman. In addition to the universities and colleges, the BC Institute of Technology (BCIT) was established in Burnaby in 1964, and six vocational schools were opened outside the Vancouver region between 1960 and 1966.

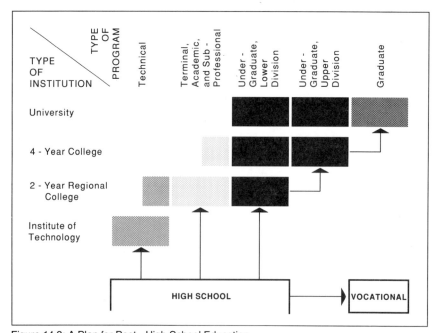

Figure 14.3: A Plan for Post - High School Education

By the end of the decade three streams of programs were available in the province — academic, career/technical, and vocational. In addition a significant degree of spatial dispersion had been accomplished, especially outside the metropolitan region of Vancouver, and the first coordinating governance and advisory structures were in place.

Rounding Out the System:1975-87

A second wave of innovation in the post secondary system emerged with the appointment of two academics as Minister and Deputy Minister of Education respectively, Dr. Patrick McGeer, Professor of Neuroscience and Dr. Walter Hardwick, Professor of Geography. They introduced new ideas about the role of science, research, and communications in education, about system-wide management, and about open learning. The construction of college facilities in regional centres continued; two specialty institutes (Justice and Marine), the College of Art in Vancouver and the Open Learning Institute were established. The latter was based on the principle of dispersing programs to the individual rather than bringing individuals to university and college centres. A College and Institute Act was passed by the Legislature divorcing Colleges from the School Act. The Discovery Research Parks were opened, the Science Council of B.C. incorporated, and a number of programs initiated to expand intelligence-based enterprises in the province.

Consolidation and Access: 1987-92

With the election of the Social Credit government of Premier William Vander Zalm in 1985 a Ministry of Advanced Education and Job Training was created with Gary Mullins, a geographer, as Deputy Minister. Reacting to continued public demands for increased access to post secondary institutions, in late 1987 a Provincial Access Committee was appointed to develop a plan to increase participation throughout the province. The issue of university programs outside the metropolitan areas was revisited and as a result the Ministry created a number of affiliation agreements among colleges and universities. In 1990, a University of Northern BC was announced with a main campus to be built at Prince George. A Human Resource Development Project (1992) reported to government on the need to further cultivate the two interrelated goals of empowering people to achieve "their learning objectives and participate in our common social and economic future; and to provide a solid base for the economic development of our province".

For the most part, geographic isolation has been diminished and at present persons resident in any community in the province have access to university and college programs. By 1992, the limitations are less geographic and more the result of insufficient capacity and difficulties arising from entry into and movement among components within the system as well as the financial capacity of institutions themselves.

Geographic Analysis

The Post-Secondary System: 1962

The case for an expanded post-secondary system was only hazily acknowledged in the 1950s. The Department of Education in Victoria was a schools ministry and had no planning capability. The President and the Senate of UBC were aware that the schools were burgeoning, but, in a period of relative fiscal restraint, they were more concerned with funding the University itself than with initiating new institutions.

Like residents of many natural resource-rich regions, British Columbians saw their increasing wealth as a product of the resources themselves, rather than the people who enabled their extraction, initial processing and sale. When skilled workers were required, the normal practice was to recruit outside Canada, often in Europe and the British Isles. A general view was that the resources themselves played a causal role in creating wealth and the agents of the task were somehow disembodied. So a combination of raw material determinism, and an ease of importing skilled labor dulled policy-makers' sense of urgency for an expanded post-secondary system.

Questions of equity of opportunity for post-secondary education had been raised since the 1960s. Over half of the residents of the province are clustered within an eighty mile radius of downtown Vancouver, itself located in the southwest corner of the province. The balance reside in cities and towns strung along the narrow valleys of the mountainous interior or the coastal inside passage. The small size and linear pattern of settlement rarely provided the threshold population required for the on site provision of a wide range of services. The variability in the range of services between the urbanized south-west and the interior was great indeed, and the adjustment of this inequality became a top priority of government. Schools were improved everywhere as property taxes for school purposes were equalized across the province. The expansion of highways to the interior and the extension of rural electrification and the BC Hospital Insurance plan substantially raised the service levels. But post-secondary education beyond Grade 13 remained unavailable in the interior and the north. So the issue of regional equity was raised as a rationale for an expansion of post-secondary education.

Then there was the issue of demographic change. As mentioned, Chapman had been invited into the UBC President's office to start an academic planning enterprise, and in the process started forecasting enrollments. Already a large high school cohort of post-war baby-boomers was moving through the schools, and provincial in-migration from other parts of Canada and abroad was strong. Inevitably the young people would be pressing the limits of UBC and the other available programs.

Hardwick had spent some time in California in 1954 and attended summer school at the University of Wisconsin in 1956. In both states he was impressed with their comprehensive system of colleges and universities. He argued that the necessary conditions existed in BC for a comprehensive system. In 1957 he published a paper while he was on a Masters program under Chapman's supervision. He stressed the need for expansion to be seen in systems terms rather than as a set of discrete institutions, the mode of thought of the day.

In discussions within the Department of Geography of UBC, the role of humans in resource development, the public service equity issues, the demographic forecasts of Chapman, the systems vision of Hardwick became the topics of a great interplay of ideas. They were brought together in a 1960 report to the University Senate on the dimensions of and location of new institutions of higher education for the province. The issues of location drew on contemporary geographic discourse and the catalytic role of humans in regional development was at the forefront of this analysis (Zimmermann, 1951). These insights naturally lead to a call for a concerted drive to expand the education and training of an indigenous workforce. Both central place and gravity models (Figure 14.4 and 14.5) were used in the location analysis.

That 1960 report to the UBC Senate might have become another paper on the shelf of a vice-president. However, it was shared with the incoming President, Dr. John. B. Macdonald. Macdonald was familiar with trends in higher education in the United States and immediately saw in it the basis for a fundamental restructuring of the post-secondary system in BC. He soon met the Premier, W.A.C. Bennett, who agreed to receive recommendations from him on the future of higher education in the province.

In 1961 the President of UBC formed a team, including Chapman and Hardwick, to advise him on the preparation of a report. After travelling throughout

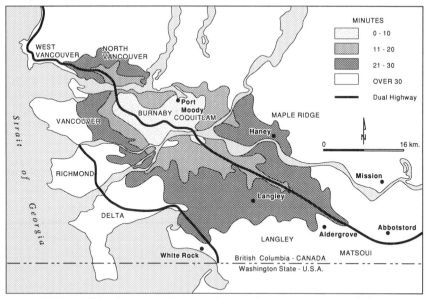

Figure 14.4: Travel Time by Automobile from Stormont Interchange, Burnaby B.C.

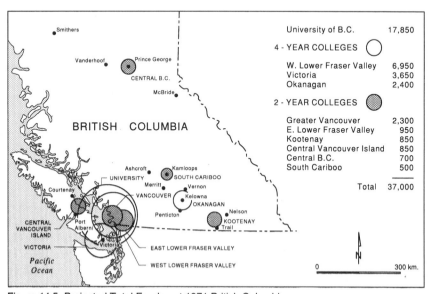

Figure 14.5: Projected Total Enrolment,1971 British Columbia

the province and receiving briefs from a variety of interests groups, a report was completed (Macdonald, l962). In order to encourage a favourable reception to the report and action on its recommendations, the president personally carried the report to Victoria for a special meeting with the Premier and his cabinet.

To encourage the government and the Legislature to act, in anticipation of the wave of young people flowing from the schools to the post-secondary system, faculty and students initiated a "Back Mac" campaign. It resulted in a petition with ten thousand signatures from people in every part of the province which was delivered to the Legislature by the Member of the Legislative Assembly for Point Grey, Dr. Pat McGeer, a UBC professor in the Faculty of Medicine.

The W.A.C. Bennett government agreed to act and in a short period the University of Victoria and Simon Fraser University were incorporated and a mechanism was created for the formation of regional colleges under the Public Schools Act. The term "regional" reflected the Chapman/Hardwick view of the role of the colleges. Later they bent to North American convention and the regional colleges became "community colleges". Hardwick, in association with Ronald Baker, assisted in the planning of several regional colleges in ensuing years, Capilano (1965) Kwantlen and Fraser Valley (l967).

Geographic Analysis and Post-Secondary Education: l976

When Walter Hardwick was appointed Deputy Minister of Education, Science and Technology under the Honourable Minister, Dr. Patrick McGeer, a second wave of planning and action was initiated. In this round, rather than acting as geographer/researcher influencing Presidents and Premiers, Hardwick was in a position to direct himself. Hardwick had secured a commitment from government for a substantial discretionary policy development budget so that the system could be planned and directed, and public support for implementation would be encouraged.

This was a new departure, for up to this time when government felt there was need for policy change they either set up a Royal Commission, such as the Chant Commission in l960, or accepted outside advice as they had with Macdonald. The Ministry personnel were seen as administrators, not initiators. McGeer and Hardwick had directional plans that had been expressed earlier, McGeer in his book, *Politics in Paradise,* (1972) and Hardwick in various reports and papers. The intellectual underpinnings of the system had deep roots in public arguments by both McGeer and Hardwick, and they naturally flowed from the 1962 analysis. Common to both their views was that the cultivation of the human resources of the province was essential to its viability in an increasingly inter-dependent world. Like Macdonald earlier, McGeer had developed his views in the United States as a graduate student at Princeton and as a researcher at DuPont. The elements in rounding out post-secondary system were:

1) the initiation of an effective management system in an information-rich environment — the "co-management" strategy;

2) the initiation of Science policy and centres of excellence;

3) the establishment of Discovery Research Parks;

4) the creation of an open learning system; and

5) the construction of additional colleges and institutes.

One of the first steps was the initiation of plans for a College and Institute Act that would give the institutions independent status outside the Public School Act, and a revision of the Universities Act. Toward that end several task forces were appointed to look at vocational education, continuing education, distance education, science policy, and university programs. The task forces were not expected to devise programs for the government as much as provide intelligence on the status of the system and raise public awareness of the pertinent issues so that when legislation and institutions were put in place there would be broad public support for them. Two geographers John Chapman and Gary Gates, played influential roles in these processes and Chapman soon became a member of an institute and then a college Board, and an influential member of a system-wide Council.

The Science initiatives came from the Minister. He knew intimately the role of Stanford University in the incubation of the Silicon Valley industries, and he was aware of the initiatives of an UBC alumnus, Cecil Green of Texas Instruments, in tele-education among high-technology workers in north Texas. His convictions lead to the establishment of the Science Council of BC, Discovery Research Parks adjacent to the Universities and BCIT, and a set of awards to Ph.D. and post doctoral students in Science, Engineering, and the Health Sciences.

The "co-management" model that gave structure to the post-secondary system was derived from Hardwick's systems view. It was designed to create a management information system that would provide province-wide information as well as institutional and district data to decision makers within school districts, colleges and institutes, and the universities. The information was wide ranging and included an inventory of public education facilities, faculty and teacher numbers and loads, program costs, and in the school sector, learning assessment results. A number of educators welcomed the challenge and once it was available, the numbers of delegations visiting the Ministry for concessions dropped.

Even in the new information rich environment the coordination function remained with pre-existing units such as the Universities Council. Its ability to act was often questioned by Presidents because voting members of the Council were not generally university people. Under the Colleges and Institute Act a troika of Councils emerged, the Management Advisory Council (MAC), the Occupational Training Council (OTC), and an Academic Council. MAC comprised College and Institute Board members, and was advised by representatives of the college principals and senior Ministry officials. Although a critical analysis of MAC is yet to be undertaken, many of the members found it a valuable and rewarding experience. However its powers were limited to advising on capital, major operating budget matters, and a library union catalogue. MAC was seen as a top policy institution in a co-managed system and its composition was deliberate. However college principals, who implemented policy and programs, resented their Board members participation, and saw MAC as an impediment to their access to Ministry officials, who had previously maintained power through restricting information flows.

Program coordination and direction was assigned to the OTC and the Academic Council. The OTC existed because the Ministry of Labour wished to control apprenticeship training and, in their view the OTC provided a forum to meet with labor leaders outside the Labor Code. Dr. McGeer was not willing to pressure his old colleague, the Honorable Allan Williams, the Minister, and his Deputy, Jim Matkin a superb bureaucratic infighter, to bring all education and training into his Ministry. The Academic Council was established to balance the OTC.

The Deputy Minister, Hardwick, had favoured a single Council modelled on MAC as a component of the "co-management model" of post-secondary education. The idealized information rich system model in which deciders at the institutional level would have as much information as central administrators, and therefore act without central direction, partially floundered in agency overkill.

Much more successful were the Open Learning initiatives. These had been on Hardwick's agenda for years. They were frustrated by Macdonald who largely withdrew UBC from university extension work across the province. However, they were advanced by the construction of the Woodward Instructional Resources center at UBC, initiated by Dr. W.C. Gibson, and equipped so as to be a possible site of a "University of the Air," an idea explored by Hardwick in his short term as UBC Director of Continuing Education. Upon becoming Deputy he challenged the universities to devise an open university system and under the leadership of Dr. Jack Blaney and Dr. Glen Farrell, they nearly made it. However, some Presidents were so shrill in their condemnation of the open university proposal that Dr. McGeer concluded that a Ministry-initiated Open Learning Institute (OLI) was the only option and it was formed in 1978.

Within its mandate, OLI was enabled to offer university, college and adult basic education programs, and to develop a television component. The first Principal of the institute, Dr. John Ellis, rejected the television function, but proceeded rapidly to develop a curriculum in the designated fields (Moran, 1991). The next year when the Canadian government sought parties to experiment with satellite delivery of education and training, a demonstration project was initiated under the auspices of the Deputy Minister's office and in cooperation with several institutions including BCIT. The outcome was Knowledge Network, one of the first satellite-based educational television networks is the world (Hardwick, 1984). It was seen as a means of finally meeting the equity issue of post-secondary education. Because of the satellite, a signal could be delivered at equal cost to homes and learning centres anywhere in the province and the friction of distance was overcome. Geographers John Bottomley and Warren Gill and planner Pat Carney acted as researcher/ planners, and the former two as administrators.

In 1988, a bill to give legitimacy to both open learning and the Knowledge Network was passed by the Legislature, ten years after its inception. As its first chairman, Hardwick implemented the policy of the 1970s of integrating educational television and open learning.

These various initiatives were intended by Hardwick to initiate a self-organizing and self-guiding post-secondary education system. It was enabled by an information rich environment into which decisions could be devolved to the college, university, and even to specific programs.

However, the idealistic goal was frustrated by the flaws in the Council system, and the incredulity on the part of administrators who had been conditioned by an adversarial environment that government would enable them to operate in a self-organizing manner. The whole experiment came to a crashing end with the government's program of financial restraint in 1983. At that time the management information system was used for a detailed centrally-controlled down-sizing of the whole educational enterprise as part of their restraining of government. Hardwick went back to Geography at UBC.

Geographers and Policy: 1988-1992

With the election of the Social Credit government of Premier William Vander Zalm, the residents of the interior and north reasserted their calls for universities. One had been recommended for the Okanagan by the Macdonald Report, and for a number of years a private university existed in the town of Nelson. The Minister appointed a Provincial Access Committee to improve access to post-secondary education. The conclusion lead to the University/College affiliation agreements at Okanagan, Cariboo, and Malaspina. Later Fraser Valley College was added with studies being initiated by geographer John Pierce. In 1990, the University of Northern British Columbia in Prince George was announced. Some of the preliminary justification for the project was undertaken by geographer Peter Ostegaard. J.D. Chapman became a member of the founding Board, and a pro-active advisor on many aspects of the planning.

The interest in systemic planning was again initiated by geographer, Gary Mullins, the Deputy Minister. A three year planning cycle was initiated for all components, and initiatives were taken to improve the participation rates in the province. A Human Resource Development Project was initiated with the Deputy Minister as Chairman. Its goals were to estimate the education and training needs of the province over the next two decades. Under Mullin's leadership many of the issues of the 1960s are being revisited, those of forecasting enrollment, the concern for a trained and skilled labor force as a catalyst for the provincial economy, issues of equity among regions and social groups within the province, and research for an appropriate form of system coordination. However after a change in government and an enlargement of the committee, the 1992 report contains only broad policy and directional statements (Human Resources Development Project, 1992). A few of them such as "Our several separate education and training systems need to operate as parts of a single, integrated but differentiated network", are reminiscent of previous goals of the system. Unlike the initiatives of the 1970s, however, the 1992 report only deals with goals and is silent on means of accomplishing them.

Conclusion

In conclusion, geographers with their synoptic views have consistently demonstrated an ability to see post-secondary education as a coherent system. They have placed the province of British Columbia in its continental perspective by using the insights and tools of the discipline. The focus on regionalization and economic development, and their use of trend analysis, locational modelling, and cartography were vital in working toward the common goal of viable regions enabled by a trained and skilled labor force.

References

British Columbia (1960) *Royal Commission on Education,* Victoria, B.C.

Dawe, A. (1959) *The Kelowna Junior College Survey,* Kelowna: Kelowna Printing Co.

Hardwick W. G. (1957) "Is this the answer? A proposal for junior colleges," *B.C. Teacher,* Vol. XXVII(3): 125-128.

Hardwick, W. G. (1960) *A Plan for Higher Education in B. C.,* A Report to the University of B. C. Senate, mimeograph.

Hardwick, W. G. (1984) "The knowledge network: A satellite educational response to the geography of British Columbia," *Space, Communications and Broadcasting,* Elsevier Science Publisher, 27-32.

Human Resource Development Project (1992) *Report of the Steering Committee,* Vancouver, B.C., 85 pages.

Macdonald J. B. (1962) *Higher Education in British Columbia and A Plan for the Future,* Vancouver, B. C.: University of BC.

McGeer, P. L. (1972) *Politics in Paradise,* Toronto: Peter Martin and Associates.

Moran, L. (1991) "A social history of open learning in British Columbia," Vancouver B.C., University of B.C., unpublished Ph.D. dissertation.

Zimmermann, E.S. (1951) *World Resources and Industries,* 2nd edition, New York: Harpers.

Chapter 15

Preparing for Coastal Management: A Human Ecological Approach[1]

J. G. Nelson and P.L. Lawrence
University of Waterloo

Introduction

Coastal zone planning and management in Canada and other countries are plagued by difficulties and slow progress on a number of fronts (CCREM, 1978; Dorcey, 1983; Harrison and Parkes, 1983; Hildebrand, 1989). The very idea itself is subject to questions. What do we mean when we speak of the coast and the shore or shoreline, especially in terms of outlining scope and associated government and private responsibilities for planning and management? Many activities in the coastal area also continue to be dealt with ineffectively in terms of their economic, social and environmental impacts (Davidson-Arnott and Kreutzwiser, 1985; Day and Gamble, 1990). Examples include conflicts among competing land uses, loss of wetlands and other environmentally significant areas, pollution and decreasing water quality, and continuing flooding, erosion and other hazards (Day et al., 1977; Jessen et al., 1983).

Many reasons have been given for slow progress on coastal problems. These include lack of understanding of the dynamic processes at work on coastal areas, fragmentation of planning and management among many federal, provincial (state) and local agencies, lack of awareness of the importance of the coast economically, socially and environmentally, and failure to learn from historic experiences (Sorenson et al., 1984; Hildebrand, 1989; RCFTW, 1992). Of particular concern in regard to coastal management is the tendency to repeat maladjustments of the past, particularly in

---

[1] This paper has also been published as Nelson, J.G. and Lawrence, P.L. (1993) "Developing a human ecological approach to coastal management: Case studies from the Great Lakes", in Lawrence, P.L. and Nelson, J.G. (eds.), Managing the Great Lakes Shoreline, Occasional Paper 21, Heritage Resources Centre, University of Waterloo, pp. 91-115.

regard to flooding, erosion and hazards (Needham and Nelson, 1978; Kreutzwiser, 1987). Land use and economic policies and practices are closely related to flood and hazard damages, loss of wetlands, loss of citizen access to the beach and declines in water and environmental quality (Clark, 1983). Without careful assessment, residential or other developments push human occupance into wetlands, dunes, flood and other high risk areas and bring economic, social and environmental losses in their wake (Nelson et al., 1975; ; Kreutzwiser, 1988; Dilley and Rasid, 1990).

In this chapter we wish to describe briefly, the attempts that a group mainly of geographers at the University of Waterloo Heritage Resources Centre has been making to deal with shore or coastal zone problems more effectively in the Great Lakes area (Figure 15.1). The attempts are based on what we call a human ecological approach. By this we mean an approach that is comprehensive, dynamic, interactive and adaptive (Nelson, 1991a). The approach stresses planning and management based on understanding the interrelationships among humans and the environment, in this case within the coastal zone. By comprehensive we mean inclusive of all activities, features and processes, including geologic and hydrologic (abiotic), plants and animals (biotic) and economic, technical, social and political (cultural). By dynamic we mean keyed to understanding changes in processes and patterns through time. It is important to know the history of change. By interactive and adaptive we mean communicating and learning from as many sources as possible, including science as well as local knowledge.

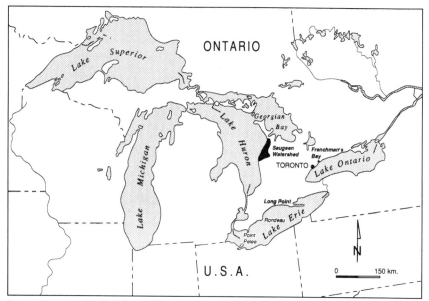

Figure 15.1: Great Lakes Study Sites

For us, a human ecological approach therefore means providing information of the foregoing kinds for use by people of different backgrounds and
interests in planning and managing the coastal zone. Our aim is to help
prepare people to deal with coastal issues by collecting and analyzing information with and for them. It is our belief that planning and management
will be made more effective if as many affected parties as possible learn
about and deal with the situation together, on the basis of as comprehensive an information base as possible. This statement presents something
of an ideal. It is of course not always attainable because of time or money
constraints, political circumstances or other factors. Given these limitations
it is important in our view, to be as open and co-operative as possible
throughout each study or project in order that as much learning as possible
is available to many interested groups and persons. We are actively working on this human ecological approach in the Great Lakes area and can
briefly present the results of some recent studies to illustrate the nature of
the work and its implications to date.

Frenchman's Bay, Lake Ontario

The first case is Frenchman's Bay in eastern Toronto (Figure 15.2). In this
case we were asked by the Toronto Waterfront Commission's office for an
assessment of the effects of proposed condominium and related developments on the Bay. We were asked also to provide views on the long term
capacity of the Bay to accommodate such development. The project involved a report to the Commission's office based upon available reports
and literature. The project did not provide support nor direction for public
meetings or other citizen involvement, although it was understood that the
results of our study would be published and so be widely available for public
scrutiny. This project began on April 1, 1991 and was completed by a team
consisting of 4 graduate students and a university professor by June 10,
1991 (Nelson et al., 1991).

The Frenchman's Bay case illustrates that a comprehensive array of information can be collected and analyzed quickly in terms of significance and
constraints bearing on a public issue. The framework for analysis in Frenchman's Bay — and the other cases to be discussed later — is the ABC
Resource Survey Method (Bastedo et al., 1984; Nelson et al., 1988, Nelson, 1991b). The technique involves the collection, analysis and interpretation of abiotic, biotic and cultural or human information in the sense
described in the introduction to this paper (Figure 15.3).

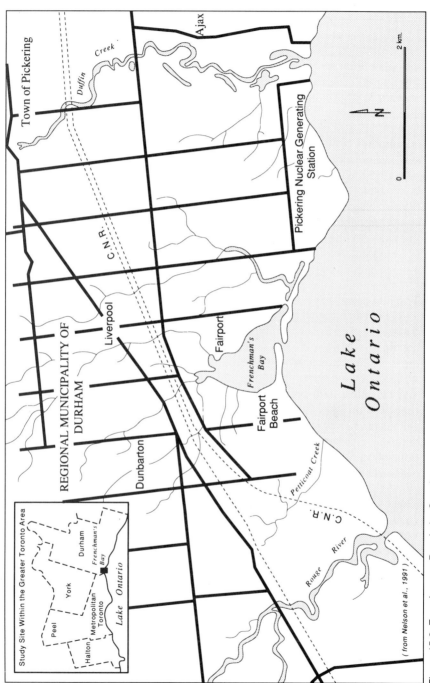

Figure 15.2: Frenchman's Bay, Lake Ontario

(from Nelson et al., 1991)

Identify Management Issues
Areas of concern
Land Use Regulations
Management Plan
Development Controls
Communications
Education
Public Participation

Level IV
Study Conclusions / Recommendations

Environmental
Significance
Map

Environmental
Constraints
Map

Level III
Summary of Significance and Constraints

Abiotic Significance Maps	Abiotic Constraints Maps	Biotic Significance Maps	Biotic Constraints Maps	Cultural Significance Maps	Cultural Constraints Maps
examples	*examples*	*examples*	*examples*	*examples*	*examples*
landforms water quality conflicts artifical fill alterations	hazards spit evolution lake levels wave energy sediments	rare species natural areas communities forest patterns	disturbance conflicts nodes corridors patterns	land use development patterns economy historical sites	use conflicts zones of tension change trends

Level II
determine Significance and Constraints
in terms of study goals

Cultural Significance Maps	Cultural Constraints Maps	Cultural Significance Maps	Cultural Constraints Maps	Cultural Significance Maps	Cultural Constraints Maps
examples	*examples*	*examples*	*examples*	*examples*	*examples*
geology sediments soils landforms topography climate	stream flow erosion deposition waves wind	ecoregions vegetation forests wetlands	succession migration change nutrient flow	land cover parks marinas roadways urban areas zoning	corridors growth nodes decline change transport

Abiotic   Biotic   Cultural

Level I
collect, synthesize and interpret information
in terms of study goals

(from Nelson et al., 1993)

Figure 15.3: ABC Resource Survey Method

Figures 15.4-15.7 are maps which provide some of the major results of the Frenchman's Bay study. The maps give important information on the geological, biological and human character of the Bay and on areas or places that are especially significant from the standpoint of environmental planning and management or sustainable development. The assessment found that development or urbanization in the area had led to stresses on shoreline erosion and geomorphic processes (Figure 15.4). Development during the past 40 years had also led to loss or decline of many valued opportunities, such as the natural, recreational and economic ones associated with wetlands which have become more and more fragmented over time (Figures 15.5 and 15.6). Historical or cultural values of the area, such as those associated with the old port and fishing history of the Bay, were likely to be modified by the proposed new residential and marina projects, along with the Bay's wetlands and other natural habitats (Figure 15.7).

With this in mind, the assessment recommended a moratorium on development for one year and called for further studies to consolidate and review information on natural and cultural values of the Bay in a more comprehensive, interactive coordinated manner. Since the completion of the study it has been used in discussion among provincial and municipal governments and other stakeholders leading to public purchase of several hectares of key bay wetlands.

Saugeen Watershed, Lake Huron

The second case study, of the Saugeen coast on Lake Huron, was conducted in partnership with the Saugeen Valley Conservation Authority (SVCA). In this case the SVCA had requested assistance in the preparation of a shoreline management plan. From the outset, it was possible to conduct the study in an open and interactive manner with concerned governments, agencies and citizens. Early discussions with SVCA and various agencies and citizens groups resulted in a decision to develop a background document to assist in preparing for planning rather than a plan itself. Subsequently a series of public meetings and numerous consultations were held with many government officials and people generally. The resulting information and views were used in completing a report over a period of about one year, from May 1991 to March 1992. The Saugeen project was also based on the ABC Resource Survey Method. One result of presentation of the material at public meetings was modification of the diagram illustrating the method in an attempt to make it clearer to the citizen (Figure 15.8).

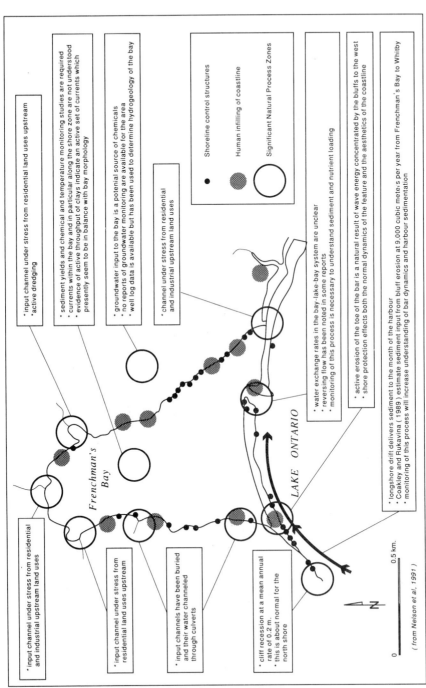

Figure 15.4: Abiotic Significant Processes and Stresses

*input channel under stress from residential land uses upstream
*active dredging

* sediment yields and chemical and temperature monitoring studies are required
* currents within the bay and in particular along the shore zone are not understood
* evidence of active throughput of clays indicate an active set of currents which presently seem to be in balance with bay morphology

* groundwater input to the bay is a potential source of chemicals
* no reports of groundwater monitoring are available for the area
* well log data is available but has been used to determine hydrogeology of the bay

* channel under stress from residential and industrial upstream land uses

Shoreline control structures

Human infilling of coastline

Significant Natural Process Zones

* water exchange rates in the bay-lake-bay system are unclear
* reversing flow has been noted in some reports
* monitoring of this process is necessary to understand sediment and nutrient loading

* active erosion of the toe of the bar is a natural result of wave energy concentrated by the bluffs to the west
* shore protection effects both the normal dynamics of the feature and the aesthetics of the coastline

* input channel under stress from residential and industrial upstream land uses

* input channel under stress from residential land uses upstream

* input channels have been buried and their water channeled through culverts

* cliff recession at a mean annual rate of 0.2 m.
* this is about normal for the north shore

* longshore drift delivers sediment to the month of the harbour
* Coakley and Rukavina (1989) estimate sediment input from bluff erosion at 9,000 cubic meters per year from Frenchman's Bay to Whitby
* monitoring of this process will increase understanding of bar dynamics and harbour sedimentation

Frenchman's Bay

LAKE ONTARIO

0   0.5 km.

N

(from Nelson et al, 1991)

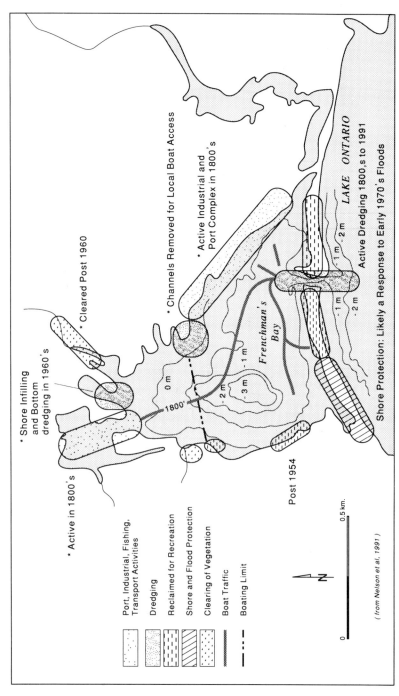

Figure 15.5: Human Impacts and Features

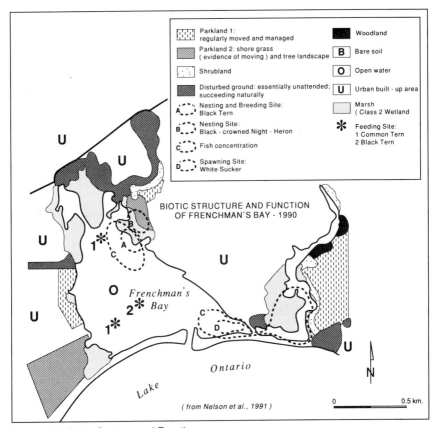

Figure 15.6: Biotic Stucture and Function

Some of the major results are presented in Figures 15.9, 15.10, and 15.11. These maps show some of the major features and processes at work along the coast. Essential abiotic features and processes were noted such as sediment transport patterns, beach/dune complexes, and stream flow (Figure 15.9). Significant biotic areas (Figure 15.10) for rare and threatened species, forest corridors, dunes and wetlands were identified by using the criteria of representativeness, uniqueness, and productivity. Four main land use changes occurred with the study area from 1954 to 1990; forest fragmentation, rural residential (cottage) extension, rural industrial development, and urban growth (Figure 15.11).

The maps also show some of the more significant features, processes and stresses which require special attention in planning and management. Valuable additional information was also made available to the research team by agencies and citizens, along with a strong indication as to the

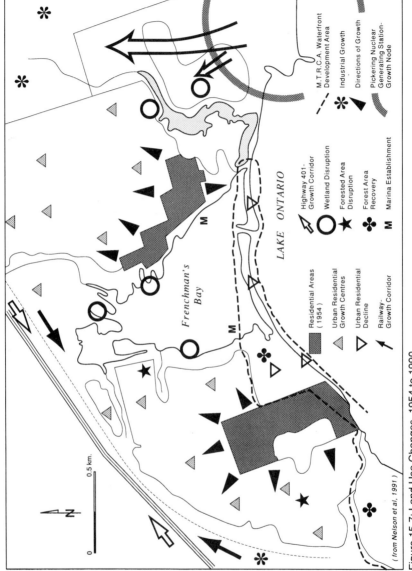

Figure 15.7: Land Use Changes, 1954 to 1990

(from Nelson et al, 1991)

priorities for action. For example, the issue of public access to the shore
was often identified as a critical one for local people, but one which was
less pressing for many of the agency professionals.

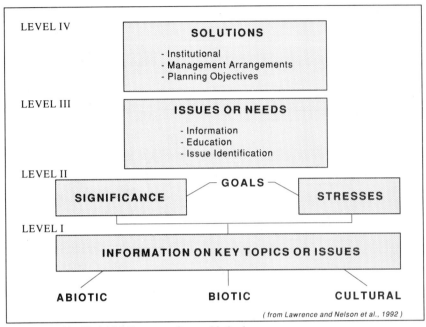

Figure 15.8: Modified ABC Resource Survey Method

The interactive process led the research team to identify several areas of
tension where significant conflicts among conservation and development
interests were either already evident or likely to develop in the future (Figure 15.12). These areas would warrant special attention in any future planning exercise concerned with the coast. Issues were also identified which
initially had not been anticipated as major ones by either the research team,
the SVCA or local people. A notable example is the degree to which coastal
forests and woodlands are being fragmented by various developments.

The final report consisted of maps and a guide to a larger repository of the
information gathered during the course of the study (Lawrence and Nelson,
1992). The HRC/SVCA assessment was undertaken on a joint basis from
the very start, sharing expertise, information and costs. This has laid the
foundation for possible HRC participation in the development of a shoreline
management plan for the area. The work provides both a basis, and a point
of departure, for further research on shoreline planning and management
along the Lake Huron coast.

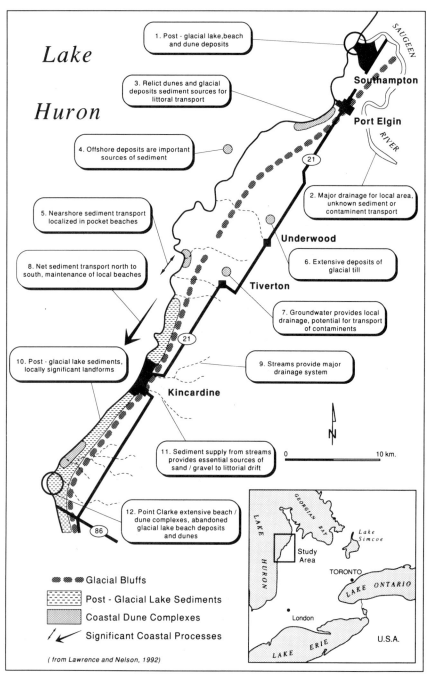

Figure 15.9: Significant Coastal Features and Processes

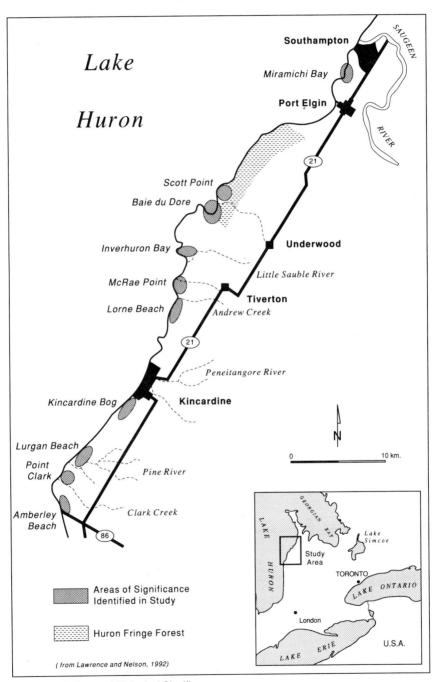

Figure 15.10: Areas of Biological Significance

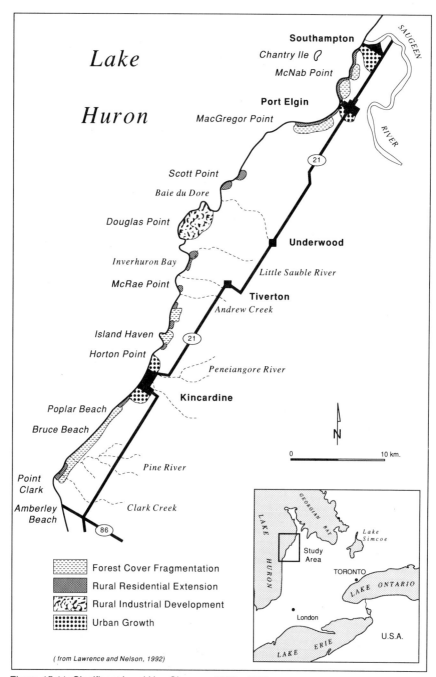

Figure 15.11: Significant Land Use Changes 1953 - 1990

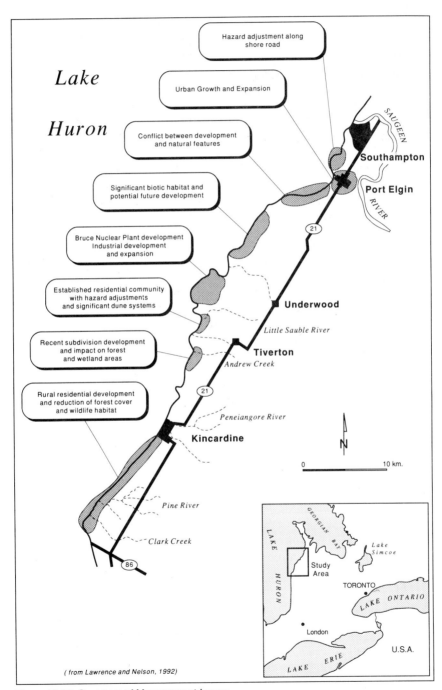

Figure 15.12: Summary of Management Issues

Long Point, Lake Erie

The third case study is of the Long Point area and this work is ongoing. The project is primarily funded by a 1992 major competitive grant from the Royal Canadian Geographical Society (RCGS), with some additional support from the Social Sciences and Humanities Research Council (SSHRC). The Canada/Man and Biosphere (MAB) program approved the nomination of Long Point as a world biosphere reserve in June 1985. In 1986 the Long Point Biosphere Reserve was officially designated by the MAB Program of UNESCO (Francis, 1985). The Long Point Biosphere Reserve (Figure 15.13) consists of a core protected area (Long Point National Wildlife Area), buffer area (defined by the 10 metre depth contour offshore and the regulatory 1:100 year flood line onshore) and an undefined "zone of cooperation" (Canada/MAB, 1990).

The shoreline is characterized by 30 to 40 metre high eroding clay bluffs to the west, the 40 kilometer long sandy spit environment of Long Point with its associated dune and wetland systems, and low-lying beaches, wetlands and bluffs to the east. The dune and wetland systems have a rich mix of habitats consisting of an open lake, shallow bays, sand bars, beaches, dunes, forests and scrub, ponds, and marshes. The region is host to a variety of land use and resource conflicts and to many significant species and habitats. Some 20 distinct biotic communities have been described on the Long Point sand spit. About 700 species of vascular plants have been recorded. 90 species are considered to be rare in Ontario and at least four occur nowhere else in Canada (Canada / MAB, 1990). The Long Point complex is a major staging area for migrating waterfowl and small migratory birds. Long Point also has a long history of human use, notably for fishing, waterfowl hunting, cottaging and other recreational and tourism purposes (Francis, 1985). The Point is also an area that is well known for flooding and erosion hazards. It is currently also an area in which the decline of tobacco farming as an economic mainstay has led to the search for other economic opportunities including development of numerous marinas and other recreational facilities and activities (Nelson et al., 1993). These developments are having incompletely understood effects on the wetlands and other resources of the productive Inner Bay and other significant places in the Long Point area.

The aim of the project is to produce an environmental folio which is seen as a means of synthesizing and graphically displaying natural and human information on the Long Point area for use by local governments and citizens in planning and management (Nelson et al., 1993). The preparation of the folio has the approval and support of the local Long Point Biosphere

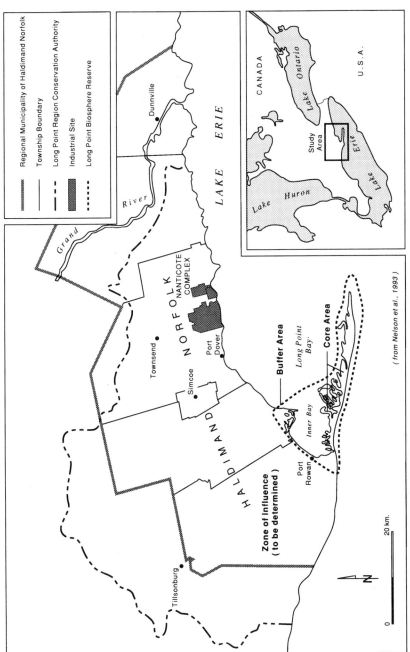

Figure 15.13: Long Point Biosphere Reserve and Region

Reserve Committee which consists of government officials and people living in the area. The Committee wants to have available information on the area put in a form where it is more widely intelligible and useful than is currently the case with scientific and scholarly articles and bibliographies. The folio will consist of maps and text built around the major concerns and issues facing the people of the area and Biosphere planning and management. Work in the first year of the project has focused on the collection of existing data from government reports, published literature, scientific studies and consultations with local people and government agencies. Topics currently under examination include geology and geomorphology (Figure 15.14), shoreline flooding and erosion (Figure 15.15) and significant natural areas and sites (Figure 15.16).

Discussion

In summary, the human ecological approach is intended to be comprehensive, dynamic, interactive and adaptive. In the current context the focus is on the interactions among humans and environment in the Great Lakes coastal zone. The approach involves working closely with local people and agencies. It is intended to assist them in preparing to address complex issues on the basis of understanding and assessing a broad information base consisting of scientific, technical and local knowledge and views. To date the approach seems to have been reasonably successful in that it has led to some significant planning and management decisions and to considerable interest and involvement in our work by local people and responsible agencies. The Frenchman's Bay study helped lead to government purchase of a key wetland in the Bay. The Saugeen project appears to have provided a good background for the preparation of a shoreline management plan. Discussion and feedback has been positive on the work to date in the Long Point area.

The approach allows for better understanding of the issues and areas of interest along the coast as a basis for a more broadly informed and participatory decision making process in land use and development planning. Though information review, public participation and expert opinion, issues such as water quality, forest fragmentation, habitat loss, disruption of natural processes, flood and erosion hazards and land use conflicts are identified and assessed. The goal of this type of research is to provide improved decision making based on an understanding of the natural environment and human use and development of resources characterizing the coastal zone such as non-renewable resources, rich biotic habitat, tourism and recreation, industrial development, and the dynamic environment of the water and land interface. In light of such factors understanding and knowledge be-

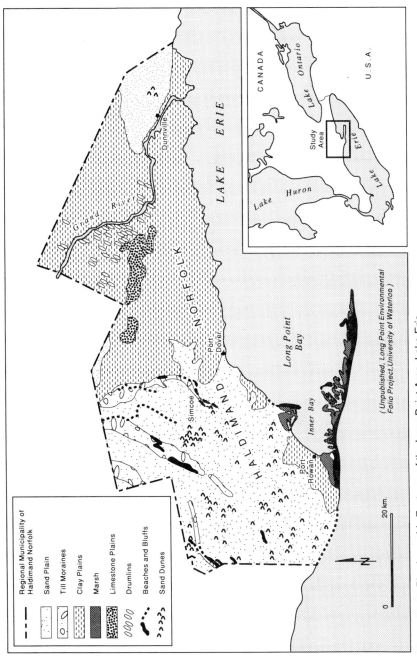

Figure 15.14: Physiographic Features of the Long Point Area, Lake Erie

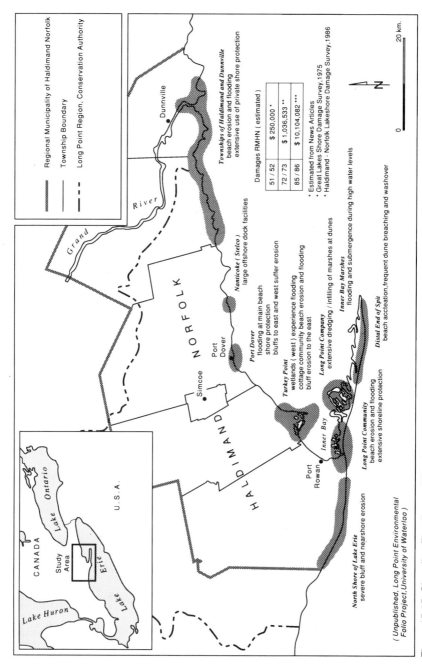

Figure 15.15: Shoreline Flooding and Erosion

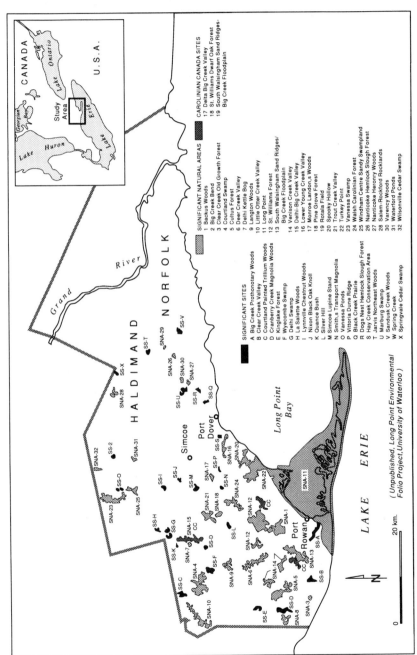

Figure 15.16: Significant Natural Areas and Sites in Long Point Area

(Unpublished, Long Point Environmental Folio Project, University of Waterloo)

CAROLINIAN CANADA SITES
17 Delta Big Creek Valley
18 St. Williams Dwarf Oak Forest
19 South Walsingham Sand Ridges-Big Creek Floodplain

SIGNIFICANT NATURAL AREAS
1 Backus Woods
2 Big Creek Bend
3 Clear Creek Old Growth Forest
4 Courtland Swamp
5 Cultus Forest
6 Deer Creek Valley
7 Delhi Kettle Bog
8 Langton Woods
9 Delhi Kettle Bog
10 Little Otter Creek Valley
11 Long Point
12 St. Williams Forest
13 South Walsingham Sand Ridges/Big Creek Floodplain
14 Venison Creek Valley
15 Delhi-Big Creek Valley
16 Lower Young Creek Valley
17 Monroe Landon,s Woods
18 Pine Grove Forest
19 Rotala Field
20 Spooky Hollow
21 Trout Creek Valley
22 Turkey Point
23 Vanessa Swamp
24 Walsh Carolinian Forest
25 Windham Centre Sandy Swampland
26 Nanticoke Hemlock Slough Forest
27 Nanticoke Heronry Woods
28 Salem-Rockford Rocklands
29 Varency Woods
30 Varency Woods
31 Waterford Ponds
32 Wilsonville Cedar Swamp

SIGNIFICANT SITES
A Big Creek Prothonotary Woods
B Clear Creek Valley
C Courtland Painted Trillium Woods
D Cranberry Creek Magnolia Woods
E Kinglake Forest
F Wyecombe Swamp
G Delhi Swamp
H La Salette Woods
I Lynnville Chestnut Woods
J Nixon Black Oak Knoll
K Quance Bush
L Silver Hill
M Simcoe Lupine Stand
N Smith,s Transport Magnolia
O Vanessa Ponds
P Vittoria Dune Ridge
Q Black Creek Prairie
R Dogs Nest Hemlock Slough Forest
S Hay Creek Conservation Area
T Jarvis Northeast Woods
U Marburg Swamp
V Sandusk Creek Woods
W Spring Creek
X Springvale Cedar Swamp

comes an essential goal in long term, proactive, comprehensive planning of the coast.

Acknowledgements

A number of individuals from the Heritage Resources Centre and Department of Geography contributed to the case studies outlined in this paper; Karen Beazley, Veronica Chisholm, Maria Healey, Kerri Pauls, Monica Quinn, Rafal Serafin, Andy Skibicki, Ron Stenson, Steve Wilcox, and Chi-Ling Yeung. Lisa Weber of the Heritage Resources Centre and Debbie Stenson assisted with text and map preparation. Special recognition is given to the agencies which provided data for the study including the Long Point Region Conservation Authority, Long Point World Biosphere Reserve Committee, Ontario Hydro, Ontario Ministry of Natural Resources, Ontario Ministry of Environment, Royal Commission on the Future of the Toronto Waterfront, and Saugeen Valley Conservation Authority. This research has been supported by financial assistance from the Royal Canadian Geographical Society, the Social Sciences and Humanities Council of Canada, Toronto Waterfront Development Office, Ontario Environmental Youth Corps, and the Saugeen Valley Conservation Authority.

References

Bastedo, J., Nelson, J.G., and Theberge, J. (1984) "Ecological approach to resource survey and planning for environmentally significant areas: The ABC method ", *Environmental Management*, Vol. 8(2): 125-134.

Beazley, K.F. (1993) Forested Regions of Long Point: Landscape History and Strategic Planning, unpublished M.A. Thesis, Waterloo, Ontario: Department of Geography, University of Waterloo.

Canadian Council of Resource and Environmental Ministers (CCREM) (1978) *Proceedings of the Shore Management Symposium*, Victoria, B.C.: British Columbia Ministry of Environment.

Canadian Man and Biosphere (MAB) Committee (1990) *Biosphere Reserves in Canada*, Canadian / MAB Secretariat, Ottawa, Ontario: Canadian Commission for UNESCO.

Clark, J.E. (1983) *Coastal Ecosystem Management,* New York: John Wiley & Sons Ltd.

Davidson-Arnott, R.G.D. and Kreutzwiser, R.D. (1985) "Coastal processes and shoreline encroachment: Implications for shoreline management in Ontario", *Canadian Geographer*, Vol. 29(3): 256-262.

Day, J.C., Fraser, J.A. and Kreutzwiser, R.D. (1977) "Assessment of flood and erosion assistance programs: Rondeau coastal experience, Lake Erie", *Journal of Great Lakes Research*, Vol. 3(1-2): 38-45.

Day, J.C. and Gamble, D.B. (1990) "Coastal zone management in British Columbia: An institutional comparison with Washington, Oregon, and California", *Coastal Management*, Vol. 18: 115-141.

Dilley, R.S. and Rasid, H. (1990) "Human response to coastal erosion: Thunder Bay, Lake Superior", *Journal of Coastal Research*, Vol. 6(4): 779-788.

Dorcey, A.H.J. (1983) "Coastal management as a bargaining process", *Coastal Zone Management Journal*, Vol. 11(1-2):.13-40.

Francis, G.F. (1985) *Long Point Biosphere Reserve Nomination,* Submitted to the Man and the Biosphere Programme, Ottawa, Ontario: Canadian Commission for UNESCO.

Harrison, P. and Parkes, J.G.M. (1983) "Coastal management in Canada," *Coastal Zone Management Journal*, Vol. 11(1-2): 1-11.

Hildebrand, L.P. (1989) *Canada's Experience with Coastal Zone Management*, Halifax, Nova Scotia: Oceans Institute of Canada.

Jessen, S., Day, J.C. and Nelson, J.G. (1983) "Assessing land use regulations in coastal wetlands: The case of Long Point area, Lake Erie, Ontario", *Coastal Zone Management Journal*, Vol. 11(1-2): 91-115.

Kreutzwiser, R.D. (1987) "Managing the Great Lakes shoreline hazard", *Journal of Soil and Water Conservation, Vol. 42(3): 150-154.*

Kreutzwiser, R.D. (1988) "Municipal land use regulation and the Great Lakes shoreline hazard in Ontario", *Journal of Great Lakes Research*, Vol. 14(2): 142-147.

Lawrence, P.L. and Nelson, J.G. (1992) *Preparing for a Shoreline Management Plan for the Saugeen Valley Conservation Authority*, A Joint Study of the Heritage Resources Centre, University of Waterloo, Waterloo,

Ontario and the Saugeen Valley Conservation Authority, Hanover, Ontario.

Needham, R.D. and Nelson, J.G. (1978) "Adjustment to change in coastal environments: The case of fluctuating Lake Erie water levels" in *Coping with the Coast*, Proceedings of the Fourth Annual Conference of the Coastal Society, Arlington, Virginia, pp. 196-213.

Nelson, J.G. (1991a) "Research in human ecology and planning: An interactive, adaptive approach", *Canadian Geographer*, Vol. 35(2): 114-127.

Nelson, J.G. (1991b) "A step towards more comprehensive and equitable information systems: The ABC resource survey method," in *Greenways and Green Space on the Oak Ridges Moraine*, Occasional Paper #14, Peterborough, Ontario: Department of Geography, Trent University, pp. 27-34.

Nelson, J.D., Battin, R.A. and Kreutzwiser, R.D. (1975) "The fall 1972 Lake Erie floods and their significance to resources management," *Canadian Geographer*, Vol. 20(1):.35-58.

Nelson, J.G., Grigoriew, P., Smith, P.G.R. and Theberge, J. (1988) "The ABC resource survey method, The ESA concept and comprehensive land use planning and management," in Moss, M. R. (ed.), *Landscape Ecology and Management*, Proceedings of the First Symposium of the Canadian Society for Landscape Ecology and Management, University of Guelph, May 1987, Polyscience Publications Inc., Montreal, Canada, pp. 143-175.

Nelson, J.G., Lawrence, P.L., Beazley, K., Stenson, R., Skibicki, A., Yeung, C.L., and Pauls, K. (1993) *Preparing an Environmental Folio for the Long Point Biosphere Reserve and Region*, Long Point Environmental Folio Publication Series, Working Note 1, Waterloo, Ontario: Heritage Resources Centre, University of Waterloo.

Nelson, J.G., Skibicki, A.J, Stenson, R.E. and Yeung, C.L. (1991) *Urbanization, Conservation and Development: The Case of Frenchman's Bay, Toronto, Ontario*, Heritage Resources Centre, Technical Paper 5, Waterloo, Ontario: University of Waterloo.

Royal Commission on the Future of the Toronto Waterfront (1992) *Regeneration - Final Report*, Toronto, Ontario: Government Printer of Ontario.

Sorenson,J.C., McCreary, S.T. and Hershman, M.J. (1984) *Institutional Arrangements for Management of Coastal Resources,* Research Planning Institute, Coastal Publication No. 1, Columbia, South Carolina.

Chapter 16

Paradise Lost : Public Policy Obstacles to Sustainable Landscape Development

A. G. McLellan and D. C. Baker
University of Waterloo and University Northern British Columbia

Introduction

Many land uses that are clearly essential to the public interest also generate potentially negative impacts on the social and physical environment. A large number of these uses, such as sanitary landfill sites, low-cost housing, or aggregate mining operations, have been labelled LULUs (Locally Unwanted Land Uses). Although such uses serve a greater need within society, at a local level they are not perceived as being in the community's benefit and generally stimulate a hostile reaction.

In many cases, the public or the community interest is not well served by institutional arrangements which polarise the issues in adversarial arenas where:

1) the local community attempts to defend its perceived private self-interests in restricting noxious land uses;

2) the proponents advocate their self-interests in developing land uses; or

3) there are conflicting government mandates at the municipal and provincial levels ("agency Balkanisation").

Frequently, new initiatives perceived in the broader public interest, such as sustainable resource development, are addressed only when they meet the agenda of one of the disputing parties. A healthy, balanced, and integrated mix of land uses is commonly sacrificed by the conflicting parties.

The focus of this paper is to examine methods of resolving public land use conflicts at the local level by addressing the substantive interests of all disputing parties. An enhanced approach to the extraction of aggregate resources will be used as an example of a LULU which can provide a "net community gain" rather than a land use which has traditionally been viewed as degradational.

In order to demonstrate new initiatives and a different means to address aggregate extraction, the authors will examine two case studies in southern Ontario. The first case study, in Puslinch Township, will outline the present public policy and legislation that deal with conflict and aggregate extraction. The problems experienced in Puslinch continue to be the status quo in southern Ontario. The second case study, Snyder Flats, also in southern Ontario, provides an alternative approach to the present planning methods for designing and coordinating aggregate mining as an interim land use.

Paradise Lost : The Fall

The planning control of construction aggregate extraction has evolved as a result of heated municipal and provincial exchanges over a period of two decades. At the provincial level, the Pits and Quarries Control Act (1971) provided the first comprehensive legislation in Canada which attempted to regulate the aggregate industry. The Act set out site plan preparation, licensing procedures, and rehabilitation requirements. The provincial controls focused on an attempt to regulate the most evident negative environmental effects of gravel pits. This legislation was modified in the ensuing years and has subsequently been replaced by the Aggregate Resources Act (1989), but environmental disputes over aggregate mining continue to be a major land use conflict.

Municipalities attempted to control the environmental problems associated with aggregate development through the Official Plan where the Province had failed to regulate the negative impacts of pits and quarries with the Pits and Quarries Control Act and environmental legislation. The Official Plan is a planning document that sets out land use restrictions and zoning regulations within a township. Municipalities have the option to control hours of operation, set-back requirements, noise and dust levels, and other restrictions such as limitations on truck traffic.

There is a traditional conflict between the Municipality and the Province in the control and planning of resources. The management of aggregate resources provides a good example of provincial expertise and "provincial interest" attempting to enforce legislation and policy on municipal governments which are often reluctant to follow the guidance of provincial mandates (Baker, 1993). Municipal governments tend to be more responsive to local citizen concerns and often elected municipal counsellors support politically expedient , anti-aggregate sentiments within the townships. For example, a municipal election was recently decided in Eramosa Township of southern Ontario on the basis of a strong anti-aggregate stand by the victorious councillors. Local responses to the environmental problems caused by aggregate mining are frequently enacted in local municipal politics and then formulated within the Official Plans. Often, municipal councillors in response to public pressure, restrict the mining of aggregate resources because of the potential negative impacts. Pressure has been frequently placed on local politicians to ban aggregate mining, with many local municipal elections based on "for or against" aggregate extraction. A failure of the different planning agencies to coordinate and manage the extraction of aggregate mining can be attributed in many cases to the lack of communication and different mandates between municipalities and the province.

The present planning system and legislation alienates local people in terms of benefits derived from a local resource. Aggregate resources, as a local product, are being exported with little compensation being returned to the community from which they are derived. Aggregate production involves a considerable environmental and social impact resulting from both mining and transportation of material. Residents and municipal coffers are faced with infrastructure costs and environmental uncertainty as a result of mining. However, there is minimal compensation paid to the people affected by these externalities.

The present means to resolve conflict for the development of aggregate sources are based in both substantive efforts to regulate the resource with the Official Plan and legislation, and procedural attempts through the Ontario Municipal Board (OMB) hearings. The OMB is an appointed board that holds regulatory tribunals to resolve land use conflicts and planning issues within the Province of Ontario. The hearings are conducted on a formal basis and involve testimony from expert witnesses, cross examination by legal counsel, and rules for the admission for evidence. The process is based on an adversarial system.

The conflict that has characterized aggregate development appears to be a recurring theme. Over 130 "aggregate" OMB hearings have convened since 1971 to settle disputes involved with objections to aggregate mining. These disputes are costly and often embitter opponents with distinct winners and losers. There has been a tradition of "aggregate wars" in southern Ontario over the past 20 years. With this tradition have come entrenched positions for parties that have rallied for or against the development of aggregate resources. For example, the Foundation of Aggregate Studies operated an information and resource centre based in Toronto to oppose many aggregate developments while the Aggregate Producers Association lobbies in favour of aggregate extraction.

The polarization of groups "for and against" aggregate mining has served to impede the resolution of conflict at a local level. The entrenchment of positions is a frequent consequence of ongoing or long term disputes and forms a difficult obstacle to a possible resolution of conflict. The OMB, in many cases, may not resolve conflict between disputing parties. Although the hearings may rule on a particular dispute at a specific site, the process may not address the basis for the resolution of conflict within a given area or township. As a result, often if residents are not satisfied with an OMB ruling for one site, the resentment and dissatisfaction continues within the area or township. The planning process may attempt to resolve conflict on the basis of legislation or the "set rules," but this does not mean that the conflict is resolved at the "interest" level for all parties concerned. The OMB hearings may exacerbate conflict in many cases because of:

1) the adversarial nature of the hearings;

2) the inequity of resources in the form of scientific information and legal counsel between citizens and aggregate companies at the hearings; and

3) the costs of the hearings for both producers and opposition are extremely high.

The land use conflict that has been generated by aggregate extraction has been an expensive exercise in planning and decision-making. It is continuing to demand time and resources from citizens, municipalities, proponents, and the province. The dimensions of this problem consist of :

1) a long tradition of conflict of approximately 30 years that has polarized sides and public opinion;

2) a struggle for control of aggregate resources between several actor groups that include: the aggregate industry, municipalities, local land owners, and provincial interests;

3) the OMB hearing system, which may not serve to mitigate conflict; and

4) the issue of compensation to the individuals and communities affected by aggregate mining.

The substantive and procedural basis for planning is inadequate to address the present diversity of interests, and lacks the flexibility to accommodate creative solutions to resolve the conflict that has developed with the mining of aggregate resources.

Lost Opportunities: The Puslinch Aggregate War

The recently completed OMB hearings in Puslinch Township are one of the longest hearings on record in Ontario, requiring 161 days and costing tax-payers and industry an estimated $5 million in professional fees (Globe and Mail, July 5, 1990). The rural Township of Puslinch (population 6,000) spent $275,000 alone in hearing fees. The long and costly hearings involved a challenge to the Official Municipal Plan of Puslinch by aggregate producers and the Ministry of Natural Resources of Ontario (MNR). Five site specific proposals for aggregate extraction appealed the Official Plan on the basis of "inadequate designations" and "overly restrictive zoning policies." The Township, ratepayers, and special interest groups supported the Official Plan designations and attempted to curb aggregate extraction within the township because of the uncertain environmental and social impacts of increased mining.

Essentially, the issue of conflict and what the Puslinch OMB hearings had to determine was: who was going to control aggregate resources, with what means, and for what reasons. The Township of Puslinch attempted to address the negative environmental and social impacts of aggregate mining, with over 800 hectares already licensed for aggregate mining, by revising its Official Plan to control the opening of more gravel pits.

In 1986, the Township adopted a new Official Plan that changed the aggregate extraction designations from the previous 1984 Official Plan. In the 1984 plan, the aggregate extraction designation was identified by Plate C, which had dated from the 1973 Official Plan of the Guelph and Suburban Planning Board in which Puslinch had previously been included. Plate C in the previous plan had defined 3 areas within the township as potential gravel sites, where by-laws permitted aggregate extraction without the need for any Official Plan amendment. In the past, Plate C had been consistently interpreted by various panels of the OMB and the courts as representing a designation of "Extractive" for this purpose. However, in the re-designation of the Official Plan in 1986, Plate C was changed to Policy Area No.2 which identified other land uses, such as agriculture, as higher priority land uses. The result was that new aggregate extraction in this area would require an Official Plan amendment rather than only a by-law approval. In addition, Section 16.2(2) of the adopted plan, which describes the

Policy Area No.2 identification, stipulated "need" — economic and social — as a requirement that must be demonstrated to Council's satisfaction before an amendment would be considered. A producer's individual construction needs were insufficient to fulfil this requirement (This section was redrafted during the OMB hearings to remove the condition of need — however, citizens opposing the pit developments maintained that need should be a governing criterion for the establishment of pits.).

As well, the 1986 plan attempted to control excavation below the water table with Development Agreements (Section 40 of the Planning Act), which stipulated a specific contract agreement between a proponent and the Township. Development agreements would restrict aggregate extraction to no less than one meter above the water table. Thus, the Township attempted to control environmental impacts of gravel mining through regulatory control in the Official Plan.

The revised aggregate designations in the Township Official Plan challenged the authority of the provincial MNR and the policy set by the Mineral Aggregate Resources Policy Statement (MARPS). The local community was attempting to place both mining and environmental controls on the extraction of aggregate resources. The history of aggregate mining conflict in the community of Puslinch had been on-going for twenty years and the designations in the 1986 plan were a continuation of the hostilities between local residents and aggregate producers. As noted by the OMB members in their final decision of the hearing, "the Board has perceived an ingrained reluctance on the part of Council to support extraction in this community, certainly within the lifetime of its Official Plan" (p. 15).

The final OMB ruling, in June 1990, decided against municipal authority in the regulation of aggregate resources. The OMB found against the development agreement clause that the municipality had adopted to control excavation below the water table, and also ruled against the Policy Area No. 2 exclusion of the Extraction designation. The vested provincial interest in aggregate resource management, as outlined in MARPS, overruled any attempt by the municipality to regulate the development of this resource.

However, with regard to the environmental impact of mining, the OMB placed a series of conditions for the approval of one of the license applications; the approval listed 46 additional conditions for the formulation of the site plans which outline the staged mining of the 188 hectare property of the University of Guelph. (The final licence contains 42 conditions.) These conditions fall under the jurisdiction of MNR and are subject only to the inspection of this Ministry. A second license, that of the Paving license, also contains a comprehensive number of conditions (34) that calls for ground water monitoring, noise emission monitoring, and defined haul routes.

The Actors

Within the context of the changes to Plate C within the Official Plan, the Ontario Ministries of Natural Resources and Transportation appealed to the OMB for a change in the designation of land within Policy Area No. 2 (to Extractive). As well, three different site specific appeals for zoning by-law amendments (under Section 34 (11) of the Planning Act) were lodged by the University of Guelph, TCG Materials Ltd., and Capital Paving Inc. for an extractive designation. In addition to these interests, the OMB hearing generated appearances from the Aggregate Producers of Ontario (APAO), Preston Sand and Gravel, and Cox Construction, all represented by counsel in opposition to the township plan and its aggregate policies.

Support for the township plan came from the Township of Puslinch and local residents. Particular site specific opposition was generated against the TCG and University of Guelph proposal from the Ontario Federation of Anglers and Hunters (OFAH) and the Presbyterian Church of Canada with respect to their nearby Crieff Hills property.

The Issues

The concerns expressed by the Township of Puslinch primarily dealt with increasing aggregate extraction, with approximately 4.5 million tonnes of gravel being mined in 1989. Prior to this, extraction volumes within Puslinch Township had steadily increased from 1.6 million tonnes of aggregate production in 1982. Over this seven year period, aggregate mining had almost tripled in its production volumes. The high quality Puslinch sources that are found in Puslinch provide some of the major aggregate reserves for the construction industry to service the large Toronto market. Their proximity to Highway 401 and to the Greater Toronto market make them a competitive product for the high demand that has been generated with the growth of Toronto.

The Township of Puslinch attempted to use their Official Plan as a means to regulate the growth of aggregate mining to protect Class 1 and Class 2 agricultural land, and local groundwater reserves. Although agricultural land is protected under the Foodland Guidelines, the Guidelines are not recognized as an official Provincial Policy. Thus, MARPS, as an Official Policy, takes precedence and so do the recognized aggregate resources.

With regard to groundwater resources, although the quality of the water is protected by statute, the limited knowledge of groundwater makes it very difficult to demonstrate environmental problems. Complex flow regimes, and the general nature of aquifers are poorly understood. The burden of proof to demonstrate a negative environmental effect falls upon the objector to an aggregate proposal. The onus is on the pit objector to demonstrate the need to restrict the pit or quarry development. The Township of Puslinch attempted to place the burden of responsibility on the shoulders of the aggregate producers by having them demonstrate that the resulting environmental impact on the watertable would be minimal. Extraction below the ground water table was prohibited by Section 14.3 (8)(g) of the Official Plan. The Township attempted to control extraction beneath the water table because of the uncertainty involved in water contamination and the potential loss to the residents of the township.

The Official Plan also attempted to regulate the mining of aggregates by introducing the issue of "need" in the Official Plan. The extraction of aggregates was to be balanced with other land uses based on the recognized need for aggregate mining within the community. As previously mentioned, the attempt by the township to place a "need" criterion on the mining of gravel was overruled by the OMB because the need for aggregates is outlined by MARPS as a provincial need, not to be superceded by local interests.

The residents' position is clearly stated in the following quotes from a submission to the OMB (Exhibit 28):

> "The extraction industry is considered a transitional land use. However, the number of years it may spend as a gravel pit can be considerable. While in the extractive stage, the land use is quite disruptive to the area in which it is located. The presence of heavy gravel trucks travelling on Township, County or Provincial roads both increases the rate of deterioration of the road, as well as increasing the level of dust, noise and traffic hazards. The presence of equipment digging, sorting, grading, etc. on the site also produces new levels of noise and dust never before present in the area" (p.4).

and

> "Although the Township understands it must share the responsibility of having aggregate resources, it must also weigh that responsibility against that of providing a suitable living environment

for its existing residents. There are limitations to the degree of disruption that residents can tolerate. It is the belief of this Council that the toleration level has been met" (p.8).

Further resident concerns dealt with groundwater loss and issues of future supply; mining below the water table and the resulting creation of lakes; the rural character of Puslinch Township being destroyed by gravel mining; the loss of agricultural land and the lifestyle associated with farming; and the hours of operation of pits and the resulting noise.

The Ontario Federation of Anglers and Hunters (OFAH) challenged the University of Guelph proposal on the environmental evidence for the protection of a cold water trout stream (Mill Creek), and an adjacent Class I wetland. Issues that were stressed in the OMB Hearings by OFAH were:

- the need for more base-line and quantitative ecological data on the proposed sites

- inadequate threshold parameters of the ecosystems determined

- inadequate boundary definition for the resulting impacts, the "larger picture" of the surrounding environment has been ignored by only site specific considerations of individual proposals

- the need for an adequate monitoring system to assess potential damage to the wetland and Mill Creek from the mine excavation

- the biological mitigation strategies proposed for the wetlands are not suitable to prevent potential damage because they lack adequate data and are based on simple qualitative assessments.

Alternatively, the aggregate producers were faced with quite different issues with regard to the problem of aggregate extraction. The following points summarize the arguments from the proponents of aggregate extraction, including MNR:

- The designation on the Puslinch Official Plan of Policy Area No. 2 is in contravention to the intention and spirit of MARPS. The municipality does not have the legal right to designate and control aggregate reserves, as they are of provincial significance. As a result of the policy designation of MARPS, aggregates should be viewed as a land use of the highest priority, and should take precedence over other land uses such as agriculture.

- The proposed designation in Policy Area No.2 contradicts the previous extraction policies that had been previously designated in Plate C and supported by previous OMB and court decisions.

- The Policy Area No.2 designation, requiring an official plan amendment, can prolong or eliminate the chance of getting an extractive designation. This increases expenses for the licensing process — where presently it can cost up to $500,000.00 to licence a source before any aggregate is produced.

- There is an increasing need for the high quality sand and gravel resources in the Puslinch Township to service the high market demand in the Toronto area. The Puslinch area, one of the nearest large reserves remaining near Toronto, provides a large source of mineral aggregates that is highly competitive due to its nearness to market. The University of Guelph property could be the single largest source remaining in southern Ontario, with a minimum estimated volume of approximately 34.4 million tonnes.

- The Official Plan should provide a permanent extractive designation for future settlement reference, so that people moving into the community are aware of the designation areas for aggregate mining and land use conflict can be avoided.

- The local concern for groundwater is not based on evidence. There are no scientific data to indicate that mining under the watertable will affect the local groundwater regime. The environmental fears for groundwater could "sterilize" approximately 75 per cent of the aggregate reserves that are located under the watertable.

- The environmental considerations for mining impact are incorporated in the Aggregate Resources Act and this is adequate to resolve concerns on a site specific assessment.

The aggregate producers' position is based on desire for open access to the resource without excessive municipal restrictions. MNR supports this position recognizing the need to ensure an adequate supply of sand and gravel for market sources and provincially determined needs.

Summary

The issues that characterise the Puslinch case study are similar to many community-aggregate mining conflicts that have occurred in Ontario over the past 10 years, and continue on a routine basis. For example in 1991, in nearby Paris, a land use battle occurred between Dufferin Aggregates and a community group of approximately 400 people entitled Communities United Against Dufferin Aggregates. The conflict that has been generated by aggregate mining is a function of many issues that may operate independently or together. Local residents' concern stem from fear of lower property values, the changing rural character, or truck traffic hazards. Environmental uncertainty is also an important factor that has motivated considerable community outcry against aggregate mining. Within the Puslinch case study, the environmental problems that were considered important were mainly the uncertain effects of mining on the local groundwater resources, and the adjacent wetlands. In addition, the altering of the landscape by mining beneath the watertable, would create several large lakes in the area. Many of these potential problems are created beyond the site specific assessment that is required for the site plan of a gravel pit.

The present means of planning for aggregate resources and dealing with the local conflict alienates local concerns in order to achieve provincial objectives. The rivalry between townships and the Province of Ontario also impedes any cooperative attempts to mitigate impacts created by aggregate mining. The adversarial nature of the OMB hearings does little to improve relations among disputing parties, and often incurs high costs and hard feelings. Indeed, the basis and the execution of the present public policy for the planning of aggregate resources in Ontario is a costly and antagonistic experience.

Paradise Regained

The development of construction aggregate sources requires an "interest-based" approach in order to resolve much of the conflict that is generated through mining activity. Ury et al. (1988) advocate the need to build an effective conflict resolution strategy on the basis of party interests rather than the defined "rights" of parties, or a solution that is contingent on "who is most powerful." The present system of planning in Ontario uses both a rights and power based method to resolve conflict. The continuation of the three decade old "aggregate wars" indicates the ineffectiveness of this conflict resolution strategy.

The authors suggest that there are "windows of opportunity" that can enhance an interests-based approach to resolve some of the difficulties of mining aggregate resources. As aggregate mining is an interim use of land, parties can search for things to trade which they may value differently (Susskind and Cruikshank, 1987). Thus, in many cases there is an opportunity to remove mineral aggregates from a site, and restore a wildlife corridor or wetland habitat according to the area's biotic needs. This approach focuses more on substantive means of settling disputes between parties by creating opportunities of mutual gain for most of the interests affected by mining. We emphasize "most" because not everyone can be appeased or compensated; some people will always be opposed because of their moral or personal stands.

A substantive approach to resolving conflict among disputing parties goes beyond singular, unilateral compensation strategies. Rather, this method of dispute resolution incorporates bilateral participation in the compensation process, where the proponent and affected parties determine the context of aggregate extraction in the community. As Lake (1987) has observed, locational conflict often arises when decisions are made separately from the process of facility siting.

Inherent to the resolution of localized conflict are a series of steps that provide a base to ensure that development and community interests can be compatible: site specific inventory, community "net gain," local expertise, and agreement on what cannot be mitigated.

Site specific inventory

The assessment of the potential site must be comprehensive. An inventory of the geological, ecological, and cultural characteristics will enhance sensitive design. The proponent must accept responsibility for an exhaustive study and possible restrictions on mining operations. The site inventory provides a baseline data source from which to evaluate potential environmental and social impacts of the operation and determine the potential landscape changes.

Community "net gain"

The mining of aggregate resources needs to be placed in the context of the community, and should no longer be tolerated as a degrading practise. With this approach in mind, a physical and/or social enhancement of the community can be incorporated with the extraction of sand, gravel, or bedrock resources. Aggregate extraction is an interim use of the landscape. Part of the profits realised from aggregate production should also benefit the community in various ways, such as the creation of desired habitat and recreation sites, or the design of new landscapes for future intended land uses.

Local expertise

An important part of the site design process is to incorporate the local resident's expertise. This is not always easy. Often, hostile groups take an adversarial stand, and oppose the project. It is essential to realise that the public who is against the project is not to be ignored and must be incorporated into the design process. The local residents must be given a chance to inform the proponents about their local environment and what is important to their lives. Local opposition should be encouraged to bring constructive amendments to the process and the proponent's plans.

Agreement on what cannot be mitigated

Even after considerable consultation to ensure a sensitive site design, not all the impacts of aggregate mining can be mitigated. For example, with truck haul routes, there will still be disruption to the residents along roads with the additional heavy traffic. It must be recognized that in the public's interest, inevitable intrusion on private lives will occur. In cases where people are affected by the negative impacts of pit or quarry development and mitigation strategies are not possible, individuals should be compensated for the inconvenience. In these situations, the proponents may have to provide at their own cost: site specific landscaping, noise scaping, or appropriate personal services (such as air-conditioning for houses).

Snyder Flats - Bloomingdale, Ontario

In Ontario, Conservation Authorities have a statutory mandate for conservation and water management within watersheds. A primary objective of Conservation Authorities has been to control flooding, and in the past this has involved the construction of numerous dams and reservoirs. Their flood control policies have decreased flooding, but in doing so, the floodplains and lower terraces have no longer been inundated by flood waters. This has the unfortunate effect of removing the traditional spawning habitat of many species of fish, and has decreased ecological diversity and the presence unique aquatic and terrestrial environments.

Conservation Authorities have been traditionally opposed to extraction of aggregate resources in areas within their jurisdiction. The floodplains and terraces of major rivers in southern Ontario, now contain much of the remaining aggregate resource base of the province. However, they are also considered sensitive, valuable ecological areas for habitat protection and recreation. Until recently, the Conservation Authorities have been reluctant to allow access to the valuable aggregate resources they contain, and often have vehemently opposed aggregate mining in proposals near to their properties.

A proposal by an aggregate company to the Grand River Conservation Authority offered an opportunity for a pit to expand its operations into a river meander bend, below the water table. Normally this type of operation is restricted by provincial licensing regulations, floodplain controls, and the municipal Official Plan. However, after detailed site examinations, it was discovered that the 100 hectare site at Bloomingdale, which is owned by the Grand River Conservation Authority, could actually be enhanced in terms of its ecological diversity by a judicious plan of aggregate removal. The plan involved aggregate extraction above and below the water table, and in so doing, created ecological niches no longer found on the site. For example, the following new habitats are incorporated into the mining plan: cold water ponds fed only by groundwater for cold water fish species; warm water habitat which is seasonally flushed by river waters; and prairie-savanna grasslands.

Some problems with the site design were encountered due to complete removal of aggregate materials and vegetation. Leaving a portion of the available aggregate resources with the landscape and vegetation intact could have cost less than rebuilding a new landscape and provided for more rapid habitat rehabilitation. Additional site problems consisted of: difficulties with diverting river waters through the system without creating flood erosion and bank instability; reforestation during drought conditions; and the reconstruction of promontories into several lakes for species habitat.

Despite these problems, the project has been remarkably successful and already the number and diversity of seasonal migratory waterfowl has increased. For example, in April, 1992, Common Mergansers, Buffleheads, and Canada Geese were observed on the created habitats. The fish habitat that has been carefully constructed in below water-level areas and contains old tree stumps and sheltered areas to ensure maximum fish spawning opportunities. From a habitat perspective, the completed design as illustrated in Figure 16.1 is considered a success by the Grand River Conservation Authority which is now using the Snyder Flats experiment as a "show piece" to demonstrate the enhanced river habitat that has been realised by the extraction of several million tonnes of sand and gravel. In addition to the creation of a valued and enhanced ecological landscape, the Conser-

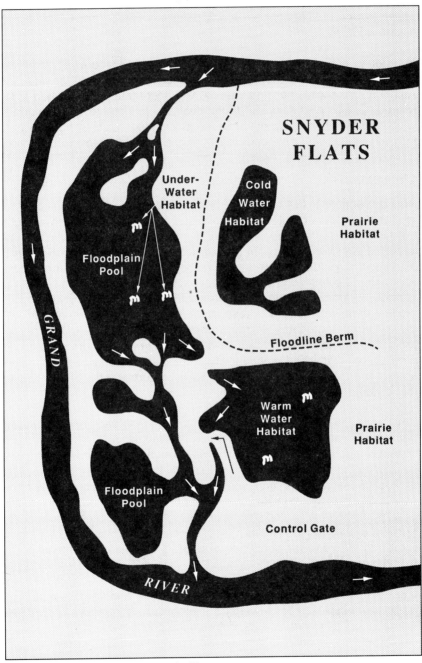

Figure 16.1: Bringing Nature back to the River

vation Authority gained over a million dollars in mining royalties from the project over a ten year period, which in times of budget duress are a welcomed addition.

In order to achieve both the economic and ecological benefits from the Snyder Flats site, the traditional battle lines between the Conservation Authority, provincial licensing agency, and aggregate producer had to be altered. Common ground was found over a considerable time horizon in which the site changed from barren excavation to a restored habitat. Input from all parties, with continuous monitoring, ensured interests were fulfilled.

Conclusion

Hostile reactions to LULUs are still an obstacle to overcome. The history of land use conflict generated by the mining of aggregate resources in southern Ontario provides an insight into how people can be entrenched into positions with very little room for compromise. The present policies and planning that regulate aggregate extraction do little to change these positions. The substantive and procedural basis for planning is inadequate to address the present diversity of interests, and lacks the flexibility to accommodate creative solutions to resolve the conflict that has developed with the mining of aggregates. In many cases the interests of disputing parties are not addressed, and compromised solutions are not accommodated. As a result, opportunities for community enhancement and sustainable landscapes are missed because of the planning forum and the public policies that divide agencies and the public.

What is required is a more cooperative approach to decision-making and public policy that supports community interaction in the planning and design of aggregate sites. Sectorial resource planning needs to be incorporated into the community to avoid narrow provincial agency objectives and policy that may enhance conflict. Co-management approaches to resource development provide potential opportunities to unite municipal and provincial concerns for the mining of aggregates. This might be achieved with regional stewardship committees in areas of potential conflict, such as Puslinch, where large quantities of aggregate resources remain to be mined in the future.

It is significant to note that the attempts to initiate and develop strategies for conflict resolution for aggregate mining have come from consultants acting on behalf of proponents, not from the public nor regulating government agencies. In order to overcome the traditional hostility between "pro" and "anti" aggregate stands, mining is seen as an opportunity rather than a constraint. Mining proposals should examine in detail, with local residents, the potential opportunities for net environmental and social gains to the community. The vision that the landscape change concomitant with aggregate removal will lead to community benefits and landscape enhancement could be seen as a positive gain in changing current social attitudes in southern Ontario.

Creative and imaginative landscape change can often ensure that perceived incompatibilities are readily overcome. In many cases, mining, instead of being a degradational activity can create new landscapes that better fit future intended land uses, and can yield substantial financial benefits whilst creating new ecological and land use opportunities. Unfortunately, the present means of planning for aggregate extraction in Ontario provides more obstacles than opportunity for the possibility of sustainable landscape development.

Acknowledgements

The authors gratefully acknowledge input from their colleague Darryl Shoemaker.

References

Baker, D. C. (1993) "Land Use Conflict in the Rural-Urban Fringe," *Plan Canada*, March Issue, pp. 24-30.

Lake, R. W. (1987) *Resolving Locational Conflict,* Rutgers, N.J.: Centre for Urban Policy Research.

Susskind, L. and Cruikshank, J. (1987) *Breaking the Impasse: Consensual Approaches to Resolving Public Disputes,* New York: Basic Books Inc.

Ury, W., Brett, J., and Goldberg, S. (1988) *Getting Disputes Resolved: Designing Systems to Cut the Costs of Conflict,* San Francisco: Jossey-Bass Publishers.

Chapter 17

Policies and Procedures for Cumulative Impact Management

Michal J. Bardecki
Ryerson Polytechnic University

Introduction

Substantial changes in the manner in which we integrate environmental issues into decision-making have resulted from the appearance of environmental impact assessment (EIA) as a formal process. On January 1, 1970 then-president Richard Nixon symbolically signed into law the first piece of United States federal legislation of the new decade — the National Environmental Policy Act (NEPA). Since then, the provisions and requirements of NEPA have been widely emulated. Soon after NEPA's introduction, the Canadian federal government and the provinces introduced environmental assessment procedures. By these, prior to any approvals being granted, a systematic analysis of the environmental consequences of major undertakings may be required. The result has been a greater recognition of the significance of environmental issues in proper planning and, to a certain extent, the integration of environmental considerations with other evaluations (e.g., financial, engineering, legal) prior to activities being initiated.

EIA has become largely institutionalized in that the basic nature of the techniques, methods, policies and procedures are reasonably well established. Nonetheless, there are continuing reappraisals of "direction" of the process (e.g., Maclaren and Whitney, 1985) and its administration (e.g., FEARO, 1990; Ontario Ministry of the Environment, 1990). Among the significant issues which remain under active debate and examination are those associated with cumulative impacts.

A rapid expansion of interest in the issue of cumulative impacts has occurred (vide Williamson and Hamilton, 1987) and there is increasing acceptance of the need to address the concerns arising from them. Much of this has arisen through the legal requirements of environmental assessment procedures. Indeed, a dominant view is that the consideration of cumulative impacts simply involves a "good" EIA which recognizes the potential for additive and interactive impacts (Munro, 1986; Baskerville, 1986). However, managing cumulative impacts also may be considered an equivalent to integrated resource management (Glantz and McKay, 1986; Cairns, 1990), a means for framing the regulatory control of the net environmental effect of a number of activities (Bardecki, 1990), a means for assuring the equitable distribution of development rights (Ankerson, 1986), or a tool for regional planning (e.g., Cooper and Zedler, 1980; Dickert and Tuttle, 1985; Hall, 1977; Merrill, 1981).

Evidently, there are a variety of circumstances in which the consideration of cumulative impacts may have a central role. Certainly, the literature on cumulative impacts is broad; but it exhibits somewhat of a paralysis in developing pragmatic policies and procedures to address the concerns associated with these issues. Much of this results from cumulative impacts being considered principally in the context of EIA.

What are Cumulative Impacts?

Cumulative impacts are pervasive. They arise in a myriad of situations. In fact, many common environmental problems are fundamentally issues of cumulative impact. Examples include non-point loading of nutrients into bodies of water, long-range transport of air pollutants, emission of greenhouse gases, agricultural chemical use, lakeshore development, habitat fragmentation, and urban encroachment on farmland. In each case, impacts arise as a result of many decisions — any one of which contributes only a small portion of the total problem. Thus, cumulative impacts often arise as a consequence of the collective effect of seemingly minor individual actions.

In a formal sense, from a variety of definitions (e.g., Horak et al., 1983; Witmer, 1985; CEARC and U.S. NRC, 1986; Williamson et al., 1986), the essence of "cumulative impacts" involves:

1) the existence of additive or incremental impacts arising from the ongoing operation of a single undertaking or from a number of separate projects in such a way that the impacts occur so frequently in time or space so that they cannot be assimilated;

2) the interactive and synergistic impacts of a number of undertakings; and

3) at least the potential for the existence of de minimis impacts (i.e., impacts which, although individually too minor to be considered from a regulatory perspective, in composite are significant).

EIA and Cumulative Impacts

Regulations published by the U.S. Council on Environmental Quality under the National Environmental Policy Act require all affected agencies to "bear in mind that the effect of many Federal decisions about a project or complex of projects can be individually limited but cumulatively considerable" (38 C.F.R. §1500.6). The first research publications specifically addressing the NEPA requirements for cumulative impact assessment appeared in 1975 (vide Williamson and Hamilton, 1987). By the late 1970s, cumulative impacts were increasingly being acknowledged in final Environmental Impact Statements prepared under NEPA.

Only recently has there been a movement in Canada to incorporate the same concerns over cumulative impacts as seen in NEPA. For example, the Canadian Environmental Assessment Act that received Royal Assent in 1992, contains a requirement for the consideration of "any cumulative environmental effects that are likely to result from the project in combination with other projects that have been or will be carried out." More generally, cumulative impacts have been a focus for recent concern in Canada, most notably by the Canadian Environmental Assessment Research Council (CEARC and U.S. NRC, 1986; Peterson et al., 1987; CEARC, 1988).

The body of literature on cumulative impacts, particularly that dealing with method and policy, is, with few exceptions, set within the context of how to incorporate cumulative impacts into EIA. However, the appraisal of cumulative impacts is distinct in several ways from that of the environmental impacts arising from a single project, which has been the province of conventional EIA. Three specific points are worth emphasizing.

First, managing environmental impacts arising from a single project initiative involves a predictive approach. That is, it provides for the assessment of proposed activities and the mitigation of (or otherwise addressing) concerns anticipated to arise in the future. Counter to this, the management of cumulative impacts is normative in that it needs be undertaken through providing an assessment against some goal, some ideal future end state or some acceptable threshold and using this to provide a standard against which to evaluate and manage environmental change.

Second, the particular realm of cumulative impacts is in the consideration of the multitude of smaller transformations (the "cumulative effects syndrome" (Brown, 1986) — none of these being individually of sufficient importance to warrant an environmental assessment. These occur in many different potential developments with differing scales, locations, time horizons and interests. The complexity of dealing with such issues is beyond the scope of EIA. Even if environmental assessments are undertaken, the crucial impacts may be de minimis from the point of view of the individual undertaking, although of significance cumulatively.

Third, EIA is not all-encompassing. The provisions are invoked only in situations where major initiatives are proposed. By way of illustration, there are only a few hundred EIAs undertaken annually in the U.S. under NEPA (U.S. Council on Environmental Quality, 1990) and many fewer in Canada. This is inadequate to deal with the variety and number of situations where cumulative impacts arise. Adding to this is the fact that the requirements for EIA are applied inconsistently. In Europe, Italy undertakes 50 EIAs a year, the United Kingdom 500 and France 5000 (Mudge, 1993). How is it that three jurisdictions of roughly similar populations, who are supposedly following the same policy (European Community Directive 85/337), can exhibit such disparity in their response to the EIA process?

Conventional procedures and structures of EIA are not designed to accommodate cumulative impacts. Dealing with cumulative impacts through EIA necessitates fitting the process of evaluating individual undertakings into broader conceptual, spatial and temporal scales. As a result there has been a search for tools that would provide for the incorporation of cumulative impacts into EIA procedures. Most are extensions or new applications of general methods that have been proposed in the past for EIA. Cumulative impact assessment methods include examples of: the use of simple scoring methods (Contant and Ortolano, 1985); modelling of the affected environments (Klock, 1985; Stakhiv, 1988); depicting impacts in matrices (Bain et al., 1986; Cada and Hunsaker, 1990; U.S. Federal Energy Regulatory Commission, 1986); methods that involve the assessment of cause-effect linkages (Clark, 1986; Sonntag et al., 1987; Horak et al., 1983; Williamson et al., 1987); methods which integrate mapping and geographic information systems (Johnston et al., 1988; Sebastiani et al., 1989; Abbruzzese et al., 1990; Winn and Barber, 1986); the determination of coefficients and indices to assess impacts (Cobourn, 1989; Weaver et al., 1986); and the use of indicators to represent a broader range of impacts (Gosselink and Lee, 1987).

Most of these methods either are fairly elementary or have been developed for a relatively narrow scope of circumstances or impact types. The current situation in developing procedures to handle cumulative impacts seems to parallel that of EIA generally. In the early 1970s, following NEPA's introduction, there was a proliferation of methods proposed for EIA — most of which have seen limited use. Then, as now, the utility of standard methods is restricted.

The administrative demands of existing EIA processes have been the catalyst for much of the interest in cumulative impacts. The result is a literature that focuses on what is in reality a peripheral portion of the matter — and one in which the essential problems that are created by cumulative impacts cannot be addressed adequately.

In fact, the assessment of cumulative impacts should involve:

1) a "landscape" level of analysis (Gosselink and Lee, 1987);

2) a holistic (Vlachos, 1985) or ecological perspective;

3) an anticipatory form of planning (Gosselink and Lee, 1987);

4) adaptive methods (Williamson et al., 1986);

5) institutional memory to allow "individual impacts to fit into a cumulative process of regulation just as individual impacts fit into a pattern of cumulative impacts" (Gosselink and Lee, 1987); and

6) a "higher" order of analysis (Horak et al., 1983).

These characteristics are, of course, precisely what EIA was touted to be from the start. However, as it has developed historically, EIA has not addressed these well.

Cumulative Impact Management — Regulation

The more universal questions that need be posed with regard to cumulative impacts are not related to how cumulative impacts may be accommodated into EIA, but rather, more fundamentally, how might the problems resulting from cumulative impacts best be addressed? The concise answer is remarkably uncomplicated — focus on how cumulative impacts have been addressed in the past and how they continue to be dealt with. Whereas EIA deals with the occasional undertaking deemed to have potential environmental impact, it is regulation that has been used, albeit on an ad hoc basis, as the day-to-day run-of-the-mill process to ensure environmental goals involving cumulative impacts.

The management of a great range of cumulative impacts is already being accomplished in a variety of situations in most jurisdictions. Although generally not described in terms of "cumulative impacts," there are numerous examples of regulatory policies based on such principles. Indeed, among the most notable "successes" in dealing with environmental concerns are situations where regulatory controls have been imposed to address issues of cumulative impact. For example:

• Technical predictions of flooding impacts from cumulative development in a watershed and the establishment of appropriate regulations are well established.

• In land development, control of cumulative impacts from storm water flows is regulated by "no net runoff" standards.

• Probable attainment of acceptable ambient air quality is used as a means of regulating the cumulative impacts from pollution-causing developments.

• The loss of developable aggregate resources by incremental urban development can be regulated through the planning process that controls development until the resources are extracted.

• The cumulative impacts of recreational development in lake planning can be assessed using regulations derived from an understanding of eutrophication.

In none of these is EIA likely a significant process. The regulatory approach potentially accomplishes the significant goals sought in dealing with issues of a cumulative nature in that the issues are explicitly recognized; there is a consideration of the extent of change that is allowable; and management occurs so as to ensure that unacceptable change does not occur.

Comprehensive analyses of the merits of regulation and of its appropriate use and form are found in a number of reviews of application to various types of environmental issues (e.g., Nemetz et al., 1981; White, 1981; Franson et al., 1982; Smith, 1992). Such issues, although often not explicitly recognized as such, are, in essence, often cumulative in nature. While there are many philosophical and practical questions that arise in applying regulatory powers, from a pragmatic perspective, regulatory systems are teleological in nature. Should analytic procedures capable of dealing with the scope of potential cumulative impacts be limited, regulation can lean more heavily towards an adaptive, evolving process. The procedures can become more heuristic. In fact, the continuing "nibbling" nature of many cumulative impacts is well suited to being administered by regulatory routine.

Even given that the setting of objectives may be the most taxing process in the assessment of cumulative impacts (Gosselink and Lee, 1987), one obvious advantage of regulatory approaches is their use of more-or-less explicit objectives. The decision-maker is faced with a visible accounting of the effect of any given action through the explicit identification of which goals may be jeopardized.

The Case of Lake and Lakeshore Planning in Ontario

A description of the lake and lakeshore planning process in Ontario exhibits the typical nature of policies regulating cumulative impacts.

The lake and lakeshore planning process assesses the carrying capacity of lakes under use from a variety of perspectives. This involves an attempt to assess the repercussions of several planning options that might be implemented as part of a lake management plan. The basis for lake management is normative, involving, in advance of development proposals, the establishment of planning objectives at a municipal level based on the Official Plan. The process involves specific stages:

- Seventeen agencies participate in the plan review stage to assure that the objectives are in compliance with the provincial planning process (Ontario Ministry of Natural Resources, 1983).

- A specific role for cottaging, fishing, wildlife management and other uses is given to each lake and its shore.

- This role is evaluated by a series of constraint models (i.e., land use, water quality, fisheries and wildlife habitat).

- From these, the capacity of the lake for various potential uses is quantified and the cumulative impact of development alternatives on the lake is assessed (Ontario Ministry of Municipal Affairs and Housing, 1982).

- A series of alternate zoning plans is produced which regulate the lake's use. These plans may be rated based on cumulative environmental impact, economic benefit and protection of social values.

As an example, the water quality constraint model is based on an assessment of trophic status and phosphorus inputs since phosphorous levels relate closely to water quality. Natural phosphorous inputs are evaluated by assessing geology, land use and precipitation. Given specific goals for the use of the lake, a threshold for acceptable cumulative phosphorus inputs from all sources, natural and man-made, can be determined. Knowledge about sewage disposal systems and use intensity related to different forms of development can be used as a basis to regulate an appropriate cap on cottage development and/or to regulate appropriate mitigation measures for development (Michalski and List, 1986).

This process meets the necessary criteria for dealing with cumulative impacts as outlined above. It involves a "landscape" level of analysis; is holistic and involves an ecological perspective; is an anticipatory form of planning; is adaptive; permits an institutional memory; and involves a "higher" order of analysis. Even minor changes in the lakeshore use may be regulated whereas it is unlikely that EIA procedures could be invoked except for the most significant of undertakings.

Conclusion

The issues arising from cumulative impacts are ubiquitous in environmental management. Their importance is recognized but the issues are not readily addressed within EIA. However, because of the dominance of the EIA perspective for cumulative impacts, the literature on cumulative impacts remains without focus and is misdirected. The emphasis to date has been on definition and method in response to the stimulus of the requirements of EIA; it has not been on the broader management and policy issues.

Nonetheless, a wide range of cumulative impacts has been dealt with through regulation on an ad hoc basis — and with success. One of the chief benefits of explicitly recognizing the principal role of regulation in addressing issues associated with cumulative impacts is that it can redirect the dominant interest in cumulative impacts away from the restricted perspectives of how they can be incorporated into EIA and into more relevant questions of more universal application. Greater value in resolving issues arising from cumulative impacts can be gained by focusing research on such regulatory issues as how one might best:

1) coordinate various jurisdictions with the mandate to deal with cumulative impacts;

2) monitor and encourage compliance with regulatory controls;

3) assess the role of mitigation in the regulatory framework;

4) assure equity given the changing "restrictive" nature of regulation through time;

5) establish the mechanisms for appropriate standard setting (from both technical perspectives and within the social/political milieu);

6) determine appropriate thresholds and criteria;

7) assess the potential of various predictive methods;

8) evaluate the relationship of ambient conditions to regulated measures; and

9) appraise the appropriateness and application of specific indicators as surrogates for broader systematic impacts.

It is said with some insight that there are three rules for success in real estate — "location, location, location." Similarly, it can be argued that there are three rules for successfully addressing the requirements of issues of cumulative impact — "regulation, regulation, regulation."

References

Abbruzzese, B., Leibowitz, S.G. and Sumner, R. (1990) *Application of the Synoptic Approach to Wetland Designation: A Case Study in Washington*, Corvallis, OR: Environmental Research Laboratory, U.S. Environmental Protection Agency.

Ankerson, T. (1986) "Cumulative impacts in Florida environmental decision-making: Finding the straw that break's the camel's back (and equitably distributing all the others)," in Estevez, E.D. Miller, J. Morris, J. and Hamman, R. (eds.), *Proceedings of the Conference: Managing Cumulative Effects in Florida Wetlands*, Madison, WI: Omnipress, 235-284.

Bain, M.B., Irving, J.S., Olsen, R.D., Stull, E.A. and Witmer, G.W. (1986) *Cumulative Impact Assessment: Evaluating the Environmental Effects of Multiple Human Developments,* Argonne, IL: Argonne National Laboratory.

Bardecki, M.J. (1990) "Coping with cumulative impacts: An assessment of legislative and administrative mechanisms," *Impact Assessment Bulletin,* Vol. 8: 319-344.

Baskerville, G. (1986) "Some scientific issues in cumulative environmental impact assessment," in Canadian Environmental Assessment Research Council and U.S. National Research Council, *Proceedings of the Workshop on Cumulative Environmental Effects: A Binational Perspective,* Ottawa, 9-14.

Brown, M.T. (1986) "Cumulative impacts in landscapes dominated by humanity," in Estevez, E.D., Miller, J. Morris, J. and Hamman, R. (eds.), *Proceedings of the Conference: Managing Cumulative Effects in Florida Wetlands,* Madison, Wi: Omnipress, 33-50.

Cada, G.F. and Hunsaker C.T. (1990) "Cumulative impacts of hydropower development: Reaching a watershed in impact assessment," *Environmental Professional,* Vol. 12: 2-8.

Cairns, J. (1990) "Gauging the cumulative effects of environmental activities on complex ecosystems," in Gosselink, J.G., Lee, L.C. and Muir, T.A. (eds.), *Ecological Processes and Cumulative Impacts: Illustrated by Bottomland Hardwood Wetland Ecosystems,* Chelsea, MI: Lewis, 239-256.

CEARC (Canadian Environmental Assessment Research Council) (1988) *The Assessment of Cumulative Effects: A Research Prospectus,* Hull.

(CEARC) Canadian Environmental Assessment Research Council and U.S. NRC (National Research Council) (1986) *Proceedings of the Workshop on Cumulative Environmental Effects: A Binational Perspective,* Ottawa.

Clark, W.C. (1986) "The cumulative impacts of human activities on the atmosphere," in Canadian Environmental Assessment Research Council and U.S. National Research Council, *Proceedings of the Workshop on Cumulative Environmental Effects: A Binational Perspective,* Ottawa, 113-124.

Cobourn, J. (1989) "Cumulative Watershed Effects (CWE) analysis in federal and private forests in California," in Woessner, W.W. and Potts, D.F. (eds.), *Proceedings of the Headwaters Hydrology Symposium,* Bethesda, MD: American Water Resources Association, 441-448.

Contant, C.K. and Ortolano, L. (1985) "Evaluating a cumulative impact assessment approach," *Water Resources Research,* Vol. 21: 1313-1318.

Cooper, C.F. and Zedler, P.H. (1980) "Ecological assessment for regional development," *Journal of Environmental Management,* Vol. 10: 285-296.

Dickert, T.G. and Tuttle, A.E. (1985) "Cumulative impact assessment in environmental planning: A coastal wetland watershed example," *Environmental Impact Assessment Review,* Vol. 5: 37-64.

(FEARO) Federal Environmental Assessment Review Office (1990) *Federal Environmental Assessment: New Directions,* Fact sheets, Ottawa.

Franson, M.A.H., Franson, R.T. and Lucas, A.R. (1982) *Environmental Standards: A Comparative Study of Canadian Standards, Standard Setting Processes and Enforcement,* Edmonton: Environment Council of Alberta.

Glantz, M.H. and McKay, G.A. (1986) "Cumulative atmospheric impact assessment," in Canadian Environmental Assessment Research Council and U.S. National Research Council, *Proceedings of the Workshop on Cumulative Environmental Effects: A Binational Perspective,* Ottawa, 131-140.

Gosselink, J.G. and Lee, L.C. (1987) *Cumulative Impact Assessment in Bottomland Hardwood Forests,* Baton Rouge: Center for Wetland Resources, Louisiana State University.

Hall, R. (1977) "MEIRS — a method for evaluating the environmental impacts of general plans," *Water, Air and Soil Pollution,* Vol. 7: 251-260.

Horak, G.C., Vlachos, E.C. and Cline, E.W. (1983) *Methodological Guidance for Assessing Cumulative Impacts on Fish and Wildlife,* Fort Collins, CO: U.S. Fish and Wildlife Service.

Johnston, C.A., Detenbeck, N.E., Bonde, J.P. and Niemi, G.J. (1988) "Geographic information systems for cumulative impact assessment," *Photogrammetric Engineering and Remote Sensing*, Vol. 54: 1609-1615.

Klock, G.O. (1985) "Modeling the cumulative effects of forest practices on downstream aquatic ecosystems," *Journal of Soil and Water Conservation*, Vol. 40: 237-241.

Maclaren, V.M. and Whitney, J.B. (eds.) (1985) *New Directions in Environmental Impact Assessment in Canada*, Toronto: Methuen.

Merrill, F. (1981) "Areawide environmental impact assessment guidebook," *Environmental Impact Assessment Review*, Vol. 2: 204-208.

Michalski, M.F.P. and List, R. (1986) "Limnology and official plans: The Muskoka, Ontario experience," *Canadian Water Resources Journal*, Vol. 11(2): 41-53.

Mudge, G. (1993) "Environmental assessment — present problems and future prospects," in International Academy of the Environment, *Capacity Building in Environment and Development*, Geneva, 9-11.

Munro, D.A. (1986) Environmental impact assessment as an element of environmental management, in Canadian Environmental Assessment Research Council and U.S. National Research Council, *Proceedings of the Workshop on Cumulative Environmental Effects: A Binational Perspective*, Ottawa, 25-30.

Nemetz, P., Sturdy, J., Uyeno, D., Vertinsky, P., Vertinsky, J. and Vining, A. (1981) *Regulation of Toxic Chemicals in the Environment*, Working Paper 20, Ottawa: Economic Council of Canada.

Ontario Ministry of Municipal Affairs and Housing (1982) *The Ontario Lakeshore Capacity Simulation Model: An Introduction*, Toronto.

Ontario Ministry of Natural Resources (1983) *An Approach to Municipal Planning of Waterbodies and their Shorelands*, Toronto.

Ontario Ministry of the Environment (1990) *Toward Improving the Environmental Assessment Program in Ontario*, Toronto.

Peterson, E.B., Chan, Y.H., Peterson, N.M., Constable, G.A., Caton, R.B., Davis, C.S., Wallace, R.R. and Yarranton, G.A. (1987) *Cumulative Ef-*

fects Assessment in Canada: An Agenda for Action and Research, Hull: Canadian Environmental Assessment Research Council.

Sebastiani, A., Sabrano, A., Villamizar, A. and Villalba, C. (1989) "Cumulative impact and sequential geographic analysis as tools for land use planning, A case study: Laguna La Reina, Miranda State, Venezuela," *Journal of Environmental Management*, Vol. 29: 237-248.

Smith, Z.A. (1992) *The Environmental Policy Paradox*, Englewood Cliffs, NJ: Prentice Hall.

Sonntag, N.C., Everitt, R.R., Rattie, L.P., Colnett, D.L., Wolf, C.P., Truett, J.C., Dorcey, A.H.J. and Holling, C.S. (1987) *Cumulative Effects Assessment: A Context for Further Research and Development*, Hull: Canadian Environmental Assessment Research Council.

Stakhiv, E.Z. (1988) "An evaluation paradigm for cumulative impact analysis," *Environmental Management*, Vol. 12: 725-748.

U.S. Council on Environmental Quality (1990) *Environmental Quality — Twentieth Annual Report*, Washington.

U.S. Federal Energy Regulatory Commission (1986) *Final Environmental Impact Statement for Seven Hydroelectric Projects in the Owens River Basin, California*, Washington.

Vlachos, E. (1985) "Assessing long-range cumulative impacts," in Covello, V.T., Manipower, J.C., Stallen, J.M. and Uppuluri, V.R.R. (eds.), *Environmental Impact Assessment Technology Assessment and Risk Analysis*, Berlin: Springer Verlag, 49-80.

Weaver, J., Escano, R., Mattson, D., Puchlerz, T. and Despain, D. (1986) "A cumulative effects model for grizzly bear management in the Yellowstone ecosystem," in Contreras, G.P. and Evans, K.E. (eds.), *Proceedings — Grizzly Bear Habitat Symposium*, General Technical Report INT-207, Ogden, UT: U.S. Forest Service, 234-246.

White, L.J. (1981) *Reforming Regulation: Processes and Problems*, Englewood Cliffs, NJ: Prentice-Hall.

Williamson, S.C., Armour, C.L. and Johnson, R.L. (1986) *Preparing a FWS Cumulative Impacts Program: January 1985 Workshop Proceedings*,

Biological Report 85 (11.2), Washington: U.S. Fish and Wildlife Service.

Williamson, S.C., Armour, C.L., Kinser, G.W., Funderburk, S.L. and Hall, T.N. (1987) "Cumulative impacts assessment: An application to Chesapeake Bay," *Transactions of the North American Wildlife and Natural Resources Conference 52*, 377-388.

Williamson, S.C. and Hamilton, K. (1987) *Annotated Bibliography of Cumulative Impact Assessment*, Biological Report 89(11), Washington: U.S. Fish and Wildlife Service.

Winn, D.S. and Barber, K.R. (1986) "Cartographic modelling: A method of cumulative effects appraisal," in Contreras, G.P. and Evans, K.E. (eds.), *Proceedings — Grizzly Bear Habitat Symposium,* General Technical Report INT-207, Ogden, UT: U.S. Forest Service, 247-252.

Witmer, G. (1985) "What are cumulative impacts all about?," in Estevez, E.D., Miller, J., Morris, J. and Hamman, R. (eds.), *Proceedings of the Conference: Managing Cumulative Effects in Florida Wetlands*, Madison, Wi: Omnipress, 13-22.

Chapter 18

Managing Natural Resources for System Sustainability

Edward W. Manning
Principal, Environmental Consultancy
Consulting and Audit Canada

The achievement of a long-term sustainable relationship between humans and the natural environment will require a renovation of the way we plan and manage natural resources. This will require a much enlarged focus on the range of functions supported by natural environments. But our current assessment procedures remain too limited, and the results often inaccessible to the decision-makers who must understand and use them. If the results of our research are to affect the decisions being made about resources and the environment, they must visibly aid in solutions, and identify practical options and realistic choices. But there remain important barriers to effectively influencing the decision process.

Too little is known about the range of functions supported by the biophysical characteristics of particular ecosystems. Few models exist which clearly identify the sensitivity of productive, life-support and carrier functions to alterations in biophysical variables. In many cases we do not even have the basic data which would identify the existence of these attributes, much less clear information which demonstrates that their value is important. At the same time, it is becoming clear that resource management decisions will occur within a widened framework of public expectations — where the manager's role becomes one of steward of many different values deriving from the resource base he or she manages. Managers of forests need to recognize and internalize, for example, aesthetic, toxic buffering, water control, habitat, tourism and recreational values into their management schemes. The key challenge lies in building the linkages between critical attributes of particular environments and the benefits that humans and the other inhabitants of the planet derive from them. While some success stories are emerging, few good models can be found which systematically address this problem. Yet increasingly, managers and planners are being held accountable for their broader impacts — on other sectors, other regions, and coming generations.

The prevailing practices of resource and environmental management which have served us in the past no longer seem capable of dealing with the significant stresses caused by human activity on the environment. Globally, burgeoning populations and increased material consumption have caused demands for the products and services supported by the environment to grow exponentially. In many areas, soils, forests and water supplies have been depleted or degraded, sometimes beyond recovery. In the more developed nations, demands on the resource base, powered by consumption, have frequently outstripped the capacity of those resources to respond — leaving eroded areas, unrestocked forests, drained wetlands and polluted streams. The byproducts of our resource development and industrial activities are contributing to continental-scale pollution and to potential global-scale environmental changes. In large parts of the world we have been living off our environmental capital — in effect, drawing down the basis of our livelihood (Kumar and Murck, 1992). Empirical research in many ecosystems and cultures leads to the conclusion that many current patterns of resource development and consumption do not appear to be sustainable in the long term. To effectively deal with this global and local problem, to build towards the goal of sustainable development, many research and policy needs remain inadequately supported.

Management within the paradigm of sustainability will require better information on the environment, improved analytical tools, changed institutions, and an altered decision-making process. Most policy makers are handicapped in that they are not specialists in environmental management themselves, yet they do not have effective processes in place which aid them to integrate environmental factors routinely into their decisions. In this paper it is suggested that there is an emerging new paradigm within which they will operate and which is based on an altered system of ethics and values — one which views and treats the environment as a common resource base on which all human activity depends. Based on work with decision-makers in several natural-resource based industries, and on research designed to support more holistic integration of environmental and social values into the planning process at all levels, it has become clear that most of those who allocate resources, and who take development decisions, have inadequate access to key information which is needed if they are to be able to accept an expanded accountability for environmental and social objectives.

Public and private policy makers require better information, analysis and planning advice in the area of human-biosphere relationships at all scales. This opens a clear opportunity for geographers. The challenge encompasses the traditional research foci of geographers in the analysis of the links between human activity and the environment — e.g. impact analysis, spatial integration of human and natural phenomena, analyses of human reaction to biological and physical change. Managers are seeking answers — directions which will reduce the risk to their enterprises (Manning, 1992). What are the limits to use of sensitive natural environments? How can a manager identify downstream effects of land use options, or cultural effects of conversion of natural systems to managed systems in subsistence economies? Where are the resource opportunities? If geographers are to use their knowledge effectively to support policy decisions, they will increasingly be faced with the need to move beyond analysis into normative areas. This paper is phrased largely in normative terms — building conclusions on a range of empirical analysis and iterative work with policy makers in the agricultural, environmental planning, natural resource development and tourism development and management sectors. If parts of this essay seem prescriptive, they are so by design; decision makers may be interested in the results of geographic research, but they are more interested in learning what it may mean for their actual decisions.

The global challenge will involve an holistic approach to ecosphere management at all scales. How we ask the questions influences and limits the answers we seek and the disciplines and approaches we involve. The conceptual model put forward in Figure 18.1 is a tool which has proven useful in dialogue with decision-makers and helps broadly define a perspective of what overall system sustainability may mean. To some extent it is phrased in terms of something they know — the notion of supply and demand. The left side of the model represents the environment, the source or supply of the biophysical properties on which all of the functions supported by the environment are based. On the right side of the model are the demands which we place on the environment. The nature of the demands are modified by the attitudes and expectations of individuals/societies, yielding a list of wants or needs for goods, services or experiences. Ideally, our understanding of these demands includes those which are not directly anthropocentric. Because the products of the environment are seldom identical to and in the same place as the demands, we have created transformation processes to move, alter, combine, safeguard, or enhance the natural products and services provided by the environment. Many of these transformation processes have feedback effects which can alter the characteristics of the environment, frequently reducing the ability of the environment to support many of the functions which depend on it. This model was initially developed as a means to integrate the reporting of the state of Canada's environment within a stress-response framework and to identify the key areas where human interventions could begin to bring management to problematic areas of the system (Manning et al., 1990; Government of Canada, 1991). In subsequent use as a broad framework for the development of means to support site and ecosystem analysis for wetland conversion (Bond et al., 1992) and for the evaluation of tourism site development options, it has proven a good means to both clarify problems to decision-makers, and to identify key areas for management response.

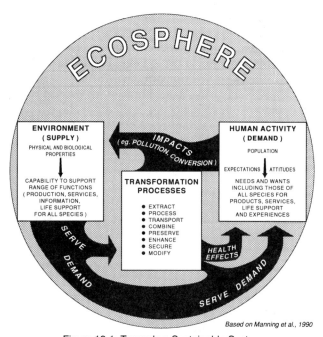

Based on Manning et al., 1990

Figure 18.1: Towards a Sustainable System

For most of our history, we have altered the environment to satisfy our demands, or created transformation processes to serve these demands. If in the long term, we are to sustain a system which provides life-support for humans and other species, we will need to adjust our demands to the limits and opportunities of the environment. The ecosphere model indicates that through many of our transformation processes, we are altering the biophysical characteristics of parts of the environment so that they are less able to support the other functions deriving from the environment, functions which serve other sectors, other societies, or other regions. The conversion, for example, of Prairie wetlands to enhance capacity for grain production has clearly come at the expense of waterfowl habitat and water retention capability and quality, as sloughs are drained and chemicals used to promote growth of particular cash crops (Bond et al., 1992). Similarly, actions to enhance tourism experiences and levels of use at destination sites have often resulted in the degradation of the sites themselves, sometimes including the critical attributes (clean water, unique ecosystems, animal species) which attracted the tourists in the first place (Manning, 1992).

In addressing questions of sustainability, we need to address all three of the areas — supply, demand, and transformation processes — to seek long-term sustainable solutions. Broader perspectives are required on management of parts of the environment. Farmers, for example, can be required or subsidized to manage their land to maintain habitat values or to provide soil management for their own need and those downstream (e.g. North American Waterfowl Management Plan). Planning processes can be made more integrative — to recognize the values of many sectors from the outset. Many of the transformation processes can be altered to be more efficient, and less degrading. Examples include the reduction of wastewater contamination through better treatment or changes in manufacturing processes, the recycling of waste materials into secondary raw materials, and the creation of more energy efficient transportation and processing technologies — often for economic as well as environmental gain (Government of Canada, 1991). Ways can also be sought to modify and manage our demands and to better suit them to the carrying capacity of the environment.

A key problem is that system capacity and key thresholds for critical values deriving from the environment are usually not known. Through the World Tourism Organization, for example, work is under way to develop international indicators of system stress and to provide standards and evaluative approaches for tolerable levels of site stress or carrying capacity. These kinds of applied measures will support the management and possible redirection of demand by industry managers in ways designed to safeguard their own product, and at the same time limit the stresses placed on sensitive environments (Manning, 1992). From examples like these it has become clear that managers and policy-makers need better ways to understand the interrelationships of their actions to environmental stress. This will allow them to move towards more sustainable overall management of the human impacts on the ecosphere and its component parts. Further, to choose between different (hopefully sustainable) futures, we need to seek broad strategies as long term guides for any interventions we may make in the system. Many of the effects of individual actions are cumulative in their effects on the environment and very difficult to evaluate on their own. Often the drainage of a single slough may seem insignificant, as can the construction of a single hotel on an island, or the removal of a few hectares of forest. Yet each may be part of a cumulative assault on specific attributes of a larger system and can be very significant when viewed at that scale. In fact, nearly half of the original Prairie wetlands of Canada have been drained through thousands of individual actions by farmers (Government of Canada, 1991; Bond et. al, 1992). In Malta, the government has estimated that the cumulative result of addition of tourist facilities is that at peak season there is less than 30 cm of beach per tourist (Globe 92 Conference — Tourism Stream). Each is a key indicator of potential environmental stress as a result of the cumulative effects of many individual actions.

Because of the magnitude of current interventions, humans have the ability to affect the function and integrity of the entire system at not only local but global scale. In Rio at the United Nations Conference on Environment and Development in 1992, this was made clear in the litany of presentations which showed the global assault on many attributes of the ecosphere including the ozone layer, the chemistry of the atmosphere, many classes of natural ecosystems of the planet and the overall biodiversity of the global system. But it is also clear that the broad global concerns need to be translated effectively to real decisions at much more local levels if these global level concerns are to be systematically addressed. The managers require greater guidance in a form which can be used to modify day to day decisions on individual programs and projects.

The natural resource base, (i.e. the environment), is the common source of our goods, services and experiences. Any environment can support a range of environmental functions, based upon its particular mix of biophysical attributes. Rudolf deGroot (1986), a Dutch environmental economist, has identified four categories of functions which are supported by the environment. These are:

• productive functions — such as food or fibre production

• carrier functions — such as the provision of habitat or fresh water

• buffering functions — such as the ability to cleanse pollutants or to absorb and neutralize toxins

• information functions — such as the ability to educate or provide experiences

All of these functions are supported to some extent in any ecosystem. All have value as the source of the products, services and experiences needed by the inhabitants of this planet. All are dependent upon a particular set of biological and physical characteristics in a particular synergistic relationship on a particular place, which provide the carrying capacity for diverse functions. If any are altered, as has become clear from work on wetlands (Bond et. al., 1992), other functions are directly affected.

All environments are multipurpose environments. Even though a manager may view an area as being "in forestry" or as "farmland," these environments serve a wider range of functions than just wood production or food production. Forest ecosystems are habitats for many species, sources of recreation, groundwater recharge, genetic diversity and carbon sinks. A farm is also habitat, and may as well be an area of aquifer recharge, or a source of recreation or aesthetic values. Areas managed or enhanced for the provision of one good or service are in fact being altered relative to their ability to serve other functions and the needs of other current or potential users. A farm devoted to continuous monoculture is frequently destructive of wetland systems and may involve removal of woodlands and shelter belts. These features are the source of many values, including wind protection, habitat, ground water recharge and conservation of the soil itself. If we do not understand the full range of functions which derive from an area under our management, we will not be able to include those values into our management plans (Manning et al., 1991). Figure 18.2 is a summary of the range of functions discovered in a five year program to establish the range of values deriving from potentially impacted wetland environments, and incorporates additional classes of functions developed through work for the Foundation for International Training to encompass other types of ecosystems (Bond et al., 1992; Manning and Sweet, forthcoming).

Increasingly, the public is demanding that resource managers are accountable for more than single sector values. Foresters are being called upon to include many environmental factors centrally in their forest management plans. They are increasingly being required under the conditions of public land leases to manage for values such as habitat preservation, watershed values, recreational values, aesthetics and landscape diversity. In the Canadian Prairies, through the North American Waterfowl management plan, farmers are being encouraged, and in fact paid, to preserve and enhance habitats on their farms and to undertake more comprehensive conservation plans for soil, water and habitat on their properties. Mine managers and resort operators are increasingly being held responsible (and legally liable) for their impacts on site and on surrounding environments. As we come to understand the costs of downstream impacts from poor management, the pressures to effectively internalize even more values and functions into our management will only grow. This will affect all sectors, from mining to recreation to transport, as well as renewable resource production. A key research challenge will be to document clearly the productivity-response relationships for each product or service in ways which are readily understandable to policy-makers.

Figure 18.2
Translating Environmental Functions
into Benefits Valued by Society

Functions	Capabilities	Examples of Products, Services and Experiences Supported by Ecosystems	Examples of Benefits to Society Derived from these Functions
Life-Support	A) Regulation/ Absorption	climate regulation, toxin absorption, stabilization of biosphere processes, water storage, cleansing	flood control, (lives, $ saved) contaminant reduction, clean water, storm damage reduction, health benefits, erosion control, carbon sink
	B) Ecosystem Health	nutrient cycling, food chain support, habitat, biomass storage, genetic and biological diversity	environmental quality, maintenance of ecosystem integrity, risk reduction and related option values
Social/Cultural	C) Science/ Information	speciments for research, zoos, botanical gardents, representative and unique ecosystems	greater understanding of nature — locations for nature study, research, education (field trips)
	D) Aesthetic/ Recreational	non-consumptive uses such as viewing, photography, birdwatching, hiking, swimming are supported	direct economic benefits to users, personal enjoyment and relaxation, benefits to tourist industry, local economy
	E) Cultural/ Psychological	uses may be part of traditions of communities, religious or cultural uses, future opportunities, space	social cohesion, maintenance of culture, value to future generations, symbolic values, "home"
Production	F) Subsistence Production	natural production of birds, fish, mammals, reptiles, plants, (e.g. canes, rushes, wild rice, muchrooms, wild fruits, nuts, etc.)	food, fibre, self reliance for communities, import substitution, maintenance of dietary traditions
	G) Commercial Products	production of foods, (e.g. fish, crops) fibre, (e.g. wood, straw) soil supplements (e.g. peat, manures)	products for sale, jobs, income, contribution to GDP

From Bond et al., 1992.

Natural resources can be portrayed as environmental capital — the assets which we have inherited and which we will pass on to our children. This can be a useful way to gain understanding from decision-makers who may not be familiar with the vernacular commonly used in research reports. An example developed for use with corporate sector managers is shown in Figure 18.3.

Development which occurs at the expense of our resource stocks or the quality of the environment, diminishes long term capability in many ways. Actions or inactions can limit the range of functions which a given area can support, or reduce the capacity of particular functions, and therefore diminish the goods, services and values which they may support. Over the past five years several seminars have been held involving researchers, industry representatives and bureaucrats aimed at examining evolving environmental ethics. Much of this has occurred with the support of the Social Science and Humanities Research Council of Canada (e.g. workshops held at Vancouver Island, 1991; Killarney, Ontario, 1992; University of Western Ontario, 1992). One result of these multi-party discussions has been a growing realization that government and corporate decision-makers must understand and manage for costs and effects much more broadly than they have done traditionally. In essence, the public ethic has changed and is demanding that they accept a much broader accountability. In addition to effective management of supply of the resource upon which individual or corporate economic success is directly based, resource managers will need to manage for:

1) downstream effects such as erosion, pollution, solid waste, impacts on water supply, impact on adjacent habitats;

2) costs at different scales such as the effects of their management on the region, the ecosystem, or global scale concerns (e.g. carbon dioxide emission levels, genetic diversity, global warming);

3) risk reduction (environmental, economic, social) such as flood risk, health risk, particularly at a community level;

4) long-term integrity of the ecosystem of which they are part;

5) maximum use of resource harvested, through minimization of waste stream, re-use, recycling; and

6) efficient management of energy use.

Response to the need for more holistic resource management will require more and better information on the attributes of the environment and the values derived from given environments. New approaches to planning will be needed. To adequately respond to these changing community demands,

---

Figure 18.3
Would you invest in a firm managed as we manage planet Earth?

Consider the case of Earth Inc., a multinational conglomerate with a comprehensively diversified range of products and services. Earth Inc. has, for some time, allowed a group of preferred shareholders to take dividends at a level which is supportable only if the enterprise continues to allow its capital equipment and resource stocks to deteriorate. The burgeoning number of common shareholders of Earth Inc., dependent upon the success of the firm for their entire livelihood, have received a very small portion of the benefits of significant growth. Meanwhile, management of the firm has continued to deplete its natural resource stocks in the hope that the research department will discover something which will propel the firm into a continuous growth mode. To continue the analogy, in recent years the firm has all but eliminated the maintenance department and has failed to pay its insurance premiums; apparently the money was used to redecorate the executive suite and to pay for increased security patrols around the manager's club and at stockholders' meetings. Recently, some major regional subsidiaries have folded, or been put into receivership. Management is concerned that on the futures market, Earth Inc. stock is being sold short, and significant blocks of shareholders are demanding a shakeup in management.

These images are used to demonstrate that normal business approaches and common sense, applied at a global scale, might yield different patterns of management and investment for the greater security of each shareholder and of the global commons. Good environmental management is fully compatible with good business practice, and in the long term is essential for the survival of businesses and of the planet.

From Kumar, Manning and Murck (forthcoming).

often expressed directly through Conservation strategies or public consult-ation procedures for project proposals, planning will likely involve larger regional scales. Integration of environmental and community interests very early in the planning and development process will become more neces-sary, even in rural and remote areas. As has been evolving in Ontario, a more comprehensive environmental impact assessment procedure may become compulsory as an integral part of the regional planning process. These institutional changes are occurring to fully reflect the changing ethics and expectations of society relative to the environment, the future and the rights and obligations of individuals and organizations. Few managers or organizations have the training and techniques which will permit them to easily accept this added responsibility, yet their future success may be de-pendent upon their ability to manage within this enlarged paradigm. A straightforward site-specific, largely biophysical review procedure after the project has been proposed or even designed will no longer be adequate within this framework.

Because of the rapidly changing ethics and expectations, resource manag-ers are finding themselves at the front lines, making decisions that deter-mine which functions and values will be sustained. Their management will therefore have to be set within a broader framework (Manning, 1990b).

- longer term — to be better able to anticipate and prevent problems and risk-reduce our decisions

- multisectoral — to include the full range of functions of the environ-ments they manage

- ecosystem based — to recognize the cumulative and synergistic ef-fects of their (and others') actions

- wider — to recognize the impacts of their actions on other sectors, regions, and communities

- deeper — to recognize that the causes and consequences of the prob-lems they seek to solve may involve others and other institutions

- full-cycle — to consider the full context of resource use from extraction to processing, to end use, recovery and re-use

These imperatives will challenge individual resource managers who may have neither the information nor the technical capacity to deal effectively with these new areas. How will geography, and the other implicated disciplines respond effectively to support better decision-making incorporating these dimensions?

Sustainable development of renewable resources means sustained-yield management framed in terms of all important functions supported by the environment. In practice, this will require that managers, supported by planning and other government bodies, seek to identify the functions supported by the environment in their management area. Plans need to recognize those attributes of the environment which are critical to the support of the key functions. In many areas, the supporting data are currently not in place, and there is thus a need for increased development of baseline information and indicators. Initiatives are under way, deriving from the Green Plan, (Government of Canada,1990) to assist in better environmental monitoring, the development of useful indicators of change and impact, and in the provision of better environmental information in support of better decisions. Increasingly, international organizations like the Organization for Economic Cooperation and Development, the World Tourism Organization, and United Nations agencies are turning to the development of indicators which will aid managers to understand the factors which can influence their outcomes, and to help them measure the impacts for which they are increasingly held responsible.

Sustainable management of natural resources will necessarily include management of demand as well as supply. How do we manage the system so that the demands do not overstress the supply capabilities? In the past, resource management was focused on efficiency in serving a given demand for a product. If people wanted more shingles, more meat or more coal, we set out to supply that commodity.

We must now look to managing the demand as well — with the long term goal of suiting the demand optimally to the long term capacity of the resource base (Weiss, 1989; Milbrath, 1989). This will involve a broader concept of resource management — one which looks to managing the whole system for an acceptable and environmentally sustainable outcome (Manning et al., 1990). For example, with respect to energy utilities, it implies equal attention in planning for conservation as for generation in order that supply equals demand. In practice, this will mean greater efficiencies in use, more cradle-to-grave management of resources and the products derived from them, greater reliance on re-use and recycled materials, and more attention to appropriate resource pricing to achieve these objectives.

Success will depend on our ability to change public attitudes — particularly those regarding waste generation and levels of material consumption (Daly and Cobb, 1989). Already many success stories exist, where individual entrepreneurs are making money by serving an environmentally sensitive demand (e.g. Environment Canada's Success Stories Bank). In the tourism industry, much more attention is being given to the management of levels of demand so that it does not damage the attributes of the natural resource base on which its prosperity depends (Tourism Canada, 1990). This will involve not only the development of new, lower impact tourism products (e.g. ecotourism,) but also the application of more effective environmental planning procedures to tourism development, and the cleanup and retrofitting of older facilities to enhance energy efficiency and to reduce pollutant emissions. In the longer term, industries like tourism, forestry, hunting, and agriculture, which are directly dependent upon specific attributes of the shared environment, will need to become more proactive as part of community level planning processes, to identify and collaborate in protecting the attributes of environments on which they depend. These steps were identified at Globe 92 where the Tourism industry sought to define key challenges in pursuit of a sustainable future for the industry. Because of intersectoral dependencies, no sector can easily act alone. The tourism stream at Globe saw a clear need for much more integration between sectors, involving both renewable and non-renewable resource planning and management, to achieve joint objectives.

Despite the apparent inconsistency, sustainable development concepts can also be applied to non-renewable resources. The crux is that the social goal is not to sustain production of a particular substance or sustain the life of a particular productive unit, but rather to sustain the key functions and necessary products and services derived from the environment. In seminars held for managers of natural resource sector departments, (at Mt. Ste. Marie Quebec) the following were identified as key steps in the application of the philosophy of sustainability to non-renewable resources:

1) minimization of negative impacts on other attributes of the environment during the siting, development, extraction, transportation, and use of the resource;

2) reduction, re-use, and recycling of non-renewable — in effect treating them as reusable (renewable) resources;

3) replacement of non-renewable with renewable, or less-scarce non-renewable;

4) research into substitutes, and efficiencies of use — aimed at ensuring continuous ability to serve societal needs; and

5) management of demand for products manufactured from non-renewable substances.

(Manning and Wiken, 1990)

The objective of planning for multisectoral sustainability is to find win-win solutions early in the process, before monetary and personal investments have been made in particular solutions or localities, and positions become fixed. Often, there are alternative locations for projects, or means of staging development so that the key needs or wants of other users of the environment need not be adversely affected (Crerar, 1986). The renovation of review procedures for regional economic development programs to include sustainable development objectives (Bond, Manning and McKechnie, 1989) focused on the early identification of non-zero-sum alternatives — in essence an approach stressing the opportunity cost of each site. Why site a mill in an area where critical habitat or recreational values will be directly impacted, if five miles away is an equally economic site with no such potential confrontations or costs? Why use a process which has a high risk of polluting when less risky alternatives exist? To take full advantage of such options will, however, require a much more cooperative approach than is traditional from firms, communities and governments. The costs of confrontation are escalating and therefore the benefits of such approaches are becoming increasingly tangible, if only in reduced time delays in reaching acceptable solutions.

Conservation or sustainable development strategies are a means to identify common goals and the means to achieve them. Through conservation or sustainable development strategies, it is possible to identify particular problems or sensitivities very early in the overall planning process and to devise consensus solutions to them (Jacobs and Munro, 1987; Manning, 1990a). If we can identify the broad goals of communities and regions, and relate these to the opportunities and constraints of the environmental resource base, we will have a much improved ability to avoid conflicts and to build on strengths. These also provide opportunities for groups who have not traditionally been active participants in the planning process (women, natives, small businesspersons, youth, labourers, religious groups) to identify the attributes of the natural and cultural environment which they value, and to lobby publicly for the full recognition of these in the plans which follow.

The Prince Edward Island Conservation Strategy, and the Yukon Conservation Strategy are promising models of what is possible (P.E.I., 1987; Yukon, 1990). Both strategies are now serving as consensus frameworks for long-term planning in those jurisdictions, and as central points of reference for specific, more local, development initiatives. These are the forerunners of similar efforts in most Canadian jurisdictions. As of 1991, all Canadian Provinces and Territories were developing similar strategies, or had established round table mechanisms to facilitate community involvement. Such strategies help to mobilize the efforts of firms, governments and communities for common goals, and to identify the steps needed and respective roles in building towards a sustainable future. They in effect identify and reflect the collective ethic — providing a benchmark against which proposals can be measured.

Governments and their programs will continue to be an important part of any effective solution. Through regulations, subsidy programs, research, infrastructure, planning, and review criteria, governments have a major impact on resource development and environmental management. In recent years, some government activities have been identified as barriers to environmentally sound solutions, and these are now being re-examined at the Federal and other levels to determine whether they can be made more supportive of sustainable development. In some jurisdictions, new programs (e.g. the Canada-Nova Scotia Sustainable Development Sub-Agreement) are being put in place to help develop strategies, to identify environmental limits and opportunities, and to provide the information needed for environmentally sensitive decision-making. In other cases, new conditions are being appended to funding — in effect requiring a measure of cross-compliance to environmental objectives for eligibility (new Federal-Provincial Development Agreements). Nevertheless, we still often reward and even subsidize behaviour which is in the long term damaging to our own or others goals'. Girt (1990), for example, has clearly documented what is in fact a subsidy to farmers to plough marginal land or to drain valuable wetlands to produce crops for which there is already a surplus and a depressed price. There is evidence that much inadvertent damage to natural resource values comes as a result of insufficient knowledge of the impacts of programs and policies and the inability to monitor effects and to consider a wide range of alternatives (Government of Canada, 1990; Bond et al., 1986).

Managers will increasingly be charged to accept responsibility for their impact on other sectors and other regions. The global, national and local systems are responding to reinforce this accountability...in effect to force managers to build the environmental factors and costs in. New laws such as the Canadian Environmental Protection Act (1988) and environmental impact assessment legislation are reinforcing the legal basis and requirement for more environmentally sound decisions and actions. Stricter and broader environmental enforcement continues to receive strong public support, and our management of natural resources will have to change to accommodate this. This will require better access to information by resource managers and decision-makers, to allow them to effectively consider cumulative effects, cross-sectoral impacts, and broad scale effects on other regions. Systems will have to be devised to provide the needed information, and means (perhaps standards) devised for integration of these factors into specific decisions. The new environmental impact assessment procedures will place enlarged demands on proponents to clearly document the range of functions present in impacted environments, and to link them clearly to the benefits which society obtains from them. There is a paucity of empirical work identifying these relationships, and is also a dearth of effective post-hoc evaluations of past assessments.

Improved resource accounting will be an important step. Better decisions will require better information at all scales. At the global and national scale efforts are being made to better integrate environmental values into economic decisions. One building block is the development of environmental or natural resource accounts (Pearce et al., 1988). The objective is to take account of resource stocks, and to identify whether economic objectives are being attained by building on the strengths of the environment, or by drawing down these stocks. In essence, stock accounting will be done, and the results either kept as a parallel means of reporting on resource stocks (a form of state of environment reporting), or built right into current indicators such as GNP and Balance of Payments. This will clearly place demands on resource managers for new and better information on the natural capital they manage and on changes in its state. But inventory of the stocks of commercial resources will not be enough. The work on wetland evaluation has shown that non-market values often are more important than those which are readily seen in the marketplace. If managers are to be sensitive to these values, it will be particularly important to develop means to assess the non-market values such as risk-reduction, maintenance of biodiversity, aesthetics and existence values — and not to only incorporate commercial natural resource stocks in accounting. Even where markets exist,(e.g. tourists willing to pay to see something) many values have proven particularly difficult to document. What is the sensitivity of tourism to aesthetic changes — how bad does it have to get before they leave? A challenge remains to identify the sensitivity of ecosystem health to alterations in many different biological and physical characteristics to allow full consideration of the implications of particular human interventions.

There remain some significant challenges. Full incorporation of environmental objectives into our decisions will not come easily. To understand more fully the environments we manage, we must clearly develop better information on the environment and on the impacts we have on it. We will need better analytical methods so that we can anticipate and prevent problems which will effect the environmental resource base and the functions and dependencies related to it. A critical step will be to identify success stories — what works in practice, why does it work, and what can we learn from good examples which can be replicated elsewhere? Another critical element lies in identifying the productivity response of a wider range of the goods, services and experiences we derive from the environment to alterations in environmental characteristics. Are there thresholds? If so, what are the cumulative effects or synergistic impacts of a wide range of different actions on these? In work to develop indicators of sustainability for tourism (Manning, 1992) it became clear that many of the nations who clearly required good information to support major changes in tourism policy and standards did not have ready access to key variables. Much information was not collected, or if collected had variable standards and was seldom comparable to that from other nations. Without adequate information informed decisions cannot be made.

Managers will need to re-examine management structures and institutions to more effectively internalize environmental factors. Do we need new institutions to provide us with the needed information, better scientific support for sound management, or an altered legislated base which allows us or encourages us to behave in an environmentally sound way? Are our institutions at the right scale? Do they involve the right partners? Do they comprehend entire problems, or only have mandates for partial solutions? Do they encourage or discourage environmentally sound decisions and actions (Milbrath, 1989; Adams, 1990)? Are there ways to establish accountability for environmental effects and can we augment the training programs of managers and professionals to help them to deal with this accountability? Can, for example, existing financial institutions, through full internalization of environmental risk factors into their calculations of investment risk, become a strong catalyst for environmentally sound investment. Through their willingness to fund development, such institutions provide strong messages regarding what is sound and what is risky. Used effectively, this financial leverage could be a keystone to long term sustainability to the benefit of both society and the lending institutions (Cassils, 1992).

Sometimes the tools we use to support our decisions are inadequate. Even if we understand the full range of functions which we must consider in our management, how will we handle the inevitable tradeoffs? Current economic evaluation tools handle questions involving such factors as habitat maintenance, common use values, and existence values only with great difficulty. Long term investments or conservation investments are difficult to defend, particularly if there is little direct benefit for many years (Bardecki et al., 1988; Manning et al., 1991). Good models of evaluation and integrated planning are in short supply, and as yet hard to replicate. These are critical areas for research and methods development if we are to be able to improve our decisions relative to sustainable development.

How can we measure our progress and reward, rather than penalize, good practice? Many current institutions and their practices are antithetical to our overall goals. Often we have great difficulty defining broadly acceptable goals which reflect a common, yet changing ethic. How are the managers to respond in a way that leads towards, rather than away from a sustainable future? These are difficult questions for the management of Earth Inc., and for its shareholders. But these are real questions, and the future of our common enterprise depends upon how effective we are in finding good answers. And unlike other corporations, if Earth Inc. goes out of business, there is no golden parachute for the management, no alternative employment for the workers, and no competing firm to fill the void. Clearly Franz Boaz' statement "everything is connected to everything else" applies to resource management, as does the perceptive observation by Garret Hardin that "you can never do just one thing" (as adapted in Future Systems Inc., 1990). The need to respond globally and locally to these challenges is becoming more evident. But much remains to be done to put in place the key building blocks. Geography as a discipline holds many keys, as it is by its nature integrative and crosses many of the boundaries which currently constrain many development decisions. But to be effective, the discipline must be seen to not only help define the problem, it must be seen to help in providing solutions. A key challenge to the discipline is to take the best of its research and analysis, and translate this into effective tools and advice for the front line decision-makers in the effort to manage a sustainable system.

References

Adams, W.M. (1990) *Green Development: Environment and Sustainability in the Third World*, London: Routledge.

Bardecki, M., Bond, W.K. and Manning E.W. (1988) *Wetland Evaluation and the Decision-Making Process*, Toronto: Ryerson Polytechnical Institute.

Bond, W.K., Bruneau H.C. and Bircham, P.D. (1986) *Federal Programs with the Potential to Significantly Affect Canada's Land Resource,* Ottawa: Lands Directorate, Environment Canada.

Bond, W., Manning, E. and McKechnie, R. (1989) *Federal Economic Instruments and the Achievement of Environmental Objectives: An Overview of Opportunities and Achievements,* Ottawa: Sustainable Development Branch, Environment Canada.

Bond, W.K., Cox, K., Heberlein, T., Manning, E.W., Witty, D.R. and Young, D.A. (1992) *Wetland Evaluation Guide,* Ottawa: Wildlife Habitat Canada and Environment Canada.

Cassils, T. (1992) *The Financial Service Industry and Sustainable Development: Managing Change, Information and Risk,* Ottawa: National Round Table on the Environment and the Economy and the Institute for Research on Public Policy.

Crerar, A. (1986) "Anticipate and prevent," Policy Options, Nov. 3-8.

Daly, H. and Cobb, J. (1989) *For the Common Good: Redirecting the Economy toward Community, the Environment, and a Sustainable Future,* Toronto: Oxford University Press.

DeGroot, R.S. (1986) *A Functional Ecosystem Evaluation Method as a Tool in Environmental Planning and Decision-making,* Wageningen, Netherlands: Nature Conservation Department, Wageningen Agricultural University.

Future Systems Inc. (1990) *General Systems Notes, The Innovative Learning Series,* Minneapolis, Minnesota: Future Systems Inc.

Girt, J. (1990) *Common Ground,* Ottawa: Wildlife Habitat Canada.

Government of Canada (1988) *Canadian Environmental Protection Act,* Ottawa: Revised Statutes of Canada, 35-36-37 Elizabeth II.

Government of Canada (1990) *Canada's Green Plan,* Ottawa: Minister of Supply and Services.

Government of Canada (1991) *The State of Canada's Environment,* Ottawa: Minister of Supply and Services.

Jacobs, P. and Munro, D.A. (1987) *Conservation With Equity: Strategies for Sustainable Development,* Cambridge, United Kingdom: International Union for the Conservation of Nature and Natural Resources.

Kumar R. and B. Murck (1992) *On Common Ground: Managing Human-Planet Relationships,* Toronto: Wiley.

Kumar, R., Manning, E.W. and Murck, B. (forthcoming) *The Challenge of Sustainability,* Toronto: Foundation for International Training.

Manning, E. W. (1990a) "Conservation strategies: Providing the vision for sustainable development," *Alternatives,* Vol. 16(4): 24-29.

Manning, E. W. (1990b) "Sustainable development: The challenge," *Canadian Geographer,* Vol. 34(4): 290-302.

Manning, E. W., Rizzo B. and Wiken E. (1990) "Conservation strategies, sustainable development and climate change," in Wall, G. and Sanderson, M. (eds.), *Climate Change: Implications for Water and Ecological Resources,* Waterloo, Ontario: Department of Geography Publication Series No. 11, University of Waterloo, pp. 299-309.

Manning, E. W., Bardecki, M. and Bond, W.K. (1991) "Measuring the value of renewable resources: The case of wetlands," Proceedings of the First Annual Conference of the International Institute for the Study of Common Property Resources, Duke University.

Manning, E. W. (1992) *Indicators of Sustainable Tourism: Towards a Global Working Set.,* Madrid, World Tourism Organization,Ottawa: Tourism Canada.

Manning, E.W. and Wiken, E. (1990) *Implementing Sustainable Development: Report of the Interdepartmental Workshop on Sustainable Development in Federal Natural Resource Departments,* Ottawa: Environment Canada, Sustainable Development and State of the Environment Reporting.

Manning, E.W. and Sweet, M.F. (forthcoming) *Environmental Evaluation Guidebook,* Toronto: Foundation for International Training.

Milbrath, L.W. (1989) *Envisioning a Sustainable Society,* Albany, N.Y.: State University of New York Press.

Pearce, D., Barbier, E. and Markandya A. (1988) *Sustainable Development and Cost Benefit Analysis*, London: London Environmental Economics Centre.

Prince Edward Island, Government of (1987) *A Conservation Strategy for Prince Edward Island*, Charlottetown.

Tourism Canada (1990) *Tourism on the Threshold*, Ottawa: Industry Science and Technology Canada.

Weiss, E.B. (1989) *In Fairness to Future Generations: International Law, Common Patrimony and Intergenerational Equity*, Tokyo: United Nations University.

Yukon (1990) *Yukon Conservation Strategy*, Whitehorse: Department of Renewable Resources.

Chapter 19

Improving Monitoring and Assessment for Environmental Decision-Making

J. Gordon Nelson and Rafal Serafin
University of Waterloo

Monitoring and assessment are widely recognized as essential to effective environmental decision-making. This recognition arises from the desire to understand what is happening in a more coherent way so as to anticipate and prevent undesirable impacts on environment and encourage sustainable development in the future. Interest is growing, therefore, in extending and improving theory and practice in monitoring and assessment for environmental decision-making. (See for example, Krawetz et al., 1987; Wathern, 1990; World Bank, 1991; Jacobs and Sadler, 1991; Tolba et al., 1992; Therivel et al., 1992; Nelson and Serafin, 1993a).

The June 1992 UN Earth Summit in Rio de Janeiro has served to highlight alarming trends in environmental degradation across the planet and has provoked a growing sense of urgency among governments, industry, non-government organizations (NGOs) and citizens generally. The critical importance of improved understanding of and more effective responses to the interactions among environment, economy and society is coming to be more fully appreciated. These interactions are occurring at increasing scales and with growing intensity, threatening the global life-support system as never before (World Commission on Environment and Development, 1987; Tolba et al., 1992).

Amid the worsening trends of environmental degradation and economic decline, there is a widely held and deep rooted conviction that improved monitoring and assessment will help strike a more lasting balance between conservation and development. But what is not so clear is how improvements can be achieved, especially in parts of the world where environmental and economic concerns are growing more serious (Tolba et al., 1992; Nelson and Serafin, 1993a).

With this context in mind, some ideas for improving monitoring and assessment for environmental decision-making are discussed in this paper. The ideas are based on experience gained during nearly a decade of research at the Heritage Resources Centre (HRC) at the University of Waterloo, Canada. The work of the HRC in linking the environment and heritage fields suggests that there are many different meanings of monitoring and assessment in practical environmental decision-making. These meanings are related to the motivations, understanding and needs of those involved in environmental decision-making and environmental change. In recent years, attempts have been made by those at the HRC to make sense of a broad range of practical experience in research for monitoring and assessment and to promote a more interactive, participative or civics-oriented approach to environmental management and planning (Nelson, 1991a; Serafin, 1991; Serafin and Nelson, 1992; Serafin et al., 1992; Nelson and Serafin, 1992; Nelson and Serafin, 1993a, 1993b).

Some Definitions

Broad agreement appears to exist at a general level as to the meaning of the terms "monitoring" and "assessment". Monitoring refers to regular observations or measurements undertaken by specialists or citizens aiming to describe changes in environment and their links to changes in economy and society (Izrael and Munn, 1986; Krawetz et al., 1987; Cartledge, 1992). Typically, monitoring is undertaken for two reasons: (i) to further understanding of some aspect of change largely for its own sake, albeit with implications for management and planning or (ii) to guide decision-making in ongoing management and planning. In both cases, information generated through monitoring is typically intended to provide guidance to decision-makers who must increasingly deal with a wide array of unexpected, partially understood and often surprising changes.

Assessment is usually taken to refer to a process which attempts to make judgements about ecological, economic and social impacts of development proposals and activities as a basis for improved projects, programs, policies and other activities in future. Environmental assessment is often undertaken formally, for example, through hearings with the public and professionals. More typically, however, assessment is informal, being based on reviews of relevant literature, some field knowledge, consultations with relevant professionals and less often with those affected or potentially affected by environmental impacts (Wathern, 1990; Jacobs and Sadler, 1991).

Both monitoring and assessment activities are always unfinished because new information is always becoming available and the complexity of change in any place can only be partially understood. Moreover, despite apparent agreement as to definitions at a generalized level, on ground implementation and actual practice of monitoring and assessment differs from place to place. Some for example, consider "snapshots" of change through historic air photo analysis at several year intervals as monitoring, others as assessment. In addition the variety of legal, administrative and institutional arrangements for making use of information from monitoring and assessment in decision-making adds another dimension in which distinctions between monitoring and assessment come to be blurred (Serafin, 1991; Nelson and Serafin, 1993a).

Most professionals would agree that their motivation for both monitoring and assessment in many situations is to understand change, prompted by a desire to influence that change for the benefit of conservation and development. With this motivation in mind, it is helpful to think of monitoring and assessment as elements of a single process that can be of two broad types. The first type might be referred to as professionally-oriented or "managerial." It emphasizes the role of those designated by governments as responsible for making environmental decisions. The second type might be called the citizen-oriented or "civics." It underscores the importance of actively involving those who must bear the costs and benefits of environmental decision-making.

The managerial type is the more familiar and typically refers to a process of understanding environmental change as a chain of elements that stretches from underlying causes through effects to perceptions of costs. Understanding and describing this change can provide a basis for possible preventive or control actions to safeguard or modify all or some of the elements of the chain (Armour, 1977; World Bank, 1991). In this context, monitoring focuses on selecting phenomena of interest or significance from a frequently complex management situation in order to study them more closely — often under highly idealized and artificial assumptions. Assessment involves combining, interpreting and judging the findings to build an overall picture of the situation which is then presented or considered as if the context or the things initially left out did not matter too much. Bureaucracies also force findings to fit institutional arrangements, such as laws, policies, guidelines and other procedures, that in turn influence the interpretation and decision-making that follows (Lang and Armour, 1979).

The managerial type is strongly associated with the classical model of environmental assessment introduced in the 1969 U.S. National Environmental Policy Act (NEPA). This type of assessment brought with it the notion of a synoptic or rational-comprehensive decision-making process. Consider all the alternatives. Select the best one on the basis of the evidence. Implement the desired alternative. Record and respond to feedback during project implementation. Manage any problems that might arise in an ongoing way.

The civics type is perhaps less familiar, but nonetheless has a long tradition in geography and human ecology. Here monitoring and assessment hinges on trying to take into account the context of a situation at all times. This means thinking about phenomena of interest as a set of populations made up of individuals who together comprise a particular situation or place. The interconnections or associations among phenomena of interest that are often left out in managerial monitoring and assessment may be regarded as very important particularly to certain interest groups, if not crucial to building a more complete understanding of environmental change and its implications in a particular place (Hagerstrand, 1976; Butzer, 1990; Serafin and Nelson, 1992).

In the civics approach, both monitoring and assessment strive to describe how human activities affect their cultural and natural setting and how they might affect that setting in the future. The approach endeavors to encompass geological, biological, archaeological, cultural, historical, marine, aesthetic and other aspects of our surroundings, as well as policies and institutions for planning and management. In many cases, the goal is to build a picture of a situation that goes beyond the tangible things to address the intangibles that often matter to people most: to the ideas, beliefs and ways of life that people value and use to understand and adjust to change in their surroundings and circumstances. Basically, the civics approach is oriented to preparing citizens for involvement in the decision-making process. A central theme is emphasis on involving a wide range of people and groups in understanding and taking responsibility for their impact on the dynamic interaction among ecosystems, human activities and institutions. This is important because, all too often, such interactions are treated largely as remote and independent concerns of different professional or disciplinary interests, such as biology or sociology, or as the concern of no one because they fall between disciplinary fields or areas of perceived responsibility.

Over the past decade, researchers at HRC have sought to develop and apply a more civics-oriented approach to monitoring and assessment by linking the environment and heritage fields. Testing and developing monitoring and assessment ideas have involved undergraduate and graduate

students and faculty in a wide range of practical environmental management studies and work. A distinct feature in nearly a decade of research has
centred on extending the managerial approach to monitoring and assessment into a more civics-oriented one. Three recent examples of assessment studies undertaken by HRC are presented to illustrate this
progression.

The move from a managerial to a civics approach in assessment can be
thought of as comprising three general types or stages: (1) the analytical,
(2) the interpretive and (3) the adaptive (Figure 19.1). The typology cuts
across what is the customary division of assessment into environmental,
social, economic, risk and other types, each of which appears pre-occupied
with a particular aspect of the environment or of human interactions with
that environment. A basic reason for proposing the three generic types —
and there may be others — is to encourage more thought about the con-
textual or background issues which are so often neglected or else not
spelled out very clearly in managerial assessments. Yet these often ill-de-
fined background issues, such as changes in ways of life, language, land
use, employment and economic vitality are often the ones that most pro-
foundly affect people and issues which people care about deeply. Indeed
in conventional managerial assessments, the history of conservation and
development in a locale is typically given little attention, as is the issue of
how that history relates to the purpose of the assessment and the interests
it is intended to serve (Serafin et al., 1992).

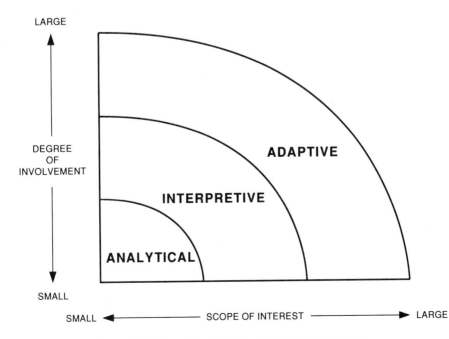

Figure 19.1: Three Steps to Civics - Oriented Assessment

Analytical Assessment

Shetland and Offshore Oil and Gas Development

The first step in assessment is often rooted in a managerial concern about a project, program, or policy and in the decision to analyze the situation. Analytical assessment relies on identifying problems and then breaking them down into units susceptible of analysis by appropriate techniques and methods rooted in scientific disciplines such as geology, biology, sociology and economics. The stress is on identifying objectives and measuring anticipated and actual changes in relation to these objectives. Consultations of varying kinds and completeness are often made with potentially affected individuals and groups in order to gain their views and consider them in analysis and decision-making. In disputed and contentious circumstances, compensation, mitigation and other forms of adjustment are offered to people who are judged by analysts and those responsible for management to have been or to be potentially adversely affected by changes arising from the proposed project, program or policy.

Conflicts can be dealt with effectively, if they are conflicts over information that is primarily concerned with disagreements over facts or data. For this reason, HRC projects often begin with some form of analytic assessment. An example that illustrates the analytical mode is assessment of planning for the environmental, land use and socio-economic effects of North Sea petroleum development in Shetland (Figure 19.2). Shetland has long had a reputation for efficient and effective planning and management of oil effects on the islands since petroleum began to be developed in the North Sea in the early 1970s. Managers of projects and programs in various parts of the world, visited the islands in order to learn from this experience.

The interest of the first author in this topic began about 1977 when the Alaska Highway Pipeline Panel — a quasi-independent group of scientists and persons with environmental management experience — supported some research on Shetland in order to gain information for use in planning for a possible gas pipeline from Alaska through the Yukon to western Canada and the U.S. Subsequently the Canadian Department of Environment arranged for more comprehensive research on this topic for use in planning for petroleum development in the western Arctic ocean (Nelson and Jessen, 1981).

In these two assessments the focus was on gaining information for use at the strategic or policy level rather than for specific programs or projects. Contacts were made and interviews held mainly with local government, U.K. government and the Scottish Office, as well as with key people in the

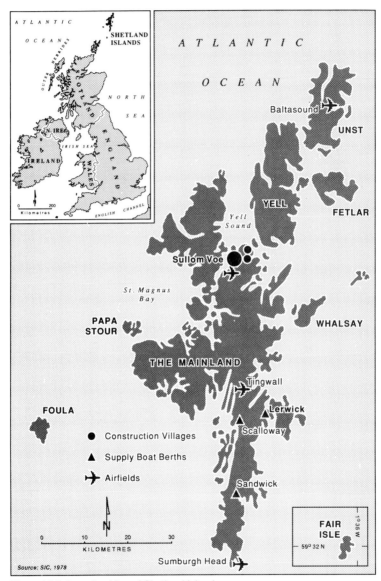

Figure 19.2: Location Map of Shetland Islands

oil industry, fisheries, and non-government organizations. In the interviews and in subsequent analysis of documents and publications secured during the research, interest centred on the key elements in planning and management and the degree to which these contributed to Shetland goals and objectives.

One of the strengths of the Shetland system was that the goals and objectives were established by the Shetland Council in an unusually clear manner. The politicians and many of the people of Shetland saw that even though people were often reluctant about oil development, it was unavoidable because Shetland was the closest and most economic landfall for North Sea oil in the U.K. and because the government in London was determined to exploit the new fields as quickly and profitably as possible.

The decision was therefore made by Shetland Islands Council (SIC) to allow for some oil development and to secure maximum local economic benefits from this, while protecting fishing, textiles, crofting and other traditional local industries and Shetland lands, waters and environment as much as possible. The SIC commissioned a major consulting company to assess the Shetland situation and to make recommendations with regard to the implementation of these goals. As a result of such research and consultations with people in Shetland, the objectives were linked to a strategy and some key implementation measures.

The "isolate and contain strategy" adopted by Shetland led to a decision to allow approximately 29 oil companies to build only one oil terminal where pipelines would come ashore at Sullom Voe on the northern edge of Mainland island, Shetland. The major servicing, shipping and other facilities would be built at the capital and major seaport at Lerwick. One major airport would be built south of Lerwick at Sumburgh. Thousands of construction workers from overseas would be housed temporarily at new quarters or on boats near the new terminal, reducing the social impacts on the small towns of Shetland.

The Shetland Council also worked to provide a promising legal framework for its goals and strategy through the passage of a new Shetland Act by the U.K. government. Among other things this Act provided for Shetland to participate in oil development and income through oil shipment fees and the like, and to control the nature and extent of development in the coastal lands and waters of the islands. These provisions in turn led to the creation of a Shetland Port Authority and to navigation, loading, and other controls and a computer-based monitoring system for tanker traffic approaching and leaving the island, all paid for by oil income.

These plans and arrangements were sufficiently impressive to warrant re-commending to the Canadian Department of Environment that a similar system be created for oil development in western Arctic Canada (Nelson and Jessen, 1981). In particular it was recommended that a coastal zone planning system be introduced and that provision be made for the high level of local involvement and control which played such a strong role in Shetland.

Later, in the late 1980s, an opportunity arose to do further research in Shetland and to learn something of the effects of the oil planning and management system in the intervening years (Nelson and Butler, 1993). This research initially involved interviews primarily with local and senior government people and oil companies as well as a limited amount of field reconnaissance work. In general this assessment indicated that the system had worked well. Income to Shetland had been substantial. The traditional industries were in good condition. Only one significant oil spill had occurred at the terminal and this had been controlled effectively enough, although some otter and sea birds were killed as well as some sheep grazing on oiled seaweed. Water pollution around the terminal was generally well within national and international standards.

Aside from the interviews and research in libraries and in the field, this research also involved a considerable amount of rapid rural survey work including observations of daily life, conversations in pubs and restaurants, reading of local newspapers and listening to local radio. As a result we became concerned that not all parties or groups in Shetland might share the very positive conclusions that had been reached based on interviews mainly with government officials and oil company staff. Further research was conducted to assess this possibility.

This second phase of research involved more interviews, analysis of documents and field studies. Interviews were held with people belonging to commercial fishing, commercial agriculture, crofting, aquaculture, tourism, the media, and other groups. Detailed analysis was undertaken of newspapers over about two decades. The minutes and other documents of Council were reviewed, including submissions by rate-payers and other groups on controversial land-use and other changes. Extensive field work included outlying islands such as Foula, 24 miles west of Mainland in the Atlantic.

This more pluralist research effort did not lead to any basic changes in the earlier conclusions. With minor exceptions the people of Shetland believed that they have derived considerable economic benefit from North Sea oil and that, while there may have been some inequities, the returns have been distributed reasonably equitably. Environmental impacts were thought to have been kept to an acceptable level and the Shetland way of life protected reasonably well. The January 19, 1993 wreck of the oil tanker, the Braer, with its 84,000 tonnes of crude oil, on the south Mainland coast, occurred well after this field work and its effects are still not well understood.

In the second phase of our work interviews were conducted in depth with well informed persons representing the different backgrounds and interests. Confidence in the results is therefore high. However, more analysis through workshops and small discussion groups as well as greater use of local researchers would have provided more detail, for example on how extensive the feeling was that "many a good strong lad with little ken of schooling" had "missed out on a chance to strike it rich" because of SIC's policy of limiting Shetlanders involvement in the construction phase of oil development. Outsiders were favoured in this context, to come and go, leaving the fewer permanent jobs primarily for Shetlanders. Contact with more Shetlanders also would have made our work and findings more widely known and allowed people to react to or act on them as they saw fit.

In sum, most environment and development situations, such as the Shetland Islands case, are typified by many affected groups and individuals, and by many responsible agencies. Indeed new groups, and individuals tend to keep appearing as more time is spent on planning or research. In such circumstances moving from analytical forms of assessment toward more interpretive assessment can be helpful to many of those concerned. In this sense analytical assessment can be seen as preliminary or strategic in nature in that it may lead to the identification of issues requiring more wide-ranging attention and perspectives — an interpretive type of assessment. In contrast to analytical assessment, which is more focused, disinterested or arms-length and objective in character, interpretive assessment is wide-ranging, pluralist, and educational in nature. A recent or ongoing example of an assessment that illustrates the interpretive mode is the work on planning for biodiversity which is currently underway at HRC.

Interpretive Assessment

Biodiversity in the Great Lakes, Ontario

The growing importance of biodiversity on the world scene owes much to the work of E.O. Wilson and other biologists, particularly during the last fifteen years (Wilson, 1988). Much of their concern about biodiversity arose as a result of widespread logging and destruction of the rainforest in tropical areas such as Southeast Asia, central Africa and Brazil. It was feared that this destruction would eliminate many of the plants and animals of the tropical rainforests before many of them were even known to biologists and certainly before their economic value for agriculture, forestry, medicine or other purposes was understood. Such concerns were also held for other biologically rich areas such as the grasslands, wetlands or coastal areas of the world.

Not all groups and people were convinced that biodiversity was so important or that a crisis was at hand in regard to it. Some observers have argued that growing anxiety about biodiversity is alarmist and exaggerated and have referred to it as the "biodogma response" (Nelson and Serafin, 1992). On the other hand, many of those who have seen biodiversity as a major public issue have argued that the evidence is sufficient to warrant large scale research, monitoring, planning and management efforts in the name of "Conservation Biology". The latter group has been successful in persuading many of the leaders and nations of the world to approve a Global Biodiversity Convention at the Earth Summit at Rio de Janeiro, 1992.

It was in the context of the push for a global convention that the HRC's work on biodiversity developed. Concern about the issue arose in various HRC workshops on coastal zone, national parks, and related topics in the late 1980s. Students and faculty with biological, geographical, planning and related backgrounds began to think about and study biodiversity. Some of this work adopted a "human ecological response" to understanding and planning for biodiversity. The basic assumption here is that biodiversity is not of interest solely from a biological or even a resources standpoint, i.e. in terms of its value to humans. Rather biodiversity itself can largely be seen as the outcome of human hunting, fishing, collecting and gathering, farming and other land uses over thousands of years. Biodiversity is the outcome of the human transformation of the earth over the millennia.

These ideas were presented at scientific meetings in Sweden and other parts of Europe (Nelson and Serafin, 1992). We developed four major propositions which apply to and illuminate the biodiversity issue from a human ecological perspective. These are:

1) Considerable evidence does exist for rapid loss of species and habitat through human activities in different parts of the world;

2) Conserving biodiversity over the long run requires understanding past and present human land use and effects in a comprehensive way;

3) Institutions deserve special attention in relation to their influence on land use, biological and other ecosystem characteristics, including biodiversity; and

4) Broader inventory, assessment and monitoring systems are needed to collect the range of biophysical and human information that is needed in a human ecological approach to planning and managing for biodiversity and related matters.

These propositions were supported by case studies of the results of human activities in several parts of the world, including the western plains of North America, the Grand River Valley area of southern Ontario, The Broads of England, The New Forest of England and the Segara Anakan of Java. In all these cases, areas with seemingly high levels of wildness or naturalness were shown to owe much of their species composition and successional character — the distribution of plants and animals in space and time — to shifting agriculture, burning, mining, drainage, land-use management and other human activities, even in national parks and other protected areas. Those who argue for protection of plants and animals in such conservation reserves therefore have to face the fact that plants and animals often owe their presence there to past and current human activities. This human history has to be understood as a basis for planning for biodiversity and other goals in national parks and protected areas.

In addition to studies like the foregoing and associated bibliographical work, HRC began to respond to the interests of others in biodiversity by organizing workshops and seminars and by assessing plans for coastal areas and other situations in terms of their treatment of biodiversity. Our review of coastal planning for a number of states and countries showed among other things, that few of them even referred to biodiversity as an objective or major concern. Four levels of definition or interest have been identified by professionals especially concerned with planning for biodiversity. These four are the genetic, the species, the community or ecosystem, and the landscape or regional level. These levels or definitions are not recognized in the coastal plans reviewed by us, even though coasts are characterized by wetlands, coral reefs, and other communities previously recognized as rich and productive biologically. Where it exists, the focus of concern in coastal and related regional and state planning is on the species. Relatively little information seems to be available on the genetic, community or landscape levels in most cases.

More detailed work on biodiversity is underway at HRC in order to provide a better conceptual and methodological basis for planning and management. The areas of particular interest are three major peninsulas of the north Lake Erie shore, i.e. Point Pelee National Park, Rondeau Provincial Park and Long Point Biosphere Reserve (Figure 15.12). The latter area includes a national wildlife area, a provincial park, a waterfowl management area, and privately owned wetland primarily used for conservation and hunting of waterfowl (Skibicki and Nelson, in press).

All three peninsulas have long and diverse land use histories and the state of their forests, wetlands and other communities owes much to centuries of agriculture, fishing, cottaging, fire control and other conservation activities including protection of deer and migratory birds, flood and erosion control and waterfowl hunting. The extent and nature of these human activities and their biological effects are not well understood but are known to differ within and among the three peninsulas. Identification and description of plant and animal species have been extensive, but much remains to be done. Insects, amphibians and the like are not as well understood as are the mammals and birds. Some community or ecosystem mapping has been completed and this shows that the peninsulas differ considerably in terms of plant and animal associations and assemblage. The associations or communities of Rondeau Provincial Park have been mapped according to at least four different typologies by biologists and scientists in the last fifty years. Which of these, if any, is to be the typology to be used for planning for biodiversity?

The previous findings of HRC biodiversity planning work to date underscore the need for an interpretive approach. A plurality of biological and scientific views exists in regard to biodiversity and how it should be identified, mapped, planned and managed. Professionals differ, along with citizens, in their preference for certain species or communities so that deer culls are being advocated to prevent what is perceived to be excess deer grazing of Carolinian or other deciduous vegetation which is relatively rare in Canada. The scene is rich with differences in scientific and general understanding of what constitutes or is most significant in regard to biodiversity and what the human role and effects have been in the past and should be in future.

Interpretive assessment in which such differences are recognized along with opportunities for mutual learning and informed judgements about future directions, seems to be the best route forward in such circumstances. Conflicts can be dealt with effectively, if they are "conflicts over communication" — i.e. they are primarily concerned with disagreements over translation and understanding. With this in mind, much of the analytical work at HRC moves to more interpretive forms that stress holding workshops, seminars and other kinds of meetings at which mixed groups of scholars, government staff, professionals and citizens are usually involved. In such circumstances, earlier research or analytical work including bibliographies, maps and other information, can be made available to a wide range of groups, people and interests. Information can be updated and expanded as a result, and can be transformed completely as key concerns, groups, individuals and management arrangements become more completely understood through interaction, communication and interpretation among concerned parties. This route is being followed in our three peninsulas work through the convening of a workshop/seminar on the general topic of Biodiversity and Ecosystem Health: The Case of Lake Erie. An attempt will be made to involve scientists, planners, managers and citizens not only from the three Peninsulas area but other parts of Ontario as well as people from the southern or U.S. side of Lake Erie where similar challenges are present in planning for biodiversity and related concerns.

In many environment and development situations, such as that of biodiversity planning, it is increasingly difficult to identify who should be involved in an assessment and related planning and management. This is because interested and affected groups may change along with changes in conservation and development activities — and because many more widespread concerns, such as biodiversity loss, climate change, or ozone depletion are not adequately represented by any single group. Moreover, the nature or scope of the "management problem" is not well known nor understood completely by any single agency, group or individual. In such circumstances, a further step towards a more adaptive assessment, based on learning and understanding change may be warranted. An underlying basis for such an assessment is to help citizens prepare to deal with changes and impacts that may affect their lives, for example by building up local institutions.

Adaptive Assessment

The Grand as a Heritage River

Adaptive assessment has several important characteristics that do not appear as prominently in the earlier two approaches. First, adaptive assessment does not seek a focus on certain types of goals and objectives nor on identifying certain key interests in the sense of the analytical assessment. Adaptive assessment is rooted in a belief that a wide range of interests, preferences, goals and objectives are important in any environmental management situation; moreover these interests tend to elaborate or evolve with time.

The need to have many different interests working together is central to adaptive assessment. But the need is dealt with differently because there is less concern with maintaining central control in management and planning. Indeed the very notion of command-and-control inherent in the concept of management is not a priority. Cooperation, compromise and accommodation are granted higher status. The focus is primarily on the process of preparing individuals and groups to participate in decision-making in mutually beneficial ways. Value differences are recognized and discussed in regard to science, economics and other matters. Communication and dialogue are actively encouraged as is initiative, resourcefulness, and responsibility at the personal, group and community levels. Conflicts can be dealt with effectively, if they are "conflicts over values" i.e. they are primarily concerned with disagreements or uncertainty over goals, priorities and methods.

As HRC activities mature through analytic and interpretive assessment steps, adaptive forms of assessment come to dominate. In such situations, the HRC has strived to remain very much involved but as one of many groups and individuals working together on a partnership basis, sharing information, resources and ideas about what is happening and how the situation of interest is changing. Workshops, seminars and other kinds of meetings are typically convened at regular intervals not just by the Centre, but also by other groups — public and private — who have become involved in ongoing management. Management responses evolve along with growing appreciation for the uncertainties and for common information and goals.

A recent example of studies undertaken by a research team from the HRC that led to adaptive assessment were the studies to determine whether the Grand River Valley, Ontario, would qualify for Canadian Heritage River designation (Nelson and O'Neill, 1989; 1990; Nelson, 1991b).

Until 1950, when the Grand River Valley Conservation Authority (GRCA) was created, there had been little coordinated management and planning of the Grand River basin at the watershed scale. But despite the efforts of the Authority, the environment in the basin has been subjected to escalating stresses leading to cumulative land use changes, associated with industrial and urban growth, notably in the cities of Kitchener, Waterloo and Cambridge. Recreational demands and pollution have also grown to threaten the natural and cultural heritage of the area. In response to this situation, the GRCA, Ministry of Natural Resources and Canadian Heritage Rivers Board (CHRB) sponsored the HRC to do an assessment of the heritage values of the Grand River valley. A research team assembled at the HRC was asked to assess whether the Grand River would qualify as a Canadian Heritage River. This entailed an assessment of the quality of the natural, historical and recreational resources of the valley, as well as of the institutional arrangements relating to their use and protection — past and present and future (Figure 19.3).

In 1988, the first of two assessment studies was completed, using criteria provided by the CHRB as a basis. Historic and current information was gathered on abiotic or geological features, such as landforms; biotic features such as vegetation, animal life and water quality; and land use, cultural and institutional features (Nelson et al., 1987). Frequent formal and informal meetings were held in various parts of the watershed during the course of the study, resulting in considerable interaction with interested persons and groups in the Grand River area.

The assessment remained interactive throughout as the initial inventory study led to a second study that provided a basis for nominating the Grand River for Canadian Heritage River status. As the studies proceeded, however, the designation or non-designation of the Grand as a Heritage River proved less important to many of those involved than the growing realization that management and planning of the watershed had to be improved and made more effective generally. Commitments to the collective interest and to cooperation and thinking in watershed terms, were all encouraged as the basis for getting agencies, groups and citizens to work together more closely in environmental and development management and planning. The initial inventory study, the nomination document and the constituency building and awareness raising efforts established a shared platform for further initiatives by the various agencies and groups with an interest in the Grand River Valley.

In 1990, the Grand was nominated as a Canadian Heritage River on human and recreational grounds, its dams preventing natural status. Following nomination, the "assessment function" has been adopted by the GRCA which has accepted responsibility for preparing a management plan, undertaking follow-up studies on cultural or human heritage in the area, and hiring an information and communications officer to coordinate and promote networking in the watershed. The HRC has continued its interest in the Grand and helped to ensure a continuity of interest in the management plan among people and groups in the watershed by convening seminars, workshops and encouraging graduate and undergraduate research on relevant topics, such as the creation of a Natural Heritage Trust for the Grand River Watershed (Martin, 1991).

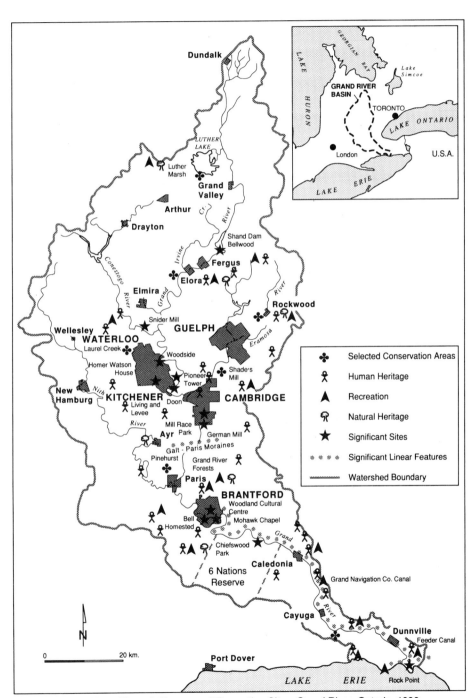

Figure 19.3: Significant Natural, Human and Recreation Sites, Grand River, Ontario, 1990

With the help of the Ontario Public Interest Research Group (OPIRG) at Guelph and the Grand River Environmental Education Network (GREEN), the constituency building efforts of the HRC contributed to the creation of a Citizens Watershed Congress for the Grand River. The motivation for the Congress was to bring together a variety of citizens and native groups from across the watershed in an effort to establish a common interest for promoting conservation of the heritage values of the river. The Congress has continued to organize and convene public meetings in various parts of the watershed, publish a newsletter, and has come increasingly to act independently of the GRCA and other agencies. In recent months, an increasing tension has become more and more evident between the Congress and the GRCA mainly because relatively little progress that has been made in preparing the management plan required to retain Heritage River status. Progress in developing the plan has been slow in part because of difficulties in securing sufficient funding by the GRCA.

The assessment function in the Grand River case is adaptive and evolving in that an assessment capability, initially prompted and later supported by HRC efforts, has developed among not only the responsible agency — the GRCA — but also among a wider constituency of citizens and professionals living in the area. The HRC study and the maps that were prepared in the initial inventory and nomination documents have helped create a point of reference or platform for ongoing assessment and monitoring of progress with environmental management and planning in the Grand River Valley.

The HRC assessment is adaptive and evolving in that it engendered and sustained a link between research and assessment to promote cooperation, transparency, responsibility and accountability in Grand River management. The strength of the approach is that disagreements over goals, priorities and methods often came to be treated as research questions or issues for discussion, thereby allowing them to be addressed in a cooperative way through the workshops and other activities involving the various groups active in the area. In the Grand as in many other areas, no single group or individual can hope to resolve or even deal with the management issues on its own. Workshops and meetings are an indispensable pre-condition or prerequisite for more effective and more sustainable environmental management.

Redefining the Role of the Citizen and Professional

The participative orientation that characterizes the adaptive step is central to the civics approach because it requires citizens to take a more active and responsible part in decision-making that affects them and others. The ideas inherent in the civics approach may be perceived as idealistic and ultimately unattainable. But practical experience suggests that such criticism is better directed at managerial regimes relying on analytical assessments and related methods which tend to have a relatively narrow focus in terms of goals, research and the involvement of concerned parties. In fact, such criticisms are gaining support among many citizens and professionals because after nearly two decades of environmental decision-making at the national and international level based on the idea of improving managerial approaches to environmental problems, environmental degradation appears to be worse than ever and more people than ever consider themselves to be affected detrimentally (Meadows, 1991; Serafin, 1991; Nelson and Serafin, 1993).

The scientific and technical solutions offered as part of the managerial approach have so far proven unable to identify and solve many major environmental problems. This is because dealing with environmental problems, such as polluted air, water and soil is not just a technical matter, but inevitably involves making economic, social and political choices in assessment and management about the distribution of costs and benefits. These choices in turn raise fundamental questions about the nature of 'progress'. Moving beyond the scientific in monitoring and assessment through analytical, interpretive and adaptive stages, to a more civics-oriented approach requires more active involvement of all those concerned or affected.

The key elements in the civics approach can be thought of as an interacting set of responses to change in an environmental management situation. The set includes understanding, communicating, assessing, planning, implementing, monitoring and adapting (Figure 19.4). The responses are not envisioned as occurring hierarchically or in any particular order. Rather they are viewed as interactive and iterative processes that persons and groups must inevitably go through in making decisions about the effectiveness of conservation and development. Understanding is fundamental and demands a comprehensive view or framework for organizing the range of choices available for improving conservation and development activities. Understanding is made possible by communication in its various forms, by assessment activities of a regular or irregular type, by implementation involving research and experiment, by monitoring of different kinds of information, and by adapting in more or less constant fashion to changing economic, social, environmental and political circumstances — which must often remain unpredictable and unanticipated (Nelson and Serafin, 1993a, 1993b).

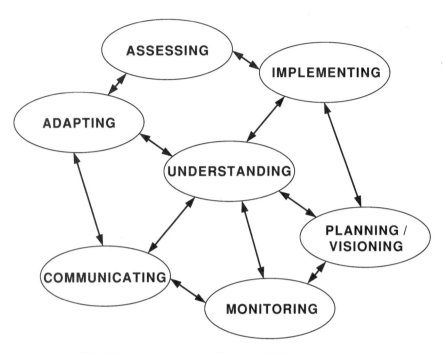

Figure 19.4: A Civics View of Environmental Decision - Making

The demands and costs of promoting and implementing a civics approach to monitoring and assessment are however, likely to be high as frequent calls must be made on the time and effort of citizens for a whole variety of reasons. At the moment, citizens frequently are not well motivated nor are they well prepared for dealing with the demands of participating in decision-making in an ongoing way. The problem of how to prepare citizens and groups to participate fruitfully in decision-making poses a major challenge for educational and other institutions.

Growing interest in adopting a more civics-oriented approach in Canada and other areas has been enhanced by widespread loss of confidence that government can, in fact, solve the economic, social and environmental problems that citizens now face. In part, the loss of confidence stems from growing recognition of the limitations of the managerial approach that has relied on decision-making based on a command-and-control stance domi-nated by professional specialists. In part also, the loss of confidence stems from growing funding and debt problems that have affected national and local governments, as well as the private sector and their capability to devote resources to environmental issues.

In Canada and elsewhere, an underlying difficulty in all this is the institutional and political context in which assessment, management and decision-making must inevitably be conducted. The recent government in Canada, for example, has persisted in emphasizing top-down or analytically-based management solutions rather than encouraging a stronger civics-orientation in environmental management and planning. The disciplinary, the multi-disciplinary and the sectoral remain the general rule not the inter-disciplinary, the cross-sectoral or integrated. Professionals still generally tend to view environmental monitoring and assessment as basically a scientific or technical task requiring specialized expertise in which affected parties, and the public or citizens, are to be consulted but not actually involved in or have basic responsibility for decisions.

The professional is still seen as doing things for or on behalf of citizens — or in consultation with citizens — too often using obscure language and behaving in less than receptive ways. The professional defines, stands upon and proceeds on the basis of a special position or expertise, even though the community affected may include people of equivalent or greater professional knowledge. Indigenous, local and related forms of knowledge are still rarely applied in assessment and heritage situations through processes that allow the people themselves to do part or all of the work with the support and assistance of professionals and governments.

If HRC experience is to be any guide, there is little prospect that technical "quick fixes" or "silver bullets" will be able to solve environmental problems, not only in Canada, but also in other parts of the world. Given this situation, one promising path lies in preparing people to participate in environmental management situations through the various elements of the civics approach. But to move in this civics-oriented direction, more stress needs to be placed on citizens acquiring the communication, assessment and learning skills that are increasingly required to adapt to and participate in a world that seems to be changing ever more rapidly and in ever more surprising, unanticipated and partially understood ways.

Acknowledgements

Thanks are extended to the Social Science and Humanities Research Council of Canada (SSHRC), and the Canadian International Development Agency (CIDA) for funding for research on which this paper is based. The paper is an amended version of earlier presentations at Washington, D.C. in August, 1992, and the Broads, U.K. in October, 1992.

References

Armour, A. (1977) "Understanding environmental assessment," *Plan Canada*, Vol. 17(1): 8-19.

Butzer, K. (1990) "The realm of cultural-human ecology: adaptation and change in historical perspective," in Turner, B.L., Clark, W.C., Kates, R.W., Richards, J.F., Mathews, J.T. and Meyer, W.B. (eds.), *The Earth as Transformed by Human Action*, Cambridge: Cambridge University Press, pp.685-702.

Cartledge, B. (ed.) (1992) *Monitoring the Environment*, Oxford: Oxford University Press.

Hagerstrand, T. (1976) "Geography and the study of interaction between nature and society," *Geoforum*, Vol. 7: 329-334.

Izrael, Yu. A. and Munn, R.E. (1986) "Monitoring the Environment and Renewable Resources," in Clark, W.C. and Munn, R.E. (eds.), *Sustainable Development of the Biosphere*, Cambridge: Cambridge University Press, pp. 360-374.

Jacobs, P. and Sadler, B. (eds.) (1991) *Sustainable Development and Environmental Assessment: Perspectives on Planning for a Common Future*, Ottawa: Canadian Environmental Assessment and Research Council.

Krawetz, N.M., MacDonald, W.R. and Nichols, P. (1987) *A Framework for Effective Monitoring*, Ottawa: Canadian Environmental Assessment and Research Council.

Lang, R. and Armour, A. (1979) *Environmental Planning Resource Book*, Ottawa: Environment Canada, Lands Directorate.

Martin, V. (1991) *The Prospects for a Natural Heritage Trust in the Grand River Watershed*, Waterloo, Ontario: Heritage Resources Centre, University of Waterloo.

Meadows, D.H. (1991) *The Global Citizen*, Covello, CA: Island Press.

Nelson, J.G. and Jessen, S. (1981) *Scottish and Alaskan Offshore Oil and Gas and the Canadian Beaufort Sea,* Ottawa: Faculty of Environmental Studies and Canadian Arctic Resources Committee.

Nelson, J.G., Grigoriew, P., Smith, P.G.K. and Theberge, J.B. (1987) "The ABC resource survey method, The ESA concept and comprehensive land use planning and management," in Moss, M. R. (ed.), *Landscape Ecology and Management,* Proceedings of the First Symposium of the Canadian Society for Landscape Ecology and Management, University of Guelph, May, Montreal, Canada: Polyscience Publications Inc. pp. 143-175.

Nelson, J.G. and O'Neill, P.C. (eds.) (1989) *The Grand River as a Canadian Heritage River,* Occasional Paper No.9, Waterloo, Ont: Heritage Resources Centre, University of Waterloo.

Nelson, J.G. and O'Neill, P.C. (eds.), (1990) *Nominating the Grand as a Canadian Heritage River,* Occasional Paper No.13, Waterloo, Ont: Heritage Resources Centre, University of Waterloo.

Nelson, J.G. (1991a) "Research in human ecology and planning: An interactive, adaptive approach," *Canadian Geographer,* Vol. 35: 114-27.

Nelson, J.G. (1991b) "Canadian heritage rivers with special reference to the Grand River in Ontario," in Mitchell, B. (ed.), *Ontario: Geographical Perspectives on Economy and Environment,* Waterloo, Ont: Department of Geography, pp.269-291.

Nelson, J.G. and Serafin, R. (1992) "Assessing biodiversity: A human ecological approach," *Ambio,* Vol. 31(3): 212-218.

Nelson, J.G. and Serafin, R. (1993) "Environmental, socio-economic and geopolitical changes and decision-making in North America: A geographical perspective," *Professional Geographer* (submitted).

Nelson, J.G. and Butler, R. (1993) "Assessing, planning and management of North Sea oil development effects in the Shetland Islands," *EIA Review,* Vol. 13: 201-224.

Serafin, R. (1991) *The Politics of Communication,* Ph.D. Thesis, School of Urban and Regional Planning, Waterloo, Ont: University of Waterloo.

Serafin, R. and Nelson, J.G. (1992) *Signposts for the Future: Environmental Assessment and Heritage in Canada,* Occasional Paper No.18, Waterloo, Ont: Heritage Resources Centre.

Serafin, R., Nelson, J.G. and Butler, R. (1992) "Post Hoc assessment in resource management and environmental planning," *EIA Review,* Vol. 12: 271-294.

Shetland Islands Council (SIC) (1978) *Shetland's Oil Era,* Lerwick: SIC.

Skibicki, A., Nelson, J.G. (in press) *Biodiversity in the Coastal Zone: The Cases of Long Point, Rondeau and Point Pelee, Lake Erie,* Heritage Resources Centre, Technical Paper No. 9, University of Waterloo.

Therivel, R., Wilson, E., Thompson, S., Heaney, D. and Pritchard, D. (1992) *Strategic Environmental Assessment,* London: Earthscan.

Tolba, M.K., El-Kholy, O.A., El-Hinnawi, E., Holdgate, M.W., McMichael D.F. and Munn, R.E. (eds.) (1992) *The World Environment 1972-1992: Two Decades of Challenge,* London: UNEP and Chapman & Hall.

Wathern, P. (ed.) (1990) *Environmental Impact Assessment,* London: Unwin Hyman.

Wilson, E.O. (1988) *Biodiversity,* Washington, DC: National Academy Press.

World Bank (1991) *Environmental Assessment Sourcebook,* 3 Volumes, Washington, DC: Environment Department.

World Commission on Environment and Development (1987) *Our Common Future,* Oxford: Oxford University Press.

University of Waterloo
Department of Geography Publication Series

Available from Publications, Department of Geography
University of Waterloo
Waterloo, Ontario N2L 3G1

Monograph Series

40   Sanderson, Marie, editor (1993) *The Impact of Climate Change on Water in the Grand River Basin, Ontario*, ISBN 0-921083-48-3, 435 pp.

39   Lerner, Sally, editor (1993) *Environmental Stewardship: Studies in Active Earthkeeping*, ISBN 0-921083-46-7, 472 pp.

37   Nelson, J.G., Butler, R. and Wall, G. (1993) *Tourism and Sustainable Development: Monitoring, Planning, Managing*, ISBN 0-921083-44-0, 306 pp.

36   Day, J.C. and Quinn, Frank (1992) *Water Diversion and Export: Learning From Canadian Experience*, ISBN 0-921083-42-4, 236 pp.

35   Mitchell, Bruce and Shrubsole, Dan (1992) *Ontario Conservation Authorities: Myth and Reality*, ISBN 0-921083-41-6, 388 pp.

34   Mitchell, Bruce, editor (1991) *Ontario: Geographical Perspectives on Economy and Environment*, ISBN 0-921083-37-8, 311 pp.

33   Preston, Richard E. and Mitchell, Bruce, editors (1990) *Waterloo Lectures in Geography, Volume 4, Reflections and Visions: 25 Years of Geography at Waterloo*, ISBN 0-921083-33-5, 312 pp.

32   Charette, Roxanne and Krueger, Ralph (1992) *The Low-Temperature Hazard to the Quebec Orchard Industry*, ISBN 0-921083-30-0, 166 pp.

31   Bunting, Trudi and Filion, Pierre, editors (1988) *The Changing Canadian Inner City, Essays on Canadian Urban Process and Form IV*, ISBN 0-921083-28-9, 175 pp.

30   Coppack, Philip M., Russwurm, Lorne H. and Bryant, Christopher R., editors (1988) *The Urban Field, Essays on Canadian Urban Process and Form III*, ISBN 0-921083-25-4, 249 pp.

29   Guelke, Leonard and Preston, Richard E., editors (1987) *Abstract Thoughts: Concrete Solutions: Essays in Honour of Peter Nash*, ISBN 0-921083-26-2, 332 pp.

28   Dufournaud, Christian and Dudycha, Douglas, editors (1987) *Waterloo Lectures in Geography, Vol. 3, Quantitative Analysis in Geography*, ISBN 0-921083-24-6, 140 pp.

27   Nelson, J. Gordon and Knight, K. Drew, editors (1987) *Research, Resources and the Environment in Third World Development*, ISBN 0-921083-23-8, 220 pp.

26   Walker, David F., editor (1987) *Manufacturing in Kitchener-Waterloo: A Long-Term Perspective*, ISBN 0-921083-22-X, 220 pp.

25   Guelke, Leonard, editor (1986) *Waterloo Lectures in Geography, Vol. 2, Geography and Humanistic Knowledge*, ISBN 0-921083-21-1, 101 pp.

24   Bastedo, Jamie, D. (1986) *An ABC Resource Survey Method for Environmentally Significant Areas with Special Reference to Biotic Surveys in Canada's North*, ISBN 0-921083-20-3, 135 pp.

23   Bryant, Christopher, R., editor (1984) *Waterloo Lectures in Geography, Vol. 1, Regional Economic Development*, ISBN 0-921083-19-X, 115 pp.

22   Knapper, Christopher, Gertler, Leonard and Wall, Geoffrey (1983) *Energy, Recreation and the Urban Field*, ISBN 0-921083-18-1, 89 pp.

21   Dudycha, Douglas J., Smith, Stephen, L.J., Stewart, Terry O. and McPherson, Barry D. (1983) *The Canadian Atlas of Recreation and Exercise*, ISBN 0-921083-17-3, 61 pp.

20   Mitchell, Bruce and Gardner, James S., editors (1983) *River Basin Management: Canadian Experiences*, ISBN 0-921083-16-5, 443 pp.

19   Gardner, James S., Smith, Daniel J. and Desloges, Joseph R. (1983) *The Dynamic Geomorphology of the Mt. Rae Area: High Mountain Region in Southwestern Alberta*, ISBN 0-921083-15-7, 237 pp.

17   Wall, Geoffrey and Knapper, Christopher (1981) *Tutankhamun in Toronto*, ISBN 0-921083-13-0, 113 pp.

16   Walker, David F., editor (1980) *The Human Dimension in Industrial Development*, ISBN 0-921083-12-2, 124 pp.

15   Preston, Richard E. and Russwurm, Lorne H., editors (1980) *Essays on Canadian Urban Process and Form II*, 505 pp. (Available only in microfiche)

13   Mitchell, Bruce, Gardner, James S., Cook, Robert and Veale, Barbara (1978) *Physical Adjustments and Institutional Arrangements for the Urban Flood Hazard: Grand River Watershed*, ISBN 0-921083-10-6, 142 pp.

12   Nelson, J. Gordon, Needham, Roger D. and Mann, Donald (1978) *International Experience with National Parks and Related Reserves*, ISBN 0-921083-09-2, 624 pp.

10   Russwurm, Lorne, H., Preston, Richard E. and Martin, Larry R.G. (1977) *Essays on Canadian Urban Process and Form*, 377 pp. (Available only in microfiche)

8   Walker, David F., editor (1977) *Industrial Services*, ISBN 0-921083-07-6, 107 pp.

7   Boyer, Jeanette C. (1977) *Human Response to Frost Hazards in the Orchard Industry, Okanagan Valley, British Columbia*, 207 pp. (Available only in microfiche)

6   Bullock, Ronald A. (1975) *Ndeiya, Kikuyu Frontier: The Kenya Land Problem in Microcosm*, ISBN 0-921083-06-8, 144 pp.

5   Mitchell, Bruce, editor (1975) *Institutional Arrangements for Water Management: Canadian Experiences*, 225 pp. (Available only in microfiche)

4   Patrick, Richard A. (1975) edited by Bater, James and Preston, Richard, *Political Geography and the Cyprus Conflict: 1963-1971*, ISBN 0-921083-05-X, 481 pp. (Reproduced in photocopied form, 1989; available also in microfiche)

3   Walker, David F. and Bater, James H. editors (1974) *Industrial Development in Southern Ontario: Selected Essays*, 306 pp. (Available only in microfiche)

Occasional Papers

16   Wall, Geoff (1993) *Impacts of Climate Change on Resource Management of the North*, ISBN 0-921083-47-5, 270 pp.

15   Wall, Geoff (1992) *Symposium on the Implications of Climate Change for Pacific Northwest Forest Management*, ISBN 0-921083-43-2, 244 pp.

14   Hucal, Darlene and McBoyle, Geoff (1992) *Job Opportunities for Geography Graduates, 8th edition*, ISBN 0-921083-40-8, 178 pp.

13   Sanderson, Marie, editor (1991) *Water Pipelines and Diversions in the Great Lakes Basin*, ISBN 0-921083-39-4, 131 pp.

12   Wall, Geoffrey, editor (1991) *Symposium on the Impacts of Climatic Change and Variability on the Great Plains*, ISBN 0-921083-38-6, 376 pp.

11   Wall, Geoffrey and Sanderson, Marie, editors (1990) *Climate Change: Implications for Water and Ecological Resources, An International Symposium/Workshop*, ISBN 0-921083-36-X, 342 pp.

10   Chalmers, Lex (University of Waikato), and MacLennan, Mark (State University at Buffalo, New York) (1990) *Expert Systems in Geography and Environmental Studies: An Annotated View of Recent Work in the Field*, ISBN 0-921083-35-1, 92 pp.

8   Adeniyi, Peter O. and Bullock, Ronald A., editors (1988) *Seasonal Land Use and Land Cover in Northwest Nigeria: An Atlas of the Sokoto-Rima Basin*, ISBN 0-921083-32-7, 32 pp.

7   Adeniyi, Peter O. (1988) *Land Use and Land Cover in the Central Sokoto-Rima Basin, Northwest Nigeria (Map)* ISBN 0-921083-31-9.

6   Bryant, Christopher, R., LeDrew, Ellsworth, F., Marois, Claude and Cavayas, François, editors (1989) *Remote Sensing and Methodologies of Land Use Change Analysis*, ISBN 0-921083-29-7, 178 pp.

5   Guelke, Leonard (1987) *The Southwestern Cape Colony 1657-1750: Freehold Land Grants* (Map) ISBN 0-921083-27-0.

3   Bunting, Trudi, E. (1984) *Kitchener-Waterloo - The Geography of Mainstreet*, ISBN 0-921083-02-5, 117 pp.

2   Kesik, Andrzej and Kresovic, Walter, editors (1984) *Selected Annotated Bibliography on Application of Satellite Images of Thematic Mapping*, ISBN 0-921083-01-7, 176 pp. (Available only in microfiche)

1   Diem, Aubrey, editor (1984) *The Mont Blanc-Pennine Region*, ISBN 0-921083-00-9, 186 pp.